ENGLISH LITERATURE OF THE MIDDLE AGES

Dr Stephen Coote was educated at Magdalene College, Cambridge, where he was an exhibitioner; and at Birkbeck College, University of London, where he was Sir William Bull Memorial Scholar. After a period of teaching and working as an examiner in English Literature, he was principal of tutorial colleges in Oxford and London. He has written a number of books for Penguin and is General Editor of the Penguin Passnotes series and joint General Editor of the Penguin Masterstudies in English Literature.

Forthcoming titles in this series:

English Literature of the Renaissance
English Literature of the Eighteenth Century
English Literature of the Romantic Age

STEPHEN COOTE

ENGLISH
LITERATURE
OF THE
MIDDLE AGES

PENGUIN BOOKS

PENGUIN BOOKS

Published by the Penguin Group
27 Wrights Lane, London W8 5TZ, England
Viking Penguin Inc., 40 West 23rd Street, New York, New York 10010, USA
Penguin Books Australia Ltd, Ringwood, Victoria, Australia
Penguin Books Canada Ltd, 2801 John Street, Markham, Ontario, Canada L3R 1B4
Penguin Books (NZ) Ltd, 182–190 Wairau Road, Auckland 10, New Zealand

Penguin Books Ltd, Registered Offices: Harmondsworth, Middlesex, England

First published 1988

Made and printed in Great Britain by
Richard Clay Ltd, Bungay, Suffolk
Filmset in Monophoto Times

I wish to save history; we cannot approach literature innocent and naked. We must know what a poem meant before we can fully know what it means.

Morton W. Bloomfield, *Essays and Explorations*

CONTENTS

CHAPTER 7 POPULAR ROMANCE, BALLAD AND LYRIC 278–301

PREFACE AND ACKNOWLEDGEMENTS

A history of seven hundred years of literature in half as many pages calls for some words of explanation. What has been attempted here is an account of much of the poetry and some of the prose created between the period of King Alfred and the death of Caxton. Individual chapters discuss major poets, genres and developments. The extended treatment of *Troilus and Criseyde* is designed to suggest something of the range of concerns than can be brought to a medieval text. While all these chapters may be read separately, they are also connected by a series of short essays, distributed through the book as a whole, which discuss particular medieval circumstances and ways of thought. Knowledge of such matters is essential, and the location of these essays is indicated by cross-references and in the contents pages and the index.

Throughout the preparation of this book I have received the support of many friends: Donald McFarlan, who waited patiently for a long script; my copy-editors, Christine Collins and Elizabeth Bland; and Brian Stone, with whom I discussed a number of Chaucerian matters. I would particularly like to acknowledge Dr C. W. R. D. Moseley of Magdalene College, Cambridge, who first pointed out to me the relationship between *Sir Gawain and the Green Knight* and St Paul's letter to the Ephesians and who also read early drafts of the text, making many helpful suggestions and improvements. Those errors that remain are solely my responsibility.

For permission to reproduce translations and passages from scholarly editions, the publishers are grateful to the following:

Edward Arnold: D. S. Brewer (ed.), Sir Thomas Malory, *The Morte D'Arthur: Parts Seven and Eight*, York Medieval Texts, 1968; Andrew Malcolm and Ronald Waldron (eds.), *The Poems of the Pearl Manuscript: 'Pearl', 'Cleanness', 'Patience', 'Sir Gawain and the Green Knight'*, York Medieval Texts, second series 1978.

Cambridge University Press: G. R. Owst, *Literature and Pulpit in Medieval England*, 1933.

J. M. Dent: W. W. Comfort (trans.), Chrétien de Troyes, *Arthurian Romances*, Everyman's Library, 1914, reprinted 1975; Eugene Mason (trans.), Wace and Layamon, *Arthurian Chronicles*, Everyman's Library, 1912, reprinted 1962; A. V. C. Schmidt (ed.), William Langland, *The Vision of Piers Ploughman: A Complete Edition of the B-text*, Everyman's Library, 1978.

Faber and Faber: R. T. Davies (ed.), *Medieval English Lyrics: A Critical Anthology*, 1963; E. J. Dobson and F. Harrison (eds.), *Medieval English Songs*, 1979.

Hutchinson & Co.: R. W. Southern, *The Making of the Middle Ages*, 1953; J. E. Stevens, *Medieval Romance: Themes and Approaches*, Hutchinson University Library, 1973.

Longman: F. Barlow, *The Feudal Kingdom of England, 1042–1216*, 1955, revised ed. 1972.

Manchester University Press: G. L. Brook (ed.), *The Harley Lyrics: The Middle English Lyrics of Ms. Harley 2253*, Old and Middle English Texts, 1956, revised ed. 1978; A. C. Cawley (ed.), *Everyman*, Old and Middle English Texts, 1961.

Oxford University Press: J. A. W. Bennett and G. V. Smithers (eds.), with a glossary by Norman Davis, *Early Middle English Verse and Prose*, 1966, revised ed. 1968; Douglas Gray (ed.), *A Selection of Religious Lyrics*, 1975; F. N. Robinson, *The Works of Geoffrey Chaucer*, 1957, revised ed. 1966.

Penguin Books: Michael Alexander (trans.), *Beowulf*, Penguin Classics, 1973; *The Earliest English Poems*, Penguin Classics, 1966; J. F. Goodridge (trans.), *Piers the Ploughman*, Penguin Classics, 1959, revised ed. 1966; Peter Happé (ed.), *English Mystery Plays*, Penguin English Library, 1975; *Four Morality Plays*, Penguin English Library, 1979; Simon Keynes and Michael Lapidge (trans.), *Alfred the Great: Asser's 'Life of King Alfred' and Other Contemporary Sources*, Penguin Classics, 1983; Betty Radice (trans.), *The Letters of Abelard and Heloise and Historia Calamitatum*, Penguin Classics, 1974.

Prentice-Hall, Inc.: Walter Hoyte French and Charles Brockway Hale (eds.), *Middle English Metrical Romances*, 1930, selections reprinted in *Middle English Verse Romances*, ed. D. B. Sands, Holt, Rinehart & Winston, Inc., 1966.

Princeton University Press: B. F. Huppé and D. W. Robertson, *Fruyt and Chaf: Studies in Chaucer's Allegories*, 1963.

Routledge & Kegan Paul: A. C. Baugh and T. Cable, *A History of the English Language,* 1951, revised ed. 1978.

CHAPTER 1

OLD ENGLISH LITERATURE

1

Our history begins early and in defeat. The Battle of Hastings in 1066 brought large areas of Anglo-Saxon culture to a sudden and almost total close. Among their many achievements, that which most clearly marks the degree of civilization these people had attained is their creation of the first native and post-classical literature in Western Europe, a body of work fashioned from a language now known as Old English. Some 30,000 lines of Old English verse survive, while there also remain those translations of 'books . . . most necessary for all men to know' which had been produced either by King Alfred (871–99) or with his encouragement to shape for his people an effective prose.

These translations are of interest for several reasons. First, they suggest that the speech of the Anglo-Saxons was sufficiently flexible to become a literary language. This was a far from predictable advance since the spoken word does not necessarily lead to the written text, which is invariably a later development. Though we now take the writing of prose for granted, be it the hurried note or a word-processor creaking with its cargo of paragraphs, the creation of prose in fact requires a high degree of linguistic sophistication. Old English began to achieve this under Alfred and, since it is the basis of a language now used by over 400 million people, we should endeavour to know something of its qualities.

Old English is the name given to the several dialects of a Germanic tongue brought to the country from about 500 A.D. by waves of conquering Jutes, Saxons and Angles. Four of these dialects eventually established themselves as being of major importance, but that spoken by the West Saxons (a people inhabiting the larger part of the country south of the Thames and the Severn estuary) is the form of Old English in which the greater part of its literature is preserved. Economic development ensured that the Anglian version underlies contemporary English, but none of these Saxon tongues is approachable without special study. Old English is, for example, an inflected language. This means that, unlike its modern descendant, certain grammatical relations are shown by changes to the last syllables of nouns and adjectives rather than by prepositions and the order of words in the sentence. In addition, the nouns have genders: masculine, feminine and neuter. These have no necessary connection with the gender of the object denoted but crucially determine the form of the adjective, pronoun and definite article. The loss of such complications has been a distinct gain to modern English, though there remains in the language something of the original division of verbs into those which are 'strong' and change their tense by altering the root vowel as in *sing, sung, sang*, and those 'weak' verbs that take the form *talk, talked, talked*.

The vocabulary of Old English is of particular interest. The greater part –about 85 per cent – is no longer in use, but, beneath changes in spelling and pronunciation, a number of words expressing basic concepts are still recognizable. For example, *mann, wif*, and *cild* present few problems while, when we know that *þ* and *ð* represent *th, sh* is written *sc*, and *æ* indicates the 'a' in *mat*, then *wiþ, sceap*, and even *bæð* become familiar.

The most marked difference between Old English vocabulary and that of today, however, is the absence of those French and the greater part of the Latin resources that make the present language so rich. How, then, could Old English provide the range a literary prose requires? One answer lies in its ability to employ prefixes and suffixes with such ease that a single word could develop a host of derivatives. Professors Baugh and Cable cite *mod* as an example, a word which, naturally enough, gave rise to the modern *mood* or mental state. In Old English, *mod* suggests 'mind', 'heart' or 'spirit' and, as a result, 'courage' and even its attendant 'haughtiness'. By writing *modig*, 'high-spirited' is achieved; *modiglic* gives 'magnanimous'; *modiglice* makes 'boldly' or 'great-heartedly'; while *modignes* signifies 'pride'. A few suffixes thus develop the root word from an adjective to a moral concept. Further, by combining this root with another noun such as *hord* or 'treasure' – we get *modhord*: 'mindhoard' or 'understanding', an evocative concept indeed.

The range of such self-explanatory compounds meant that Old English was practical, concrete, and able to express abstract ideas without losing touch with the world of things. It also had a further quality which has always been a characteristic strength of the language: a willingness to absorb useful elements from other vocabularies. This flexibility is of the greatest importance. With the arrival of Christian, Latin-speaking missionaries in the sixth century, for example, Old English acquired the means of becoming a sophisticated instrument of European thought and feeling. A whole range of ecclesiastical terms, educational words such as *school* and *master*, names of household items, even the exotic *phoenix*, became available. Although a basic knowledge of the language requires detailed study and quotations from Old English will be given here mostly in translation, the following passage – the Lord's Prayer – may be cited here in the original. Through it can be heard the cadences of what probably became the most widely read of all writings in English, the King James version of the Bible:

> Fæder ure,
> þu þe eart on heofonum,
> si þin nama gehalgod.
> Tobecume þin rice.
> Gewurþe ðin willa on eorðan swa swa on heofonum.
> Urne gedæghwamlican hlaf syle us to dæg.
> And forgyf us ure gyltas, swa swa we forgyfað urum gyltendum.
> And ne gelæd þu us on costnunge,
> ac alys us of yfele. Soþlice.

This passage beautifully suggests the continuity of the language. It also shows the ability of Old English to join the intellectual and spiritual life of the country to the mainstream of European thought, in particular its Latin inheritance and Christian traditions. This too is a major quality of King Alfred's translations.

2

In Alfred's Wessex, an attempt to be reunited with the sources of European culture was a matter of the greatest urgency. Repeated Viking raids, first on the kingdoms of the north and south-east, then through central Mercia, and finally into the heart of the last Christian kingdom, had resulted in the sacking of churches and the burning of libraries. Destruction and retreat are the constant refrain of the chroniclers, and by 878 Alfred himself appeared as little more than the captain of a beleaguered band hiding in the obscure, waterlogged fastnesses of Somerset. Yet, remarkably, the final humiliation did not take place. Two months after celebrating Easter, the young king gathered the local men about him and, routing the Vikings at the Battle of Edington, obliged them to retreat into that part of the country which was soon to be called Danelaw. The long struggle to rebuild a kingdom could begin, and it is a testimony to the strength of Alfred's imaginative vision that he saw this not simply as a process of fending off an enemy without – the Vikings whom he held at bay with a system of *burghs* or fortified dwelling-places – but as a struggle against the enemy within: illiteracy, a disregard for the things of the mind and spirit, which are the sterile fruits of fear and long fatigue.

Recalling a time before the Viking raids, a period when, under Bede (673–735) and his contemporaries, the country had been at the forefront of the Catholic and Latin scholarship of Europe, Alfred realized that to create his kingdom afresh he needed both to develop its language and revive its traditions. These aims he set out in the Preface to one of his most important works, his translation of St Gregory's *Pastoral Care* (trans. before 896). This takes the form of a letter addressed to the leading English churchmen of the day and is a document of exceptional interest. The Preface begins with a frank recognition that learning has decayed, that Latin is all but unknown, and that the greater part of the books in which Latin culture was preserved have been destroyed. Alfred continues:

When I reflected on all this, I wondered exceedingly why the good, wise men who were formerly found throughout England and had thoroughly studied all those books, did not wish to translate any part of them into their own language. But I immediately answered myself, and said: 'They did not think that men would ever become so careless and that learning would decay like this; they refrained from doing it through this resolve, namely they wished that the more languages we knew, the greater would be the wisdom in this land.' Then I recalled how the Law [i.e. the Bible] was first composed in the Hebrew language, and thereafter, when the Greeks learned it, they translated it all into their own language, and all other books as well. And so too the Romans, after they had mastered them, translated them all through learned interpreters into their own language. Similarly all the other Christian peoples turned some part of them into their own language. Therefore it seems better to me – if it seems so to you – that we too should turn into the language that we can all understand certain books which are the most necessary for all men to know, and accomplish this, as with God's help we may very easily do provided we have peace enough, so that all the free-born young men now in England who have the means to apply themselves to it, may be set to learning (as long as they are not useful for some other employment) until the time that they can read English writings properly. Thereafter one may instruct in Latin those whom one wishes to teach further and wishes to advance to holy orders.

What shine through this passage are a sense of continuity and a belief that England is part of a European tradition, the hope that the native language can be a means of preserving these, and a commitment to education and the spiritual life. The Preface to *Pastoral Care* is nothing less than a programme for the recreation of a culture.

The books Alfred chose either to translate himself or have others work on confirm this idea. At first sight they may seem a strange collection, pieces it is now difficult to regard as either central to the mainstream of the classics or even, in some cases, as the most interesting their original authors wrote. This will not seem a serious limitation, however, if two further ideas are borne in mind. First is the fact that the classical tradition itself is a process of constant rediscovery. Many of the works we now regard as fundamental were only circulated in England much later than Alfred's time and were simply not available to him. Secondly, a great strength of authors reviving the classical past has always been the courage to choose what is most useful to them. Indeed, the Greek and Latin authors in which the society of a particular period shows an interest are often a key to its deepest and most pressing concerns. As a result, the presence of the classics in English literature is rarely the product of dry academic enquiry. Rather, it is an excited and often grateful attempt to absorb what has been inherited. Nowhere is this clearer than in two further aspects of Alfred's versions: the idea that translation is an important patriotic activity, a means of enriching the native language, and secondly that it is not (or need not be) solely a matter of dictionaries and strict linguistic accuracy. A passage possibly written by one of Alfred's colleagues declares that Alfred himself sometimes 'set down word for word, sometimes sense for sense, rendering . . . as clearly and intelligibly as he could'. There was nothing particularly novel about this freedom, but we may go further and say that, as Alfred gained in confidence, so he resolved to edit his originals and add passages gleaned from commentators and his own experience. These qualities make his translations both more personal and more clearly directed towards his great self-imposed task of preserving wisdom for the nation.

The books translated were all directed to contemporary needs. The earliest, which was probably the work of Waeferth of Worcester, was the *Dialogues* of St Gregory (trans. *c.* 880). This was a popular collection of the lives of the saints and a record of their miracles which showed an exhausted people the preservation of Christian life under adversity. The form was to remain important for many centuries and underlies some of the finest medieval literature. We have seen that Alfred himself translated Gregory's *Pastoral Care*, and for generations this was to provide a basic manual of the clerical life, a vision of the priesthood imitating the Good Shepherd and a work that, directly or not, was profoundly to influence Chaucer's creation of his Parson in *The Canterbury Tales*. Gregory was clearly of central importance to Alfred and his contemporaries. This was partly because, up to the eleventh century, he was the major exponent of a Catholic theology rooted in authority, dwelling on the terrors of Hell and emphasizing penance. Gregory was also revered, however, for his ecclesiastical initiative and for the lofty spirit of order with which he remodelled the Church along the lines of the Late Roman Empire. Both Gregory's works that were translated appealed directly to the laity and to priests, and were clearly essential to re-founding the Church and so halting the process of cultural decline.

But there was a further significance in the decision to translate Gregory, a significance made clear in a passage from the third book Alfred had rendered into Old English and the most important work of Northumbrian Latin culture: Bede's *Ecclesiastical History of the English Nation* (original 731, trans. *c.* 880). It is Bede who tells of the British conversion to Christianity. In a famous story he shows the young Gregory, moved by the fair faces of some English boys in the slave market at Rome, vowing that their race should be converted and so become not Angles but angels. This was a promise partly fulfilled when, in 597, Gregory sent St Augustine to England as head of the first Christian mission. It is the history of the country subsequent to this event (an occurrence which brought both renewed faith and literacy to the island) that is Bede's chief concern. It is a narrative he tells with devotion, with a critical concern for accuracy unique in his time, and a skill with anecdote that still gives pleasure. Here, in what is perhaps the best-known passage from the *Ecclesiastical History*, a courtier of King Edwin (616–32) suggests reasons for his master's conversion:

'Your Majesty, when we compare the present life of man on earth with that time of which we have no knowledge, it seems to me like the swift flight of a single sparrow through the banqueting-hall where you are sitting at dinner on a winter's day with your thanes and counsellors. In the midst there is a comforting fire to warm the hall; outside, the storms of winter rain or snow are raging. The sparrow flies swiftly in through one door of the hall, and out through another. While he is inside, he is safe from the winter storms; but after a few moments of comfort, he vanishes from sight into the wintry world from which he came. Even so, man appears on earth for a little while; but of what went before this life or of what follows, we know nothing. Therefore, if this new teaching has brought any more certain knowledge, it seems only right that we should follow it.'

The speech is perfectly achieved, a blend of pathos and intelligence. It seems also to have had its effect. The success of Christianity was swiftly if not regularly achieved, and, despite a series of arguments about organization and quarrels with Celtic priests over that most tendentious matter, the dating of Easter, we have seen that the Church in England became a stronghold of learning in an otherwise dark age. In Northumbria especially, preserved by Bede and his masters, a Christian culture that richly blended the inheritance of Greece, Rome and Byzantium nurtured the teachers who were to lead Charlemagne's renaissance on the continent. These men now appeared to Alfred, engaged on a similar enterprise, as essential figures to emulate. If the Alfredian version of the *Ecclesiastical History* is considerably shorter than the original (translating, incidentally, the beautiful image of the sparrow into the biblical 'twinkling of an eye'), it provided both a glimpse of the culture of eighth-century Northumbria and of the development of English history under God's guidance. Both were of central importance to securing a new sense of national identity, for without an informed concept of the past there is no sense of the future.

The Alfredian translation of the *Universal History* of Orosius (trans. *c.* 880) – an encyclopedic account of the growth of the Christian faith – is clearly supplementary to Bede and is again a severely edited version of the original. It is a work containing some lively travel writing, however, which the Elizabethan Hakluyt was to use when compiling his history of English sea voyages. Alfred's prose translation of the Psalms, which he was perhaps at work on when he died, was another part of his revival of learning, since the Psalter served as an elementary text in the teaching of Latin and the training of the priesthood. Alfred no doubt felt a personal sympathy with their ancient author who put his trust in the Lord while striking out against his foes, but it is important to remember that of all the books of the Bible – itself the most influential text of the age – it was perhaps the Psalms that became the most widely and intimately known. Finally, Alfred's translations of Augustine's *Soliloquies* (trans. 880) and Boethius's *Consolation of Philosophy* (a work of seminal influence on the Middle Ages but one most usefully discussed in the context of Chaucer, another of its translators) again show his abiding interest in philosophical problems and his appreciation of the central figures of early medieval thought. Like all his works, these latter translations reveal Alfred's commitment to his native culture, to Christian truth and that intellectual endeavour which are the foundations of his achievement.

3

The Old English of the translations was also employed by writers of *The Anglo-Saxon Chronicle* (*c.* 871–1154). Again, this is a work we owe to Alfred's initiative though probably not to his hand. Where Orosius had provided a European view of Christianity and Bede had told the history of England from the earliest times to his own, *The Anglo-Saxon Chronicle* is a laconic record of contemporary national events and thus a vital source of information on Alfred's and subsequent reigns. It survived the Norman Conquest, and entries in the version from Peterborough (one of the seven centres at which the *Chronicle* was kept) continue into the reign of King Stephen (1135–54). While the narrative rarely rises to the level of literature, what is chiefly remarkable about the *Chronicle* is its very simplicity at a time when Latin authors in England and abroad were striving for elaborate rhetorical effect.

Conscious artifice, a concern with style and fluency, were clearly of interest among later vernacular prose writers. This is particularly true of those associated with the Benedictine revival which took place during the reign of King Edgar (959–76). In this prolific period, the time when the manuscripts in which Old English verse survives were written, the learning fostered by Alfred was placed on a firm foundation after the troubles that succeeded his reign. A large quantity of alliterative prose sermons survive. Some of them, forcefully decrying the evil of the times, see further Viking raids as a divine punishment foretelling the end of the world. However, it is the particular mark of Old English prose in this last great period that it was considered capable of dealing with almost any subject, be it history, romantic adventure such as we find in the translation of *Apollonius of Tyre* (*c.* 1050), righteous indignation or the subtleties of theological argument. Indeed, fifty years before the Norman Conquest the sermons of Aelfric (d. *c.* 1020) and Wulfstan (d. 1023), along with a quantity of medical, legal and scholastic prose, reveal a complete mastery of the medium.

4

But the glory of Old English is its verse. The remaining 30,000 lines are mostly preserved in four manuscripts dating from 1000 A.D. Barely surviving fire, dispersal and other hazards (including, in one case, use as a chopping board and a beer mat) these precious volumes contain relics of a once oral poetry that is variously heroic and elegiac, visionary and riddling. Nevertheless, such variety is only a fragment of what had once been created, and it is important to remember that our knowledge of Old English poetry is based on the most partial evidence. We are told, for instance, that Bede had a considerable reputation as a vernacular poet, but only one of his poems in his mother tongue survives. It is five lines long. The monasteries were naturally committed to Christian literature, and so an interest in preserving secular verse was not uppermost in their minds. Even those works they did copy out suffered neglect in the Middle Ages and destruction at the Reformation. As a result, there is often little material for comparison. The corpus of Old English verse, for example, contains nothing to equal its greatest work – the epic *Beowulf* – yet so assured a poem can hardly have been unique. Such difficulties are further complicated by the fact that in the rare cases where several manuscripts of a poem survive they differ considerably. The text, in other words, is not absolutely certain. But, above all, those transcriptions that do remain are versions of poems often composed in Mercia or Northumbria yet only written down in the southern dialect of Wessex as much as three centuries later. Loss is thus compounded with uncertainty. Nonetheless, if a degree of caution is essential when surveying what remains, one fact is abundantly clear: Old English verse is – and was meant to be – deeply enjoyable. The poet or *scop* was sometimes referred to as a *gleoman* or 'gleeman', and his works were originally sung, often in the halls of local princes.

The communal and oral nature of Old English verse accounts for a number of its most characteristic features, all of which made it easier for the bard to improvise and his audience to understand. For example, each line, divided into halves of two stressed and a varying number of unstressed units, is symmetrical and alliterative. The language is also marked by vivid poetic diction and variations on well-known phrases. Alliteration and the rhythm of Old English verse offer a pattern and flexibility that appeal directly to the ear, while its poetic diction (frequently a matter of *kennings* or compound words, such as 'whale's acre' for the sea or 'Spear Danes' for a nation) helps to set the verse apart from normal speech while providing great linguistic vividness.

It is, however, a third characteristic of Old English verse – its use of a formulaic means of composition – that offers the surest clue to its oral nature. Accounts of popular events (fights or feasts, for example) are usually constructed from similar verbal units according to patterns that were clearly part of a traditional and unwritten inheritance. The use of such formulaic construction is fundamental to the literature of an oral culture, and its presence has been traced in the poetry of Homer and the long folk-tales improvised in this century by illiterate bards in Eastern Europe.

Finally, and analogous to such devices, there are many passages in Old English poetry that show the poet drawing on the abundance of parallel or alternative expressions for a single idea contained in his 'wordhoard' – the common stock of poetic vocabulary – and thereby displaying the wealth of his resources. The following lines, even in translation, suggest something of these qualities. Being the only verses directly attributable to Caedmon, they have additional interest as the earliest datable specimen of English poetry (657–80) whose author is known by name:

> Now [we] must praise the Keeper of Heaven's Kingdom,
> The Maker's might, and His conception,
> The deed of the Father of Glory; as He of all wonders
> – The Eternal Lord – established the beginning.
> He first created for the children of men
> Heaven as a roof, the Holy Shaper;
> Then Middle Earth [did] Mankind's Keeper,
> The Eternal Lord, afterward ordain,
> The earth of men, the Almighty Lord.

5

In these nine lines there are no less than eight periphrases for the name of the Lord and two for human beings. Caedmon has drawn heavily on the 'wordhoard', and each of his epithets for God contributes to an enhanced sense of supernatural power, marvellous in its works and intellect. Mankind, on the other hand, is seen in all its earthbound mortality, living in a universe irradiated with divine creativity. For the first time, as far as we are aware, a Christian theme has been presented in the style and diction of Germanic poetry. Such is the nature of the 'Caedmonian revolution'. The pleasure which is always to be found in new poems of this sophisticated kind lies in the virtuoso display of epithet linked to a serious vision of man's place in the cosmic order, a vision at once grateful and rapturous.

Bede had no doubt that Caedmon's poetry was divinely inspired. A passage from his *Ecclesiastical History* relates how this herdsman, though illiterate, received the gift of song from God. Bede tells how the sleeping Caedmon had a vision of a man who commanded him, despite his confessing his inability, to sing. 'What must I sing?' the future poet asked. 'Sing of the beginning of created things,' came the reply. According to Bede, when Caedmon received this answer 'he immediately began to sing verses in praise of the Creator'. They are those reproduced here. The following day, Caedmon was taken before St Hild, Abbess of Whitby, and so impressed was she and those literate people about her that they made Caedmon a lay brother and offered him instruction in order that, having remembered all he had learned 'and turning it over like a clean beast ruminating', he could transform theology into verse. *Perplacida histriola*, 'a charming little tale,' wrote Milton, who surely realized the biblical tradition of divine inspiration underlying the passage, a tradition he was himself to invoke in *Paradise Lost*.

Bede also provides a list of Caedmon's works on subjects ranging from the Creation to Doomsday. Of these, only the nine lines quoted here

survive, recent scholarship having shown that the four poems *Genesis,
Exodus, Daniel* and *Christ and Satan* belong to that more minor
phenomenon, the 'school of Caedmon'. Other biblical and Christian
narratives of the period include works by Cynewulf (late eighth or ninth
century), who is the only Old English poet besides Bede and Caedmon
who is known by name. Such pieces, though developing the techniques
of the 'Caedmonian revolution', are generally of a lower quality, overly
didactic and sometimes melodramatic in their intention. They are sometimes of more interest for their methods of biblical exegesis than for their
poetic effect. One vernacular Christian poem from this period, however,
towers above all others: *The Dream of the Rood* (c. 698).

6

'Rood' is the Old English for a processional cross, and devotion to this
most famous Christian symbol was well established by 700 A.D., the date
of the magnificent stone crucifix from Ruthewell. This is one of the
masterpieces of Anglo-Saxon art, and fifteen lines from the Old English
poem are actually incised round its stone panels. They are appropriate,
for the poem is an intense meditation on Calvary, a history of the True
Cross and the all-involving paradox that the Crucifixion was at once a
symbol of human sin and an assertion of divine love.

The cross itself, now glorious in heaven, appears to the poet in a dream.
Hymned by angels, clad in precious metal and encrusted with gemstones
symbolic of Christ's five wounds, the glorious apparition recalls a fabulous
reliquary fashioned by some Saxon goldsmith. As the poem progresses,
so tree and gold, shame and victory, mingle in visionary paradox:

> Around angels of God
>   all glazed upon it,
> since first fashioning fair.
>   It was not a felon's gallows,
> for holy ghosts beheld it there,
> and men on mould, and the whole Making shone for it
> – *signum* of victory!
>   Stained and marred,
> stricken with shame, I saw the glory-tree
> shine out gaily, sheathed in yellow
> decorous gold; and gemstones made
> for their Maker's Tree a right mail-coat.

The gemstones – the wounds of Christ – have now become part of the
armour of a Saxon warrior. If the cross is an aspect of the glory of

Heaven, its continuing power on earth is that of a soldier. But when the cross is made actually to tell of its bitter experiences and describes Christ's eager mounting of the gallows, the heavy embrace of his body and the mourning after his death, we are also offered that intense, riddling experience of the universe which, along with the dramatic pathos of warrior heroism, are qualities found again in the Elegies and *Beowulf*:

> I was reared up, a rood.
>   I raised the great King,
> liege lord of the heavens,
>   dared not lean from the true.
> They drove me through with dark nails:
>   on me are the deep wounds manifest,
> wide-mouthed hate-dents.
>   I durst not harm any of them.
> How they mocked at us both!
>   I was all moist with blood
> sprung from the Man's side
>   after He sent forth His soul.

With the fading of the vision comes repentance. The heavens close and the poet is left on the dark, worthless earth. Mortal existence is nothing. The cross had warned him of death and Doomsday, and he now turns to his own plight. 'I have not many powerful friends on earth.' The familiar sense of isolation, timeless and so often expressed in Old English verse, returns. Faith is the only consolation. Summoning the renewed forces of his devotion, the poet imagines a time when he will be released from the travails of 'middle earth' and will be able to join the blest in Heaven. As the poem comes to a close, so we are led more surely to know its author, to see him not through the incidental details of his life and character, but on that most intense plane of his being – his faith.

7

The stoic endurance and sense of transitoriness that partly characterize *The Dream of the Rood* are also the subjects of the Elegies, that handful of poems preserved in the Exeter Book, which, along with *Deor* (*c*. 643), make up the most directly affecting works in all Old English literature. The names by which these poems have come to be known are: *The Wanderer*, *The Seafarer*, *The Ruin*, *The Wife's Lament*, *The Husband's Message* and *Wulf and Eadwacer* (*c*. 780). Each concerns loss and isolation, and coldly through the greatest of them blows a salt-edged wind and a knowledge of the heaving wastes of the sea. These build to a sense of universal desolation. Huddled at the edge of the known world, the narrators brave out their despair: 'That went past; this may too.' The poet of *Deor* mouths his refrain through the clenched teeth of exile and a jealousy of happier men. The narrator in *The Wanderer*, deprived by the death of his patron, tries to contain his despair as he seeks out another prince:

> 'So must I also curb my mind,
> cut off from country, from kind far distant,
> by cares overworn, bind it in fetters;
> this since, long ago, the ground's shroud
> enwrapped my gold-friend. Wretched I went thence,
> winter-wearied, over the waves' bound;
> dreary I sought hall of a gold-giver,
> where far or near I might find
> him who in meadhall might take heed of me,
> furnish comfort to a man friendless,
> win me with cheer.'

But the gold and friendship are mere remembered joys. Before the poet stretch the fallow waves, the ghosts of friends and the enforced wisdom of pain. He urges himself to suffer in silence, but knowledge of personal defeats builds to a picture of worldwide decay:

> 'A wise man may grasp how ghastly it shall be
> when all this world's wealth standeth waste,
> even as now, in many places, over the earth
> walls stand, wind-beaten,
> hung with hoar-frost; ruined habitations.
> The wine-halls crumble; their wielders lie
> bereft of bliss, the band all fallen
> proud by the wall.'

God has laid the buildings waste, and an echo of Babylon is perhaps intended here as it more certainly is in *The Ruin*. There, with the belief that the present world is an image of timeless biblical truth (an important characteristic of much literature for the next millennium), the poet offers a picture of the decay of Roman Bath that is intended to conjure images of the destruction of the Old Testament cities of the proud.

This sense of doom and decay, though the dominant impression of the incomplete *Ruin*, is not the only mood expressed in *The Wanderer* and *The Seafarer*. Yet to say these works breathe a confidence in salvation would be facile. There is about them both – and it is important to be responsive to such shifts in the tradition of the Christian life – a profound sense of the arduous and sinful brevity of existence that is especially characteristic of faith in the first Christian millennium. *The Seafarer* in particular conveys an impression of near despair in the face of physical hardship, mental suffering and spiritual exertion. These moods are both subtle and apparently autobiographical. 'The history is of myself,' the poet declares, and he recounts the gruelling life of a man rowing in the longships, an exile's existence broken only by the screeching gulls:

> Hail flew in showers,
> there was no sound there but the slam of waves
> along an icy sea. The swan's blare
> my seldom amusement; for men's laughter
> there was curlew-call, there were the cries of gannets,
> for mead-drinking the music of the gull.
> To the storm striking the stone cliffs
> gull would answer, eagle scream
> from throats frost-feathered. No friend or brother
> by to speak with the despairing mind.

Such things, the poet says, are incomprehensible to the gregarious town-dweller and his world of youthful ardour. Yet the very strenuousness of the sea-life is an imperative, and, as the narrator obeys its call, so the physical rigours of his journey take on a metaphysical dimension. The ocean becomes an image of the perilous sea of faith. England is the fast-corrupting world best left behind by a white-haired man. He sees how the old, heroic values with their warrior cult of honour have dwindled to disuse. Pagan beliefs (the burial of the dead with their golden artefacts, for example) are contemptible because useless. There is no possibility of secular fame or spiritual salvation in a heathen world gone bad. As the Seafarer sets out once again, rejecting the corrupt, braving the ocean, his last thoughts are of

> ... the anger of God
> towards a soul sin-freighted.

There is no sense of divine mercy here. Rather, and in a more heightened form than is found even in *The Dream of the Rood*, there is a view of redemption in which man, in the words of Sir Richard Southern, 'was a helpless spectator in a cosmic struggle which determined his chances of salvation'. God and the devil dispute for man's soul while man himself remains frightened, guilty and as powerless as a mariner in a storm. What is absent here – absent because not yet fully realized – is an image of the compassionate and suffering Jesus, the loving Saviour made man, which was to be developed for its emotional impact by St Anselm and a later epoch.

8

Before moving to a discussion of *Beowulf* – the greatest of the surviving works of Old English literature – a number of short but excellent poems need to be mentioned. Of these, the Riddles form the most extensive group. In these often curious but frequently attractive pieces there is a deliberate and playful obscurity, but, more richly pleasurable, a verbal exhilaration that sometimes amounts to awe in face of the natural world and its beauty.

Of three other outstanding groups of verse from the tenth century, *The Phoenix* – a poem interestingly derived from a pagan Latin verse – best conveys that sense of wonder which is sometimes found in the Riddles. It too is a work that calls for unusual means of interpretation, ways of thought that are, nonetheless, of the greatest importance. Though superior in imaginative resourcefulness to *The Panther* and *The Whale*, *The Phoenix* should be considered along with these works since, in intention, each expresses the idea that the creatures of the world we perceive or imagine around us signify the invisible things of God. The Phoenix, for example, living in a vividly realized paradise, is a symbol of Christ. A passage from the end of the poem sees its rebirth from its own ashes as an image of both the Resurrection and man's redemption after the Fall. By contrast, the Whale, beguiling mariners into thinking it is an island, lets sailors anchor off itself and even kindle a fire on its back. When the men have settled to sleep, the Whale submerges and, revealing its true colours as an image of the devil, draws the hapless sailors down to Hell and destruction.

There is an obvious pleasure in such ways of thought, a satisfying feeling that the natural world is a vast encyclopedia which can be read for timeless moral truth. To the early medieval mind such a belief was axiomatic. 'All creation, like a book or picture, is a mirror to us – a true figure of our life, our death, our condition, our lot,' wrote the twelfth-century scholar Alain de Lille. Such ideas, once commonplace but now so unfamiliar, are essential features in the background of much medieval poetry, and we must appreciate that behind what Alain says lies the curriculum of studies laid down by St Augustine in *De Doctrina Christiana*. Here all human learning – logic and languages, mathematics, natural and human history – are shown to be ancillary to the study of the Bible. In other words, knowledge of fact brings man to the gateway of spiritual truth, and this superior world is expressed through imagery and allegory.

Perhaps no other current of medieval thought is more typical or initially more foreign than this. To St Augustine and later scholars, however, the belief that below physical appearances and the literal sense of the Scriptures there existed layers of allegorical meaning that showed man in relation to Christ and redemption, to the conduct of life and the future of the soul, was a matter of 'infinite sweetness'. It was the clearest expression that God's love and purposes irradiate the universe, giving even the humblest insect its useful place in a cosmic economy. As a means of interpreting literary texts especially, this allegorical mode is of the greatest importance and we shall return to it often. To read it is to begin to read the medieval mind.

Equally important to Old English and later poetry is an interest in biblical narrative. This was sometimes written to suggest that events in the Old Testament prefigure those in the New – a way of thought already present in the Gospels and in St Paul – and sometimes, as in the magnificent *Judith* (*c.* 911–*c.* 918), for sheer delight in the drama and the poet's skill. The accommodation of the original to a Saxon ethos is admirably achieved in *Judith*, while the detail and vivacity (something not always to be found in similar but later works) appear again in those re-tellings of Old Testament narratives attributed to the fourteenth-century author of *Sir Gawain and the Green Knight*.

Judith also contains an excellent battle scene, but the two tenth-century poems that most clearly express the heroic warrior ethos are *Bamborough* and the finer *Battle of Maldon*. The latter, though incomplete, is the record of a historical Saxon defeat at the hands of the Vikings in 993. Its scenes of action are vivid, but most moving and characteristic are the speeches of the warriors at the close as they face a certain death:

> 'Courage shall grow keener, clearer the will,
> the heart fiercer, as our force faileth.
> Here our lord lies levelled in the dust,
> the man all marred: he shall mourn to the end
> who thinks to wend off from this war-play now.
> Though I am white with winters I will not away,
> for I think to lodge me alongside my dear one,
> lay me down by my lord's right hand.'

9

Such suffering and duty, a love of wisdom and the recognition of an uncertain, malign universe, partly characterize the longest and most famous Old English poem: the epic *Beowulf*. Though composed in a relatively sophisticated Christian court in eighth-century Mercia or Northumberland, the work is deeply sympathetic to the heroic tradition expressed in *The Battle of Maldon*, to that view of human activity characteristic of the pagan world in southern Scandinavia during the fifth and sixth centuries. This heroic view of life is Germanic in origin and was depicted by the Roman historian Tacitus as early as the first century A.D. It clearly remained a living tradition, and many of its characteristics, such as personal loyalty to a lord, the expected rewards of horses and feasting, valour, glory and the pursuit of deathless fame, are fundamental to *Beowulf*.

These heroic qualities are at once social and literary, for here was a way of life in which poetry immortalized the warrior's most prized possession, his fame, and so inspired a similar bravery in others. The communal, oral and traditional nature of Old English verse thus came into its own with the epic. In the following passage from *Beowulf*, which shows poetry being improvised as a band of warriors rides back from seeing the result of the hero's first great struggle, we have a useful description of these qualities:

> ... a fellow of the king's,
> whose head was a storehouse of the storied verse,
> whose tongue gave gold to the language
> of the treasured repertory, wrought a new lay
> made in the measure. The man struck up,
> found the phrase, framed rightly
> the deed of Beowulf, drove the tale,
> rang word-changes.

It follows that the verse largely reflects an aristocratic ethos, a life of fights and feasting, of ceremony, brilliant gold and sudden darkness. Here are pride in birth and physical strength. In secular terms, the poem shows a world of blood and kinship loyalties, sacred obligations, feud and vengeance. Beyond this, the forces of *wyrd*, or fate, seem to control man's destiny with mysterious omnipotence, while evil is both primordial and monstrous, something to be outwitted and destroyed by physical strength wherever possible. As the Christian poet explains, introducing values by which we may choose to understand but not simply to judge his heroes:

> Such was their practice,
> a heathen hope; Hell possessed
> their hearts and minds: the Maker was unknown to them,
> the Judge of all actions, the Almighty was unheard of,
> they knew not how to praise the Prince of Heaven,
> the Wielder of Glory.

Beowulf's own name encapsulates a number of these admired pagan qualities since 'Beowulf' is itself a *kenning* derived from 'bee-wolf', in other words a raider of hives and so a 'bear'. *Beorn*, Old English for a heroic warrior prince, seems originally to have meant 'bear' as well, and these princely but animal elements – the sheer glorying in physical strength – are evident in Beowulf himself. Near the close of the work he remembers killing with the force of his hug a man who was defending his own home:

> 'It was not my sword
> that broke his bone-cage and the beatings of his heart
> but my warlike hand-grasp.'

The speech that follows expresses Beowulf's public vow to slay the dragon that has been harrying his people and so suggests something of the poem's mythical elements – the slaying of the dragon contains clear folk-lore motifs – while the speech again reveals a number of qualities characteristic of the heroic world:

> Beowulf made speech, spoke a last time
> a word of boasting: 'Battles in plenty
> I ventured in youth; and I shall venture this feud
> and again achieve glory, the guardian of my people,
> old though I am, if this evil destroyer
> dares to come out of his earthen hall.'

Boasting (a traditional social and literary accomplishment) as well as a love of battle are evident here. So too is the proper role of the king as the guardian of his people. The resolve to destroy something incomprehensible and evil – a threat to that prized symbol of warrior society, the hall – is stirring, but the pathos lies partly in the fact that Beowulf will be destroyed in the fight and his fame will be ensured by his death. Glory and destruction, the fundamentals of the heroic ethos, are here inseparable. Beowulf himself is described as *lofgeornost*, 'most eager for praise', while in the same passage – that which describes the mourning after his death – the grandeur of the melancholy and a feeling for the intensity of warrior bonds during the brief span of life again display the values of the society in which the poem is set:

> Then the warriors rode around the barrow,
> twelve of them in all, athelings' sons.
> They recited a dirge to declare their grief,
> spoke of the man, mourned their King.
> They praised his manhood and the prowess of his hands,
> they raised his name; it is right a man
> should be lavish in honouring his lord and friend,
> should love him in his heart when the leading-forth
> from the house of flesh befalls him at last.

It is against these human qualities that the monsters of the poem are pitted. There are three of them: Grendel, his mother and finally the dragon. Their appearances form the main elements of a diffuse action which is further complicated by digressions that place the hero in the context of the struggle between his own Geatish people and the Swedes, as well as in the broader sweep of Scandinavian history with its complex interlacings of feud, treachery, vengeance and accidental slaughter. While these digressions help establish the poem in a world of recorded events, the battles with the monsters relate it to myth. There are, as we have seen, mythopoeic elements in the struggles themselves, in the magic regions in which they sometimes take place, and in the supernatural help the hero occasionally receives. It is, however, a third quality of the work, the nameless poet's ability to draw on traditional resources and present an all-involving view of man and the supernatural, war and peace, life and death, that helps to give the poem its status as a heroic elegy.

The imaginative power that results from this fusion is clear in the opening section. Here, in the hall of Hrothgar the Dane, a poet is singing of creation to the company after their feast. This is in many respects the world of Caedmon; but outside, envying the display of warrior glory, lurks incarnate evil – Grendel, descendant of Cain, the first murderer:

> With the coming of night came Grendel also,
> sought the great house and how the Ring-Danes
> held their hall when the horn had gone round.
> He found in Heorot the force of nobles
> slept after supper, sorrow forgotten,
> the condition of men. Maddening with rage,
> he struck quickly, creature of evil;
> grim and greedy, he grasped on their pallets
> thirty warriors, and away he was out of there,

> thrilled with his catch: he carried off homeward
> his glut of slaughter, sought his own halls.
> As the day broke, with the dawn's light
> Grendel's outrage was openly to be seen:
> night's table-laughter turned to morning's
> lamentation. Lord Hrothgar
> sat silent then, the strong man mourned,
> glorious king, he grieved for his thanes
> as they read the traces of a terrible foe,
> a cursed fiend. That was too cruel a feud,
> too long, too hard!

Grendel's repeated raids have sapped the nation's strength, and it is only with Beowulf's arrival – a rich passage of traditional episodes which clearly portrays the formalized, glory-seeking world of warrior heroism – that Grendel is destroyed. The passage describing the fight has exceptional physical vividness; but, in another shift in the register of the poem, splendour returns to Heorot when, at the close, the Danish king lavishes praise and gold on his deliverer.

Grendel's mother, however, is lurking in her Mere. Eventually she stalks to Heorot to avenge her son. Beowulf is summoned a second time, and the description of his arming, his underwater struggle and final victory (the latter achieved with the help of a divinely fashioned sword) again mingles traditional motifs with a sense of both a mythical hero and a providential benevolence. The Christian poet is confident that even in this pagan world God cares for the virtuous. When Beowulf has finally slain Grendel's dam, a second period of celebration occurs, treasure is lavished on the victor and he returns to his home, his fame immeasurably increased. Yet Hrothgar's words in the midst of proud rejoicing cannot be forgotten:

> 'Beloved Beowulf, best of warriors,
> resist this deadly taint, take what is better,
> your lasting profit. Put away arrogance,
> noble fighter! The noon of your strength
> shall last for a while now, but in a little time
> sickness or a sword will strip it from you:
> either enfolding flame or a flood's billow
> or a knife-stab or the stoop of a spear
> or the ugliness of age; or your eyes' brightness
> lessens and grows dim. Death shall soon
> have beaten you then, O brave warrior!'

This is the turning point in the poem and marks the transition from the brilliance of youthful achievement to the shadow of death.

The final main passage in the poem is the episode with the dragon. It moves on an altogether more mythopoeic level. The dragon has come to destroy Beowulf's hall, for the hero, now some fifty years older, has become the ancient and revered king of his Geatish people. They are harried by the dragon because of a theft from its hoard of gold. About both the dragon and its treasure hovers an ominous sense of destruction and obscure malevolence. With his spirit 'gloomy, death-eager, wandering', Beowulf seems to realize something more than human in this last encounter.

In the heat of battle all his companions desert him, save one. Recalling the bonds of duty that bind warrior to lord in the heroic ethos, Wiglaf alone goes to help his master and stays to wash his mortally wounded body. He is then sent to fetch the dragon's treasure. The dying Beowulf, his sacrifice complete, stares at it and passes his kingship to his one loyal thane. But even before the magnificent funeral, the burial of Beowulf along with the fatal gold, Wiglaf knows that the cowardice of his companions spells an end to the heroic, pagan world. Its own values cannot sustain it. Destruction and exile wait for all:

> 'Now there shall cease for your race the receiving of treasure,
> the bestowal of swords, all satisfaction of ownership,
> all comfort of home. Your kinsmen, every one,
> shall become wanderers without land-rights
> as soon as athelings over the world
> shall hear the report of how you fled,
> a deed of ill fame. Death is better
> for any earl than an existence of disgrace!'

The poem closes with Beowulf's funeral. During the work's long progress, mythic struggles and human values merge with a vision of the rise and fall of communal and individual life. All are shown in conflict with destiny and the *aglaecas*, the 'monsters' or 'terrible ones'. If the poet himself, fashioning these matters in the traditional patterns of epic, was aware of a different and Christian view of life, he also honoured the older forms: heroic death and warrior pride as exhibited on the *wælstow*, or 'place of slaughter'. It was this last phrase, so charged with associations, so thoroughly Old English, that the writer of the *Chronicle* was also to recall when he was obliged to recount the destruction of the last Saxon army at the Battle of Hastings – an event which we may choose to see as both the last Norse invasion (the Normans were 'the men from the North') and as the start of a new era.

CHAPTER 2

EARLY MIDDLE ENGLISH AND ITS LITERATURE

1

Language in both its written and spoken forms is a series of symbols subject to change and even to decay. It is also the principal means of social co-operation and to that degree a powerful tool of social control. Much of this is illustrated by the effects of the Norman Conquest. Though at the age of forty-five King William set out to learn the Old English of his subjects, he seems to have abandoned the project, and the depredations following the Battle of Hastings during which he secured his grasp on the country ensured that a Norman dialect of French established itself as the principal language of government. The Anglo-Saxon aristocracy was depleted and, while Norman soldiers built castles to defend their new lands, Norman prelates were placed on the thrones of English cathedrals. Though the formidable Saxon Bishop Wulfstan (d. 1095) maintained his see at Worcester and preserved something of the traditions of Old English literature, even he was ridiculed by Lanfranc of Canterbury for his inability to discuss politics in the new language of power.

In addition to becoming the principal tongue of government and school education, the Saxon defeat meant that Anglo-Norman also established itself as the medium of aristocratic literary culture and, eventually, of the law. It produced its own body of excellent work, including religious allegory, saints' lives, history and narrative poems. All of this work forms an essential European context for the later rise of vernacular literature and so must be considered. In addition, while a quantity of Old English homily, prose translation and copies of earlier work was still written in the monasteries, Latin soon became virtually the sole language of the Church and scholarship, the tradition of Old English as a religious teaching language being eclipsed for some time in most areas. It is possible that a popular tradition of oral alliterative poetry in English survived, contributing to the vernacular verse of the following centuries, but the sundering of intellectual life from the speech of the majority and the decay of a great prose were grievous losses. Though writers in Peterborough continued *The Anglo-Saxon Chronicle* into the twelfth century (its depiction of the horrors of the reign of King Stephen is justly famous), a language without a commonly approved and constantly refreshed literary standard is vulnerable. While it would be wrong to suggest that the Normans were actively hostile to Old English, the problems arising in a bilingual nation were vividly described by the chronicler Robert of Gloucester as late as 1300:

> þus com lo engelond in to normandies hond.
> & þe normans ne couþe speke þo bote hor owe speche
> & speke french as hii dude atom, & hor children dude also teche;
> So þat heiemen of þis lond þat of hor blod come
> Holdeþ alle þulke spreche þat hii of hom nome.
> Vor bote a man conne frenss me telþ of him lute.
> Ac lowe men holdeþ to engliss & to hor owe speche 3utc.
> Ich wene þer ne beþ in al þe world contreyes none
> þat ne holdeþ to hor owe speche bote engelond one.
> Ac wel me wot uor to conne boþe wel it is,
> Vor þe more þat a mon can, þe more wurþe he is.

(*Lo, thus England came into the hands of Normandy. The Normans could only speak their own language and so they talked in French as they did at home, teaching their children likewise; and the highly placed in the land who are descended from them continue to use this language which they derive from them. Unless a man speak French he counts for little. But lowly men still keep to English and to their own way of talking. Apart from England, I think there are no other countries in the world that do not use their own language. Yet men know it is a good thing to learn both languages, for the more a man knows, the more he is worth.*)

This passage makes clear that the division between those who chiefly spoke Anglo-Norman and those who continued to communicate largely in Old English was a social one. The new aristocracy maintained their associations with France, used their own language in their business, and for nearly half a century showed only an incidental interest in Old English. William himself was buried in his native Normandy and left England to his second son, reserving his dukedom for his first. This bias was maintained throughout the storms of the next century and a half and, with the marriage of Henry II (1154–89) to Eleanor of Aquitaine, the English king found himself controlling an empire that stretched from the borders of Scotland to the Pyrenees and which included some of the most culturally active areas in the South of France. The primacy of French at court thus seemed assured.

Nonetheless, on a humbler and in some respects more significant level, contact between conquerors and conquered was bound to take place. Orders had to be given, estates controlled, babies nursed and business conducted. The result was a very gradual merging of the two nations, and, by the close of the twelfth century, it was possible for a jurist to write: 'Now that the English and Normans have been dwelling together, marrying and giving in marriage, the two nations have become so mixed that it is scarcely possible today, speaking of free men, to tell who is English, who of Norman race.' The social qualification – 'speaking of free men' – is important, for information on the distribution of French- and English-speakers at this period comes largely from the upper levels of society rather than from feudal serfs. What this information suggests, however, is that fifty years after the Conquest a knowledge of both languages was becoming widespread among those nobles and more prosperous town-dwellers who were normally resident in the kingdom. By 1200, ladies were being advised to read both French and English. Among churchmen and in other educated circles a knowledge of English seems to have been expected, while among those who had to convey a landowner's wishes to his serfs an ability to speak both languages was normal. We should therefore ask what this particular stage of English was like.

The language of the chroniclers and recorded poets was, we have seen, a form of the West Saxon spoken in Wessex and the nation's old capital at Winchester. It had an extensive vocabulary, it was inflected, and its nouns had genders. It was also to prove itself remarkably adaptable. Even before the Conquest it was changing, inflexions in particular weakening and finally passing virtually out of use by the close of the twelfth century. Once Old English had been forced to surrender its status as the language of record, this process was accelerated. Pronouns were simplified, the use of strong verbs declined, and the arbitrary system of attributing gender was placed on a natural basis. French-trained scribes, searching for the phonetic equivalents of Old English, allow us to hear shifts in pronunciation, while contacts between Normans and English led to an enormous widening of vocabulary. It was perhaps this development in an already fluid language that was the change most obviously attributable to the Conquest.

As the speech of the Anglo-Saxons changed into what is now called Early Middle English, many Old English words died or became synonyms. Readers of Sir Walter Scott's *Ivanhoe* – that very romantic view of Norman England – may remember the opening scene where the Saxon serfs Wamba and Gurth complain that although the names of living animals such as *ox*, *swine* and *calf* are all English, when they are cooked they become French: *beef, pork* and *veal.* By the middle of the thirteenth century some 900 words had been absorbed from Anglo-Norman, the greater part being learned from the invaders rather than, as is the case with the more extensive adoption of French vocabulary after this date, being words imported by native speakers of French now learning English. Most of these new words were religious, some were legal or educational, but many were abstract terms suggesting an increasingly civilized way of life. Among these are *courteous, honour* and *noble.*

Despite this proliferation, a number of structural words deriving from Old English remained. Prepositions (*on, to, for, by*), relatives (*who, which, what*), conjunctions (*and, but*), modal verbs (*shall, will*), most pronouns and some adverbs (*full, very*) are all native, as is much of the basic vocabulary of existence: *life, love, work* and *death.* The resulting combination of Saxon with a usually more abstract phraseology deriving from French and Latin is what helps to make modern English so richly expressive.

2

These linguistic movements, so subtle an index to the energies released in the people, are paralleled by changes in the literature produced during the next three centuries that are equally profound and quite as far-ranging. Though the loss of a language is permanently disabling – its nuances and uses, its particular personality, can never be re-established or fully conveyed through translation – a number of factors need to be borne in mind when considering the works of the ensuing epoch. First, Norman culture was far from unknown in the courts of the last Saxon kings and could, therefore, never be wholly alien. Secondly, the widespread use of Latin and Anglo-Norman not only enriched the native language but, just as importantly, gave English life and thought access to the tumultuous achievements of a renaissance that was spreading across Europe like a sudden spring. Lastly, particularly in areas removed from London, something of Old English literary traditions remained active, not only preserving the past but looking forward to the future.

The longevity and resilient patriotism of Bishop Wulfstan may be held partly responsible for the continued copying of Old English texts in the west. The area was comparatively remote from the capital in a period when the country was markedly regionalized, but, above all, the late development of a French prose style meant that the preservation of the Old English homiletic tradition had an important function. Though copying could lead to the preservation of a merely literary form of Old English, a language out of contact with the spoken tongue, a lively form of West Saxon which shows the influence of a Mercian dialect is clear in three saints' legends which are freely translated from Latin and form part of the 'Katherine' group of manuscripts (*c.* 1200). This is a collection of work in rhythmical prose. Included with these pieces are the allegorical homily *Sawles Warde* ('The Guardian of the Soul'), which again is a translation, and *Hali Meiðhad* ('Holy Virginity'), for which no foreign original has been found. The following passage from *Sawles Warde* (which owes little to its original but much to Old English traditions of prose) is an interesting example both of the alliterative style of these works as a whole and of one type of experience from which this particular author drew his inspiration:

O helle, deaðes hus, wununge of wanunge, of grure ant of granunge, heatel ham ant heard wan of alle wontreaðes, buri of bale ant bold of eauereuch bitternesse, þu laðest lont of alle, þu dorc stude ifullet of alle dreorinesses, Ich cwakie of grisle ant of grure, ant euch ban schekeð me ant euch her me rueð up of þi munegunge, for nis þer na steuene bituhhe þe fordemde bute 'wumme', ant 'wa is me' ant 'wa beo þe' and 'wa beo þe'. 'Wa' ha ȝeieð ant wa ha habbeð, ne of al þet eauer wa is ne schal ham neauer wontin. þe swuch wununge ofearneð for ei hwilinde bliss her of þisse worlde, wel were him ȝef þet he neauer ibore nere. Bi þis ȝe mahen sumdel witen hwuch is helle . . .

(*O Hell, house of death, dwelling of want, of terror and of misery; habitation of hate and dreadful home of every danger; city of suffering and abode of all bitterness, thou most loathed land of all, thou dark place full of every weariness. I quake with terror and fear, and each of my bones shakes and every hair stands up at the memory of you, for there is no sound among the damned but 'Woe is me!' and 'Woe to me!' and 'Woe to you!' 'Woe,' they cry and woe they have; nor shall any woe ever be wanting to all who earn such an abode for any passing pleasure here in the world. Well might he wish he had never been born. From this you may know something of what hell is like . . .*)

The later modification of such penitential melodrama is a most interesting and important development in the spiritual life of the period. In a somewhat similar vein, *Hali Meiðhad* presents, with a shrewd if somewhat gruesome accumulation of detail, the woes of marriage and the advantages to women of a life of cloistered seclusion. Such an existence is also the subject of a work from this period which, with its greater emotional refinement, is unquestionably a masterpiece: *The Ancrene Riwle* (*c.* 1200).

This book was written for the guidance of three well-born women, perhaps from Herefordshire, who had forsaken the world to live as anchoresses in an enclosed cell built on to a church. A particularly accurate version of the text known as *The Ancrene Wisse* suggests the popularity of the work and the wide adoption of the life it examines. So demanding an existence – the decision to suffer mortification greater than normal living can offer and so identify with Christ's suffering that he would eventually come in love to the soul – inevitably presents problems for the modern reader. Great religious devotion (which should be distinguished from emotional extremism) may for many be repellent. This is an important difficulty, and *The Ancrene Riwle* raises in heightened form an issue common to every encounter with the literature of the past: the fact that we must ask first what its contents meant to contemporaries if we are truly to ascertain what they may mean for ourselves. Such a questioning is best approached in this case by a brief outline of *The Ancrene Riwle* followed by an analysis of the images in a passage from it.

The Ancrene Riwle consists of eight sections, the first and last concerning devotional practices and the ordering of daily existence. Between these come passages on the inner life: on controlling the senses, regulating the heart, avoiding temptation, the importance of confession, penance and, in the great seventh section, the pursuit of divine love. Throughout, the anonymous, highly cultured yet reluctant author, though profoundly aware of human sinfulness and the constant, subtle threat of the devil, emphasizes moderation, a refusal of the extremes of mortification and self-neglect. Cleanliness, decorum and refinement suggest that the anchoress's stern vocation is a noble one, a life regulated by prayer, silence and scrupulous self-examination. Its description, deepened by a constant interpretation of the Scriptures in the allegorical manner prescribed by Augustine, is also brought to life by vivid observation. Particularly memorable is the author's portrayal of such moral types as the backbiter pulling a long face and hesitating before discharging his load of venom. We all know him. The closing section is again a tenderly observed picture of daily life. An arduous vocation thus becomes both dignified and humane. With the sixth and seventh passages, however, the emphasis on the anchoress's proper identification with Christ's sufferings and the human need for divine forgiveness and love rises to a climax in this passage of sustained allegory:

A leafdi wes mid hire fan biset al abuten, hire lond al destruet, ant heo al poure, inwið an eorðene castel. A mihti kinges luue wes þah biturnd upon hire, swa unimete swiðe þet he for wohlech sende hire his sonden, an efter oðer, ofte somet monei; sende hire beawbelez baðe feole ant feire, sucurs of liueneð, help of his hehe hird to halden hire castel. Heo underfeng al as on unrecheles, ant swa wes heard-iheortet þet hire luue ne mahte he neauer beo þe neorre. Hwet wult tu

mare? He com himseolf on ende; schawde hire his feire neb, as þe þe wes of alle
men feherest to bihalden; spec se swiðe swoteliche, ant wordes se murie, þet ha
mahten deade arearen to liue; wrahte feole wundres ant dude muchele meistries
biuoren hire ehsihðe; schawde hire his mihte; talde hire of his kinedom; bead to
makien hire cwen of al þet he ahte.

Al þis ne heold nawt. Nes þis hoker wunder? For heo nes neauer wurðe forte
beon his þuften. Ah swa, þurh his deboneirte, luue hefde ouercumen him þet he
seide on ende; 'Dame, þu art iweorret, ant þine van beoð se stronge þet tu ne maht
nanesweis wiðute mi sucurs edfleon hare honden, þet ha ne don þe to scheome
deað efter al þi weane. Ich chulle, for þe luue of þe, neome þet feht upo me ant
arudde þe of ham þe þi deað secheð. Ich wat þah to soðe þet Ich schal bituhen
ham neomen deaðes wunde; ant Ich hit wulle heorteliche, forte ofgan þin heorte.
Nu þenne biseche Ich þe, for þe luue þet Ich cuðe þe, þet tu luuie me, lanhure
efter þe ilke dede dead hwen þu naldest liues.' þes king dude al þus – arudde hire
of alle hire van, ant wes himseolf to wundre ituket ant islein on ende, þurh miracle
aras þah from deaðe to liue. Nere þeos ilke leafdi of uueles cunnes kunde, ჳef ha
ouer all þing ne luuede him herefter?

(*There was once a lady who was completely surrounded by her enemies, her land
was all laid waste, and she herself was destitute in an earthen castle. But a king of
great power loved her so much that he sent messengers to her one after another, and
often several together, with many fair jewels, and with food to sustain her, and he
sent his noble army to help her in the holding of her castle. She accepted it all
unthinkingly, and was so hard-hearted that he could never come any nearer to her
love. What more would you? At last he went himself. He let her see the beauty of his
face, the face of one who of all men was the fairest to behold. He spoke so very
tenderly, and spoke words of such delight that they might have raised the dead to
life. He worked many wonders and wrought great marvels before her eyes, revealed
to her the power that he had, told her of his kingdom and asked that he might make
her queen of all he possessed.*

*All this availed nothing. Was it not strange, this disdain? For she herself was not
worthy to be his handmaid. But love had so vanquished his tender heart, that at last
he said, 'Lady, thou art assailed, and thine enemies are so strong that thou canst
by no means escape their hands without my help, which can prevent their putting
thee to a shameful death after all thy misery. For love of thee I will take this
fight upon myself and deliver thee from those who seek thy death. I know without
any doubt that among them I must receive my death-wound, but I will gladly
meet it in order to win thy heart. Now I beseech thee, for the love I show thee,
that thou shouldst love me, at least after my death has been accomplished, who
wouldst not while I live.' The king carried out all this, delivered her from her
enemies, and was himself outrageously tortured and finally slain. But by a miracle
he rose from death to life. Would not this lady be of an evil nature had she not
loved him thereafter beyond everything else?*)

When we compare this passage from *The Ancrene Riwle* with earlier
examples of religious literature such as *The Seafarer, The Dream of the*

Rood, or even the prose homilies, it at once becomes clear that a bene-volent and profound change has taken place in spiritual awareness. The finger of an angry God no longer points to the sin-freighted soul. Instead, Christ comes as a knightly lover to his lady. Explorations into new places of the heart, a concern with emotional quest and movement, mean that human society and human love can now serve as allegories for the far greater force of divine redemption and Christian compassion. In three anchoresses' chaste, mortifying withdrawal from the world, a vocabulary for delicate possibilities of introspection has been found, a new interest is shown in the primacy of the feelings, and a novel emphasis has been placed on the humanity of Christ and the possibilities of romance.

3

All these were the flowers of a renaissance that blossomed across Europe between *c.* 1050 and the middle of the thirteenth century, a renaissance that revived the monasteries, helped to inspire the Crusades, and urged a new interest in learning, society, poetry and the self. It was a movement deeply rooted in the French-speaking culture of the Loire and the Seine (areas that had particularly benefited from the vigorous expansion of economic life) and one which, with the Norman Conquest, England too could join. Indeed, drawn into the sphere of Norman influence and so having a place in a territorial initiative that stretched from the Scottish border to the Sicilian court where Greek and Arabic culture rubbed shoulders with Latin scholarship, Englishmen in the century after Hastings are found in France, in southern Italy and Spain, searching out treatises on astronomy and mathematics and joining pilgrimages and crusades. The twelfth century was, as great ages always are, both an international period and a multilingual one. As we observe the Church building up its vast body of systematic knowledge and developing a rich and inward life; as we see the formation of the chivalric mystique that led to the writing of a literature of romance; and as we watch the growth of an educated, increasingly secular class founding in the court of Henry II an administrative system of remarkable sophistication, so we can also hear the English language and the ideas it has to express being enriched by contact with a newly invigorated but refined love of life.

Nowhere is this new vigour more evident than in the monasteries. The Rule of St Benedict (*c.* 529), which had organized the asceticism of the early Christian desert Fathers and then spread across Europe, slowly became encrusted with formality and a measure of worldliness. Despite this, the daily round of the great monasteries, divided into eight parts by the canonical offices of the Church, the enrichment of the liturgy with further prayers and offices, and the continuous reading – public and private – of the Bible and the Church Fathers, ensured that religious texts were fully absorbed into the atmosphere of life and thought. Monastic devotion – often abused, frequently satirized, and yet central to the period – provided the ground-bass for a form of worship that was only to be silenced with the Reformation. Plain-chant and the sacred texts are heard constantly beneath the violent tenor of medieval secular life and the discoveries of its literature. But if monasticism emphasized a retreat from the world and encouraged a constant awareness of the divine, it also fostered a degree of scholarship. From the eleventh century onwards, both this and the monastic ideal itself were given a new impetus that deeply affected the creation of literature.

To take scholarship first. The syllabus of studies prescribed by St Augustine (itself derived from the courses offered by the schools of the Late Roman Empire) had made theology the queen of the sciences and shown the importance of secular intellectual effort while defining and limiting its purpose. In the monasteries of the so-called Dark Ages, the skills needed for ordering daily life (telling the time and basic mathematics, for example) were also developed, while the requirement to study set down in the Benedictine Rule resulted in the slow, regular extraction of passages from past literature and the creation of *florilegia*, or anthologies collected in the course of a monk's reading. Dull work perhaps, but, comparing themselves with foraging bees, the Benedictines' command of Latin and their digests of patristic and pagan literature were the storehouses which provided material for the massive efforts of intellectuals in the twelfth and thirteenth centuries, the great age of encyclopedias. On this material poets also were to draw.

The monastic schools were again important to the preservation of knowledge, and their syllabus, based on the division of studies into the *trivium* (grammar, rhetoric and logic) and the *quadrivium* (music, astronomy, arithmetic and geometry), was profoundly to influence all medieval and later education. The emphasis on grammar or the learning of Latin examples was designed to prepare clerics for the study of the Scriptures so that they could edit them and then write commentaries. This basic training in scholarly techniques meant that, along with a deal of patristic writing, knowledge of Virgil, Ovid and Statius – albeit highly allegorized – was also preserved. However, the *trivium*'s concern with rhetoric and logic is equally important to future developments.

The *trivium* provided a schooling in the arts of communication, and rhetoric – a concern with the effective presentation of ideas – is a skill that is fundamental to most literature until the close of the eighteenth century. In medieval manuscript illuminations, Rhetoric often appears personified as a gracious lady whose robes are emblazoned with the weapons of her profession: figures of speech. She thus represented the ability to invent material, arrange it in convincing patterns with the aid of known rules, and array it in ornaments of style that are both beautiful and effective. Rhetoric, though now in ordinary speech often a term of disparagement, was once a formal skill of the greatest importance. It was important not only as a means of relating literature to the classical tradition of Aristotle, Cicero and Quintilian from which the developing body of rhetoric itself derived, but for its implication that the construction of verse and often of prose at this period was not a matter of random inspiration but of recognized procedures, known patterns and traditional formulas. This is made clear in a central passage from the *Poetria Nova* (1200), an influential Latin treatise on rhetoric written by the Englishman Geoffrey de Vinsauf. Though this work is perhaps best known for the sly satire on its pretensions in Chaucer's *The Nun's Priest's Tale*, Geoffrey's belief that literature is not a question of spontaneous expression but of long-considered form and careful preparation is revealed again by Pandarus in lines from the first book of *Troilus and Criseyde*, which are in fact a translation from the *Poetria Nova*:

> For everi wight that hath an hous to founde
> Ne renneth naught the werk for to bygynne
> With rakel hond, but he wol bide a stounde,
> And sende his hertes line out fro withinne
> Aldirfirst his purpos for to wynne.

wight: person *founde:* build *rakel:* rash, thoughtless *bide a stounde:* wait a while
aldirfirst: firstly

For the medieval writer, the carefully considered idea came first, and only when it was fully realized in the mind could it achieve expression through practical craftsmanship.

Rhetorical skills were thus the common tools of the writer's craft and the scholar's learning. They were as familiar to a medieval audience as today's belief that a writer should be original. But this was not all. In addition to providing the rules by which poems, sermons and letters were constructed (in nearly all cases from received material), rhetoric also indicated how they should be received and interpreted. Indeed, in many cases, a virtuoso playing with the rules of rhetoric is part of the pleasure a work has to offer, a skill many members of a contemporary audience would have relished as we now consciously enjoy good editing and exciting camera-work in a television programme.

Rhetoric was thus used in the overall construction of a work and in determining the relation between its parts. It was the means by which emotions were raised, arguments propounded, proofs offered and examples drawn. Rhetorical rules defined what style was appropriate to the matter in hand, the adornments to be used and even the syntax. Rhetoric provided categories for different types of literature, be it epic, epigram, debate or sermon. Determining the forms of these, it also allowed a writer to show his skill in manipulating the rules and revealed the copiousness of his invention. This gave pleasure to his audience. But, above all, rhetoric provided an acknowledged system in which literature could operate, a critical vocabulary and a set of principles which directed the creator of verse and prose outwards from private concerns towards the communal experiences he shared with his audience. Hence the constant appeal to ancient authorities in the period, the belief that the learned poet should hand on the received wisdom of the past.

As a basic skill, rhetoric is something to which we shall have constantly to return. While for major writers its techniques were the means by which more fundamental ideas and feelings were conveyed – the medium through which literature operated and not its end – a knowledge of rhetorical forms and practices will be of considerable importance if we wish to understand a work in the ways in which its contemporaries would have received it. Indeed, it is often the case that only when we realize the rhetorical purpose of a particular passage shall we really understand its true function and appreciate the poet's effect.

If rhetoric was a means of ordering received truth, logic – the third element in the *trivium* – was the means of ordering fresh experience. Its renewed importance in the twelfth century was again partly a matter of rediscovering the classical traditions which had been imperfectly preserved in some of the works of the early Fathers and, above all, in the translations and original texts of Boethius (*c.* 470–525). Boethius was the man who, more than any other scholar, had handed on the philosophy of the declining ancient world to the dark ages. From among such works, a student learnt to classify the objects of knowledge and experience, to reason and to criticize arguments. Then, after the first quarter of the twelfth century, contact with the Arab world brought a new and fuller knowledge of Aristotle to the West. Logic, the reduction of the apparently chaotic flux of appearance to a number of categories which seemed to account for all experience and forms of reasoning, provided men with a revelation of the possibilities of order, system, the powers of the mind. The immense variety of subjects discussed by Aristotle (physics, biology, ethics and politics, as well as the other branches of philosophy) meant that Aristotle and many subsequent scientific writers from Greek antiquity became, along with Arabic commentaries on them, the focus of intellectual effort from the end of the twelfth century. Many of these works formed part of Chaucer's reading, and the passion they engendered for order, for logical rigour and analysis, spread out to the law, to political theory, theology and rhetoric. By the thirteenth century, disputation in the manner of Aristotle was a chief feature of cathedral schools and of undergraduate studies in Oxford and Paris. This new intellectual curiosity was also reflected in a restless desire for knowledge. The students who now wandered Europe as an international, Latin-speaking community that was sometimes serious and sometimes wittily satirical, open to religious love or the attractions of a girl, witnessed to a newly aroused curiosity as they sought out the great teachers of the age, such as Peter Abelard (1079–1142).

Abelard, the tragic hero of the twelfth-century renaissance, has an abiding place in the martyrology of love, but his technique of examining problems raised in the Scriptures and patristic writings by marshalling arguments for and against – *Sic et Non* – stressed the new role of a classically inspired use of human reason. 'I preferred the weapons of dialectic to all the other teachings of philosophy,' wrote Abelard in his *Historia Calamitatum* ('Story of my Misfortunes'), 'and armed with these I chose the conflicts of disputation instead of the trophies of war.' One of the central issues of this conflict was the debate as to whether universal categories such as 'mankind' have more than merely grammatical status (a position known as 'realism') or whether only individual things or people (a position known as 'nominalism'). Abelard's belief that faith could be enhanced by the rigorous, aggressive logic through which he achieved a qualification of these extremes showed a remarkable and, to many contemporaries, dangerous confidence in the intellect. This new awareness of the powers of the mind, however, pointed forward to that magisterial synthesis, the detailed, ordered and encyclopedic reconciliation of Aristotelian thought and divine revelation evident in the *Summa Theologica* of St Thomas Aquinas (*c.* 1225–74). This work, which became the cornerstone of Catholic orthodoxy and the intellectual movement know as 'scholasticism', is a towering achievement of the twelfth-century renaissance and, in its penetrating and comprehensive scope, was the fulfilment of the boast recorded by the greatest English classical scholar of the period, John of Salisbury:

Bernard of Chartres [John of Salisbury's teacher] used to compare us to dwarfs perched on the shoulders of giants. He pointed out that we see more and farther than our predecessors, not because we have keener vision or greater height, but because we are lifted up and borne aloft on their gigantic stature.

This passage clearly reveals a new if self-deprecating confidence in a developed culture, a confidence based partly on a recovery of the past.

4

The view from this journey outwards – the relation achieved between the received classical and Christian traditions – was accompanied by an inner pilgrimage, and parallel with an emphasis on system came a new concern with subjectivity. This, too, was of vital importance to literature.

In order to explore the private recesses of the spirit, some degree of solitude is essential, and in what had become the busy, formalized round of the monasteries, richly endowed and enjoying their highly developed, corporate life of prayer, long periods of self-communing were not easily found. To escape this atmosphere, an English monk, who had been dedicated to the religious life at the time of the Norman Conquest, broke his vows and wandered Europe. Finding himself in France, he became involved in a controversy between conservatives and those who wished to return to a more simple ideal of monasticism. Stephen Harding, as modern scholarship names him, eventually became Abbot of Cîteaux (1110–33). The Cistercian order whose ideals he promoted (in Latin, of course) placed a renewed emphasis on meditation, spiritual friendship, even on mysticism, and so became one of the most active religious initiatives of the time. It was an initiative which succeeded because it answered a mood that had been felt for the previous half-century.

Excita mentem tuam, St Anselm (*c.* 1033–1109) wrote, 'enter into the chamber of your mind and exclude all else but God and those things which help you in finding him; close the door and seek him'. Though Anselm of Canterbury was a major political figure and a great theologian who developed an influential proof of the existence of God, a new subjectivity is at once clear in his devotional writings. Faith now seeks understanding through the feelings. There is an emphasis on inner development, the ardent self-disclosure of sin, and a longing for redemption. In the prayers Anselm wrote when Prior of Bec (1063–8), and which were circulated especially among the great women of Europe who play so important a role in medieval literature, this emotion becomes centred round a new tenderness for the sufferings of Christ and his humanity. Christ is now fully God become man and Saviour. His love and voluntary self-sacrifice are seen as central to salvation, while, in their turn, human feelings draw the heart to him. The battle for the soul revealed in *The Seafarer* is no longer a duel between God and the devil. A mediating and suffering Christ has become central to devotion and to art. The believer's own desires have their special place and frequently pour out in such lyrical poetry as these widely transcribed lines from a twelfth-century English Cistercian:

> Dulcis Jesu memoria,
> dans vera cordi gaudia,
> sed super mel et omnia
> eius dulcis praesentia.

The poem was rather freely translated in the fourteenth century as:

> Jhesu, swete is the love of thee,
> Noon othir thing so swete may be;
> No thing that men may hear and see
> Hath no swetnesse agens thee.

The hymn is still sometimes sung today as 'Jesu! the very thought is sweet'.

Then, with St Bernard of Clairvaux (1090–1153) – the furious opponent of Abelard's logic and the inspirer of the Second Crusade – the physical humanity of Christ becomes central to a mystical form of devotion. In his twentieth sermon on the Song of Songs (part of a collection of seminal importance) St Bernard declared: 'God wished to be seen in the flesh and to converse with men, that he might draw all affections of carnal men, who were unable to love except after the flesh, to the saving love of his flesh, and so step by step lead them to spiritual love.' Carnal love thus seeks its spiritual object, and spiritual friendship becomes a subject in the Latin works of Aildred of Rievaulx (*c*. 1110-66), a great English Cistercian. Bernard's rapturously spiralling and prayerful theology suggested to the whole of Europe how, when the word of God has chastened the reason into humility and the Holy Ghost has kindled charity, then Christ appears to the soul in a mystic union as bridegroom, physician, father and (of central importance to *The Ancrene Riwle*) as knightly lover. For St Bernard, the language of the Troubadour love poets of Provence, their fresh discovery of refined human emotion and their exalted cult of *fine amour*, helped suggest the words of love between God and the soul. This newly tender form of devotion was soon to be popularized by Franciscan preachers, and, in recreating his image of

Christ as the knight and the soul as his lady, the author of *The Ancrene Riwle* has drawn (not without reservations) on the most advanced theology and the most recently discovered aspects of secular love. English writers are now completely at home in a revived European culture.

5

In Early Middle English vernacular poetry, this delicate intensity of emotion is best revealed in a new form – the lyric. There is nothing that quite corresponds to this in Old English literature, but it is clear that by the thirteenth century, drawing partly on French traditions and the rhymed, accentual Latin verse of the wandering scholars or *vagrantes*, a body of lyric poetry was well developed in England. Much of it we must presume is lost – a constant problem with so distant a period – but in the following stanzas, taken from that remarkable manuscript collection known as the Harley Lyrics (*c.* 1310), the new emphasis on the humanity of Christ we have been tracing is deepened by his words to his mother and by Mary's replies:

> 'Stond wel, moder, vnder rode,
> byholt þy sone wiþ glade mode,
>   blyþe, moder, myht þou be!'
> 'Sone, hou shulde y bliþe stonde?
> Y se þin fet, y se þin honde
>   nayled to þe harde tre.'

> 'Moder, do wey þy wepinge.
> Y þole deþ for monkynde,
>   for my gult þole y non.'
> 'Sone, y fele þe dedestounde,
> þe suert is at myn herte grounde
>   þat me byhet Symeon.'

> 'Moder, merci! Let me deye,
> for Adam out of helle beye
>   ant his kun þat is forlore.'
> 'Sone, what shal me to rede?
> My peyne pyneþ me to dede.
>   Lat me deȝe þe byfore.'

> 'Moder, þou rewe al of þi bern,
> þou wosshe awai þe blody tern;
>   hit doþ me worse þen my ded.'
> 'Sone, hou may y teres werne?
> Y se þe blody stremes erne
>   from þin herte to my fet.'

rode: cross   *byholt:* behold   *blyþe:* happy   *fet:* feet   *do wey:* stop   *þole:* suffer
gult: guilt   *dedestounde:* hour of death   *suert:* sword   *Symeon:* a just man who was
promised sight of Jesus and who prophesied his death and Mary's suffering
Adam, etc: The Harrowing of Hell   *kun:* kin   *forlore:* lost, damned
rede: help   *rewe al of þi bern:* grieve for all your children   *tern:* tears   *werne:* restrain
erne: run, flow

It is no longer the symbolic rood that speaks, but God incarnate as a
suffering man involved with his mother as both her Saviour and her son.
The humanity of the anguish, its detailed and colloquial expression, stirs
the mind to contemplate its divine significance. Such devotion now
becomes a central feature of Christian life.

6

The religious lyrics of the Harley manuscript draw on the liturgy, the
Bible, the Latin Fathers and, like St Bernard and the author of *The
Ancrene Riwle*, on secular love poetry as well. It was reported that
Thomas, Archbishop of York (d. 1100) could not hear a popular verse
without converting it to a hymn of Christian praise, and this was not a
simple resolve against the devil having all the best tunes. As the gently
ironic contrasts between two Harley lyrics – *The Way of Christ's Love*
and *The Way of Woman's Love* – show, such borrowing was partly a
recognition of the fact that the new-found emotionalism of faith and the
humanity of Christ could be expressed in the new-found language of
human love. Certain Harley lyrics thrill with these fresh possibilities:

> When þe nyhtegale singes þe wodes waxen grene;
> lef ant gras ant blosme springes in Aueryl, y wene,
> ant loue is to myn herte gon wiþ one spere so kene,
> nyht ant day my blod hit drynkes; myn herte deþ me tene.
>
> Ich haue loued al þis зer, þat y may loue namore;
> ich haue siked moni syk, lemmon, for þin ore.
> Me nis loue neuer þe ner, ant þat me reweþ sore.
> Suete lemmon, þench on me, ich haue loued þe зore.
>
> Suete lemmon, y preye þe of loue one speche;
> whil y lyue in world so wyde oþer nulle y seche.
> Wiþ þy loue, my suete leof, mi blis þou mihtes eche;
> a suete cos of þy mouþ mihte be my leche.
>
> Suete lemmon, y preзe þe of a loue-bene;
> зef þou me louest ase men says, lemmon, as y wene,

ant ȝef hit þi wille be, þou loke þat hit be sene.
So muchel y þenke vpon þe þat al y waxe grene.

Bituene Lyncolne ant Lyndeseye, Northamptoun and Lounde,
ne wot y non so fayr a may as y go fore ybounde,
Suete lemmon, y preȝe þe þou louie me a stounde.
      Y wole mone my songe
      on wham þat hit ys on ylong.

tene: grieves   *ich:* I   *siked . . . syk:* sighed . . . sigh   *lemmon:* beloved
for þin ore: for your favour   *þench:* think   *ȝore:* for a long time
oþer nulle y seche: will not look for another   *leof:* beloved   *eche:* increase   *cos:* kiss
leche: doctor   *loue-bene:* love-boon   *wene:* think   *wot:* know   *may:* maiden
fore ybounde: in love fetters for   *stounde:* a while   *mone:* sadly sing
on wham, etc.: about the cause of my complaint

The purity of this lyric has survived through seven centuries and is what, first and last, makes the piece so attractive. Early Middle English, its vocabulary unencumbered with tired modern associations, exactly expresses the pristine clarity of green woods and the call of the nightingale. It is as if mankind had fallen in love for the first time. Nonetheless, we should be wary of thinking of the poem too simply as a spontaneous overflow of powerful feelings. Technically – and this needs to be stressed – the lyric is an example of what is known as a *chanson*, a form of poetry that is a clearly recognized type behind which lies a Latin and French tradition derived ultimately from the high sophistication of Troubadour verse. The invocation of spring, the picture of the desperate state to which the lover has been reduced, the praise of his lady's beauty and the plea for her favour are common to many hundreds of such poems. They are, in fact, conventional – and rhetorical convention, which we have seen is essential to medieval literature, frequently causes problems.

We often like our writers, our poets in particular, to be extreme. 'Byronic' is an adjective applicable as much to a way of life as to a manner of writing, and it is sometimes assumed that if poets are not eccentrically individual then they are not doing their job properly. Such a concern with personal expression pays scant regard, however, to the fact that many of our deepest emotions are aspects of experience common to us all and which we have developed conventions to explain and articulate. Without these conventions, much of our existence and many of our feelings would be intolerable. Indeed, many of our emotions might not even exist. Medieval literature, frequently operating on the highest planes of feeling, is firmly rooted in this observation. The devices of its rhetoric are part of it too, for the conventional means by which a work is constructed suggest the shared nature of the ideals expressed. Of course, in the hands of a minor versifier, a dull, insensitive application of the rules results in a dull and insensitive poem. But this lyric is evidently not like that. It has the bloom of complete mastery. Its striking contrasts, its recreation of direct speech, its formal control and apparent unselfconsciousness are achievements of the highest order. Though seeming so simple, the poem is the very opposite of naive, and its anonymity shows how rhetorical conventions allow a great writer to reveal the full extent of his mastery.

Aside from their lyrical beauty, verses such as these are also of interest in so far as they show, perhaps for the first time since the ancient world, that love between the sexes is a proper subject for poetry. Few literary developments are of such importance. Passion once again expresses itself in terms of the man's abasement before his lady, but (in this instance at least) sexual ardour is not the intense, annoying intrusion it can be in Horace, or the witty, comic aberration it is sometimes shown as being in Ovid. Rather, like a saint, the lady of medieval literature can confer grace on her unworthy supplicant and, like a feudal lord, receive pledges of his undying service. The idealized forms of literary emotion thus reflect the newly idealized forms of religious and social life. These social ideals in particular are aristocratic in tone, and to appreciate them fully we need to trace the developments that had taken place in the concept of the fighting man – at its broadest, the metamorphosis of Beowulf into Lancelot. This change, so fundamental to European life, is focused on the word 'chivalry'.

7

Chivalry was in part at least both a political initiative designed to solve the problem of what to do with armed retainers in the growing nation state and a development of older notions of warrior companionship. It was also an ecclesiastical response to the evils of war. The appearance of chivalry further coincided with the development of the mounted soldier. The professionalism of Chaucer's Knight in *The Canterbury Tales*, for example, is partly suggested by the excellence of his horses, while the Lancelot of the French poet Chrétien de Troyes (late twelfth century) – an important author to whom we shall return – receives universal contumely for riding in an executioner's cart. But the interest of chivalry is far from merely equestrian. A song inspired by St Bernard's preaching of the Second Crusade declared that 'God has ordained a tournament between Heaven and Hell, and sends to all his friends who wish to

defend him, that they fail not'. Religious devotion and political initiatives
here borrow, in a manner typical of the rich interlacing of the different
strands of medieval life, the vocabulary of the knight.

The religious aura that came to surround the institution of knighthood
– the vagueness is deliberate – stemmed from the fact that while the
knight held his lands by feudal obligations which placed him under legal
restraints, his admission to the brotherhood of chivalry took on a sacramental appearance which established his status as an ideal figure. For
John of Salisbury, the perfect knight existed to protect the Church and
the poor, attack infidelity, reverence the priesthood, keep the peace, shed
his blood and, if necessary, lay down his life for his fellow men. In an
age that believed ideal forms have great philosophical validity – that
they are, finally, more 'real' than their particular and individual embodi-
ments – this image of perfect knighthood was for many a truth deeper
than, for example, the sometimes dishonourable behaviour of noblemen
in the fluctuating fortunes of the Crusades or the Hundred Years War.
Chaucer's Knight embodies John of Salisbury's ideal, just as his Parson
represents the priest as Good Shepherd defined by St Gregory. Such a
technique is a crucial aspect of the medieval approach to characterization
and we ignore it at our peril.

But for many medieval authors, including Chaucer, the literary character of the knight was usually incomplete without a refined appreciation
of sexual love. The hero of *Sir Gawain and the Green Knight*, for example,
is admired by some for his prowess but by others for his 'luf-talkyng', his
social and emotional grace. If the comradeship of *Beowulf* became the
chivalry of Camelot, the image of Hrothgar's wife filling the mead horns
became transformed into the historical Countess of Champagne ad-
judicating for her followers the fine-drawn, wittily legalistic problems
they had posed on the nature of *fine amour* or high romantic love.
Chivalry is intimately connected with this intense and newly serious
refinement of personal emotion and lends it its exclusive, aristocratic
tenor. Such a civilizing of the feelings was now seen as the groundwork
of personal, social and even moral excellence, and it showed wholly new
possibilities in human existence compared with which, as C. S. Lewis
once declared, the Renaissance was but a ripple.

8

In narrative literature, as in life, this impulse towards the ideal is best
summed up in a single word: 'romance'. Like many such words, romance
expresses a variety of concepts – fulfilment of erotic desire, escapism and

the imaginative enhancement of reality, for example – but in origin it was a verb that meant 'to compose in the vernacular' rather than in Latin. This suggests the popular and secular appeal of most romance which is a literature that explores the nature of courtly life perfected. This was a matter which literary decorum decreed as most suitably discussed in the vernacular languages. As a result, the subjects of medieval romance were the preoccupations of medieval aristocratic existence: love, courtesy and chivalry. Its form was often that of the quest, a journey both outwards to adventure and inwards across landscapes of the mind. Romance is an abidingly useful literary form and, by going beneath the surface detail of life, disencumbering characters of the limiting round of common cause and effect, the writer of medieval romance could present men, women and events as a series of psychological, social and even moral possibilities.

The deepest concerns of the medieval secular audience are usually offered in romance through symbolic and thus conventional situations: the recurrent and often marvellous images of the lone journey, test, forest, garden, sea; the meeting with the evil giant or the encounter with the beautiful beloved. Many of these motifs were developed from the repertory of French-speaking Breton storytellers, who seem to have been particularly active at the start of the twelfth century. Refashioned by poets with an aristocratic culture, the ideal figures of romance, exemplifying the most refined and obsessive tenets of chivalry, love and courtesy, then rise to the surface of understanding dressed in the heightened forms of daily life and invested with the intuitive power of dream and possible perfection. We know these figures are not 'true' but we are sure they embody some 'truth'. With its long, complex interlacing of significant events and development of a wide variety of fictional techniques, romance, superseding the older heroic poetry of *chanson de geste* such as *The Song of Roland* (early twelfth century), stands to medieval literature as the novel does to our own. At its finest it was not a mode of escape but of exploration and subtle experiment. It also required from its audience a new delicacy of apprehension.

9

Romance found one of its earliest mature expressions in the Anglo-Norman *lais* of Marie de France (late twelfth century), and her exquisite *Laüstic* is a poem that offers something of the refinement we have mentioned. The plot of *Laüstic* is simple but suggestive. A lady at her bedroom window is keeping a rendezvous with her lover who stands admiringly by. A nightingale (*le laüstic*) is singing. The physical distance, the tower, the garden and the voice of the bird are all exact yet tremulously evocative. They are both themselves and representative of the quality of the affair itself. The lady is then forced to tell her interfering husband (the adultery is characteristic but not essential to such relationships, and certainly not condemned by the poet) that there is no joy in the world for those who do not listen to the nightingale's song. Laughing with spiteful anger, the husband has his servants catch the bird which he then kills in front of his wife, throwing its little corpse at her breast and telling her that she will now be able to sleep in peace. Both his cynical understanding of the lovers' secret symbol and his violence condemn this conventional figure of the jealous husband out of hand. The sorrowful lady then wraps the nightingale's body in a samite cloth richly embroidered with scenes from the tragedy and sends it to her friend. He, a proper lover and no *vilain* or churlish man, places the corpse in a golden reliquary and has it carried before him constantly. There is no comment, only the perfect expression of rare and natural beauty destroyed, of refinement, savagery, and an infinite, noble sadness.

10

Since the great flowering of Middle English romance – Chaucer's *Troilus and Criseyde* (1386–7), a number of *The Canterbury Tales*, *Sir Gawain and the Green Knight* (*c.* 1385), certain aspects of the alliterative *Morte Arthure* (*c.* 1360) and the works of Malory (d. 1471) – stems largely from this European and particularly French tradition, it will be useful to suggest here something of the earlier techniques these English works absorb and develop, so placing them in a proper European context.

We may begin with the romances of Chrétien de Troyes and a passage from near the close of *Erec and Enide* (*c.* 1170) – his earliest work in the form – known as the 'Joy of Court'. As with *Laüstic*, this episode relies on the creation of a subtle and even ambiguous image that has both an erotic and a social significance: the garden of earthly delights where a restrained couple, entangled by desire and courtesy, live in an eternal spring. The loveliness of the garden is at once visible to observers yet protected by a magic column of air. In the middle of the garden, reclining on a silver couch, lies a woman of fabulous beauty who has entrapped her knightly lover Mabonagrain who can only be freed after defeat at the hands of a challenger. A narrow gate allows entrance to this equivocal paradise, but facing it is a pallisade surmounted by the severed heads of those who have tried the dangers of the place and come to grief.

In its combination of exuberance and terror, the garden subtly conveys the pleasures and claustrophobia of a joy which is paradoxically its own entrapment.

For Erec, the 'Joy of Court' is his last great challenge, the *aventure* that will allow him to show his fully idealized potential as a knight. To see why this is, we should know that Erec himself has won his bride through his chivalry – the public display of his valour at a tournament – but has then lost his reputation by preferring the delights of his bed to the challenge of arms. By successfully fighting Mabonagrain, Erec will at once prove his rediscovered excellence and free his opponent from a plight similar to that which he has himself escaped. The balance between the two great themes from romance – prowess and love – is thus the central issue here and, at the risk of presenting so subtle a writer as Chrétien simply as a moralist, we may say that while *Erec and Enide* is concerned with this problem of balance from the viewpoint of a knight who has indulged in excessive passion, *Yvain* (*c.* 1170) looks at the equation from the other direction: a knight too exclusively given to arms. What both works suggest is that in these romances Chrétien is concerned to analyse the connection between a refined, intense inner life and the demands of society. As a result, we can see the importance of the romance form as a means of showing medieval men and women in relation to an idealized view of their world. This is an important matter indeed and one central to *Troilus and Criseyde*, to a number of *The Canterbury Tales*, and to *Sir Gawain and the Green Knight*.

How does this intense inner life reveal itself? The defeated Mabonagrain tells Erec that he has made his mistress a rash promise. Immediately after he has been dubbed a knight it rebounds on him:

My lady, who is sitting there, at once recalled me to my word, and said that I had promised her that I would never go forth from here until there should come some knight who should conquer me by trial of arms. It was right that I should remain, for rather than break my word, I should never have pledged it. Since I knew the good there was in her, I could not reveal or show to the one whom I hold most dear that in all this I was displeased; for if she had noticed it, she would have withdrawn her heart, and I would not have had it so for anything that might happen. Thus my lady thought to detain me here for a long stay; she did not think that there would ever enter this garden any vassal who could conquer me. In this way she intended to keep me absolutely shut up with her all the days of my life. And I should have committed an offence if I had had resort to guile and not defeated all those against whom I could prevail; such escape would have been a shame.

This is a very elegant problem and one that goes to the heart of the courtly life: a knight must keep his word and never challenge his lady. However, trapped by his oath into a false situation, Mabonagrain's honour immures him in a shameful state just as his valour imprisons him in a perverted chivalry. He can only be rescued from moral confusion by a greater integrity, by defeat at the hands of the newly perfected Erec. The male 'character' here reveals itself less through the purely personal and subjective than through the presentation of a witty yet very serious problem. On the level of plot, the two knights (Mabonagrain especially) have the interest of people trapped in a legal nicety. However, just as important, the solution to Mabonagrain's dilemma lies in the power of Erec's ideal values, the strength that issues from the proper relation of man to himself, his love and his world, and which lies at the very heart of romance life. This is an integrity which can only be fully known when the false 'Joy of Court' has been replaced by the true. At the close of the poem, and when Erec has freed Mabonagrain by defeating him, the pleasures of newly found well-being (delicately glancing at those archetypes of fulfilment we all share) are expressed by the sumptuousness of the feasts that attend the victory and by Erec and Enide's later coronation as king and queen of their own court, a delight made all the more vivid by Chrétien's pleasure in creating beautifully limned vignettes of the noble life and the fact that true joy has been won after intense inner and physical struggle.

The richness of the 'Joy of Court' episode reveals a number of further elements characteristic of medieval romance. The encounter is, for example, an exclusively aristocratic business, the climax of a quest which is itself a purely aristocratic prerogative. A moment from *Yvain* helps to define this life of a noble elite. Near the start of the poem, we are shown a knight faced by a giant loutish herdsman. The situation is far from uncommon in medieval romance and we should know that giants and dwarfs were conventionally considered evil. Chrétien's knight is eventually told by the hideous herdsman that he himself uses his strength only to master his beasts. The knight, by contrast, defines his own role as questing for adventure – a way of life, a civilized and humane employment of muscle, that the *vilain* simply cannot understand. The contrast here is thus between brute strength and chivalry, brawn and refinement, courtesy and vulgarity. In other romances the *vilain* is the bourgeois, the man of money merely, who, in one poem, buying a beautiful garden as such men will, is made to look ridiculous by the little talking bird who preserves the garden's loveliness. Eventually the bird flies away and the secret place becomes a desert. Potency together with natural beauty, it would seem, cannot belong to the vulgar.

Neither can they belong to the knight if he errs, and, with their loss, he too becomes part of a feral existence. When Erec encounters Mabona-grain, for example, he finds his opponent is again a giant (in fact a man a foot taller than everyone else and so not too perverse, we may suspect) while Yvain, giving himself over to an excessive pursuit of chivalry, loses first his wife and then his reason. His loveless and desperate wandering in a state of untamed nature (a motif again developed in the Tristan romances, themselves deriving from the Anglo-Norman of Thomas) is a symbol of his unnatural state. His slow struggle back to integrity reveals Chrétien's art at its most sophisticated.

Reduced to an animal existence, Yvain is eventually saved by an animal: a lion who accompanies his adventures. Of course, the lion is a symbol, a suggestive image of natural values and integrity, even, in what we have already seen as the complex world of medieval animal sym-bolism, of Christ. Such suggestions are latent in the lion's every appear-ance and reveal an aspect of medieval literature which is one of its most subtle delights: the fact that the narrative level – the *matière* – sometimes sheers away into learned and allusive areas of *sens* or specialized inter-pretation which make us ponder its significance. *Matière* and *sens* are thus important critical terms. We shall refer to them often and should cite here this significant passage from Chrétien's *Lancelot, or the Knight of the Cart* (*c.* 1170) as our source:

> Del CHEVALIER DE LA CHARRETE
> comance Crestïens son livre;
> matiere et san li done et livre
> la contesse, et il s'antremet
> de panser, qui gueres n'i met
> fois sa painne et s'antancïon.

(*Chrétien here begins his book concerning the Knight of the Cart. The material and the underlying meaning are given and furnished to him by the Countess* [Marie de Champagne] *and he is only trying to carry out her concern and intention.*)

This division between surface meaning and underlying intention is a vital quality of much medieval narrative technique. We should be aware of its presence in nearly all the major works, be they as different as *The Miller's Tale* or *Piers Ploughman*. In all such poems the physical world becomes an allegory of the metaphysical, casting on to daily life the light of eternity.

What we might not have expected, however, is the fact that while Chrétien is being deeply serious in *Yvain* he can also treat his lion with an almost Disney-like comic sentiment, an element of burlesque, such as the moment when the unhappy beast tries to commit suicide. This dextrous, witty change of register reflects a playfulness, a self-delighting and self-conscious artifice, which adds immeasurably to our delight in the romance as a work of art. We are clearly in the presence of a highly sophisticated literature. With Chaucer, such elusiveness becomes a matter of signal importance.

Conscious and explicit artifice is again clear in those passages of romance where a modern audience, trained on the novel, might expect the author to be least visible: dialogue and the characters' moments of self-analysis. But not so. Where we would look for at least the appearance of the greatest subjectivity, Chrétien's humour and artistry become most apparent, as Chaucer's often do. The presence of the author at such points of analysis is particularly directed towards elegant construction, verbal play and surface ornament – to rhetoric, in fact. We shall develop this important point later, but a delight in the patterned language of rhetoric is evident in Mabonagrain's speech to Erec, a speech which it might be more accurate to describe as an elegant and non-naturalist disquisition on a problem of courtesy which Chrétien makes sure we see he has invented and then placed on the lips of his knight for our enjoyment. In other words, he is showing us his skills.

Connoisseurship in these matters is important and takes us some way into the world of the first audience that enjoyed these works, since many of the romances suggest how a refined casuistry of love was a highly regarded social accomplishment. The hero of *Sir Gawain and the Green Knight* is its master. Yvain, delicately unravelling the paradox that he has fallen in love with a woman whose husband he has killed; that, defeated by love, he is the woman's willing prisoner but that she must eventually surrender to him, is another. In Chrétien's *Cliges* (*c.* 1170), two young people are each given long and complementary speeches on the nature of their feelings which, in truth, are more concerned with elegance and the invigorating use of traditional commonplaces than with self-revelation. Such a delight in artifice is again apparent in many speeches from Chaucer's *Troilus and Criseyde* and the laments of the two courtly heroes from *The Knight's Tale*. One of the most elegant and unusual examples of such 'luf-talkyng', however, comes in the little *Lai de Graelent* where the hero, pursued by the queen, resists her blandishments with the following speech:

'Lady,' said he, 'I love no woman, for love is a serious business, not a jest. Out of five hundred who speak glibly of love, not one can spell the first letter of his name. With such it is idleness, or fullness of bread, or fancy, masked in the guise of love. Love requires of his servants chastity in thought, in word and in deed. If one of two lovers is loyal, and the other jealous and false, how may their friendship last, for love is slain! But sweetly and discreetly love passes from person to person, from heart to heart, or is nothing worth. For what the lover would, that would the beloved; what she would ask of him, that should he go before to grant. Without accord such as this, love is but a bond and a constraint. For above all things love means sweetness, and truth, and measure; yea, loyalty to the loved one and to your word. And because of this I dare not meddle with so high a matter.'

The Queen heard Graelent gladly, find him so tripping of tongue, and since his words were wise and courteous, at the end she discovered to him her heart.

'Friend, Sir Graelent, though I am a wife, yet have I never loved my lord. But I love you very dearly, and what I have asked of you, will you not go before to grant?'

'Lady,' said he, 'give me pity and forgiveness, but this may not be. I am the vassal of the King, and on my knees have pledged him loyalty and faith, and sworn to defend his life and honour. Never shall he have shame because of me.'

With these words Sir Graelent took his leave of the Queen, and went his way.

It is a delightful irony that this near perfect description of courtly loving is spoken by a man who is seeking to avoid it. However, we should note that the passage also reveals a number of further characteristics of romance, in particular the place of women and marriage, the nature of feudal loyalty and that idealism of love which sometimes touches on the religious.

In medieval romance there is a wide variety of ways in which women are presented and in the situations in which they are placed. Very few of these noble ladies are simple reflections of the male desires of courtly love, for the greater authors at least see their female characters independently of their heroes' idealizing perceptions. These women are, indeed, quite as richly complex as the men – often rather more so – and range from those who, like Chrétien's Enide or Chaucer's Dorigen, have a particular and serious human issue to face, to such enchantresses as the moralizing heroine of *The Wife of Bath's Tale* who, like the male giants and dwarfs, is a literary device from the world of faery. Chaucer's Criseyde (surely the supreme creation of romance) thus has behind her a rich variety of female portraits, a whole range of women involved in the dramas and intricate problems of *matière* and *sens*.

The wife of Yvain, for example, an intelligent and passionate woman, falls in love for the best of political reasons – she needs the besotted knight to defend her realm; but when he breaks his vow to return after the dispensation she has allowed him, he is summarily dismissed. Chrétien's Lancelot, obsessed by the imperious and highly-sexed Queen Guinevere, is himself pursued by a woman who is completely frank about her physical needs. Chrétien's handling of the way she comes to terms with her rejection is interesting and moving. However, since we have found the 'Joy of Court' episode from *Erec and Enide* so fruitful a source of romance themes, we could perhaps return to it and show that not only is Erec reinvested with his full and ideal potential by his victory over the knight, but that Enide, leading Mabonagrain's mistress out of the enchanted garden, is also revealed as having reconciled the problem of the balance in her marriage between the demands of the erotic and the requirements of her husband's chivalry. She is no longer the unwilling cause of his lost reputation, rather she is the inspiration of his chivalry.

If the marriage of Erec and Enide resolves the problem of the relation between private desires and public responsibilities for both the man and his wife, the poem also examines the concept of marriage itself in a way that is important to many works. Briefly stated, this view sees the relation of man to wife as corresponding to that between God and the soul which owes its Maker total obedience and complete gratitude. This view has its biblical origins in St Paul's Epistle to the Ephesians. The wealthy and aristocratic Erec, for example, chooses as his bride a woman who is innately noble but very poor. Throughout the poem, both in Enide's own thoughts and in Erec's testing of her loyalty, the parallel is constantly drawn between the loving devotion of a wife to her master (who may seem to withdraw his love) and the proper, unquestioning devotion of the soul to a sometimes hidden God. Such imagery represents an important theological concept of marriage, and one that was to be treated by Boccaccio, Petrarch and, with the most subtle awareness of its limitations, by Chaucer in *The Clerk's Tale*. In *Erec and Enide*, however, it provided for a medieval audience a measure of religious grace and authority in marriage and, in particular, invested an emotional relationship with spiritual imagery. Such a view of marriage is in many ways comparable with the picture of Christ as the knight and the soul as his lady presented by the author of *The Ancrene Riwle*.

Extreme romantic passion seems inevitably to draw to itself the imagery of religious experience. The radical change effected by love in Chaucer's Troilus, for example, is presented in terms of a spiritual conversion. This is conventional in such poetry and also profoundly ambiguous. In *Aucassin and Nicolette* (late thirteenth century) – that exquisite little masterpiece of the *faux-naïf* – Aucassin much prefers thinking about the rites of love to the possibility of salvation. Such an uneasy fusion of erotic and religious imagery is again central to Chrétien's *Lancelot*. Indeed, it is fundamental to that whole aspect of courtly passion which C. S. Lewis defined as 'the religion of love'.

Perhaps the most famous passage of *Lancelot*, aside from the hero's abject veneration of a comb containing some strands of Guinevere's hair, is the moment when the hero forces his way into his mistress's bedroom. We should know that Guinevere at this stage of the romance has been abducted into a strange and twilight world of the living dead, a kingdom of inertia and violence into which Lancelot has won his way accompanied by imagery which suggests the Harrowing of Hell. This was a scene from the apocryphal Book of Nicodemus, much used in medieval art and literature, which shows Christ's descent into Satan's realm in order to free the souls of Adam, Eve and the virtuous pagans. The scene was also interpreted allegorically to suggest Christ's breaking into the darkness and error of the human soul. The deliberately ambiguous terms of Lancelot's quest or pilgrimage to save Guinevere from her captors is thus enveloped in a very serious form of religious imagery: that of Christ's winning redemption for lost souls. Against this is then contrasted Lancelot's subsequent portrayal as a passionate worshipper at that most revered sanctuary: Guinevere's bed. When Lancelot has broken the bars of Guinevere's cell (itself a most convincing psycho-sexual image) he ceases to suggest the Harrowing of Hell and becomes instead the famished pilgrim seeking his own salvation:

he comes to the bed of the queen, whom he adores and before whom he bows down, holding her dearer than the relic of any saint.

Such witty yet deeply evocative blasphemy (the image of Lancelot adoring his adulterous beloved, the woman who masters his life with an absolute and cruel fecklessness) suggests the most refined extremes of courtly passion through the imagery of a religion which condemned excessive human love as a sin, a sin which repeated Eve's dominance over Adam and hence the fall of man. By expressing romantic ardour through imagery that is at once an apt correlative of the emotional experience of *fine amour* yet morally opposed to its values, Chrétien here creates an ambiguity which proliferates an infinite suggestiveness. It echoes – now seriously, now wittily – through much medieval love poetry and asks: if we experience something of divinity in human love, how should we relate this to the Christian divine? The question is central to many of the great love poets of the Middle Ages, to Dante and Petrarch as much as to Chaucer and Chrétien, and it receives a wealth of answers.

It is probable in this case, however, that just as Chrétien's heroes are presented with refined problems of love and courtesy, express these in elegant speeches and try to resolve them through the *sens* and *matière* of the poem, so, in the case of *Lancelot* particularly, the audience is also presented with intricate problems of the author's intentions – Chrétien's particular handling of *sens* and *matière*. The audience is then asked to try to solve these problems through what might be called critical discussion but is more properly a mode of that 'luf-talkyng' which is a mark of refined courtly behaviour. If this is so, Chrétien's technique not only places the most developed examples of romance firmly in the context of the audience for whom they were written, but suggests a highly sophisticated detachment on the part of the author, an articulate and playful self-consciousness which is also a major quality of Chaucer's genius.

11

One further factor shared by many of these romances, including all those by Chrétien de Troyes, is an imagined contact with the fabulous court of King Arthur. In such works, Camelot comes to exemplify the glowing possibilities of the chivalric ideal, the lost paradise of secular perfection. The 'matter of Arthur' became both a province of the imagination and, with a measure of wistful latitude, an alleged historical reality it was promised would one day return. This attraction, supported by an interest in its mysterious and historical origins, helps to account for the rapid spread of the Arthurian legend through the twelfth and subsequent centuries. 'What place is there within the bounds of the empire of Christendom to which the winged praise of Arthur the Briton has not extended?' asked a contemporary with only slight exaggeration. Camelot and its works were soon made to constitute a myth which could be developed to express both the wide variety of the ideals of chivalry and the aspirations of romance, whether these were concerned with man in pursuit of social excellence, or, as with the Cistercian-inspired *La Queste del Saint Graal* (*c.* 1225) and Chrétien's *Percival* (*c.* 1170), in search of religious enlightenment. Something of the origins of this extraordinary phenomenon may be traced to English writers of the twelfth century and, in particular, the historians.

Of those areas of the twelfth-century renaissance in which the English were among the leading figures, the writing of history was perhaps the most important. Though we have seen that Old English literature, following the example of Bede, had created a considerable vernacular record, the slow decay of the language and the absence of an effective French prose meant that the greater part of English historical writing continued to be created in Latin, as literary decorum required. This gave it an international audience. The works of William of Malmesbury,

William of Newburgh, Roger of Hovedon, Giraldus Cambrensis and Matthew Paris, again taking something of their craft from Bede and their style from the ancients, were highly regarded. But it was the least scholarly of them all, Geoffrey of Monmouth whose *Historia Regnum Britanniae* ('History of the Kingdom of Britain') was composed in about 1137, who won the heart of Europe.

Geoffrey's work provides the first versions of the stories of Lear, Cymbeline and Arthur, but it is perhaps most useful to regard his narrative as a lucid and well-contrived prose epic, an eloquent work relying on colour, pace and oratory rather than on convincing portraits. It was also a book of enormous influence. In the tradition of historical writing at the time, Geoffrey attempts to correlate what is in this case a largely fictitious line of kings stemming from Brutus, the supposed great-grandson of Aeneas, with events in classical and biblical history. Brutus is shown as living at the same time as Eli the priest, for example, a period when the sons of Hector were ruling in Troy, and Silvius Aeneas held sway in Italy. This line of English kings eventually ended with Cadwallader in A.D. 689.

Such fantasy is not without its serious methodological aspects. An attempt to relate historical events to a providential scheme centring around the Crucifixion and Resurrection for example, the wish to see the world, in other words, in terms of God's entire plan for creation, was a form of pious scholarly method founded by Eusebius (265–340), used by Bede, and which remained fundamental to the European historical imagination for a millennium. It is a corollary of this view that the rise and fall of empires both in biblical and subsequent times was seen as being wholly in God's providence and not – as we might say – the result of economic forces, cultural initiatives or military prowess. Hence Geoffrey shows that under the glorious figure of Arthur the Britons nearly gained control of the empire of the world when his hero defeated the Roman emperor Lucius. Such possible glory was eclipsed, however, by the sinfulness of Mordred (his adultery with Guinevere in particular), and from this moment on the Britons are shown descending to ever deeper levels of humiliation until their final routing by the Anglo-Saxons and their retreat to the coasts of Wales – Geoffrey's home. That this was a divine punishment, that history is a moral pattern controlled by God who did not wish for world domination by the Britons, is made clear at the start and is revealed again at the close by an angel. Geoffrey's history is thus a vital and patriotic tale narrated against a background of foretold defeat. As such, its method is of great significance, and the book's self-evident appeal was so considerable that it was not only widely transcribed but was adapted and translated into Anglo-Norman by the poet Wace (d. after 1171). Writing for the court of Henry II, Wace lavishes on his version a lovingly detailed description of the noble life, idealizing the newly invented chivalry of Camelot to make it a paradigm for the most sophisticated aristocratic audience in twelfth-century Europe. Wace thereby becomes one of the figures to influence Chrétien. His poem is a fine work of imaginative recreation and also the principal source for one of the most important Early Middle English verse chronicles.

Layamon's *Brut* (twelfth century) – in other words 'a story beginning with Brutus'–is a work of 16,000 long alliterative lines whose form probably derives from the popular and oral tradition of such verse rather than directly from Old English texts. The poem again recounts the early and mythical history of Britain, largely in the form that Wace derived it from Geoffrey. But, once more, it would be wrong to think of the *Brut* merely as a translation. Lacking that enjoyment of courtly sophistication which characterizes Wace, the poem is principally heroic and military in its interests. In its more literary Arthurian sections it also reveals an impressive command of epic simile and a delight in hunting and battle. Indeed, it displays much of that tone at once dogged and fitfully illuminated by the supernatural which is familiar from Old English heroic poetry. This is clearest in the prominence Layamon gives to the story of Arthur. In the description of the hero's death and his final passage to Avalon, there is a parallel with the last moments of Beowulf and a suggestion of that mystery which helps to account for the enduring fascination of the 'matter of Britain':

> Arður wes forwunded wunder ane swiðe.
> Per to him com a cnaue þe wes of his cunne:
> He wes Cadores sune, þe eorles of Cornwaile.
> Constantin hehte þe cnaue, he wes þan kinge deore.
> Arður him lokede on, þer he lai on folden,
> And þas word seide mid sorhfulle heorte:
> 'Costæntin, þu art wilcume; þu weore Cadores sone.
> Ich þe bitache here mine kineriche,
> And wite mine Bruttes a to þines lifes,
> And hald heom alle þa laȝen þa habbeoð istonden a mine daȝen
> And alle þa laȝen gode þa bi Uðeres daȝen stode.
> And Ich wulle uaren to Aualun, to uairest alre maidene,
> To Argante þere quene, aluen swiðe sceone,
> And heo scal mine wunden makien alle isunde,
> Al hal me makien mid haleweiȝe drenchen.
> And seoðe Ich cumen wulle to mine kineriche
> And wunien mid Brutten mid muchelere wunne.'

Æfne þan worden þer com of se wenden
þet wes an sceort bat liðen, sceouen mid vðen,
And twa wimmen þerinne wunderliche idihte,
And heo nomen Arður anan and aneouste hine uereden,
And softe hine adun leiden and forð gunnen hine liðen.
þa wes hit iwurðen þat Merlin seide whilen:
þat weore unimete care of Arðures forðfare.

(*Arthur was wounded wondrously much. There came to him a lad, who was his kindred: he was son of Cador, the Earl of Cornwall. The lad was called Constantine, he was dear to the king. Arthur looked on him, where he lay on the ground, and said these words, with sorrowful heart: 'Constantine, thou art welcome; thou wert Cador's son. I give thee here my kingdom, and defend thou my Britons ever in thy life, and maintain them all the laws that have stood in my days, and all the good laws that in Uther's days stood. And I will fare to Avalon, to the fairest of all maidens, to Argante the queen, an elf most fair, and she shall make my wounds all sound; make me whole with healing draughts. And afterwards I will come again to my kingdom, and dwell with the Britons with much joy.'*

Even with the words there approached from the sea nearby a short boat, floating with the waves; and two women therein, wondrously formed; and they took Arthur anon, and bare him quickly, and laid him softly down, and then they made ready to go.

Then was accomplished all that Merlin once said, that there should be much grieving at Arthur's departure.)

12

Layamon's *Brut* is a work of importance in its own right, but it stands aside from the most developed area of Arthurian romance. This, we have seen, was a preoccupation of a French-speaking audience at this period, and there is nothing in the contemporary English use of the form to compare with the subtlety of Chrétien. Romance motifs were used nonetheless by fairly unsophisticated native poets. Though similar in their *matière* to a number of contemporary French works, chivalry and refined passion are less the subjects of *King Horn* (*c.* 1225), *Havelock the Dane* (mss. *c.* 1300–1325), *Athelston* (1350–1400), *Bevis of Hampton* (early fourteenth century) and *Guy of Warwick* (early fourteenth century) than the more forthright and (as their heroes' names might suggest) rough Norse pleasures of muscle and preposterous violence. These incidents form part of a series of adventures whose excitements are largely narrative, a series of thrills and spills. Though *Floris and Blancheflour* (*c.* 1250) preserves a little of the sentiment of the similar *Aucassin and Nicolette*, the women of the Early Middle English romances inspire at best a horny-handed courtesy. These poems are not works for an exclusively courtly audience but for a group whose interest in folk-heroes, marvels of strength and robust piety can be gauged from the opening of what is perhaps the best-told of these narratives, *Havelock the Dane*:

> Herkneth to me, gode men,
> Wives, maidnes, and alle men,
> Of a tale that ich you wile telle,
> Who-so it wile here and ther-to dwelle.
> The tale is of Havelok y-maked;
> Whil he was litel, he yede full naked.
> Havelok was a full good gome:
> He was full good in every trome;
> He was the wighteste man at nede
> That thurte riden on any stede.
> That ye mowen nou y-here,
> And the tale you mowen y-lere,
> At the beginning of ure tale,
> Fill me a cuppe of full good ale;
> And while I drinken, her I spelle,
> That Christ us shilde alle fro helle!
> Christ late us evere so for to do
> That we moten comen him to;
> And, with-that it mote ben so,
> Benedicamus Domino!
> Here I schall biginnen a rim;
> Christ us yeve well god fin!

yede full naked: ill-clothed   *gome:* fellow   *trome:* troop   *thurte:* might   *mowen:* must
y-lere: learn   *spelle:* relate   *moten ... mote:* must   *Benedicamus Domino:* God bless us

These lines give the impression of a lively narrator. One of his generally required skills – an ability to characterize different roles in a poem – is also suggested by the marginal indications of who speaks the various passages of dialogue in another English work from the thirteenth century: *Dame Sirith*. This narrative further introduces us to a new poetic form which is the opposite of romance and one of the great delights of medieval literature.

13

The fabliau is a usually short, often indecent and always comic narrative poem. Where romance exalts the noble, emotional and chivalric, fabliau presents a heightened view of the grotesque and very physical world of the bourgeois, the peasant and the clerk. Both romance and fabliau reorder the world into an imaginative sequence, but where the knights and ladies of romance aspire to the ideal, the heroes and heroines of fabliau live by their wits in a world of farce. Fabliau is a common form in the literature of France and Italy but, aside from the unknown author of *Dame Sirith*, Chaucer is the single major exponent of the fabliau in English. Like the tales of both the Miller and the Reeve, *Dame Sirith* is a reworking of well-known comic motifs and shows a clerk or learned man's attempts to sleep with an attractive married woman. Clerk Wilekin in *Dame Sirith*, like the similar figure in *De Clerico et Puella* from the Harley Lyrics and Absalom in *The Miller's Tale*, has fallen into a comically inappropriate state of languishing *fine amour*. Rejected by his horrified beloved, Wilekin consults Dame Sirith who suggests such a witty stratagem that it can bear to be re-told. Smearing mustard round her dog's eyes, she takes the seemingly weeping animal to Wilekin's beloved and tells her that the dog is in fact Dame Sirith's own daughter who has been transformed through the magic powers of a vengeful cleric whose advances the girl rejected. The frightened and gullible Margery immediately submits to Wilekin's desires, and Dame Sirith, adequately recompensed, leaves the couple to their delights:

> And loke þat þou hire tille
> And strek out her þes.
> God ʒeue þe muchel kare
> ʒeif þat þou hire spare,
> þe wile þou mid hire bes.

þes: thighs   *bes:* be

Such lines constitute the bawdy antithesis of romance and are to the vast body of romance what the gargoyle is to the cathedral.

14

There is, however, a further and far-ranging aspect of the twelfth-century renaissance reflected in Early Middle English verse and one which, since it is of central importance to *The Owl and the Nightingale* (*c.* 1200–1215) – the masterpiece of this literature – we should now examine. Alongside the enrichment of scholarly and spiritual life, the rediscovery of human love as a proper subject for poetry, and the development of a body of romance and situation comedy, there lies the creation of a sophisticated administrative machinery in the courts of the papacy and of Henry II. With this came the emergence both of the law as a proper field for intellectual enquiry and an intelligent, highly trained elite to use it.

An advanced legal system is an aspect of reason in action, an attempt to relate general principles and accepted practices to particular conflicts. The rediscovery of the *Institutes* of Justinian (the great codex of late Roman law) showed men the possibilities of an ordered and comprehensive legal system as rigorous and encyclopedic in its field as the *Summa Theologica* of St Thomas Aquinas. This was both attractive in itself and of great use to the eleventh and twelfth centuries when rulers, keen to exploit the profits of judicial proceedings, were also trying to consolidate their domains on a sound theoretical basis. The concordance of canon or church law compiled by Gratian under the influence of both Justinian's work and the force of scholastic logic – a book generally known as the *Decretum* (1140–50) – was a similar attempt to govern an international body on an agreed basis derived from historical and theoretical first principles rather than by confused and often crude local custom. The writing of the *Decretum* further witnesses to the vast efforts being made to centralize ecclesiastical authority around the Pope at this time, and Gratian's labours became crucial to that fierce legal conflict between Church and state in the England of Henry II, the eventual martyr of which was Thomas à Becket (1118?–70). The study of the law was particularly well established in England (Becket himself worked with some of the finest canon lawyers of the day) and a new and growing body of men, revealing their training by calling themselves 'magister' and eager to apply the disciplines of the law in royal employment, is one of the central features of the age. Nicholas of Guildford, the probable author of *The Owl and the Nightingale*, was himself such a figure, and his plea for professional recognition at the close of his work suggests that a knowledge of the law was now seen as a key to advancement.

It was perhaps inevitable that just as the allegorical reading of religious texts and the vocabulary of spiritual devotion should enrich the writing of secular literature, so too would the newly acquired intellectual power and formal processes of the law. We have already noted a distinct legalistic tone in the problems faced by some of Chrétien's heroes, and both he and the author of *The Owl and the Nightingale* were writing for royal households where a witty parody of legal procedures, the so-called 'courts of love', investigated hypothetical amorous problems and pronounced playful judgement on them. This resolution of problems of love is a central aspect of much medieval secular poetry. It is a motif given prominent if ambiguous place in, for example, the tales of both Chaucer's Franklin and his Wife of Bath. The particular distinction of the author of *The Owl and the Nightingale*, however, is the way in which he contrived a debate between two female birds representative of the life and poetry of the Church and the court, and, using the form of the *débat* or *altercatio* which was widely popular on the continent, fashioned it around the actual procedures of a contemporary English trial. He then enlivened a dispute on some of the central issues of his age with that virulent abuse or 'flyting' which was a rhetorical exercise familiar from the grammar schools. In the following passage, the Nightingale describes the respective positions of the antagonists:

> Also þu dost on þire side:
> Vor wanne snov liþ þicke an wide
> An alle wiȝtes habbeþ sorȝe,
> þu singest from eue fort amorȝe.
> Ac Ich blisse mid me bringe;
> Ech wiȝt is glad for mine þinge,
> An blisseþ hit wanne Ich cume
> An hiȝteþ aȝen mine kume.
> þc blostme ginneþ springe an sprede,
> Boþe ine tro an ek on mede.
> þe lilie mid hire faire wlite
> Wolcumeþ me, þat þu hit wite;
> Bid me mid hire faire blo
> þat Ich shulle to hire flo;
> þe rose also mid hire rude
> þat cumeþ ut of þe þorne-wode
> Bit me þat Ich shulle singe
> Vor hire luue one skentinge.

(This you also do, for when the snow lies thick and wide and everyone is feeling miserable, you sing from morning to night. But I bring such bliss with me that everyone is cheered by my efforts, rejoices when I appear and is glad before I have even arrived. The blossom starts to spring both on the trees and in the fields. The lily with her lovely face welcomes me, as you know; bids me to joy with her so that I fly to her; the red briar rose asks me to sing something for love of her.)

The contrast is evidently between two attitudes to life and the two kinds of song or poetry that reflect these. On the one hand the Owl at first appears wintry and life-denying, a conventionally learned but sinister figure obsessed with the penitential functions of literature, who declares that her song of learning and lament is sung in order to encourage men to weep for their transgressions and groan for their misdeeds. In this, the Owl seems to belong exclusively to that stern Gregorian tradition of the Christian life which such figures as St Anselm and St Bernard had greatly modified: a literature of wailing and gnashing of teeth which viewed the world as a thoroughfare full of woe, consolation as being at best a longing for Heaven, and the horrors of Hell the likely home for the soul after death. This is an attitude also expressed in the section quoted earlier from *Sawles Warde*. It was an abiding view of existence in the Middle Ages which, while it must be seriously appreciated, was one that it is suggested here is too little touched by the newly awakened tenderness of the spiritual life.

The Nightingale, by contrast, is the harbinger of spring familiar from French poetry, who appears initially as the singer of heart-gladdening if somewhat frivolous love songs. She is at first presented as the advocate of purely secular pleasure. Significantly, it is also the Nightingale who is the plaintiff in the case, the party who feels she has been unwarrantably attacked. Her first vigorous assertions relate both her and her poetry to the newly discovered delights of *fine amour*, to the world of romance and *chanson* which, establishing the claims on poetry of love and the social world, was, as we have seen, a great innovation of the twelfth century. Whether poetic endeavour may be used for such secular purposes at all, however, is one of the issues that the trial seeks to establish. It is a matter of the greatest general importance. How far a literature of fiction and human desire is proper in a world conceived ultimately in religious terms was an issue that was to preoccupy Chaucer at the end of *The Canterbury Tales* and is a central problem in much medieval writing. In *The Owl and the Nightingale*, two apparently irreconcilable contemporary attitudes to life and art are thus presented, and the ensuing debate greatly extends the possibilities of a popular form by a detailed use of the processes of law and – most remarkably – by having both protagonists modify their views in the course of their argument.

That argument, the poet tells us, is stern, strenuous, stubborn and abusive. The protagonists are first shown in appropriate habitats: the Nightingale hidden amid rich blossoms, the Owl chanting her Church hours from a tree-stump swathed in symbolic evergreen ivy. This sort of description is the conventional opening to a *débat*, but after an initial fiery exchange, the particular nature of the poem reveals itself when the Nightingale states her first indictment of the Owl.

She is, the Nightingale declares, cruel, ugly, dirty and unnatural in so far as she prefers night to day. All these charges should be read allegorically as referring to courtly distaste for clerical austerity. Since in legal practice a mere accusation is insufficient, however, the Nightingale supports what she says by references to proverbial law, a procedure that will be adopted throughout the poem. The Owl then denies the Nightingale's charges and indicates her willingness to defend her case through trial by combat. This was a standard judicial procedure and reflects an older and increasingly uncommon form of justice in which guilt or innocence was supposedly determined by the direct intervention of God. The little Nightingale cunningly refuses the offer, and her confidence in the legal process suggests her belief in the newly enhanced powers of the mind to determine issues in a manner free from violence and with a due regard for the law.

The Nightingale further suggests that Nicholas of Guildford be appointed judge of the issue since she regards him as prudent, virtuous and a connoisseur of song. The Owl agrees to this, for, as she says, although Nicholas was given to the ways of the Nightingale in his youth, his ardour has now cooled and his natural feelings incline him to her side of the case. In this way the probable author of the poem subtly reveals himself to his audience – and, he hopes, his patrons – as a mature, capable yet humane man. Nonetheless, because we only see the trial rehearsed away from his presence (the Owl finally admitting that she possesses that most revered scholastic gift of a perfect memory which she will use when they go before their judge) Nicholas is never actually shown giving his verdict. Rather, with that literary tact which marks the presentation of the author in much of the finest medieval verse, Nicholas's wise presence is felt at crucial points during the poem but never obtrudes in the form of a decision. Indeed, much of the sophisticated refinement of *The Owl and the Nightingale* lies in the fact that, while important issues are raised and firm opinions modified, an explicit conclusion is never reached. Once again, the audience is left to decide for itself.

The processes of law having been accepted, we should note some differences between legal proceedings in the twelfth century and in our own, bearing in mind that the most crucial distinction here is the fact that the case is pleaded in English rather than in the French used by the courts up to 1361. This was a factor which for contemporaries would have highlighted the element of parody in the poem. We should also note that complaints about arbitrary wrong such as this had always reached the king and that cases tried in the royal court invariably involved punishment. The decision the birds have made is thus not a light one. Secondly, a jury at this period was an instrument of royal prerogative and not a right. If it was called, it was a body representative of some local group and was sworn to tell the truth on the basis of its own investigations rather than solely on the evidence presented. In so far as the trial in *The Owl and the Nightingale* is inconclusive and the poem is directed towards an aristocratic audience who are left to wonder at the final outcome, we may choose to see that audience in the role of a jury empanelled under particular medieval circumstances, circumstances familiar enough to them but strange to us. It is just these differences we must appreciate, however, if we are to understand the poem in the ways contemporaries would have received it. This is important, for, just as Chrétien's religious imagery asks its audience to discuss issues of secular love, so the form of *The Owl and the Nightingale* asks its audience to interpret the poem in terms of judicial procedures that encouraged wide debate.

Finally, we should turn to the position of Nicholas as judge and realize that his role would have been essentially that of an umpire rather than his more powerful modern equivalent, since a characteristic of the judicial process at this period was its rigid and even stereotyped course which could not be easily changed. As Professor Barlow has written: 'Once the plaintiff had chosen a writ the trial proceeded remorselessly according to the appropriate rules. If the plaintiff had chosen wrongly he could not amend his plea nor could the judge use his discretion. All parties to the trial were shackled by the rules, and the one redeeming feature of this archaic formalistic rigidity was that it kept the judge in his place. He soon became, as he had been before, but the umpire of a complicated game.' It is just the rules of this 'game' that determine both the shape of much of the early part of *The Owl and the Nightingale* and the frequent attempts by the two birds to trip each other up.

For example, the Nightingale's formal indictment is followed by the Owl's reply and subsequent use of her right of *exceptio* by which she charges the Nightingale with a multitude of misdemeanours. Having established that her own strength is natural, her monastic retreat a dignified matter and her song a beautiful chanting of the Church hours, the Owl rebuffs the Nightingale's accusation that her singing is a churlish and wintry grumbling – an accusation that suggests the rather frivolous presentation of herself by the courtly bird at this stage. The Owl further declares that the Nightingale's song is a mere accompaniment to the rank coupling of peasants in the summer heat. This reflects the ascetic's wholesale disapproval of sex, a view which allows for no delicacy or refinement in human relations. This perhaps sways the audience or jury away from sympathy with the Owl at this point. In response, the Nightingale tries to bring another charge against the Owl, a move which, as the Owl herself points out, is strictly illegal. Rather, the Owl now exercises her own right to accuse the Nightingale of frivolity, ugliness and an obsession with the fact that, as Yeats was to declare, 'love has pitched his mansion in/The place of excrement'. Sex, she again suggests, is foul and degrading. The Owl further declares that she herself is useful, preserves the Church and, contrary to the Nightingale's assertions, is in fact a clean bird.

The Nightingale is momentarily flustered by so comprehensive an attack. Indeed the violence and cogency of the argument at this point provide much of the poem's intellectual pleasure. This aggression is a deliberate ploy on the Owl's part, however, since the trick of angering an opponent and causing him or her to make a mistake in pleading would generally result in the breakdown of the trial. But remembering King Alfred's advice that the mind is keenest when most pressed, the Nightingale puts forward her *replicatio* and, in her ensuing speeches, presents herself as a skilful singer who – unlike the Owl – charms men to Heaven. The Owl regards this claim as merely ridiculous. Weeping and wailing are the ways to God, she says, and the Nightingale's courtly frivolity does at this stage seem to condemn her. Nonetheless, she continues to defend her own beauty against the Owl's ugliness and pessimistic foreboding, for which she curses her.

But eventually the Nightingale is bound to reply to the Owl's charge that her singing of courtly love songs encourages adultery (the Owl actually cites a version of *Laüstic* to support this) and that her brief passions are corrupting. Forced into a corner, the Nightingale's reply is a serious attempt to examine the morality of *fine amour*. She is obliged to test her own position carefully and, under the pressure of greater thoughtfulness, she rejects adulterous passion and claims her song teaches young girls that love is a brief, dangerous but legitimate delight which should lead to marriage. This serious modification of the Nightingale's original position suggests a view of refined human emotion which is far more than a frivolous rebuttal of ecclesiastical asceticism. And, just as the Nightingale moves towards a more serious view of pleasure, so the Owl in her reply moves towards a more compassionate view of human relations. Her song, she now admits, comforts unhappy wives (she provides a sympathetic picture of marital strife comparable in its intensity to that in *Hali Meiðhad*) and also solaces loving spouses sundered from their husbands. Such a view is far more humane than the ascetic bigotry of her earlier view of men and women.

But the Owl overplays her hand. She has accused the Nightingale of being useless, either alive or dead, and then claims that she herself is both useful as a singer and, after her death, as a scarecrow. The quick-witted Nightingale realizes that this declaration is what was known as a *stultiloquium* – a verbal foolishness which destroys her case – for what the Owl has done by her last statement is to boast of her own disgrace. The Nightingale and her newly arrived allies now claim that the courtly bird has won the suit (as, technically, she has), but the Owl demands a proper re-trial before the excellent but apparently hard-done-by Nicholas. The law-abiding Nightingale willingly agrees. Nonetheless,

> Ah hu heo spedde of heore dome
> Ne can Ich eu namore telle.
> Her nis namore of þis spelle.

(*I can tell you nothing more about how judgement in their case was given. There is no more of this tale.*)

So this lively and beautifully constructed work comes to its inconclusive conclusion. A poem at once serious and charming, it is vividly characterized and written with a masterly control of a familiar style and in the light octosyllabics used by French verse. In its deft sophistication and the effortless way it draws to itself some of the great issues of the period – the new compassion of the religious life, the claims of *fine amour* and the rigour of both scholastic logic and the law – it is proof that by the early thirteenth century literature in English had reached a very high level of achievement indeed.

CHAPTER 3

THE RISE OF MIDDLE ENGLISH

The Owl and the Nightingale (*c.* 1200–1215) was probably written at the start of a period when profound changes were taking place in the social and political structure of England, changes that were crucially to affect both the form and status of the native language. One of the most important of these was the disintegration of the vast estates ruled by the Plantagenets and, in particular, the loss of Normandy in the reign of King John (1204). The latter had the greatest political and symbolic importance since it finally confirmed that the allegiance of an aristocracy of Anglo-Norman descent now lay with England. This in turn suggested that the country had its own interests and purposes, and that by 1250 the most valid reason for the use of French had apparently disappeared. Such a change does not mean, however, that a simple and wholesale use of Middle English occurred, for the development of the language is complicated by two further factors: first, by what came to be seen as an excessive French cultural influence in the court and senior Church circles, and secondly, by the fact that from about the year 1200 French had established itself as the international language of courtly literature, a tongue capable, as we have seen, of great refinement and subtlety.

The sophistication and broad influence of literary French was appreciated from Norway to Spain. It was literally the *lingua franca*, and as late as the fifteenth century was described by Christine de Pisan as the language 'la plus commune par l'universel monde'. This was no mere patriotic boast, and it was against such broad achievement that Middle English had to compete in its homeland. Further, under King John – and even more extensively during the long reign of Henry III (1216–72) – the hegemony of French was reinforced in England by the widespread replacement of senior native officials by Frenchmen and a consequently renewed dependence on French culture in the court. Henry was himself French on his mother's side and had married a French wife who, in her turn, brought such a crowd of foreign retainers with her that the historian Matthew Paris was forced to describe London as 'full to overflowing not only with Poitevins, Romans and Provençals, but also of Spaniards who did great injury to the English'.

There was an inevitable reaction which can be traced in three areas.

First in politics, where unofficial opposition to foreigners grouped itself around Simon de Montfort and had its part to play in the turmoil of the Baron's War (1258–65). This was a mood only reversed at the end of the century when, in 1295, Edward I summoned Parliament with a rousing challenge to face the French king's 'detestable purpose', which was, 'God forbid, to wipe out the English language'. The status of French in England at this period can also be measured by the somewhat artificial attempts to preserve what remained the language of polite society, a language supported by legal custom and business convention, but which, in its Anglo-Norman form, was a dialect increasingly regarded as somewhat crude in comparison with the French now spoken in Paris. These efforts to preserve the French tongue take the form of manuals on the language such as that of Walter of Bibbesworth (pre-1250), and such regulations as those passed by the universities which required under-graduates to converse in Latin or, if necessary, in French. The speaking of English among dons was strongly disparaged as a sign of decadence. Similar in intention (and again reflecting the growing use of spoken English) was a parliamentary decree of 1332 which Froissart describes as requiring all more prosperous Englishmen to teach their children French. Clearly, by the end of the thirteenth century, a rapidly developing form of English was widely spoken by all classes and legislation had become an increasingly ineffective means of stemming the tide.

Something of the resentment caused by this uncertain situation is evident in a passage from Ranulph Higden's *Polychronicon* (*c.* 1327) – written, it should be noted, in Latin, but which may be quoted here from an English translation made some fifty years later:

> This apayrynge of þe burþe tunge is bycause of tweie þinges; oon is for children in scole aȝenst þe vsage and manere of alle oþere naciouns beeþ compelled for to leue hire owne langage, and for to construe hir lessouns and here þynges in Frensche, and so þey haueþ seþ þe Normans come first in to Engelond. Also gentil men children beeþ i-tauȝt to speke Frensche from þe tyme þet þey beeþ i-rokked in here cradel, and kunneþ speke and playe wiþ a childes broche; and vplondisshe men wil likne hym self to gentil men, and fondeþ wiþ greet besynesse for to speke Frensce, for to be [more] i-tolde of.

apayrynge: reduction   *vplondisshe:* arrogant   *i-tolde of:* talked of

Anger at the fact that the native tongue is devalued in educational circles here combines with frank annoyance at the social ambitions which still accompanied a knowledge of French. As we shall see, John of Trevisa, the translator of this passage, added an important rider which reflects the changed conditions of his time.

But what of literature? The outstanding quality of *The Ancrene Riwle*, the Harley Lyrics, *Brut* and *The Owl and the Nightingale* witnesses to the fact that Early Middle English, though in a constant state of flux, was capable of refinement as a literary language. Nonetheless, it was still secondary to both Latin as a medium for serious discussion and to French as a means of literary expression. But slowly, as writers wished to appeal to a growing and changing audience, we find them explaining their decision to write in English. Many of these late twelfth- and early thirteenth-century vernacular works are religious and homiletic in purpose, and as such can often be allied both to the various traditions of such writing which had been sporadically maintained from the time of Wulfstan and to the influence of the preaching orders of the Franciscans and Dominicans. The so-called *Ormulum* (late twelfth century), for example, though isolated in style and a work with no obvious direct successors, is an incomplete, brave but tedious attempt to provide an English version of the Gospels as used in the Mass over the Church year, followed by their interpretation and application. The work is also of some linguistic interest since, in the attempt to establish clear and consistent pronunciation, the poet has used a system of double consonants to establish that the vowels these follow are all short. This technique can be illustrated from the following line which may also serve to illustrate Orm's monotonous metre:

þiss boc iss nemmnedd Orrmulum Forrþi þatt Orrm itt wrohhte.

Thirty-two of the planned 242 of Orm's homilies survive, and the work was intended to be read to ordinary people – a noble aim, if one that was poorly and incompletely executed. A quantity of other vernacular sermons from the period is also preserved, including some in the Kentish dialect, which are translations of the new, direct style of preaching being developed in Paris.

Rather more successful, though again not to be ranked as great imaginative literature, are collections of saints' lives such as those contained in *The Northern Passion* and *The South English Legendary* (late thirteenth century). In its earliest form, the latter contains pieces on the life of Christ, the saints and martyrs, and a further range of homilies, but, like the vast *Cursor Mundi*, the work was eventually expanded to become an encyclopedia of scriptural knowledge.

It is important to realize why such huge compilations were needed. Where we are used to a plain text of the Bible in our own language, medieval congregations almost never received it in this form. The Church reserved direct access for itself alone (hoping thereby to limit the possibilities of heresy) and taught the Scriptures to the largely illiterate masses through the carvings and stained glass of the greater churches, through preaching, drama and such collections of re-told stories as those gathered in the works we are discussing here. Even in its early version the *Cursor Mundi* contains much interesting information, both sacred and secular, including material on Thomas à Becket and such pieces as the life of St Kenelm. The latter, the story of a child martyr caught up in the machinations of his evil sister, is proudly cited by Chauntecleer in *The Nun's Priest's Tale* as one of the works he has read. The legend may have Old English origins, and its sentimental melodrama can be seen as both the ecclesiastical equivalent of the excitements of vernacular romance and as prefiguring the later, highly sophisticated use of saints' legends such as that told by the Prioress in *The Canterbury Tales*. Further, *The South English Legendary* is clearly a compilation designed for lay instruction, and this in turn is a matter which suggests both a vital element in the medieval audience and the way in which many works were designed for them. In William of Nassyngton's *Speculum Vitae* or 'Mirror of Life' (*c.* 1325), there is also an important declaration of why such poems should be written in English. Simply – importantly – English is now seen as the language most readily understood by all:

> In English tonge I schal ʒow telle,
> ʒif ʒe wyth me so longe wil dwelle.
> No Latyn wil I speke no waste,
> But English, þat men vse mast,
> þat can eche man vnderstande,
> þat is born in Inglelande;
> For þat langage is most chewyd,
> Os wel among lered os lewyd.
> Latyn, as I trowe, can nane
> But þo, þat haueth it in scole tane,
> And somme can Frensche and no Latyn,
> þat vsed han cowrt and dwellen þerein,
> And somme can of Latyn a party,
> þat can of Frensche but febly;
> And somme vnderstonde wel Englysch,
> þat can noþer Latyn nor Frankys.
> Boþe lered and lewed, olde and ʒonge,
> Alle vnderstonden english tonge.

mast: most   *chewyd:* in evidence   *lered:* learned   *lewyd:* unlettered, lay   *trowe:* believe
tane: taken, learned   *party:* some   *Frankys:* French

And so, we might add, can we. Compared with the lines quoted from

The Owl and the Nightingale, this passage reveals a grammar, vocabulary and syntax that are almost familiar.

Nonetheless, although the greatly enhanced resources of the native language at this period require it to be differentiated from earlier forms by the term Middle English, this development should be seen in the context of a marked regionalization of dialects. These fall broadly into Kentish, Southern, Northern, the West Midlands form used by the Gawain-poet which was spoken in an area bounded by the Welsh border and the Severn north to Lancaster, and the dialect of the prosperous East Midlands, a huge and subdivisible region stretching from the Humber south to the Thames and defined in the west by the Peak District. Variations and borrowings between these areas (themselves dependent on the regionalized pattern of Old English) are marked but complex, and involve changes in orthography, pronunciation and grammar that admit few ready generalizations. While a systematic account of these is not possible here, we should note that further events were to consolidate the varied development of the native language.

These events indicate a profound shift away from early medieval feudalism and its concepts towards the richly coloured, highly differentiated society which formed the first audience for Gothic art. The greatest imaginative recreation of this audience is, of course, the company of pilgrims gathered at the start of *The Canterbury Tales*. Such political and social changes can again only be lightly sketched here, but in terms of the development of English we can isolate a number of strands. For example, the early successes of the Hundred Years War (1337–1453) caused a surge of patriotism in a nation of growing self-awareness, while later defeats marked out French as the language of the enemy. Of more long-term significance were a series of social and economic changes: a general increase in prosperity and population in the first half of the fourteenth century, and, in the towns particularly, the development of free, self-governing and English-speaking communities banding together for purposes of trade and administration.

With the establishment of an urban middle class – Chaucer's parents, for example, prosperous, attached to the court, ambitious for their educated and brilliant son – there comes that subtle, important sense of individualism, of men working both for and in competition with their fellows, which slowly forced the native language into new areas of expression and expertise. Two incidents illustrate this development. In 1356, the mayor and aldermen of London required proceedings in the sheriffs' courts in the City and in Middlesex to be conducted in English, a move which clearly reflects the decision of a powerful group of men to attend to their own business in their own speech. Six years later the king's courts followed suit, since they too were aware of the 'great mischiefs' that derived from cases conducted in an unknown language. As a result, the Statute of Pleading (1361) required that all matters should be 'pleaded, showed, defended, answered, debated, and judged in the English language'. However, with a characteristic legal cautiousness which helps us see exactly into the linguistic prejudice of the time, the Statute of Pleading itself was drafted in French and required that legal records be entered and enrolled in Latin.

All these factors making for the establishment of English were perhaps predictable (many were shared, for example, by the more prosperous city states of the Italian peninsula), but perhaps the most significant cause of the reorganization of English society and the success of the English language at this period is the result of a purely natural disaster: the Black Death (1348–50). Ravaging the country, decimating the monasteries which then attracted men speaking only English, killing 40 per cent of the clergy, and creating such wholesale mortality among the peasantry that labour prices (a relatively new and deeply threatening phenomenon in a feudal society) rose to a premium, the Black Death was an instrument of profound social change. It caused feudal ties to collapse and discontent to express itself in the Peasants' Revolt (1381). Some of the elements in this confrontation are suggested by the image of a young and gorgeously bedecked Richard II, patron of the most lavish international court culture, riding out to face the rebels, ragged men who had engaged in the mass slaughter of immigrant Flemish workers, and addressing them in English. The importance of the Black Death as an instrument of linguistic change is also made clear in the additions to his original made by the translator John of Trevisa. Where the Latin of the *Polychronicon* had bridled at the hegemony of French, Trevisa now sees dangers in the triumph of English as a teaching language:

þis manere was moche i-vsed to fore þe firste moreyn and is siþþe sumdel i-chaunged; for Iohn Cornwaile, a maister of grammer, chaunged þe lore in gramer scole and construccioun of Frensche in to Englische; and Richard Pencriche lerned þat manere techynge of hym and oþere men of Pencrich; so þat now, þe ȝere of oure Lorde a þowsand þre hundred and foure score and fyue, and of þe secounde kyng Richard after þe conquest nyne, in alle þe gramere scoles of Engelond, children leueþ Frensche and construeþ and lerneþ an Englische, and haueþ þerby auauntage in oon side and disauauntage in anoþer side; here auauntage is, þat þey lerneþ her gramer in lasse tyme þan children were i-woned to doo; disauauntage is þat now children of gramer scole conneþ na more Frensche þan can hir lift heele, and þat is harme for hem and þey schulle passe þe see and trauaille in straunge landes and in many oþer places. Also gentil men haueþ now moche i-left for to teche here children Frensche.

moreyn: plague   *siþþe:* since   *sumdel:* somewhat   *leueþ:* leave   *construeþ:* interpret
conneþ: learn   *trauaille:* work

Despite Trevisa's legitimate concern – Middle English was, after all, an offshore language spoken only by a small nation – the change to its widespread use became ever more marked, and to that list of economic, social and natural forces determining its supremacy we should add the names of the two schoolmasters mentioned by Trevisa: John Cornwall and Richard Pencrich, Oxford men and largely unknown, yet innovators of the greatest possible significance. As a result of these forces, Middle English was now getting ready to take its place beside the great literary vernaculars of Europe, to absorb their techniques and extend their purposes. It was to do so in the hands of a poet of genius.

CHAPTER 4

GEOFFREY CHAUCER (*c.* 1340–1400)

1

Chaucer is 'the father of English poetry'. This popular epithet is in many ways deserved, and although nothing can explain the sudden appearance of a mind of the most acute and original sensibility, range and innovative power, it is at least possible to suggest something of Chaucer's circumstances and the traditions on which he drew, only to transfigure these with so mastering a facility that he ranks as a poet of European stature.

Numerous details survive which help us to trace Chaucer's career. We know, for example, that his parents were prosperous wine merchants and that the family, coming originally from Ipswich, had settled in London and enjoyed both an important place in the life of the City and connections with the court at Westminster. Such a background among the English-speaking middle classes is revealing. It suggests on the one hand a serious and specialized concern with work, achievement and the world, and, on the other, knowledge of a leisured, chivalric and French-based culture of the greatest brilliance. To these influences should be added an active and searching piety, the Latin education Chaucer almost certainly received, his knowledge of Italian poetry, and a speculative, humane intellect deeply concerned with rhetoric, theology, philosophy and the several branches of medieval science. From such diverse origins as these, established in the main literary languages of his time and involved with most aspects of English life, Chaucer emerges as an exceptional representative of a new breed of men: literate, strong-minded laypeople, willing to read widely, to question, and able to record their concerns.

Chaucer's father used his connections at court to advance the career of his son. He thereby introduced him to a range of culture that was largely to determine the nature of his poetry. We know much of what this world was like. The chance survival of a fragment from the account book of Elizabeth, wife of Lionel, Duke of Clarence, for example, allows us to envisage the poet on Easter Day 1357, a pageboy of about seventeen, newly dressed in a short cloak and vivid red-and-black tights. Purchased at huge expense (the outfit cost over half the annual wage of a ploughman), it suggests how Chaucer had entered a world of formalized life and conspicuous public display. Here, and later when serving Edward III in what was perhaps the most splendid court in Europe, Chaucer could observe the ceremony and etiquette that surrounded the existence of the great, the exercise of power, the intrigues and sudden reversals of political fortune, the widely based artistic endeavour, and the dreams of love and chivalry with which the nobility decorated their lives and which, as we have seen, they also enshrined in their literature.

From this time on, Chaucer was to remain firmly attached to the court and in particular to the service of John of Gaunt. In 1360 he was campaigning in France where he was captured and ransomed; then, becoming a trusted and busy civil servant, he was sent on diplomatic journeys to Italy in the 1370s. He had by this time already begun his partial translation of the French *Roman de la Rose* (a work of seminal influence, to which we shall return) and his discovery of the vernacular and Latin writings of Dante, Petrarch and Boccaccio was to be of further importance to his poetic development. Now in his early thirties, we can see Chaucer not only as an Englishman deeply committed to his own language (in particular to the dialect of London and the rich East Midlands) but also as a European intellectual familiar with his Latin inheritance, with the courts of Aquitaine and Paris and the banks of the princely merchants of Florence.

After wedding a lady-in-waiting to the queen (little is known about his marriage) Chaucer was offered administrative posts at home. He became an active Comptroller of Customs for the Port of London, responsible for the accounts and living in a grace-and-favour apartment over Aldgate. It is in this period between 1374 and 1385, the serious decade of his early middle age, that we can glimpse him reading omnivorously in both modern and traditional poetry, philosophy and theology, enjoying the company of like-minded friends, and writing works that culminate in *Troilus and Criseyde*, his finest complete achievement. Later he was briefly in Parliament, and he appears to have been welcomed into the court of Henry IV at the end of Richard II's turbulent reign. Chaucer retired to Kent in about 1385, and it was in this period that he began seriously to assemble *The Canterbury Tales*, the most famous and popular of his works. He died in Westminster in 1400, his most ambitious project incomplete, and was buried in what is now Poets' Corner in Westminster Abbey.

2

Such are some of the external details of Chaucer's career, but in one of his early works he offers a more intimate self-portrait in which he shows how, when he had finished his work at the customs house,

> In stede of reste and newe thynges,
> Thou goost hom to thy hous anoon;
> And, also domb as any stoon,
> Thou sittest at another book
> Tyl fully dawsed ys thy look . . .
>
> *dawsed:* dazed

Since Chaucer's involvement with his literary traditions is so fundamental to his art, we should now turn to his reading and ask how representative of his class it was.

Alongside the influence of a secular and ecclesiastical aristocracy whose tastes dominated his age, the growing and articulate section of society into which Chaucer was born forms a group of the greatest importance to Middle English literature. Here were people living in a thriving city who conducted extensive and often international business that required them to be literate, numerate and competent in several languages. They were men whose financial power and civic influence had ensured both their effective freedom from serfdom as well as a considerable degree of political control. They were people for whom Parliament was a means of authorizing taxation, defending the law, determining policy and developing political theory. They thus enjoyed a large measure of responsibility and self-determination. It was these men too, their piety enriched by sermons and the sacraments, who helped finance the great flowering of medieval church architecture and for whose pleasure and spiritual nourishment much Middle English homiletic and secular literature was now being written. The popularity of such work witnesses to a new and important interest in reading among this group, an interest which turned increasingly on the inner life, on love, devotion and the moral consequences of action. These are also among the great themes of Chaucer's poetry. Here, then, was a section of his audience who realized the value of literacy and whose intellectual interests were spreading out to encompass translations and commentaries on current philosophical and biblical scholarship.

How did they obtain their literacy? French was the language of international business and the court, while basic Latin – the foundation of nearly all their studies – was taught in choir schools such as that attended by the infant hero of *The Prioress's Tale*. The standard curriculum of the grammar schools allows us to look again at the Latin grammar, logic and rhetoric of the *trivium*, and, in particular, the *Distichia Catonis*, which was the common textbook of almost every young scholar whose parents realized that burgeoning educational possibilities offered their sons the chance of literacy and perhaps a place in the swelling ranks of the professions. Of course, the *Distichia Catonis* is no more exciting than we might reasonably expect any school textbook to be. It is, in fact, a collection of the *sententiae* or wise sayings of some of the great writers of classical antiquity. As such, it could hardly be more important. It introduced boys to a range of Latin thought and suggested that this work was valuable for its teaching. The past, whether pagan or Christian, was seen as a source of wisdom, the gigantic shoulders on which the present age stood. But the past was also a source of style. Both the content and the manner of these passages had to be translated (sometimes with the help of a French crib), and as children grappled with the sonorous elegance of hexameters so they used their native language at the point where it was developing most quickly: its vocabulary. To turn a literature of great formal perfection and mature insight into a still-growing speech could be profoundly challenging and provide a lifetime's excitement. In Chaucer's work many of these traits cohere, and it was such a rhetorical training that helped ally him to the great European traditions.

But school textbooks were only one of the areas in which an increasing body of literate laypeople discovered snippets from works of the past, interpreted these in the light of moral instruction, and saw classical literature as actively engaged with their own growing language. Full-scale translations (often from French intermediaries), commentaries on the Latin quotations and exemplary stories included in sermons, and the increased production of alphabetized reference books in which preachers could find the pronouncements of a wide range of authorities on almost every topic, encouraged a further diffusion of knowledge. Nor should we forget the influence of the universities. While those with prestigious intellectual gifts might graduate and pursue a career in the higher echelons of the law or the Church, others wishing to learn the humbler skills of letter-writing and business also attended the new colleges of Oxford and Cambridge and so came into contact with fresh ideas. It was here too that clerics were trained, and such forms as the sermon, where piety and philosophy debated in the native tongue, were one of the main sources of an English literary and intellectual tradition on which Chaucer could draw.

Chaucer's education also meant that he could read many works in their Latin originals. His classical scholarship was wide-ranging and untroubled by a division into ancient and medieval, but, above all, it reveals how creative a learned dependence on a foreign literature can be. Since this last is a vital element in all his poetry, we should look first at the ways in which Chaucer encountered these sources and then at how he interpreted them. In other words, we should follow him to his library.

Because of Chaucer's familiarity with a wide range of Latin poetry, he was aware of a living classical tradition of which the modern poet – with suitable modesty – could be a part. At the close of *Troilus and Criseyde*, for instance, Chaucer bids his poem take its humble station behind the works of 'Virgile, Ovide, Omer, Lucan, Stace', this last figure being Statius, who is a source for *The Knight's Tale*. However, because Latin was still the international language of scholarship, to Chaucer's own list of writers should be added the names of such later figures as Boethius, Macrobius, Bernard Silvestris, Alain de Lille (Alanus), the rhetorician Geoffrey de Vinsauf, and the satirist Nigel of Longchamps, whose *Speculum Stultorum* ('Mirror of Fools') is a source for *The Nun's Priest's Tale*.

This is an unfamiliar canon, but it is such a range of figures who, along with the Latin Church Fathers, are included in that large manuscript miscellany – a *compilatio* – which the exasperated Wife of Bath is supposed to have burnt. A number of such works still survive (they were clearly treasured in less lively households), and to their frequently corrupt texts and misattributed contents we should add the further problem that Chaucer often derived his classical allusions from *florilegia*, French intermediaries or such epitomes as that of the *Aeneid*, which one medieval anthology wrongly ascribes to Ovid. Indeed even this most famous of Latin love poets, and the one to whom Chaucer most frequently turned, was known to him only in part. The silent areas of such a major poet's work are in some respects as interesting to the historian as the widely read volumes. Further, even when Chaucer consulted the *Metamorphoses*, as he did for the story of Ceyx and Alcyone in *The Book of the Duchess*, he seems also to have looked at the French *Ovid Moralisé*. Indeed, such cross-referencing was one of his common practices, for it is often the case that when he is reworking an ancient narrative – the story of Dido and Aeneas, for example, which he tells in both *The House of Fame* and *The Legend of Good Women* – he seems to have compared details in Virgil and Ovid as well as in more recent renditions, and to have then built up a composite narrative alive with his own energy and refashioned to the tastes of his time. In *The Legend of Good Women*, for example, the besotted Aeneas ceases to be Virgil's erring pioneer and becomes instead an embroidered squire, the courtly expert in 'amorous lokyng and devys'. Classical motifs have been thoroughly medievalized.

Nowhere is this relationship between the classical and medieval worlds of Latin scholarship closer than in a series of works whose form was greatly to influence Chaucer's early poems and whose ideas can be discerned throughout his career. These include Cicero's *Somnium Scipionis* ('The Dream of Scipio') with its lengthy commentary by Macrobius, Boethius's *Consolation of Philosophy*, and the writings of two medieval poets: Bernard Silvestris's *De Mundi Universitate* and Alain de Lille's *Anticlaudianus* and *De Planctu Naturae* ('The Complaint of Nature'). Each is a visionary work. The first takes the form of a journey to the heavens in which the dreaming hero sees the smallness of the earth, learns of the vanity of worldly fame and then hears the harmony of the spheres. His guide also tells him of the immortality of the soul and reassures him that those who do well go to Heaven while the sensual and wicked are whirled round the earth in a long-enduring pagan purgatory. For Cicero, the *Somnium Scipionis* was above all an attempt to define the ideal leader in a republic. It was the culmination of his interest in political philosophy. But for the Middle Ages (a society obliged to read the work without its preceding *De Re Publica*) the fact that Scipio's vision was set in a dream and that dreams received a detailed commentary in Macrobius was of greater interest. We take from the past what we need, and dream visions, drawing on a wide tradition in classical, biblical and vernacular literature, are fundamental to much of the greatest Middle English poetry – to work as diverse as *Pearl*, *Piers Ploughman*, most of Chaucer's earlier poems and even to some of *The Canterbury Tales*.

Like the *Somnium Scipionis*, the medieval Latin works we have mentioned also presented Chaucer with a series of imagined events which have a philosophic meaning at once independent of Christian teaching and yet analogous to it. Along with the vision of Lady Philosophy, who appears to Boethius, these works provided a means of investigating human reason and morality. They also reintroduce to us an important tool of medieval analysis: allegory.

Allegory is perhaps as old as thought itself, but for writers concerned to express the developing complexity of their inner and intellectual worlds, clothing ideas in the form of living or imagined beings allowed them an attractive means of presenting philosophical problems while opening up the possibilities of plot. A plot almost inevitably means conflict, and inner struggle – the *psychomachia* – is a common feature of much of this writing. Further, since ideas were often represented as people or as gods, they could talk, argue and reveal their qualities, thereby allowing for the artistic presentation of debate. Such a technique was deeply rooted in the medieval mind and was reinforced by the belief that many of the great texts of classical antiquity (the *Aeneid* and the *Metamorphosis*, for example) could be read in a similarly allegorical fashion. It was in this guise that much classical myth was passed on to the Middle Ages and reconciled with a belief that literature should embody moral teaching. Indeed, so strong is the notion that a character represents an idea that, in considering what is undoubtedly the liveliest collection of individuals in Middle English literature, the pilgrims gathered in *The Canterbury Tales*, we should be constantly on the watch for the allegorical personifications that underlie them. Figures as diverse as the Ploughman, the Pardoner and the Wife of Bath may well convince us on the level of intuition, but we should also be prepared to see them as exemplifications of ideal faith, 'false-seeming', or the variety of allegorical personae used in discussions of the physical life. Such notions are the skeletons on which Chaucer works his very vivid depictions of the flesh. Indeed, it is possible to see his portraits as a most sophisticated combination of observation and the techniques he found in French and such Latin literature as we are discussing here.

In Bernard's work, for all its pedantic concern with rhetorical filigree, the techniques of allegory help him present a convincing portrait of the central figure in many of these Latin poems: the goddess Nature, a personification who has never quite lost her power to convince us she exists. In *De Mundi Universitate*, it is Nature who helps make man, and Bernard's discussion of mankind's powers, his ability to discover the causes of things and rule the earth, is a touching expression of the abilities with which, by the twelfth century, the human mind was seen to be endowed. However, along with the celebration of this so-called 'humanism' goes a discussion of whether man's will is really free or is controlled by higher forces through the influence of the planets. Both these issues were deeply to concern Chaucer and, as we shall see, are closely allied to the theological and philosophical speculations of his time. They are, for example, central issues in *Troilus and Criseyde*, and are widely discussed in many of the *Canterbury Tales*.

So too is a concern with human excellence, and, in the *Anticlaudianus*, the perfect man, rather more a Christian gentleman than an ascetic or saint, proves himself in a battle against the vices. This poem was again an important source for Chaucer's astronomical and astrological lore. Alanus's *De Planctu Naturae* (a title which Chaucer translates as the 'Pleynt of Kynde') is also a text fundamental to *The Parliament of Fowls*, perhaps Chaucer's most directly philosophical work. In this Latin poem Alanus tells how Nature, lamenting what she believes to be the unnatural vices of humanity, has Genius, the universal god of generation, pronounce her curse on them. The work is a pageant in praise of both natural love and Nature. Nature herself is shown preserving the balance of the world against Venus, who has grown weary of ordinary desires and passes her time with adulterous and sinful passions. The piece is, in both form and matter, a work of the widest influence.

In *The Parliament of Fowls*, Chaucer describes Nature as

> ... the vicaire of the almyghty Lord,
> That hot, cold, hevy, lyght, moyst, and dreye
> Hath knyt by evene noumbres of acord ...

hot, cold, etc.: the constituents of the physical world as the Middle Ages believed them to be

This is a summary of Alanus's conception of a benevolently controlling Nature, but it also corresponds to a passage in the secular Latin work that was perhaps most profoundly to influence Chaucer: *The Consolation of Philosophy* by Boethius.

Boethius was a great Christian scholar, a senior civil servant to the sixth-century Ostrogothic King Theodoric who eventually ordered his execution, and the writer who, perhaps more than any other, passed the intellectual traditions of the declining classical world to the early Middle Ages. Indeed, his reputation was undimmed until the seventeenth century. Boethius wrote translations of Aristotle, commentaries on a number of the great classical texts, and treatises on logic, music and theology. It is with the *Consolation*, however, a sacred dialogue in which the figure of Philosophy appears and teaches the imprisoned Boethius a portion of concealed wisdom, proving to him the existence of God in terms of classical logic rather than of theology, that his greatest influence lies. Here, in alternating passages of question and answer, prose and verse, Boethius and his mentor discuss the origins of evil, the nature of Fortune, true happiness, fate and free-will. Though Philosophy explains to him that love is the great bond of nature that keeps the natural world within its bounds, she also shows how an excessive attachment to earthly things binds man to the great wheel of Fortune which, now up and now down, causes those revolutions in human life that make existence so precarious, so painful. Eventually, Boethius's view is turned away from such false happiness, away from the world and its desires, and upwards to the realization that God is indeed the supreme good. To achieve this state, he learns that the soul must turn inwards and be guided back to its home by both its own light and a remembrance of the truth which is God indeed:

> Disperse the clouds of earthly matter's cloying weight;
> Shine out in all Thy glory; for Thou art rest and peace
> To those who worship Thee; to see Thee is our end,
> Who art our source and maker, lord and path and goal.

Such a union with the divine requires a proper understanding of God's ways of controlling the world, and Boethius eventually achieves knowledge of the state in which the soul, disentangling itself from earthly desires and rising up through a universe controlled by love, comes nearer to that still point of the turning wheel of fate which is true love, God, or, in Boethius's terms, Providence. Thus, born with a knowledge of the highest good (there is a distinct reminiscence of Plato's *Timaeus* here), man foolishly turns from his loving Maker to love what his Maker has made. Wisdom, however, permits his turning back to his divine origins, and the close of the sixth poem of Book IV, where this idea is expressed, lies behind some of the great paeans to love in *Troilus and Criseyde*. Finally, it is the involved discussion of divine foreknowledge and man's free-will – the question of how man can be truly free if an all-powerful God knows what is to happen – that the desolate young Troilus, racked by the pains of an all too human passion, rehearses in the fourth book of Chaucer's poem. Troilus is in love with the created world. He is no longer able to rise to a pure contemplation of the divine and so cannot grasp that while God, existing in a timeless present, can see all things without causing them, man, caught in the trammels of the world, appears trapped in the web of destiny.

So important was *The Consolation of Philosophy* to Chaucer that he himself translated the work with the help of a French version in about 1382. The result is a significant piece of Middle English prose, and Chaucer's labour indicates how such literate laymen as his fellow poet Gower and 'philosophical Strode' – the dedicatees of *Troilus and Criseyde* – were deeply interested in such matters as predestination, the individual's part in his salvation, and his responsibility for his life and the world about him.

Such an interest in the well-being of the world led in its turn to the creation of a large body of satirical or 'complaint' poetry in English (we shall look briefly at such work when we come to *Piers Ploughman*) and also to one monumental Latin satire: Gower's *Vox Clamantis* ('The Voice of One Crying'), which he worked on in the 1380s.

This poem is a dream or, perhaps more accurately, a nightmare vision of the turbulent period of the Peasants' Revolt. Here, in seven books, Gower sets out to determine who is responsible for the evils of the age. He examines what he and the backward-looking legal theory of the time saw as the divinely given ideal of the three states of society: the clergy, the knightly class and the peasantry. These groups were supposedly regulated by love and law under a just king, but were now being pulled apart by corruption and strife. It is interesting to note that in Gower's opinion it is men rather than fortune, fate or chance who determine history, and he attacks in turn the debilitating voices of the clergy (including scholars and monks), knights, and the detested peasantry. He further savages avaricious lawyers and issues dire warnings to the boy king Richard II whose eventual deposition Gower was to declare just.

It is important to note that in the midst of so much gloom Gower reserves high if qualified praise for the City Fathers. It is reasonable to suppose that such men, along with senior clerics, Latin-reading lawyers and administrators, formed the greater part of his audience. In other words, it was for such people and in Latin that some of the most serious and committed poetic analysis of society was now being conducted. Though Chaucer read his 'moral Gower', his artist's impulse was to admire and do otherwise. His own seriousness is of a quite different order.

Chaucer was far from immune to all Latin satire, however. Where Gower, earnestly consulting his *florilegia*, lent rhetorical dignity to his work with quotations from the classics and the Bible, other Latin satirists, blessed with the smile of high intelligence, used their scholarly training and quotations to suggest, against the severer ideals of the day, that wine is better than water and lying beside a girl more wholesome than the crabbed ambitions of scholarship. Who is to say they were wrong? And that is just the point. By showing that rigid views of the world are not appropriate to all times and places, that logic and rhetoric are not the preserve of pedants only, the so-called Golliard poets and other satirists were among those who suggested to Chaucer that the world can be looked at in many ways and is capable of many interpretations. For example, the eternal triangle of love can be seen as both the high heroics of *The Knight's Tale* and the bawdy street wisdom of the Miller's riposte – both epic and fabliau. Multiple viewpoints were now possible, and it is with such thoughts as these in mind that we should turn to a different language and a literature that was again deeply to determine the nature of Chaucer's poetry.

4

We left French romance with Chrétien de Troyes, reserving until now our discussion of a work that was to affect not just Chaucer but much Middle English literature: the *Roman de la Rose*. This poem, as monumental in size as in influence, was partly translated by Chaucer, draws on many of the Latin works previously mentioned, and contributes to a large number of the vernacular poems that remain to be analysed. It was the product of two men. Guillaume de Lorris (act. *c.* 1230–35) wrote the opening 4,058 lines, and the poem was completed by Jean de Meung (act. *c.* 1275) nearly half a century later with additions over four times the length of the original. How visible the join between their work really is remains a matter of critical dispute. The *Roman de la Rose* kindled debates down to the seventeenth century, contentious issues which have been revived in our own time. While differences of style are clear and to be expected, it is now generally believed that the two poets had a common purpose: to present a dreaming young man's erotic fantasy through allegorical personifications that stand for the social, emotional and philosophical aspects of headlong desire. And it is here that the problems begin. Since these are central to establishing an authentic critical method for reading the literature of the Middle Ages, we should address ourselves to them.

Medieval critical theory – if such a generalization may be hazarded – has an intricate history deriving ultimately from the revisions to classical rhetoric made by St Augustine and most influentially expressed by him in the *De Doctrina Christiana*. There, it may be recalled, Augustine had argued for an active and interpretative relation to sacred and secular texts, an approach in which surface beauty was perceived as a veil that allures the reader only to ask him to draw it aside to reveal doctrinal truth. Thus all literature worth the name speaks finally of God. Artistic effects are a metaphor through which 'we may comprehend the eternal and spiritual'. All knowledge and all efforts at interpretation should therefore lead the soul towards the greatest doctrinal truth which is love or, in the Pauline vocabulary favoured by Augustine, 'charity'. It is therefore necessary to understand what Augustine means by charity. The *De Doctrina* provides this definition:

> I call 'charity' the motion of the soul toward the enjoyment of God for His own sake, and the enjoyment of one's self and one's neighbour for the sake of God; but 'cupidity' is a motion of the soul toward the enjoyment of one's self, one's neighbour, or any corporal thing for the sake of something other than God.

Charity and cupidity: confusions between these two interpretations of love echo through the *Roman de la Rose*, *Troilus and Criseyde*, *The Canterbury Tales* and *Piers Ploughman*. They are, indeed, the medieval terms of the human condition. Man's deepest longing, in St Augustine's words, is for God – 'though madest us for thyself, O Lord, and our hearts are restless till they rest in thee' – but when man substitutes for such infinite love that 'cupidity' which is a wholesale desire for the finite pleasures of sex, money, status or whatever, the erring soul is, again in Augustine's words, 'lashed with the cruel, fiery rods of jealousy and suspicion, fear, anger, and quarrels'. It is these last that form much of the subject-matter of the *Roman de la Rose* and are personified in the allegorical figures who make up its *dramatis personae*.

Why were such allegorical figures thought necessary and why is the poem set in a dream? Perhaps we can best answer these questions by going some way into the work.

At a crucial moment in the hero's adventures (his name is simply Amant or the Lover) he encounters the magisterial figure of Reason. Like the similar figure of Holy Church in *Piers Ploughman*, Reason descends from her tower to offer instruction to a mortal. As the poem tells us, God made this lady in paradise and in his own image. She thus personifies the ability of the human mind to approach through logic and intuition that innate knowledge of eternal truth which, for St Paul, was written on the hearts of all men. Further, Reason also 'has the power and the lordship to keep man from folly, provided he be such that he believe her'. Needless to say, the Lover in the *Roman* is not such a one. He tells us that he was twenty when his dream took place, that he was racked by unsatisfied desire, and that he had finally fallen asleep. Reason, the most noble of man's mortal functions, was the least of his concerns.

In his dream, the erring Lover has come to a beautiful park around the walls of which are presented such allegorical figures as Hate, Crime, Avarice, Sorrow and Old Age, qualities to which Idleness, the guardian of the gate, will never allow entry. Despite the carolling birds and lovely trees, scenes that were to be endlessly reduplicated in medieval literature and which lead the Lover to think that this is the Earthly Paradise, we might well ask what the moral status of so charming a location is. Are Sorrow and Old Age really to be despised? Should Idleness truly keep the keys to paradise? How trustworthy is a Lover who thinks that the god of sexual desire is an angel straight from Heaven? Such suspicions mount as the Lover enters further into the garden which, like that other Eden, has both its Tree and River of Life. The latter is here the fountain of Narcissus into which the Lover peers, only to see reflected in two crystal stones a rosebush and, in particular, one especial bud. He is immediately struck by Cupid's arrow.

It is a common enough observation that roses fade and girls grow old, but a truly original insight that the romantic lover should fall – like Narcissus – into a fatal attraction towards some aspect of his own earthly needs apparently existing in the real world. In thus surrendering to earthly desire, however, the Lover has, as Augustine declared, descended into that enjoyment of one's self and one's neighbour 'for the sake of something other than God'. Such ultimately selfish behaviour is a sin, and at this point we may care to remember that the first sin also took place in a garden. Centuries of human endeavour had then established what might be called the psychology of this process which each sinner every day repeats. First comes suggestion to the senses, to the eyes in particular, since for Eve the apple was 'fair to the eyen, and delytable to the sighte'. Then comes joy of the heart, and thirdly (since the Fall was Adam's conscious choice to love his wife rather than honour his Creator) consent of the reason, or the corruption of man's most sacred gift. It did not escape the sharp scholastic minds of the thirteenth century that this process of falling into sin was very similar to the process of falling in love. As Andreas Capellanus, possibly chaplain to Marie, Countess of Champagne, patroness of Chrétien, defined the matter:

Love is a certain inborn suffering derived from the sight of and excessive meditation upon the beauty of the opposite sex, which causes each one to wish above all things the embraces of the other and by common desire to carry out all of love's precepts in the other's embrace.

As a couple fall in love, so there is first suggestion to the senses, then delight of the heart. In the last stage, however, Reason – the lady from the tower – gives way to 'desire'. For 'love' read 'sin'. If we miss the parallel we also miss the joke and the very serious truth that underlies it.

So far, the Lover in the *Roman de la Rose* has only fallen under the sway of the senses and the delight of the heart. These are states dangerous enough and are made all the more so by his submission to the God of Love (an ironic title indeed) who provides him with ten commandments which, as we might now expect, are partly a witty and blasphemous parody of a more famous set. And it is at this point, when the Lover has fallen into idolatry and been rebuffed by Dangier or the personification of his lady's resistance, that the far grander lady Reason arrives to admonish him and explain that, rather than following a foolish and cupidinous desire, Amant should recognize that there are other types of love. There is, for example, the natural and legitimate need man shares with the beasts, a desire kindled by the senses, and which, while it may lead to sin, is also touched by pardon if there is a true wish to continue one's self through Nature's delight in propagating the species. This is the proper function of sex and was approved by the Church. We should recall its influence when the Nun's Priest tell us that Chauntecleer desired to 'feather' his wife 'moore for delit than world to multiplye'. Such lust as this, of course, is one of the Seven Deadly Sins, but true love – the 'charity' of the Bible or the *amicitia* of the classics – is neither puffed up nor selfish. Nor, like lust and the desire for the things of this world, does it place man on Fortune's wheel (Reason, it should be noted, is fully conversant with her Boethius), and so lead to everlasting death. Reason advises that, to save his soul, the Lover should turn from his rose to her. Of course, he will do no such thing. Guillaume's part of the poem closes with the worldly Amant's deep despair.

For Freud, the interpretation of dreams was the royal road to the unconscious; for Guillaume de Lorris, innocent of the concept but elaborating no less influential a system, dreams allowed him to lay bare what we are asked to believe was his youthful unhappiness and then discuss desire in a philosophical context.

He explains at the opening of his poem that his guide to the difficult art of dreaming has been Macrobius, and it was Macrobius who declared that some dreams contain truth while others do not. Guillaume, as both the narrator of his dream and dreamer of it, is clearly a figure of ambivalent status. He might be recording profound insights, or he might be regaling us with a fantasy. At the start of his work, however, he declares that his poem conveys truth. If we give this temporary credence, then, in Macrobius's terms, it means that his dream must belong to one or any of three categories of legitimate dream: a *visio* or vision of events which actually came to pass, an *oraculum* in which a revered person provides advice (here we might think of Reason), or a *somnium* which 'conceals with strange shapes and veils with ambiguity the true meaning of the information being offered, and requires an interpretation for its understanding'.

This last is a particularly interesting category since it functions in the same way as allegorical poetry and needs to be interpreted in a similar manner. Form and content, it seems, might be one. But what of the meaningless types of dream? The *visum* or half-waking vision may be dismissed as Macrobius dismisses it, but, in view of the narrator's self-confessed misery at the start of his work, may not Macrobius's definition of the *insomnium* or nightmare which is 'caused by mental or physical distress, or anxiety about the future' and in which 'the patient experiences . . . vexations similar to those which disturb him during the day' be an equally applicable category? This is the equivalent of saying that the dream is either true or false (some dreams convey truths, others do not) or that the dream's ontological status is at best ambivalent. The only issue that is straightforward here is the fact that the *Roman de la Rose* is a highly wrought literary artefact which refuses easy definitions in its own terms.

Since the *Roman de la Rose* so elaborately draws attention to itself as a work of imaginative literature, are there guidelines which medieval critical theory can give us for interpreting the work? For example, is it an 'imitation' of some well-known form of dream literature?

For the Middle Ages, there existed a considerable body of literary dreams and visions which were either regarded as being true or in which the narrator conveys truth in a relatively unproblematic way. To the first category belong scriptural works such as the dreams of Joseph and Nebuchadnezzar as well as the visions of Ezekiel, St John the Divine, and the Apocalypse of St Paul which is now considered apocryphal. Caedmon's dream is similar. To the latter category pertain the *Somnium Scipionis*, the poems of Alanus, and, perhaps, *De Consolatione Philosophiae*. It is with these works, too, that *Pearl* and *Piers Ploughman* belong. We have already seen that the *Roman de la Rose* and its questionable narrator define themselves ambivalently against such pieces, particularly those which show a heavenly place, for in the *Roman* the description of the Earthly Paradise is of an ambiguous locale where problematic events occur. It is similar to other works and yet not the same. Thus if the poem is an imitation it is an odd one, and it defines itself better as an example of sustained and ambiguous literary artifice.

As such a work of artifice, however, if the *Roman de la Rose* is meant to serve more than 'merely to gratify the ear' there should at least be a kernel of truth beneath the surface shell, what Chaucer calls the 'fruyt' amid the 'chaf'. In words that Chaucer himself would have read in *De Planctu Naturae*,

. . . in the superficial shell of the letter, the poetic lyre sounds forth falsehood; but within, it speaks to those who hear the secret of a higher understanding, so that the exterior shell of falseness having been cast away, the reader may discover within secretly the sweet kernel of truth.

This is a clear indication that much of the greatest medieval literature requires an active and reasoned interpretation. It is not a mere flow of impressions but an intellectual sequence, rhetorically modulated, which requires interpretation in the light of received ideas. No critic from Augustine onwards, however, pretended that the interpretation of medieval literature was an easy matter. Indeed, Boccaccio, writing as both a poet and a don, vividly describes the audience's problems:

> You must read, you must persevere, you must sit up nights, you must inquire, and exert the utmost power of your mind. If one way does not lead you to the desired meaning, take another; if obstacles arise, then still another; until, if your strength holds out, you will find that clear which at first looked dark. For we are forbidden by divine command to give that which is holy to dogs, or to cast pearls before swine.

This is a memorable injunction and one which again suggests the active involvement with the text that a medieval poem requires. As he struggles with this process of interpretation, so the critic progresses (in the scale defined by Hugh of St Victor, one of the most influential exponents of exegesis) from reading the words, or 'letter', to understanding the superficial 'sense' or action, and so to the 'sentence' which is 'the more profound understanding which may not be attained except through exposition or interpretation'. We have seen that Chrétien claimed to work within similar parameters, and a full understanding of medieval literature clearly requires both a wide knowledge of medieval ways of thought and a constant awareness that serious literature points to charity and God. 'Poetry,' declared Petrarch, 'is subject to theology.'

Jean de Meung's Lover seems a long way from the practice of theology, however, and his distance defines the manner of the poem. Having dismissed Reason and so turned his back on the image of God, the Lover is plunged into a welter of desire where a multitude of figures, in a near hallucinatory whirl of nightmare deceit, self-seeking, and monologue within hugely extended monologue, dance the deluded hero ever closer to his final 'plucking' of the rose. Where lies truth when Reason has been shunned? The worldly Ami or Friend is a travesty of true friendship. False-Seeming, dressed as a prelate, offers a mock confession (this was greatly to influence Chaucer's creation of his Pardoner) in which man's spiritual guides are grotesquely parodied. Friend also creates a long and misogynistic speech by a jealous husband in which are rehearsed all the clichés of medieval anti-feminism. La Veille (a figure who was a crucial influence on the creation of the Wife of Bath) presents the opposite view: a speech in favour of free love. Through La Veille, the Lover eventually gains access to that aspect of his beloved called Fair Welcoming, but once again he is repulsed. When, after a comic *psychomachia*, he comes before Nature busily preserving the species in the only way she knows, we see how far the Lover has fallen in a world where Reason's teaching no longer applies. All that interests him about Nature now is not natural procreation but her gift of a sack of hammers – his testicles – and his pilgrim's staff, or penis, on which he relies as he travels his parodic pilgrimage towards the fragrant shrine of the rose placed in a narrow aperture between two pillars. When Genius (another figure borrowed from Alanus) appears dressed as a bishop and preaches a sermon which declares that man will only gain paradise if he lets copulation thrive, the height of confusion is reached. Now under the influence of Venus, the Lover's victory is assured. His joy over, he wakes.

Whose side is the poet on? Which of his figures speaks for him? The answer is, none of them:

> We should consider not so much what the poet says as who in the poem says it. Various figures appear, some good, some bad, some wise, some foolish, each speaking not the poet's opinions but what is appropriate for each person.

Milton describes the whole tradition. In this encyclopedia of endless contradictions there is no audible guiding voice. A world of headlong desire, a world without Reason, allows instead for an endless proliferation of false and shifting comic viewpoints and for the poet to enter the full variety of the human condition – that existence which, with all its ebullient energy and pathos, is nonetheless underpinned by our knowledge of things as they should be but almost never are. And it is this silent voice of true 'sentence' – our own reason, our own knowledge of what for the people of the Middle Ages were the fixed truths of existence – against which we should measure both the dream and the dreamer even as we delight in the variety and audacity of the fiction. It was these various qualities too that Chaucer, with a far greater feeling for the diversity of life and the possibilities inherent in different literary genres, was hugely to extend.

5

To appreciate the ways in which Chaucer developed these notions it is necessary not only to examine his sources but to recognize the special circumstances in which he created his work and his contemporaries received it. Both the medieval writer and his audience existed under conditions wholly different from those with which we are familiar – the printed book, for example, read in silent solitude and existing in thousands of identical copies – while the period also took for granted many assumptions we now need to reconstruct. Chief among these is a circumstance whose importance we have already discussed in terms of Chrétien and *The Owl and the Nightingale* – the idea that a work of literature, at least when first written, would be recited before an actual or imagined group. It was to be performed and listened to. Only when we are aware of this essential difference, the intimate and dramatic nature of Middle English narrative verse especially, will something of Chaucer's insight into the nature of medieval literary creation become apparent and a modern audience be able to appreciate the lively artistic intelligence with which he approached his contemporaries. The sophisticated and often very serious literary playfulness to which medieval conditions gave rise are exhibited even in Chaucer's earliest poems, and stem from a long line of experiment and practice. This we must now trace.

We have seen that King Alfred's ideal of creating an educated and literate aristocracy reared on the translations he had himself initiated was an attempt to unite his kingdom with European ecclesiastical traditions in which the written word had an importance it never attained in Germanic culture. The Bible and its commentaries, sermons and saints' lives existed as written Latin texts and not as the improvised accumulations of traditional formulae that constituted the oral tradition of Old English verse. As opposed to the phrase delivered in public, the sentence written in private can be altered and corrected. It can be at once more self-consciously wrought and more permanent. It can also be exactly repeated. As we have mentioned, the latter almost always meant recitation to a group – a public performance – and the passage from *Havelock the Dane* quoted on page 54 shows this relationship at its most simple. The address to the audience, the request for a cup of good ale and the blessing on the company all serve to create a friendly rapport between the teller and his listeners, as well as giving them time to settle down without missing too much. Such an intimate relationship was capable of being refined to an exceptional degree of sophistication, but even at the most elementary level the lines from *Havelock* make clear that the minstrel is offering an already finished work – a text which he or another has completed. This is a composition rather than an improvisation, and in its turn suggests the idea of authorship.

To appreciate the medieval concept of authorship we need to rid ourselves of the popular modern notion of a purely literary writer, the paid creator of fictional works who may, at times, diversify into biography, travel writing, screen adaptation, criticism and so forth. While patronage by the court or an influential nobleman was common and often had an important effect on the medieval writer's presentation of himself in his work, none made a living purely from what he produced. Chaucer, we have seen, was a diplomat and civil servant – a king's man. Nor would the writer necessarily have regarded himself as belonging to a group of the specially talented employing a rare mode of imaginative discourse. Rhetorical manuals such as John of Garland's *Parisiana Poetria* (*c.* 1220) are far less concerned with such notions than with the art of eloquence, the *ars eloquentiae* or arrangement of words in correct and effective rhetorical patterns. This was a technique as appropriate to a business letter as a love song, and to see the range and innovative daring of Chaucer's concept of authorship we must set aside assumed ideas of the poet as a visionary and replace them with the more common medieval concept of the writer as a maker of books. A passage from St Bonaventura clearly establishes this:

> There are four ways of making a book. Sometimes a man writes others' words, adding nothing and changing nothing; and he is simply called a scribe [*scriptor*]. Sometimes a man writes others' words, putting together passages which are not his own; and he is called a compiler [*compilator*]. Sometimes a man writes both others' words and his own, but with the others' words in prime place and his own added only for purposes of clarification; and he is called not an author but a commentator [*commentator*]. Sometimes a man writes both his own words and others' but with his own in prime place and others' added only for purposes of confirmation; and he should be called an author [*auctor*].

This lucid description raises many points of interest. It suggests, first of all, the degree of specialization that manuscript culture had achieved by the thirteenth century. This was a direct result of the increased demand for books fostered by the new interest in scholarship. The cathedral schools and universities, the proliferating orders of monks and the newly literate bourgeoisie, were all becoming familiar with the idea of the book as an essential repository of past traditions and current attitudes. The numbers of scribes, binders and illuminators inevitably increased. In England, the text-writers' and illuminators' guilds separated from the writers of court letters in 1373, and amalgamated to form a professional body specializing in vernacular literature thirty years later. While it should not be forgotten that the handwritten and often beautifully illustrated books of the Middle Ages were rare and expensive things, that it took a flock of three or four hundred sheep to provide parchment for a large volume (a complete *Canterbury Tales*, perhaps), the increased demand for books also led to the creation of the new and more quickly written cursive script, while, from about 1300, books themselves began to be written on a new material from the Near East: paper. The stationers who sold this and other writing materials also provided work for the swelling numbers of graduates, since, in addition to hiring out books, they operated a 'bespoke' trade for literate members of the City and others who required either romances or works of pious edification. Such volumes were copied out by section or *pecia*, perhaps the nearest form of mass-production a non-industrial society could have achieved. It was, however, a system which inevitably increased the chances of error. Though St Bonaventura describes the *scriptor* as one who 'writes others' words, adding nothing and changing nothing', this apparently simple ideal is far from easily achieved, as every author knows. A note of exasperation can be heard in 'Chaucers Wordes unto Adam, his owne Scriveyn' for example, when he somewhat sarcastically declares:

> Adam scriveyn, if ever it thee bifalle
> Boece or Troylus for to wryten newe,
> Under thy long lokkes thou most have the scalle,
> But after my makyng thou wryte more trewe;
> So ofte a-daye I mot thy werk renewe,
> It to correcte and eek to rubbe and scrape;
> And al is thurough thy negligence and rape.

Boece: Boethius   *scalle:* a scabby disease   *but:* unless   *rape:* hate

Some scribes indeed went rather further than Adam, deliberately clarifying, omitting and rewriting whole passages. A very large number of Middle English texts have come down to us in manuscripts showing wide variations, and it is important to realize that there lies behind the best recent editions generations of careful scholarly work. An 'authentic' medieval text is in many ways a modern creation.

Each of Bonaventura's four categories of writer also reveals a varying but considerable degree of reliance on the work of others, on the wisdom of the authorities of the past who, it was widely believed, had said by far the greater part of what there was to say. Even the *auctor*, though giving prime place to his own words, still adds those of others 'for purposes of confirmation'. This suggests that on the one hand there was a received and conventional notion of what an author was or might be, and secondly it prompts the rather more subtle idea that it was not originality as such that was to be prized, but the dependence – however indirect – of all literary work on its antecedents. This attitude is fundamental to an appreciation of Chaucer, who, as the most imaginative innovator in Middle English literature, expresses it in a number of places, nowhere more effectively perhaps than in these lines from *The Parliament of Fowls*, a work which is at once one of his most original and most 'bookish' poems:

> For out of olde feldes, as men seyth,
> Cometh al this newe corn from yer to yere,
> And out of olde bokes, in good feyth,
> Cometh al this newe science that men lere.

science: knowledge   *lere:* learn

These lines acknowledge a tradition that grows afresh for each generation so that all may be nourished by it. No literature, Chaucer suggests, however independent it may appear, is *sui generis*. It has its roots in the work of others.

Humility in the face of tradition is one aspect of the medieval writer's self-presentation; piety is another, and a petition either to God or to society's great patrons is one of the chief forms of self-portraiture in many medieval texts. *The Canterbury Tales*, for example, ends by requesting prayers for Chaucer's soul. The *Morte Darthur* does the same for Malory. In the closing lines of the introduction to Layamon's *Brut*, the author once more presents himself in the widest Christian context – as a soul begging for intercession. The 'runan' or written letters of the poet are hopefully to be silenced in the prayers of his audience. Secular communication gives way to divine.

Such piety was by no means the only way in which the medieval author revealed himself, however. He did not only ask for his audience's prayers. Indeed we have suggested that the relation of a poet to his public was an area of intimate contact, capable of the most developed sophistication. The self-conscious artifice of Chrétien, for instance, draws its courtly listeners into a discussion of the issues that very artistry has raised. In analysing Chrétien's meaning and appreciating his rhetoric, we also acknowledge his mastery. Again, we have seen that the author's self-portrait in *The Owl and the Nightingale* is a subtly contrived appeal for promotion. Without too explicitly declaring his personal qualities, Nicholas of Guildford quietly insinuates himself into his audience's favour. Their presence before him is a crucial aspect of the poem's purpose and meaning. His listeners are both the jury of the imagined trial at which he will be the judge, and those who may well give preferment to the author of the poem who also happens to be its narrator.

This distinction between the actual poet reading his work and the imagined poet as a figure within it – the real 'I' and the fictional, sometimes erring, 'I' of the text – is again crucial in the *Roman de la Rose*. It is the older and wiser poet who recounts the imagined follies of his youth. Throughout the course of both parts of the work, a listening medieval audience would have been aware of the subtle distinctions to be drawn between the person of the poet reading to them and his persona inside his text. The dream poem especially was useful to the presentation of the poet as a man highly conscious of himself as an artist and creating a work of fiction which, while exploring real and important issues, was nonetheless a work in which he was his own creation. Such a paradox raises intricate questions about the nature of fiction, interpretation, and the relation of author to audience. It also lies close to the heart of Chaucer's work. Because Chaucer invariably sees himself as an imagined character within his own fiction, it is not Chaucer the man whom the poet asks us to look at, but rather the ways in which the processes of literature communicate to their audience through Chaucer the poet. His persona is all-important.

It so happens that a beautifully illuminated page from a text of *Troilus and Criseyde* preserved in the library of Corpus Christi College, Cambridge, allows us to see some of the people in the audience Chaucer was writing for. Though painted after his death, and inspired perhaps by memory or the force with which the poem itself presents the relation of its narrator to his public, the illustration shows the poet standing at a lectern and reading aloud to his sumptuously dressed and noble audience, the courtiers of Richard II who also appears in the picture with his young queen. While such people may have been more used to small reading parties – the pleasant world of a 'fayre book and compaigne' such as the poem itself describes – we see here a group of men and women open to social pleasure and the civilizing effects of great writing. They are representatives of the exclusive, international world of the fourteenth-century aristocracy, a group of exceptional personal power on whose favour Chaucer's livelihood depended. To instruct and entertain them, or even – as is the case with *The Book of the Duchess*, Chaucer's first major poem as far as we know – to solace them in their grief, required strategies of elaborate tact, the most carefully contrived relation of poet to audience. This Chaucer learned in part from the French poems and *dits amoureux* that followed in the long wake of the *Roman de la Rose*.

6

The work of these later French poets made more of the possibilities opened up by the life and assumed personality of the narrator than we find in the work of either Guillaume de Lorris or Jean de Meung. Two early works by Machaut (c. 1300–1377), for example, which also happened greatly to influence *The Book of the Duchess* – the *Jugément dou Roy de Behaigne* and its complementary *Jugement dou Roy de Navarre* – illustrate this well. Each provides a debate between rounded, relatively unindividualized yet non-allegorical figures, and each also offers some touching details about the poet and the exercise of his art.

In the first poem, Machaut, meeting a mourning knight and lady, rashly declares that the lady whose lover has died suffers less than the knight whose lover has been untrue. In the companion piece, another great lady's not unreasonable objections to this verdict are heard and the King of Navarre sentences the humorously maladroit poet to a suitable punishment – the production of more verse. It is all delicate enough, and we are shown Machaut the narrator as both an expert in the apparently dangerous art of poetry and as an amusing, subservient – if mildly obtuse – follower of a court of grandees. Machaut's poems, in fact, provide the clearest source for one of Chaucer's subtlest poetic creations: himself as the sometimes bewildered, sometimes omniscient yet always deftly playful narrator of his own work. This is a technique that is most elaborately presented in *Troilus and Criseyde*, but in *The Book of the Duchess* the notion of a flexible and wittily self-conscious persona is already extensively developed. The skill with 'complaint', with passages of Boethian philosophy, and the reworking of tales from Ovid evidenced in others of Machaut's poems, again helped create the complex effects that are found in Chaucer's first poems. Though early works, *The Book of the Duchess*, *The House of Fame* and *The Parliament of Fowls* are in no sense juvenilia. They are the fruits of considered reading and the most avant-garde experiment.

THE EARLY POEMS

7

Like a fair quantity of medieval verse, *The Book of the Duchess* was written for a specific occasion. Blanche, the wife of John of Gaunt, had died in 1369, and Chaucer's poem is an offering of delicate consolation. Such origins point once again to the fact that the medieval poet was rarely conceived as an intuitive recluse writing for his own release, but rather as a public figure who laboured to beguile or instruct an audience through known literary forms. We shall see that as a young civil servant of bourgeois origins attempting to console a great feudal magnate, Chaucer played on these opportunities in *The Book of the Duchess* with a sympathy that irradiates his entire technique with courteous and humane concern.

In outline, the poem presents us with a dreaming narrator who is transported to an idealized world where, like the narrator of a *visio*, he learns a solemn truth from a great figure. *The Book of the Duchess* is thus a work that exploits with considerable originality a genre that was to be of abiding fascination to Chaucer: the dream vision. Through his earliest poems and on to the period of *The Nun's Priest's Tale* he was to be deeply interested in the problem posed by Macrobius when he declared that some dreams tell the truth while others do not. It is a characteristic of Chaucer's searching yet undogmatic intellect that even in his earliest work he investigates this idea and uses the imaginative possibilities it arouses without finally committing himself to a point of view. Subjectivity, a variety of interpretations, becomes possible. This is a central theme in all Chaucer's work and an aspect of tradition he was greatly to extend.

The Book of the Duchess opens with an expression of the poet's own melancholy which seems (the ambiguity is characteristic) to derive from an unhappy love affair. Such an opening is conventional, but it establishes a sombre and restless tone as well as both sympathy for the narrator and a foretaste of the Black Knight's despair, the latter being a figure whom the narrator meets in the middle of a forest and with whom he discusses a central Boethian theme of all Chaucer's work: man's proper response to Fortune and her apparent power over his happiness. The Black Knight, we will later come to realize, represents John of Gaunt, Chaucer's mourning patron.

'Sorwful ymaginacioun' is the keynote here, and leads the narrator to while away his time with his Ovid, in particular with the story of Ceyx and Alcyone which he re-tells in part and with a complex mixture of humour and a touching awareness of Alcyone's deep distress at the sudden loss of her love. Literature is thus seen as a consolation, while to the audience drawn in by the imaginative conviction of Chaucer's narrative this classical episode states the main theme of the poem in reverse: a man's mourning for his wife is preceded by a wife's mourning for her husband. The parallel with the real-life situation is tactfully and delightfully drawn, and suggests how words – the expression of grief – can help ease anguish. Chaucer does not, however, go on to tell of the classical couple's reunion after death. His poem will be concerned with courteous tenderness in this world and not, like the similarly elegiac *Pearl*, with more profound issues of salvation. Rather, we should note how the imaginative intricacy of this long prelude is an example of what Wolfgang Clemen has called 'the liking for an indirect method of presentation, for shrouding the theme in exuberant ornament and disguise, [which] corresponds to the *goût des complications* illustrated in the flamboyant style of late Gothic art'.

This *goût des complications* also expresses itself as a taste for paradox and ambiguity. After the lengthy prelude with its careful suggestions of the main themes of the poem, the poet offers us a somewhat comic prayer to Morpheus, the god of sleep. Sleep descends and the dream vision proper can now begin. Is it, we may ask, a result of melancholy which causes men to dream of black things, or a reflection of the poet's own concerns which make him dream of similar unhappiness? Is it even a divinely inspired vision sent by the god of sleep? To an audience drawn into the act of interpretation, the subtle construction of the poem and the elusive presentation of the narrator make each of these approaches a possibility. The paradox is presented but not resolved, but we should also note that each reading establishes an imaginative sympathy between the humble but humane dreamer and the Black Knight he is about to meet.

The narrator eventually finds this figure deep in a wood, having been led to him by a charming little dog after following a hunt. We may like to think that the hunters' pursuit of a hart leads the narrator to a man who can only pursue his heart's love in eternity. To suffer for unobtainable beauty in this way is, of course, a supreme expression of romance ardour.

The mourner then tries to explain his plight to the narrator through an analogy with a game of chess: he has lost his queen in the cosmic game played between himself and Fortune. The dreamer's humble, naive failure to understand the image, however, at last causes the man in black to describe the course of his affair more directly. His beautiful Blanche, he says, was at first sight as disdainful as she ought to have been. But her virtues were incomparable and, as a result, the knight became the perfect courtly lover, pursuing her for many years before she eventually sent him a ring. The description of Blanche he then provides follows the conventional rhetorical rules for such portraits, generalizing and universalizing his dead wife's qualities, but what is particularly effective in the poem is the narrator's gentle prompting of the mourner and the slow rise of the Black Knight's narrative until he admits with simple and complete sincerity: 'She ys ded!' The truth is told and pain a little relieved.

Chaucer's high artifice arrives at this modest but consoling statement. The poet's purpose of offering a brief reconcilement to an enduring anguish has been achieved:

> Therwyth I awook myselve
> And fond me lyinge in my bed;
> And the book that I hadde red,
> Of Alcione and Seys the kyng,
> And of the goddes of slepyng,
> I fond hyt in myn hond ful even.
> Thoghte I, 'Thys ys so queynt a sweven
> That I wol, be processe of tyme,
> Fonde to put this sweven in ryme
> As I kan best, and that anoon.'

sweven: dream

The poem ends with the vow to write in poetic form the experience the poem itself contains. Such a paradox is again typically Chaucerian and points to important developments to come. Only in the last line, as the narrator tells us that 'now hit ys doon', is the engaging play between life and literature finally stilled.

8

The tactful complexities of Chaucer's first work suggest an image of the poet reading aloud to his courtly audience during one of their frequent and very elaborate periods of royal mourning. *The House of Fame*, however, must have been written for a smaller group of initiates, quick-witted men and women of international culture, familiar not only with their Latin and French traditions but alive to the plurality of poetic worlds opened up by Italian verse, by Petrarch, Boccaccio and, above all here, by the work of Dante. *The House of Fame* is Chaucer's response to this diversity, a fact which accounts for the particular difficulty and especial interest of the poem.

The House of Fame is an intensely 'bookish' work – 'bookishness' and experience are, indeed, among its principal subjects – and we may imagine its first audience as being not simply one of listeners, but of readers like Chaucer himself, sitting before their text as 'domb as any stoon' and relishing the dextrous speed with which the writer alludes to a wide range of poetic possibilities while, amid so many 'auctoritees', remaining his own man. Something of this is suggested by the Proem to the second book:

> Now herkeneth, every maner man
> That Englissh understonde kan,
> And listeneth of my drem to lere.
> For now at erste shul ye here
> So sely an avisyon,
> That Isaye, ne Scipion,
> Ne kyng Nabugodonosor,
> Pharoo, Turnus, ne Elcanor,
> Ne mette such a drem as this!
> Now faire blisfull, O Cipris,
> So be my favour at this tyme!
> And ye, me to endite and ryme
> Helpeth, that on Parnaso duelle,
> Be Elicon, the clere welle.
> O Thought, that wrot al that I mette,
> And in the tresorye hyt shette
> Of my brayn, now shal men se
> Yf any vertu in the be,
> To tellen al my drem aryght.
> Now kythe thyn engyn and myght!

sely: blessed   *avisyon:* dream   *Isaye:* Isaiah   *Cipris:* Venus   *kythe:* know
engyn: skill, contrivance

We have heard something like these lines before. They have the rumpty-tum patriotism of much minstrel narrative, the simplest form of Middle English literature and one now increasingly old-fashioned as is revealed by Chaucer's parody of the mode in his *Tale of Sir Thopas* in *The Canterbury Tales*. The chief amusement to be derived from this opening, however, lies in the fact that no minstrel had ever written a vernacular poem like this – indeed, there had been no 'Englissh' work like it before. Nor, so Chaucer tells us, had there been a biblical or classical one either. Scriptural and Latin dreamers of vision are cited here only to be dismissed for failing to have had 'such a drem as this'. The irony of the boast lies in its being true. To appreciate this, we must turn to the start of the poem.

The House of Fame opens with the pious and rhetorically decorous hope that God will turn all dreams to our profit. Then, developing the idea that poetry was still the chief means of written instruction at this time, the ironically ignorant narrator creates a continuous fifty-line passage of great technical virtuosity in which he lists all the received opinions about dreams, only to state that he does not know which of them to believe. Some dreams convey truths, others do not. His own dream is so wonderful, however, that he will simply re-tell it and leave its deeper purposes to God. In thus suggesting the divide English thinkers especially had opened up between rational analysis and the sphere of pure faith, Chaucer gives us all the conventional clues to interpreting his work but validates none of them. His dream is both wonderful and, in the tradition of the *Roman de la Rose*, ontologically ambivalent. It is hazardous to define it as anything more than a report on imagined experience remembered subjectively – 'as I kan'. Such a technique ensured that the usual critical flails with which a medieval audience were asked to separate the 'fruyt' from the 'chaf' are recognized as inadequate. Only charity towards the narrator, trust in God and the imagined substance of the dream remain. Right at the start, 'auctoritee' turns its own conventions on their head. We are left with only the subjective narrator – a man who is the poet's own fiction.

In so literary a poem it is fitting that the dreams themselves should also be of literary subjects: the first being the story of Dido and Aeneas, which the narrator sees painted on the wall of a temple he slowly comes to recognize as belonging to Venus. Love is apparently his subject here and Virgil his authority. Taking on the useful medieval role of the commentator, Chaucer will describe what he sees in the temple and thus in effect follow St Bonaventura's description and write 'both others' words and his own, but with the others' words in prime place and his own added only for purposes of clarification'. The opening phrase of the *Aeneid* – 'armes, and also the man' – thus makes perhaps its earliest appearance in English literature, and the most famous of classical love stories unfolds.

But is it really Virgil's narrative or even the more sentimental version of Ovid that is re-told? The answer, of course, is neither. While apparently being an objective reporter, the narrator in his version in fact strips his material of Virgilian grandeur – the remorseless call of fate – as well as of its Ovidian pathos, in order to present Aeneas as a philanderer and Dido as any nice but deceived young girl. In the very temple of Venus's delight we learn that men seduce women for 'fame' (fame, in other words, can be just a kind of bragging), for specious appearances of friendship (*amicitia*), or out of straightforward lust (*cupiditas*). As for the reputation of the fallen woman, that is in the hands of gossips. So much, Chaucer seems to be suggesting, for *fine amour* and the automatic authority of a received literature of grand passion and poetic immortality. Carefully investigated, the rhetoric of tragic love can be shown as glossing over more down-to-earth motives, and love itself – the sovereign subject of so much medieval narrative verse – is revealed as a rather tawdry business.

However, by a final irony, the narrator and commentator seems not fully to realize the subjective effects his re-telling has involved. Like a dutiful tourist, he merely comments on the matchless nobility of the pictured scenes. He thereby opens up a divide between the received material of the poem and the effect of the narrator upon this material. Such a divide can only be fully appreciated by an alert and informed audience, but it suggests once again that insight into poetic ambiguity – the complexity of literary processes – which is an abiding quality of all Chaucer's work and an essential aspect of his genius.

The manner in which Chaucer describes the temple of Venus appears to cheat our anticipated response. A great tradition has been tested against more commonplace and everyday experiences and found wanting. But what alternative to human love is there for the narrator when he leaves the temple? Only a sterile desert and a sudden mock seriousness in which the narrator turns to God. Apparently in answer to his prayer, a mighty eagle descends. A great experience seems about to take place – a revelation of a higher truth, perhaps. Once again, it will be an experience shot through with a wide range of literary allusions. These we should now examine.

The eagle derives from Dante, from both the ninth canto of the *Purgatorio* and the nineteenth of the *Paradiso*. In the latter, towards dawn the narrating poet falls asleep. Dawn is, so Dante tells us, the time when the soul's visions are very near to the divine, and he says elsewhere that 'we have a continued experience of our immortality in the divination of our dreams, and these would not be possible unless something in us were immortal'. Some dreams, in other words, tell the truth. Dante's vision of a golden eagle, dreamed after an experience of the world's corruption, is one such and is intended as a powerful image of the divine concept of human and heavenly justice. The eagle is part of a *visio* and a prelude to Dante's revelation of supreme truth: *l'amor che move il sole e l'altre stelle*, 'the love that moves the sun and the other stars'. Just as Chaucer requires us to appreciate his ironic treatment of Virgil and Ovid in his first book, so here he requires us to recognize a second grandly serious web of allusion and with it to have some knowledge of the exalted self-consciousness of Italian poetry. How did Chaucer himself obtain this?

9

There were many contacts between England and medieval Italy. Church affairs necessitated these, while commercial transactions through the

Port of London, where Chaucer was a highly placed official, furthered them. There was also a substantial Lombard community resident in the capital. Finally, Chaucer himself made at least two official visits to Italy, one between December 1372 and May 1373, and a second between May and September 1378.

We should not, however, too readily assume that Chaucer the civil servant automatically came into contact with the literature that was to transform Chaucer the poet. For example, French and Latin were the languages of international exchange, and there was probably no English–Italian grammar from which Chaucer could learn the new tongue. Nor was there any considerable import of Italian books into the country at this time. Further, the production of manuscripts in Italy itself was such that the complete *opere* of a poet were not readily obtainable. Finally, there was a great deal of Latin literature written by contemporary Italians which might more easily have come to Chaucer's attention. To read the vernacular literature of Dante, Petrarch and Boccaccio, Chaucer had to learn a new language (a difficulty it is perhaps easy to over-estimate) and actively search out texts of their work. What propelled him was insatiable literary curiosity, whetted in this case by the fact that now, fifty years after his death, Dante's use of the Tuscan dialect in the *Divine Comedy* had so triumphantly established the vernacular as a language for great literature that commentaries were being written on his work and a chair of Dante studies was about to be founded in Florence. Its first holder was Boccaccio.

Chaucer's relation to Dante as he portrays it in *The House of Fame* – the relation of a man writing in English, of course, and using a range of French forms – offers a fascinating insight into a poet defining his role through his absorption of some aspects of a master's work, his rejection of others, and his portrayal of his own critical intelligence as being at once admiring but, through its exercise of humour, free. Just as Chaucer reworked sections of the *Aeneid* in the first book of his poem in a way that reshaped them with alert critical intelligence, so his use of Dante is at once daringly experimental and acutely self-aware. Chaucer borrows phrases and ideas from Dante while also recognizing the vast range of styles and thought which the *Commedia* reveals. Some of these literary possibilities were permanently enriching for Chaucer, others he played with in a way that shows he had to reject them. To appreciate this seminal relationship with Dante, some general and particular knowledge of the Italian poet is clearly necessary.

Dante's literary career began with vernacular love lyrics written in the *dolce stil nuovo*, the 'sweet new style' that his contemporaries had developed from Troubadour verse, enriching this with their own philosophical concepts of love as an irrational and destructive force. A reformulation of such a view is evident in the poems Dante later wrote to Beatrice Portinari who, though married to another and dying in 1293, lived on as the inspiration of his poetry, a heavenly figure whose image 'was of such very noble virtue that it did not suffer Love to rule me without the faithful counsel of reason'. We can see this conception of a truly heavenly Beatrice as both the ultimate development of the 'divine' beloved of conventional *fine amour* and as a profound revaluation of human love that emphasizes its holy, noble and rational aspects rather than the perils of mere sexual attraction. Beatrice is now the epitome of beauty, virtue, power and sanctity, and her creation – first fully embodied in the *Vita Nuova* – marks a huge advance in literary self-consciousness. It is an advance reinforced by Dante the layman's informed interest in philosophy and theology, in his vulgar tongue, in ethics and in his art. We can see many of these interests brought together in the following lyric:

> Le dolci rime d'amor ch'i solia
> cercar ne' miei pensieri,
> convien ch'io lasci . . .
>   E poi che tempo mi par d'aspettare,
> diporrò giù lo mio soave stile,
> ch'i'ho tenuto nel trattar d'amore;
> e dirò del valore,
> per lo qual veramente ome è gentile,
> con rima aspr'e sottile . . .

(*The sweet love rhymes I was wont to seek out in my thoughts I must now forsake . . . And so, since it now seems a time for waiting, I will lay aside my sweet style which I held to while writing of love and tell of the quality by which man is truly noble in harsh and subtle rhymes . . .*)

The poem continues as a discussion of the idea of innate nobility or 'gentilesse' which, Dante believed, is not a product of the accidents of wealth and social status but is a spiritual value placed in the human soul by God. As such, the lyric reveals how advanced philosophic ideas could be expressed in the vernacular. It also points to the fact that, in Dante's belief, man is essentially rational and that the pleasurable exercise of reason makes him aware of divine truth and the necessity of faith, hope and charity. Under the influence of neo-platonic philosophy, Dante sees human love, and indeed everything in the universe, as proceeding from God and varying in its blessedness by reason of its proximity or distance from the deity. These noble concepts of human worth, of the potential of the mind and heart, are all suggested in *le dolci rime d'amor*, and are particularly important to our present discussion since we know that Chaucer read both the poem itself and Dante's own commentary on it in the fourth book of the *Convivio* – his somewhat sprawling account of much of his early work. Dante's ideas on 'gentilesse' reappear in *Troilus and Criseyde*, in the tales of the Franklin and the Wife of Bath, as well as in Chaucer's ballade of the same name.

In his discussion of true nobility, Dante places in the mouth of a Roman emperor the erroneous view that this virtue derives from the external trappings of wealth and birth. He thereby points to another of his abiding themes: his belief that philosophy and theology belong exclusively to the Church, while purely secular matters should be controlled under a single empire. The Roman emperors and their political descendants, Dante thought, were destined to fulfil this role since God's providence had determined the conjunction of the birth of Jesus with the founding of the Roman empire. As the poet of the empire (and, it was erroneously believed, a prophet of Christ) Virgil provided for Dante an obvious model for exploring this subject. Consequently it is Virgil, the fount of eloquence and representative of all that is best in the mind unenlightened by Christian revelation, who is Dante's guide through the early stages of the *Divine Comedy*.

Dante's journey through the three regions of the afterlife (Hell, Purgatory and Paradise, which also give their names to the three *cantice* or books of the poem) is conceived as a divine mission in which Dante himself, as he becomes progressively more enlightened, is seen as the prophetic declaimer of worldly corruption and the spokesman of imperial salvation. The journey links classical antiquity with a highly developed concern for the individual's destiny, placing both these concerns against a Christian universe deeply influenced by neo-platonic thought and within a literary structure of unparalleled intricacy. The *Divine Comedy* requires of its readers that all the interpretative precepts laid down by medieval literary theoreticians – and these include Dante himself – should be used with the greatest rigour. Like Scripture and many medieval religious works, the *cantice* need to be read for their literal meaning, for their moral teaching, for their reflection of Christian doctrine and their prefiguration of the afterlife. Chaucer was fully aware of this tradition – it was universal to the Middle Ages – and while he does not fully exploit it in *The House of Fame* he uses it with great imaginative brilliance in a number of *The Canterbury Tales*.

The *Divine Comedy* is thus a vernacular poem employing a philosophical and rhetorical structure that takes the whole world of man and nature for its subject and whose style ranges from the passionate and mystical lyricism of St Bernard's concluding prayer (parts of which Chaucer was to adopt in *Troilus and Criseyde* and the tales of the Second Nun and the Prioress), through theological and even scientific exposition of great formal beauty, to encompass vivid description, characterization and dialogue. Precision is again a central aspect of the *dolce stil nuovo*, but there is also in Dante's work that intense personal realism, the direct and sharp perception of individuals, which is one of the abiding qualities of the Florentine civic ethos and was something romance conventions could never supply. Its influence on Chaucer was, of course, immense.

Of further concern to Chaucer in *The House of Fame* was Dante's high conception of the poet's role and his belief that writing poetry is its own justification. In the fourth canto of the *Inferno*, for example, Dante, guided by Virgil through the realm of the virtuous pagans, meets the shades of Homer, Horace, Ovid and Lucan. For Dante, these men represented (along with Virgil himself) the chorus of classical poetry, and their human greatness is such that it gains the favour of Heaven which permits them to live in a blaze of light amid the encircling gloom of Hell. These poets greet Virgil and then make Dante the sixth among their number. In other words, he is not to be submitted to their 'auctoritee' but, through his own ability, is to be seen as an equal among his mighty predecessors. The passage thus suggests Dante's belief in the nobility of human reason and art even while the melancholy darkness of Hell points to the necessity of Christian illumination. The greatness of the true poet wins its own light, however, and modern writers, we are shown, can equal the ancients. They can be equally inspired, call upon the muses, and trust their own intellectual powers. Dante does so himself:

> O Muse, o alto ingegno, or m'aiutate;
> o mente che scrivisti ciò ch'io vidi,
> qui si parrà la tua nobilitate.

(*O Muses, O exalted wit, aid me now! O memory that writes that which I saw, here show your worth!*)

This is an astonishing assertion of the powers of the mind and, in the second half of the Proem to Book II of *The House of Fame*, Chaucer recalls it. In under a dozen lines we move from the simplicity of a minstrel's invocation to the crowd, through scriptural authority and classical reference to divine inspiration and the 'tresorye' of the human brain. As the muses enter English poetry for the first time, so, in a mere ten couplets, Chaucer also presents the whole range of poetic possibilities open to him. This is a remarkable achievement indeed.

10

Nonetheless, among these various paths Chaucer will have to choose his own way, and he will do so with that high comic intelligence – itself the product of a free and critical mind – with which he investigated the story of Dido and Aeneas.

Though we have seen that the eagle which transports Chaucer through the heavens derives from Dante and that the narrator himself shows something of the Italian poet's fear at the start of his journey, Chaucer's voyage will not in fact be towards God and a revelation of divine love or even the human emotion he is promised. The eagle, despite all his sugges- tion of the high-soaring mind and his assimilation to Virgil, turns out to be nothing more than a loquacious and amusing pedant: bluff, kindly and tireless. He is as vivid and fully realized as anything in Italian poetry, but his lecture on the nature of sound – a strictly factual and hardly a high or edifying matter – is a delightful mockery of versified scientific explanation and the methods of medieval logic and rhetoric. Again, the comically self-deprecating narrator may see himself in the context of others who have made great literary journeys – Enoch, Elias, Aeneas, Romulus, Ganymede, Scipio, St Paul, Alanus, Bernard Silvestris and Dante himself – but he remains essentially and comically reserved. A vast and very serious literary tradition thus plays over his jaunt and this reaches its comic climax when the poet arrives amid the spheres to find not divine truth but the coarse and fickle goddess of Fame, a lady quite devoid of the imperious energy of Virgil's Fama or the august nobility of Boccaccio's Gloria. Her words to her earnest suitors betray her true nature:

> 'Fy on yow,' quod she, 'everychon!
> Ye masty swyn, ye ydel wrechches,
> Ful of roten, slowe techches!
> What? false theves! wher ye wolde
> Be famous good, and nothing nolde
> Deserve why, ne never ye roughte?
> Men rather yow to hangen oughte!
> For ye be lyke the sweynte cat
> That wolde have fissh; but wostow what?
> He wolde nothing wete his clowes . . .'

masty: sluggish   *techches:* blemishes   *sweynte:* slothful

Once again – and in a manner wholly characteristic of the poem – a mighty conception has here been brought down to earth and shown in a comic light. The temple of Fame and the nearby house of Rumour are not a glorious part of the systematic world of medieval allegory but chaotic and teeming places in which personifications are portrayed in such a way as to be no longer worthy of the grand preconceptions we bring to them. As Fame confronts her petitioners we see this clearly, and when Chaucer himself is asked if he has 'come hider to have fame' he replies:

> 'I cam noght hyder, graunt mercy,
> For no such cause, by my hed!
> Sufficeth me, as I were ded,
> That no wight have my name in honde.
> I wot myself best how ystonde;
> For what I drye, or what I thynke,
> I wil myselven al hyt drynke,
> Certeyn, for the more part,
> As fer forth as I kan myn art.'

drye: endure

He rejects the whole precarious and unfair charade: 'I wot myself best how ystonde.' He is his own man, his own critic of 'auctoritee'.

The ironically self-deprecating narrator has thus looked on many of the grand figures, thoughts and events of medieval and other poetry. Though openly admitting his bookish nature – his reliance on authority rather than experience – he has nonetheless exposed something about the less than edifying truths which may underlie many of these grandiose theoretical schemes. Such quick-witted comedy reveals a shrewd assessment of the 'bookishness' within which the poem operates and, when a man of 'gret auctoritee' arrives, perhaps to explain the whole, the work comes to an abrupt close. *The House of Fame* may well be unfinished, but it is also tempting to think that, in a poem which has cast such an ironic eye over received ideas and established truths, the final, enforced dumbness of authority itself is not without point.

11

The House of Fame may well have been composed for a group familiar with the pleasures of quiet study. *The Parliament of Fowls*, a poem probably written between May 1382 and February of the following year as part of the lavish celebrations associated with St Valentine's Day, returns us to the world of royal entertainment and the French and Latin culture of the English court. But there is this addition: Chaucer's Italian influences had exposed him to the widest potential of medieval poetry. However, the aspects of this which particularly affected him have now been so fully assimilated that, in discussing aspects of the nature of love both sacred and secular, Chaucer can move freely and critically amid his various sources, recognizing and analysing the qualities of each and juxtaposing them with confident delicacy. While we are shown the worlds of philosophically inspired charity, *cupiditas* and the natural love that leads to generation, we are not conscious of uneasy conflict between these differing views. Rather, as the poet offers us a précis of the *Somnium Scipionis* and then, seemingly dissatisfied with the other-worldliness implicit in some interpretations of *caritas*, presents us with his dream of a lovely park in which he encounters the inflamed and uncomfortable eroticism of the temple of Venus, the loving plenitude of Nature and finally the debate of the birds themselves before they choose their mates, so we have the impression of a poet fully at home in the variety of his European traditions and adapting these to reflect the complex tenor of his responses. This is indeed the creative use of received wisdom, and to appreciate the subtle allusiveness of *The Parliament of Fowls* – a poem whose small compass is almost as encyclopedic as the *Roman de la Rose* – is one of the great pleasures of medieval scholarship.

Chaucer's new fullness of mind is reflected in a new amplitude of technique. The eight syllables of the French-inspired couplet have been replaced by lines of more or less ten syllables of fairly regular scansion grouped into the sevens of the 'rime royal' stanza:

> The lyf so short, the craft so long to lerne,
> Th'assay so hard, so sharp the conquerynge,
> The dredful joye, alwey that slit so yerne:
> Al this mene I by Love, that my felynge
> Astonyeth with his wonderful werkynge
> So sore, iwis, that whan I on hym thynke,
> Nat wot I wel wher that I flete or synke.

assay: attempt   *slit so yerne:* slides away so fast   *flete:* float

This verse is an excellent example of the sophistication Chaucer's art had now achieved. It is possible to enumerate the rhetorical devices used, but it should be realized that these are not simply a matter of surface ornament but reflect ways of thought that help determine the overall plan, the *dispositio*, of the poem. For example, the opening *sententia* or 'wise saying' is a translation of the familiar and ancient Latin tag, *ars longa vita brevis* – art takes 'long to lerne', while life is short. Such acknowledged wisdom, as well as being rhetorically decorous to the opening of a poem, suggests the presence of 'auctoritees' in the work. Further, by being unexpectedly applied to love, it reveals the novel use made of authorities in the poem, as well as the fact that love itself, while an overwhelming natural force, is also to be seen as a social creation, an acquired skill. Love is both natural and manufactured, both the need to procreate and the elaborate sophistication of *fine amour*. As such, it belongs to the provinces of both deities in the poem: Nature and Venus. As the progress of the work makes this apparent, so the informed medieval audience is alerted to similar discussions in Bernard Silvestris, Alanus and the *Roman de la Rose*. Chaucer's richly suggestive but apparently contradictory juxtapositions – the proper term is *contentio* – are then repeated in the second and third lines as he continues his analysis of the paradoxical nature of love. This technique gives the poem a feeling of amplitude as well as reinforcing its fundamental concern with contrasted states of being.

There is, however, a further cluster of associations in the opening lines that need to be examined. These concern the pain and insecurity of love, the sombre anguish of the 'dredful joye' in this 'lyf so short'. Such phrases, while a wholly conventional aspect of the poetry of *fine amour*, bring with them – delicately, seriously and yet undogmatically – suggestions of a second great medieval theme: contempt for the world, knowledge of pain and death, the need for a philosophy that places all earthly existence in a timeless perspective. It is such a philosophy that Chaucer the narrator, revealing himself once again as the troubled and unworldly scholar, searches for at the start of the poem, until:

> The day gan faylen, and the derke nyght,
> That reveth bestes from here besynesse,
> Berafte me my bok for lak of lyght . . .

reveth: relieves

We have seen that the work he has been reading is the *Somnium Scipionis*, of which Chaucer, as a compiler and commentator, provides a précis. Cicero's underlying ideas of contempt for the world, the necessity of moral action, and his understanding of the divine plan are all given a Christian treatment. Mortal existence is shown as false and painful. No man 'schulde hym in the world delyte'. One must instead recognize an immortal destiny and live charitably for 'commune profit' in order to come to bliss:

> 'Know thyself first immortal,
> And loke ay besyly thow werche and wysse
> To commune profit, and thow shalt not mysse
> To comen swiftly to that place deere
> That ful of blysse is and of soules cleere.'

werche: work

Before recounting his own dream, Chaucer thus provides his audience with a serious account of the purpose of human life as it is given in an ancient *visio*. The passage is steeped in authority and is agreeable to Christian doctrine, but for all that it leaves the narrator troubled and dissatisfied. He is anxious about his own personal position and, as a reference to Boethius shows, about the general state of unenlightened man who is restless because he 'lakkide somewhat that thow woldest nat han lakkid, or elles thou haddest that thow noldest nat han had'. As the night closes round his bewildered longing and deprives him of light in which to read, so the lines in which Chaucer expresses this uncertainty associate him with Dante in his dark wood at the start of the *Inferno*:

> Lo giorno se n'andava, e l'aere bruno
> toglieva li animai che sono in terra
> dalle fatiche loro; e io sol uno
> m'apparecchiava a sostener la guerra
> sì del cammino e sì della pietate,
> che ritrarrà la mente che non erra.

(*Day was departing and the darkening air released the earth's creatures from their labours; and I alone was preparing myself for the conflict of the way and its pity which memory unerring shall recount.*)

Like Dante, the perplexed and dreaming narrator needs a guide, and, through the association of ideas it seems, one comes to him: not Virgil, but Scipio Africanus from the very work Chaucer has just been reading. Scipio tells the narrator that he will help him towards truth as a reward for studying his book.

What can account for the presence of Scipio here? The association of ideas, derived by Chaucer from a passage in Claudian, may explain it, but so also may the fact that (as Chaucer makes clear in the next stanza) his guide has been sent by the planet Venus, the beneficent force of plenty, learning, love and eloquence. It is therefore Venus who has prompted the dream and whom Chaucer now invokes as his muse. The dream has been sent by an irresistible divine power, but Chaucer's art must give it literary shape.

That shape, we have seen, is partly founded on contrast or *contentio*. The ensuing passage makes this clear. Scipio, guiding the narrator as Virgil guided Dante, brings the dreaming Chaucer to a walled park over the gate of which is a pair of inscriptions. The first describes the park as an Earthly Paradise, a place of 'hertis hele and dedly woundis cure'. The second informs both the narrator and his audience that the place is Hell. It does so through a further allusion to Dante. In the third canto of the *Inferno* Dante reads a famous inscription:

> Per me si va nella città dolente,
>   per me si va nell' etterno dolore,
>   per me si va tra la perduta gente.
> Giustizia mosse il mio alto fattore:
>   fecemi la divina potestate,
>   la somma sapienza e 'l primo amore.
> Dinanzi a me non fuor cose create
>   se non etterne, e io etterna duro.
>   Lasciate ogni speranza, voi ch' entrate.

(*By me ye go to the doleful city, by me ye go to eternal woe, by me ye go among the lost souls. Justice moved my maker on high, I was made by the divine power, the highest wisdom, primal love. Before me were made only eternal things, and I endure for ever. Abandon hope all ye who enter here.*)

Chaucer paraphrases this:

> 'Thorgh me men gon', than spak that other side,
> Unto the mortal strokes of the spere
> Of which Disdayn and Daunger is the gyde,
> Ther nevere tre shal fruyt ne leves bere . . .'

In these lines Chaucer suggests the hell of love's despair and – more subtly – the belief that this is intimately connected with love's delight. Just as both inscriptions are placed on a single tablet over one gate, so the park beyond that gate will be seen as a type of both Hell and Heaven: the paradoxical realm of Venus and her followers sweltering in over-refined emotion, and of Nature under whose guidance some at least find their ease.

Just as Dante blanched at the prospect of the journey ahead of him, so now does Chaucer. Unlike Virgil, however, Chaucer's guide does not tell the narrator that he is in the hands of a benevolent Providence. Rather Scipio shoves ('shof') him unceremoniously through the gate and tells Chaucer that the inscriptions have nothing to do with him. He is not a lover but only the inexperienced poet of love who will be allowed to glimpse the enactment of some essentially literary experiences of passion. Once again, comedy points to the ambiguous relation between books and life. It has already been suggested that the authority of books cannot solve all the problems of existence, but the poet is here offered not a direct experience to pit against 'auctoritee', but rather a *tableau vivant* curiously suspended between art and life. Such a paradox is typical. Chaucer and Scipio then part and the narrator is left to explore the park. We move from Cicero's sombre world to that of Alanus:

> But, Lord, so I was glad and wel bigoon!

A new joy in the beauty of existence – a humane response denied by the *Somnium Scipionis* – now becomes the subject of the poet's discourse. Forms of love other than austere charity will be discussed.

The garden the dreamer enters has its origins in conventional descriptions of the Earthly Paradise, and also owes much to a passage from the Italian poet Boccaccio in whose *Teseida* (later to be a vital source for *The Knight's Tale*) the allegorical park of the *Roman de la Rose* tradition is described in a less overtly didactic manner than in its original. Boccaccio assumes a knowledge of the allegories in the French poem, but his moralized landscape also takes on the heightened visual qualities of a decorative tapestry. Chaucer, greatly enriching the detail of this – his flowers have real colours, his fish 'fynnes rede and skales sylver bryghte' – creates a more subtle effect. As with the temple of Venus in *The House of Fame*, so here we are made to feel the narrator's personal perception of a real place. As he records this for us, we also sense his developing reactions to a garden that is at once an actual location and a moral sequence.

That moral sequence develops from the rhetorical list of the trees (each of which is, in its way, related to man's activities, his life and death), through the beauties of sight, sound and intellect, until we see those great sources of human emotion and destiny: the gods. We then slowly become aware of both a delicate change of moral register and Chaucer's subtle art of reference and juxtaposition. For example, 'Cupide, oure lord' is first presented in a largely agreeable way, though the presence of Lust and disfigured Craft at his side may alert us to the moral dangers of youthful affection. But it is when we come to the temple of Venus that the modulation of tone (chiefly expressed by Chaucer's alterations to his sources) becomes particularly subtle. For instance, where, in Boccaccio, Venus's temple is a construction made wholly of brass, Chaucer carefully places his 'upon pileris greete of jasper longe'. This is not the happy invention of a natural colourist. In the world of moralized nature where, as St Augustine and later scholars had shown, each natural object represents a divine truth, jasper stands for *luxuria* and infertile sex – indulgence for its own sake, and thus *cupiditas* or sin. The temple of Venus is then appropriately described as an unhealthy place full of sighs 'hoote as fayr', where 'the bittere goddesse Jelosye' fans the ardours of the frustrated, where the grotesquely phallic Priapus is an object of veneration to the lascivious, and Venus herself in her 'prive corner' is a personification of the wanton and destructive indulgence of such tragic lovers as Dido, Tristan and – a pointer of great importance for future works – Troilus. Such is the nature of unbridled sensuality.

When the narrator has left this hothouse atmosphere he almost immediately encounters a more benevolent deity: Nature. Chaucer's figure of a beautiful and orderly Nature is derived from Alanus's *De Planctu Naturae*, a work to which – confident of his audience's learning – he refers us for a fuller description. In Alanus's poem a universal joy attends Nature's coming, and she is presented as a most richly worked allegorical figure suggestive of order, creative energy and, in particular, procreation within the bounds of divine and human law. Alanus's Nature is, we have seen, 'the vicaire of the almyghty Lord', and in her earliest and most developed form she stands for the idea of the beauty of God's creation and the varying degrees of goodness it may achieve by reason of its proximity to God. Nature is thus a figure in contrast both to Venus and the tradition of contempt for the world, a tradition exemplified in both the *Somnium Scipionis* and the *De Contemptu Mundi* of Pope Innocent III, a work which Chaucer informs us he translated and whose substance is found in the Prologue to *The Man of Law's Tale*. His ability to enter all these traditions – to recognize that the earth is both despicable and glorious – is one of the most profoundly paradoxical of his attitudes and one that develops from here, through *Troilus and Criseyde* to *The Canterbury Tales*. There is no dogmatism, however. In *The Parliament of Fowls*, for example, Nature is a divine figure 'ful of grace', yet she is not presented as an answer to the issues previously raised but rather as a third element to be juxtaposed with the *Somnium* and the temple of Venus – Nature is the central figure indeed of the very subtly contrived debate or 'parliament' of the fowls.

We now learn that it is St Valentine's Day and that the birds have gathered to choose their mates under Nature's guidance. In their sheer plenitude they cover the whole surrounding area, suggesting thereby the abundance of their tutelary deity. But it is a particular mark of Chaucer's inventiveness that he has taken the birds which in Alanus's poem were merely embroidered on Nature's gown and has given them such liveliness and energy that we can readily appreciate them, grouped in hierarchies as they are, as representatives of the medieval social estates, types characterized also by temperaments variously inclined to every manner of human weakness and nobility. All, however, have gathered for a common purpose, and Nature's first speech – glancing at the manner in which the Chancellor would have addressed the opening of Parliament at Westminster – makes clear what this is:

> 'Ye knowe wel how, seynt Valentynes day,
> By my statut and thorgh my governaunce,
> Ye come for to cheese – and fle youre wey –
> Youre makes, as I prike yow with plesaunce;
> But nathelcs, my ryghtful ordcnaunce
> May I nat lete for al this world to wynne,
> That he that most is worthi shal begynne . . .'

cheese: choose   *makes:* mates   *lete:* put by

We see here Nature's legal authority, her insistence on a combination of free choice and pleasure in matters of love, and her support for the social hierarchy. In line with this, the most 'worthi' birds will choose their mates first, and we are now presented with three male eagles or tercels who state their claim for the beautiful formel eagle perched on Nature's hand. Their graceful speeches declare their total humility, length of service and exclusive loyalty respectively.

This situation has every appearance of being a *débat d'amour*, but Chaucer's playful freedom with standard genres ensures fresh variations which allow him not simply to present an interesting amatory problem, but to explore the relation of *fine amour* to the more basic needs of which courtly love is the refinement. Such refinement is made clear by the noble amplitude of the eagles' speeches. Which of them deserves to win the formel? Chaucer's skill in dramatic presentation is such that we feel the first of the speakers is the worthiest, but the raucous, comic impatience of the other birds is so insistent that Nature eventually declares that each class shall appoint a spokesman to offer a solution to the problem. The impatience of the lower birds has perhaps cast the mildest irony over the graceful *longueurs* of the eagles, yet the solutions they offer – a duel, a switch of affections and so on – reveal their own lack of refinement and the vigour of Chaucer's dialogue. We are made simultaneously aware of the beautiful yet impractical sophistication of *fine amour* as well as the emotional limitations inherent in the gaucheness and occasional sentimentality of the lesser birds. Once again it is the range of opinions, the juxtaposition of attitudes, that is important, rather than the reaching of a specific conclusion.

Indeed, by a masterly comic device, Chaucer refuses to let the parliament reach a firm decision at all. When Nature allows the formel herself to state which of her suitors she prefers, the blushing young lady delicately requests a postponement and is granted a year's delay. The whole question is passed unresolved to the audience who are thereby asked to see the beauty and mild absurdities of their cult of *fine amour* against the background of the social order and of Nature and her promptings. In other words, they are asked – as they have been throughout the poem – to examine love in a philosophical context. The emphasis is thus on search and discussion, on recognizing the complexity of the world rather than on the statement of any absolute truth.

It is in this undogmatic manner that the poem concludes. The lesser birds, unwilling and indeed unable to place those restraints on Nature's promptings that underlie the civilized refinement of the eagles, noisily and hurriedly choose their mates. Yet it would be wrong to see this as merely an undignified mêlée. The beauty and sacredness of Nature's promptings are suggested by the rondeau which is sung at the close. Though individually often vulgar, all the birds participate in a communal dignity, a long-established rite of great loveliness, as their annual song is sung. For the duration of the lyric they are at one with a force and beauty that individually they could not attain. When it is over they return to their raucous selves and their 'shouting' wakes the poet from his dream. He has glimpsed the complicated responses his culture requires but has reached no final 'auctoritee'. As he turns once more to his books, so we are given the impression of life as a continuing philosophical quest.

12

The intellectual subtlety of these early poems shows that they are in no sense juvenilia. They are profoundly literary and daringly experimental. Each reveals a progression towards a comprehensive engagement with the range of sources available to Chaucer: biblical and classical wisdom, the Latin literature of the earlier Middle Ages, French romance and the poetry of Italy. In addition, they reveal a number of traits central to Chaucer's development.

There is, first of all, the increasing subtlety of his presentation of himself as a humane, widely read, yet imagined figure within his own creations. His seemingly passive naivety, however, is in fact a most elaborate device for revealing a diversity of opinions without an obtrusive dogmatism. Secondly, we are very soon made aware of an intellect at once capacious and independent, humorous and humane, given equally to sombre moral and religious introspection and to energetic delight in the world. These two aspects combine to develop the complexity of literary processes and the relation of the narrator to his sources, his audience and his own imagined responses.

This complete engagement with the paradoxes of literature is a central feature of Chaucer's art, but what is perhaps too easy to overlook is the fact that this astonishing mind – familiar with the great international literatures of Europe – chose to express itself in the native tongue and so take that language into the most advanced areas of expression. Chaucer's early poems show Middle English to be capable of the greatest resource. His next poem – and his masterpiece – reveals how that language could also serve as the medium for a poet of European stature.

TROILUS AND CRISEYDE

13

In the early dream sequences, Chaucer was a poet of *fine amour* exploring his art against a range of literary and philosophical possibilities. In *Troilus and Criseyde* he applied this experience to a different mode, and, in one of the supreme achievements of English literature, became a master of romance.

Contact with Italy again provided the initial stimulus. Sometime around 1335, Boccaccio, then in his early twenties, had turned his attention to the 'matter of Troy'. This complex of tales, vying across Europe in popularity with those of Arthur, Alexander and the siege of Thebes, had already a considerable literary history. Setting aside Homer, an author mentioned with respect but almost never read in his original since Greek texts were few and readers of Greek still fewer, the Middle Ages preferred the accounts of their mythical ancestors provided by Latin prose translations from Dares Phrygius who was believed to be an eyewitness for the Trojan view, and Dictys Cretensis who allegedly spoke for the Greeks and had had the further advantage of a supposed interview with Ulysses. These texts from the early Christian centuries provided the information on Troilus, Breseida and Diomede that Benoît de Sainte-Maure then developed into a brief, tragic tale of parting and deception. Benoît in his turn was the unacknowledged source of the definitive medieval version of the 'matter': the *Historia Trojana* of Guido delle Colonne (act. 1257–80). In these last works especially, Boccaccio found the basis of a story whose young hero could express what is made to appear as his own despair at a separation from his beloved. The Troilus of *Il Filostrato* – 'the one made prostrate by love' – is thus an imagined, rhetorically modulated image of Boccaccio himself, and it was from a corrupt text of this poem that Chaucer derived the basis of his masterpiece. He translated and extensively adapted his original (both, as we have seen, commonplace medieval activities) to produce a poem unique in its depth and variety.

In what ways does *Troilus and Criseyde* draw on earlier practices of medieval romance? We have seen that in the work of Chrétien de Troyes, the vernacular narrative of love and chivalry, constructed around a wide variety of recurring and often marvellous motifs, allowed the poet to present an *aventure* in which the relation between the private desires and public responsibilities of his noble characters could be discussed. His audience was provided with both the narrative level of *matière* and the interpretative level of *sens*. Further, we have seen that certain carefully contrived problems of *fine amour* were introduced which the characters then discussed or analysed in soliloquies. These soliloquies, however, rather than revealing individual psychology, tended to be self-conscious and non-naturalistic rhetorical exercises which displayed both the artistry of the poet and his skill in isolating moral issues. Such artistry again showed itself in beautifully created vignettes of the courtly life and in subtly ambiguous chains of imagery which related human passion to Christian and divine love. Such delicate literary questions were among the issues Chrétien's noble audience were then required to unravel. In these ways they were drawn into the complexities of medieval poetic interpretation.

We have seen further that the sometimes ambiguous status of the narrator of romance was much developed in the work of Guillaume de Lorris and Jean de Meung. The *Roman de la Rose* presents the stages of a young man's erotic fantasy through an allegorical dream sequence in which the headlong pursuit of irrational and sinful desire allows for the presentation of several important literary techniques: a welter of shifting viewpoints, for example, the continuous contrast afforded between what we know is unreasonable behaviour as opposed to 'sentence' or the true values of society, and the creation of a narrator who relates in the most subtle manner to the material he presents. Finally, the *Roman de la Rose* offered the entire Middle Ages both a vocabulary and a scheme for describing the process of falling in love. In *Troilus and Criseyde* many of these traits are brought together under the influence of a work deeply rooted in Italian poetry, and from them Chaucer created a philosophical romance infinitely greater than the sum of its sources.

The first Proem outlines the main events of the narrative and indicates a number of the major themes:

> The double sorwe of Troilus to tellen,
> That was the kyng Priamus sone of Troye,
> In lovynge, how his aventures fellen
> Fro wo to wele, and after out of joie,
> My purpos is, er that I parte fro ye.
> Thesiphone, thow help me for t'endite
> Thise woful verse, that wepen as I write.
>
> To the clepe I, thow goddesse of torment,
> Thow cruwel Furie, sorwynge evere yn peyne,
> Help me, that am the sorwful instrument,
> That helpeth loveres, as I kan, to pleyne.
> For wel sit it, the sothe for to seyne,
> A woful wight to han a drery feere,
> And to a sorwful tale, a sory chere.
>
> For I, that God of Loves servantz serve,
> Ne dar to Love, for myn unliklynesse,
> Preyen for speed, al sholde I therfore sterve,
> So fer am I from his help in derknesse.
> But natheles, if this may don gladnesse
> To any lovere, and his cause availle,
> Have he my thonk, and myn be this travaille!
>
> But ye loveres, that bathen in gladnesse,
> If any drope of pyte in yow be,
> Remembreth yow on passed hevynesse
> That ye han felt, and on the adversite
> Of othere folk, and thynketh how that ye
> Han felt that Love dorste yow displese,
> Or ye han wonne hym with to gret an ese.
>
> And preieth for hem that ben in the cas
> Of Troilus, as ye may after here,
> That Love hem brynge in hevene to solas;
> And ek for me preieth to God so dere
> That I have myght to shewe, in som manere,
> Swich peyne and wo as Loves folk endure,
> In Troilus unsely aventure.
>
> And biddeth ek for hem that ben despeired
> In love that nevere nyl recovered be,

And ek for hem that falsly ben apeired
Thorugh wikked tonges, be it he or she;
Thus biddeth God, for his benignite,
So graunte hem soone owt of this world to pace,
That ben despeired out of Loves grace.

And biddeth ek for hem that ben at ese,
That God hem graunte ay good perseveraunce,
And sende hem myght hire ladies so to plese
That it to Love be worship and plesaunce.
For so hope I my sowle best avaunce,
To prey for hem that Loves servauntz be,
And write hire wo, and lyve in charite,

And for to have of hem compassioun,
As though I were hire owne brother dere.
Now herkneth with a good entencioun,
For now wil I gon streght to my matere,
In which ye may the double sorwes here
Of Troilus in lovynge of Criseyde,
And how that she forsook hym er she deyde.

clepe: call　*unliklynesse:* displeasing aspect　*pyte:* compassion　*unsely:* unhappy
apeired: injured

These stanzas, the most richly orchestrated English rhetoric had yet
achieved, are ripe with suggestion. Indeed, they hint at so many of the
themes the poem will develop that in isolating a number of these here we
shall begin to see the range within which the work operates. For example,
the opening lines ask us to imagine ourselves as part of a group of
initiates in the fine arts of love, and, most unusually, it is our own
experience quite as much as our knowledge of 'sentence' which will be
called upon to validate the narrative. In other words, we are invited to
use our personal and subjective intuitions as we watch the characters
in action. This is a technique Chaucer will use with subtle imaginative
enterprise throughout the poem and it will be a constant theme in our
analysis.

Again, the fact that such an ephemeral occasion as a reading has been
given an effect of permanence by a written text points to the ambivalent
status of the poem. It exists to be listened to and also to be studied when
we are alone. We are both audience and, as Chaucer makes clear when
we reach his last book, a 'redere' as well. The poem has acquired its
more or less definitive form in the intense privacy of the study and is
intended for both public occasion and solitary analysis.

The narrator further informs us that we are to be treated to a Troy story. As members of a medieval English audience, we are immediately alerted to the manifold significance of a poem about our ancestors whom it will praise as it beguiles our imaginations and gratifies our curiosity. The story of Troy is a true one (or at least what Milton called a received truth 'attested from ancient writers from books more ancient') and is also part of our own history. As Geoffrey of Monmouth among others had shown, it was the descendants of Aeneas after he had fled from Troy to Rome who founded London, or Troy Novant, thereby joining English history to a tradition of heroism and chivalry as well as to the idea of the *translatio imperii* – the transfer of empire from one state to another as those preceding lost their power through moral shortcomings. Chaucer's Troy is distant in time and space (the poet's sense of the 'pastness' of the past and the relativity of values is remarkable for the age he lived in) as well as being a moral focus of timeless significance.

Though the splendid pagan city in Asia Minor resembles fourteenth-century London in many of its tastes and customs, it differs from it in one profound respect. Where the inhabitants of New Troy (Chaucer and his contemporary audience, in other words) have a knowledge of the saving grace of Christianity, the fine folk of the classical city know nothing beyond reason and natural law. They can just attain to the idea of God as Creator, but not to faith in Christ as a personal Redeemer which is the narrator's overview at the close of the work. Such a contrast between pagan and Christian in the poem is again of the greatest importance. Though some of the Trojans can indeed rise to the true nobility of that central figure – the virtuous pagan – and thereby achieve a moral excellence which may well make an enlightened Christian audience critical of their own supposedly superior behaviour, the Trojans' unaided secular values cannot finally save them. Their 'corsed' rituals stem essentially from 'wrecched worldes appetytes'. As a result of such worldliness, there hangs over their city an assured doom wrought by Fortune from the Trojans' moral weakness. Since *Troilus and Criseyde* is part of this wider circle of the Troy story, it is worth recalling here the origins of the city's inescapable fate.

Those origins lie in the prophecy that Paris, son of Priam, King of Troy, would bring destruction to the city his grandfather had built with the help of gods he later slighted. Left exposed on Mount Ida, Paris's life was saved and he lived happily with the nymph Oenone (see Book I, ll. 652–79) until Ate, goddess of strife, asked him to award a golden apple to the deity he chose as the most beautiful from Hera, Athene and Venus. Venus successfully furthered her case by promising Paris the most beautiful woman in the world, and his resulting offer of the apple to this embodiment of sexual passion could be paralleled with Adam's choice of *cupiditas*, the desire that led to his destruction and the Fall. When Venus fulfilled her promise and Paris eloped from Sparta with Helen, wife of Menelaus, he broke the bonds of moral law and so ensured the destruction of his city. The rape of Helen – a proud act of *cupiditas* – subjected the fate of Troy to a woman. The city was now Virgil's *superbum Ilium* which the incensed gods abandoned for Rome. To the Middle Ages, certain that the pagan deities were, in St Augustine's words, 'suggesters and counsellors of crime' rather than moral agents, Troy an *exemplum* of wanton, foolish and tragic lust.

We shall see that Troilus himself (the Latin diminutive allows us to view him as a 'little Troy') epitomizes the fate of the city in both his own person and the narrative of his desires. As always in a high Gothic narrative and in a period that could not rigidly distinguish between 'story' and 'history', the focus of *Troilus and Criseyde* is on the fate of the hero conceived in terms of a philosophical and chivalric romance rather than the economic and impersonal forces that constitute much of our historiography. Chaucer's interest in his subject is thus moral and not mechanistic.

The greatness of *Troilus and Criseyde*, however, lies partly in the fact that the hero's love, despite its moral implications, is almost never openly condemned. The tragic pathos, indeed, derives from the revelation that while a limited good is still a good, so beautiful an experience as Troilus's passion should yet be deadly. Human love, as is fitting for a romance, is thus a central issue, and the Proem suggests the complexity with which it will be analysed.

The form and imagery of the first Proem make clear that human passion is to be intimately connected with religious and supernatural experience. We have seen that this is conventional in medieval romance, and what we are offered in the opening stanzas are two prayers that greatly extend this tradition.

The first is the invocation to Tisiphone, middle sister of the three Furies and a hellish figure 'sorwynge evere yn peyne'. These lines are considerably more than empty rhetorical embellishment. The Furies were the avengers of sin, the traditional spirits of remorse and despair. Boethius describes them grinning at the guilty man's terror, and in the ninth canto of the *Inferno* (from which Chaucer most probably derived the idea of the Furies weeping) they appear on the encircling walls of Dis. Here are sent those souls who have wilfully turned their backs on God and refused his truth. They are heretics, those who have followed a false religion. In evoking a classical figure of damnation in this way, Chaucer suggests the association between the pursuit of sexual passion and the punishments of Hell. He suggests, in other words, the likely results of following a pagan 'religion of love'. However, since even Pandarus knows that 'th' ende is every tales strengthe', it is necessary to contrast this opening stanza with that which closes the poem some 8,000 lines later. Turning now from the punishment of guilt and pagan despair, Chaucer (his Dante again open before him) looks to Paradise, to the Trinity and the Virgin. He prays not as a secular poet for help in composing 'thise woful vers, that wepen as I write', but as a Christian sinner who may be saved by divine grace (see Book V, ll. 1860–69). Such is the final 'trouthe' of a poem in which the imagery of a fleeting, human and pagan passion constantly mirrors, parodies and is ennobled by the permanent forms of Christian love.

Yet if Chaucer appears to set up a conflict between human passion and salvation – a conflict which results in the inevitable triumph of divine truth – it must also be recognized that *Troilus and Criseyde* is a subtle, rapturous and deeply moving account of the very human emotion its hero eventually transcends. It acknowledges in a way wholly conventional in romance yet rarely expressed with such power that in our most personal relations we may indeed experience something of the divine. God both made love and is love himself, and the second prayer of the first Proem (ll. 22–51) explores this idea with an intricacy that conditions the whole work.

This second prayer again makes clear that human passion is to be connected with religious and supernatural experience. Passion does not only lead to Hell. Love is also to be understood as the potentially joyous sexual attraction between man and woman, as the bond of charity between man and his kind, and as the love of God which both binds the world in steadfast unity and leads to salvation. We shall see that these ideas have many of their philosophical roots in Boethius and Dante, but we should note here how Christian worship lends its vocabulary to the service of Cupid. In a way wholly conventional in medieval romance, the pursuit of sexual pleasure is compared with the known forms of religious experience. Thus as the absence of God is the anguish of Hell, so the perils and failures of human passion are 'derknesse', 'hevynesse', 'adversitee', horrors to be recalled in what are made to appear as rare, fragile moments of erotic delight. This is far from being merely a witty and blasphemous parody. The narrator's feeling for the transitoriness of human joy – an essential theme of the whole poem – leads to a deep concern for fellow sufferers. Sexual love raises man's moral stature by requiring him to look charitably on his neighbour. From *cupiditas* may spring *caritas*, the greatest of Christian virtues and one that is urged here in a familiar religious way. The form of the 'bidding prayer' the narrator adopts spreads out to encompass all sorts and conditions of lovers, drawing them away from worldly suffering and the cardinal sin of despair that results from their idolatry of Cupid. Instead, the assembled company are gently led upwards to an unfailing and other-worldly love, the permanent 'solas' of true worship. As yet, the full implications of this are barely hinted at. Only at the close of the poem when the bondage of excessive mortal passion, anguish and steadfast 'trouthe' has been rewarded by the unexpected charity of divine grace, when a timeless and loving God has freed the soul of Troilus the virtuous pagan and led it to its abode among the stars, will the narrator be able to turn directly to his audience of 'younge, fresshe folkes', and urge on them the precepts of St Paul:

> Besides this you know what hour it is, how it is full time now for you to wake from sleep. For salvation is nearer to us now than when we first believed; the night is far gone, the day is at hand. Let us then cast off the works of darkness and put on the armour of light; let us conduct ourselves becomingly as in the day, not in revelling and drunkenness, not in debauchery and licentiousness, not in quarrelling and jealousy. But put on the Lord Jesus Christ, and make no provision for the flesh, to gratify its desires.

It was this passage, chanced on by St Augustine at a crucial moment in his life, that finally convinced him of the necessity of a celibate existence. Again, it is St Augustine's Pauline definition of true love not as selfish indulgence, but as charity, as 'the motion of the soul towards the enjoyment of God for its own sake, and the enjoyment of one's self and one's neighbour for the sake of God', which is the 'sentence' that underlies *Troilus and Criseyde* and, indeed, much of the great tradition of medieval secular love poetry.

That *Troilus and Criseyde* develops some of the central traditions of this literature is clear from the poet's ambivalent presentation of himself as the narrator of his work. This ambivalence is once more central to our understanding of the poem and is again a factor introduced in the first Proem. For example, just as the Pope is the *servus servorum Dei* ('the servant of the servants of God'), so the narrator casts himself as the servant of the servants of Cupid. He is the priest of secular love. However, by revealing himself in this role through the form of the 'bidding prayer' used by his spiritual equivalent, we have seen that he also shows a genuinely charitable concern for the pains and 'gladnesse' of earthly pleasure. He thereby casts his audience as a congregation. His poetry, seen in this light, is not an immoral and frivolous entertainment but, in its lowly concern for the suffering of others, an act of true charity. As such, it qualifies for the most serious critical consideration.

Chaucer's re-telling of his tragic story springs from no personal 'auctoritee', however. The narrator has, to use the other term of Chaucer's favourite equation, no 'experience' of love. He is – or pretends to be – the bumbling and simple figure familiar from the earlier poems. As a result of this supposed inexperience, he will have to rely on the authority of his alleged sources (a game of fast and loose Chaucer will play with the greatest dexterity), and on whatever wisdom can be derived from the audience's own experience. Both these devices open up subtle literary possibilities that are most fruitfully discussed when analysing the narrative itself, but it is useful to know here that in addition to drawing us into the audience and congregation of lovers – a group, we have seen, of alleged initiates – Chaucer also draws us into his poem, first by suggesting how we might question his sources about their omissions and secondly by asking his public to supply from their own superior knowledge the deficiencies both of those authorities themselves and his own art. In these ways we are often persuaded into an intuitive response to the facts and frequently asked to imagine the motivation behind the events and the conventionally elaborate, non-naturalistic speeches. Indeed, we are so often required to create the 'psychology' of the protagonists, to will them into individual life, that it is frequently we – and not the poet – who create fiction out of chronicle and turn history into story. If *Troilus and Criseyde* is, in the tired and misleading cliché, the first novel, then it is largely the audience who have created it.

We have seen that the Proem twice tells the whole narrative in brief outline. Such a lack of surprise is again entirely conventional and encourages us to think that the model for Chaucer's narrator here is derived from concepts of the medieval writer similar to those outlined by St Bonaventura. He is a humble transcriber. He is in reality very much more than this, but, accepting for the moment the traditional and prescriptive belief that there is nothing new in literature under the sun and that the best tales are the old ones, the ones we know, we should ask ourselves if Chaucer fits himself to his apparently humble role unthinkingly. The answer is, of course, that he does not. The fact that he twice gives us an outline of his story in the first Proem is of the greatest moment. We know from the opening line that we are to be regaled with the 'double sorwe' of Troilus and that as Fortune's wheel revolves so we shall see the hero progress from anguish to ecstasy and on to death when

Criseyde abandons him for another. It all appears predetermined. But while we know – or think we know – the whole story, the characters do not.

Such a clearly dramatic device has at least two important and related repercussions. First, it provides pathos through continuous narrative irony. The characters struggle to achieve a happiness we know is doomed from the start. This in its turn is an exact literary equivalent of the Boethian philosophy that provides much of the poem's intellectual groundwork. So important a matter clearly calls for some comment.

The two crucial terms to discuss here are Providence and Fortune. In the thorny sixth prose section of the fourth book of *The Consolation of Philosophy*, Boethius draws an important distinction between them. Providence is the divine idea of the universe in the unchanging and timeless mind of God. It is 'trouthe' or stable faith, the love and reason that knows past, present and future and holds the universe together, causing (among other things) the cycles of the seasons and controlling the elements. Philosophy herself compares this divine idea of the universe – this knowledge of how all things have been, are and will be – to the idea a craftsman or artist has of the whole plan of what he is going to make. In other words, just as God's Providence sees all events in the universe, so Chaucer the poet sees all the events in his poem – and he tells us what most of them are. We seem to share his God-like knowledge. But while God and the poet know all, they do not directly cause all. If they did so, man would have no free-will and thus no moral status. In philosophic terms, he would be nothing more than a faceless citizen in an authoritarian cosmic state. In literary terms, he would be a product of the poet's imagination and not a figure from a true history. Man must therefore have the right to choose. If he chooses wisely he will cleave to 'trouthe', the steadfast mind of God. This, of course, is what Chaucer urges at the close of his poem. If he chooses unwisely, however, man will cling to the mutable and untruthful things of this world, the things his Maker has made rather than his Maker himself. The more ardently he pursues these worldly pleasures the further away from God man gets.

At this point Philosophy creates a second essential image. We are now to imagine God as the still centre of the turning wheel of Fortune. While the circumference of that wheel moves in a huge circle, points nearer the centre revolve far less dramatically until, at the very centre, there is no movement at all. Without that still centre, however – without God's Providence or 'trouthe' – there would be no wheel, no universe, no Fortune. The further a man turns away from God or Providence, however, the more he becomes a victim of the cycles of Fortune and the infinite variety of ways in which the divine Idea is actually realized in the universe. If he has chosen Fortune rather than Providence, man has chosen anguish rather than peace, the predetermined patterns of cause and effect rather than the freedom of God.

In *Troilus and Criseyde*, Chaucer and his audience watch such predetermined patterns play themselves out. They are elements of a story deriving from the historical characters' acts which we know but cannot change. It seems that we too are trapped in the set course of the poem. We are told it will lead to death and destruction – and so it does. But it also leads to a sudden and surprising freedom. We have seen that Troilus, the passionate worldly lover, does not go down to Hell. He is not greeted by the Furies, to spend an eternity of despair among the damned. He is saved by inexplicable grace. God is not tied by his own rules. He alone does not have to act in a predetermined way. He can intervene. In the words of St John, his truth can set men free. At the close of the poem, when the known story has come to its end, there is a sudden and exhilarating release. Through the mercy of God (underlined by the contrivance of the poet) Troilus's soul is liberated. Human love is at last measured against the truly divine:

> And whan that he was slayn in this manere,
> His lighte goost ful blisfully is went
> Up to the holughnesse of the eighthe spere,
> In convers letyng everich element;
> And ther he saugh, with ful avysement,
> The erratik sterres, herkenyng armonye
> With sownes ful of hevenyssh melodie.
>
> And down from thennes faste he gan avyse
> This litel spot of erthe, that with the se
> Embraced is, and fully gan despise
> This wrecched world, and held al vanite
> To respect of the pleyn felicite
> That is in hevene above . . .

goost: soul   *holughnesse:* the concave inner surface of the eighth of the celestial spheres
In convers letyng, etc.: leaving on the other side each of the four elements
erratik sterres: the planets

The significance of this crucial passage (one that has caused the greatest difficulty and contention) will be a central point of our analysis. It is best approached, however, in the way Chaucer would have us do – from the events in the first book.

14

'Yt is wel wist' – the opening stanza of the narrative reminds us once again that the story of the destruction of Troy is both well known and to be envisaged as a revenge on sexual immorality. To the audience, the punishment of illicit lust and the transfer of empire seem predetermined. We have hindsight. Only one contemporary figure appears to have foreknowledge: the traitor Calkas, father of Criseyde. Aware of the fate of his city, he slips quietly away. Calkas thereby emphasizes the themes of treachery, fatalism, destruction, and the divide between public life and personal, secret desire which are so crucial to the whole work. The father of the traitor to a great and secret passion is cursed as a public traitor to his own city, and we should note here how the flowering of the secret love between Troilus and Criseyde takes place between two public events of terrible import: the treachery of the heroine's father and her own later exchange for the Greek prisoner Antenor, who will in turn cause the loss of his city's most valuable relic and so contribute to its downfall. Calkas's treason or 'untrouthe' – his failure to uphold the moral values of natural law – thus prefigures many of the themes the poem will explore.

We should also note the limited nature of Calkas's foreknowledge. Calkas may well be aware of the downfall of his city, but what he does not foresee is that his own actions (his wretched desertion and his subsequent plea for his daughter in exchange for another traitor) will play a significant part both in that downfall and in the destruction of the hero and heroine themselves. By asking for his daughter, Calkas paves the way for her desertion of Troilus and the great 'untrouthe' whereby she submits to the callous advances of the oily Diomede. The narrative ironies are woven very fine. With the first mention of the defenceless Criseyde, they also become immediately moving and point to the 'sentence' by which the Christian audience should begin to measure the tale.

We have seen that in Calkas's haste to save his own skin he has abandoned his daughter, just as she will later abandon Troilus to protect and pleasure hers. For the moment we are appalled that she should be so deserted. 'If anyone does not provide for his relations, and especially for his own family, he has disowned the faith and is worse than an unbeliever.' This passage from the fifth chapter of Paul's First Epistle to Timothy suggests the exceptional importance of biblical references and allusions in this poem and indeed in all medieval literature. It reinforces our Christian outrage at the pagan Calkas and illustrates the double focus of Chaucer's poem by which the Christian audience watch and evaluate the behaviour of those ignorant of that revelation. In line with this, Paul's text also provides an important gloss for our understanding of Criseyde's status as a widow.

In his Epistle to Timothy, Paul urges that widows are a special responsibility of the Church. He adds, in words that must partly help determine our attitude to the heroine: 'She who is a real widow, and is left all alone, has set her hope on God and continues in supplication and prayers night and day; whereas she who is self-indulgent is dead even while she lives.' This is a stern, fateful admonition, and Paul, realizing the temptation to 'idlers, gadding about from house to house', urges that young widows re-marry and raise families rather than 'wanton against Christ'. Such, then, was the Church's condemnation of the youthful Criseyde's illicit passion, her secret if rapturous exploration of *fine amour* based on the conventional denial of wedlock.

It is only after this allusion has been raised that we are told of Criseyde's beauty. The sternly moral is juxtaposed with the delightfully human. Our first view of the all too frail woman whose actions will make her a byword for deceit is ironically of a perfect, angelic creature, imagined as being above nature and almost a part of the truth of Heaven (Book I, ll. 99–105). In these respects, Criseyde might be Beatrice.

However, the 'real' Criseyde of the narrative, living in fear and threatened by her father's treason, makes her appeal to Hector. Her pathetic beauty and dignity move the mercy of the just judge to overrule his people's desire for revenge. Criseyde is returned safely to her house to live as a great widow should: in honour, stateliness and quiet withdrawal, 'ful wel biloved'. It might be the end of the matter, but Chaucer the commentator on his received text raises a question. He claims – erroneously as it happens – that the sources do not state if Criseyde had children. He refuses Boccaccio's statement that she had none and Benoît's that she was a virgin. He thus throws a mystery about his heroine. He casts a shadow of doubt concerning the range of her widow's responsibilities, and so points once again to his preoccupation with the unknowableness of the past, the ambiguity of fact, and the questionable nature of authority. Meanwhile, in a second and again original aside, Chaucer presents Fortune's temporarily equal-handed control of this war of inevitable destruction. For the moment, all is poised. Not the most strained reading could find a clue to the destruction of the city or Criseyde's later deceit – but we know both will happen.

We have seen that one of Chaucer's major additions to Boccaccio – from whom he derived the next scene – is that the passion between Troilus and Criseyde will be presented through the full and ambivalent range of imagery provided by the 'religion of love'. It is thus fitting as well as conventional that the conversion of 'this Troilus' from a callow adolescent who scorns both *fine amour* and the 'lawe of kynde' should take place in a temple. He is present at the spring ceremony where the public congregation of pagans – including the humble, stately and beautiful widow, silent as Paul required a woman should be in church – show their *pietas* to their most revered relic. For the moment, however, Troilus has neither a religious nor a secular devotion. Ignoring the service and coolly eyeing the ladies, he ironically refuses his companions' 'lewed observaunces'. Instead, he proudly exults in the false, shallow freedom of his 'wil'. Greater forces at once humble such juvenile arrogance. Cupid fires his arrow.

A passage of eight stanzas between the launch of the arrow itself and Troilus's first sight of Criseyde allows the narrator to exhort his audience, or congregation. Man's blind pride and alleged freedom, he says, are absurd. Man is a victim of circumstance and wears the harness of necessity as surely as a beast of burden. Nothing – not even rank – frees him from the human condition. It is fruitless for 'wise, proude, and worthi folkes' to rebel against love, for instance. Besides, the 'fair cheyne of love' that indeed binds the universe is both irresistible and virtuous. It is a solace and an antidote to vice and shame. Biblical references and the ambivalent priestly tone here both support and qualify the narrator's praise of secular passion, for, while it is true that love indeed 'alle thing may bynde', in its worldly form and too ardently pursued, *cupiditas* is also a species of bondage.

We can perhaps most usefully point to the wide range of Christian responses evoked by Chaucer's theological interpretation of Troilus's conversion to love by referring to three passages.

The earliest comes from the First Epistle of St John. It is the central 'auctoritee' for what we may call the extreme ascetic viewpoint, a vision of man's life in this world that is present in both the first Proem and throughout the work, but which is not its only voice. Writing to members of the early Church, St John declares:

Do not love the world or the things in the world. If any one loves the world, love for the Father is not in him. For all that is in the world, the lust of the flesh and the lust of the eyes and the pride of life, is not of the Father but is of the world. And the world passes away, and the lust of it; but he who does the will of God abides for ever.

From this central text derives the idea of sex and the physical life as the lust of the flesh, the lust of the eyes as avarice or intellectual curiosity, and the pride of life as that vainglory which places the self before God. Alongside this threefold division of sin there was then ranged a threefold division of the processes of sin. This derived from St Augustine and, by its appearance in the *Sententiae* of Peter Lombard, became the accepted teaching of medieval Christianity. As we have seen, it consisted of an analysis of sin whereby 'suggestion' – which was either from memory or the senses – was linked to the serpent's temptation of Eve. This in its turn led to 'delectation', that wavering of the will which prompted Eve's carnal appetite eventually to taste the apple. Finally came 'consent', which was Adam's rational but sinful choice to follow his wife rather than his God. Sin is thus a reasoned but perverted choice of action.

Since the world is a principal source of 'suggestion' to sin, it inevitably came to be seen first as a proper object for indifference and then in a pejorative light. Only the monastic life with its rejection of the world could be viewed as a true image of man living at his finest in the Earthly Paradise – an important location to which we shall return. Under the influence of Cistercian monastic reform especially, there then developed a literature *de contemptu mundi*, the great text of which was Pope Innocent III's tract of that name. Chaucer was familiar with this. Indeed he seems to have prepared a translation, now lost. He certainly paraphrased parts of it in *The Man of Law's Tale*. It is thus right to see the austere tradition stemming from St John as central to any medieval debate on the worth of worldly things. That this debate was entered at all, however – that the world could be viewed sometimes in all its beauty and delight – we have acknowledged to be one of the supreme achievements of the twelfth-century renaissance. It is to two texts stemming from this development that we should now turn.

The first text is the eighteenth canto of the *Purgatorio* where Virgil, the virtuous pagan, expounds to Dante the nature of human love as far as he understands it, drawing as he does so on Aquinas and the profound change Dante himself had made to the lyric tradition when he apostrophized his own passion as being essentially reasonable and virtuous. As a result of this development, a new and positive valuation of human emotion became possible. The mind, Virgil declares, is 'created quick to love'. It is moved by all that pleases, and pleasure rouses it to action. The mind then mounts upwards in spiritual movement to attain and pleasure in the thing it loves. Ideally, and in conformity with the Augustinian notion of charity by which objects and people should be loved for their proximity to the divine and not as ends in themselves, the proper and reasonable goal of love is the discovery of God. When, in the enlightened world of the *Paradiso*, Dante discusses this issue with no less a figure than St John himself, he is told: 'by human intellect and the authorities concordant with it, reserve your sovereign love for God'. But while the loving worldly heart may indeed be pure in its intentions and even longing for its Maker, the particular worldly object chosen may be evil or – if loved for its own sake – lead to evil effects. In Dante's image, the heart may be pure wax but the seal that leaves its impress on it may be bad. Moral goodness is thus seen to stem from the operation of reason on natural and involuntary desires – their proper interpretation rather than their wholesale rejection – and this in turn preserves free-will. Sin comes from abandoning or misdirecting reason and free-will, and this Troilus will partly do.

The third passage we should consider is that from Andreas Capellanus quoted on page 82, where, in a neat but suggestive scholastic joke, the birth of excessive passion is wittily described in the standard terms of falling into sin. Love, the French chaplain tells us, is an inborn suffering derived from the sight of and 'excessive meditation' on the beauty of the opposite sex. This in turn can lead to the reason's consenting to lust. In the romance tradition, however, desire can also be seen as the limited worldly excellence of *fine amour* which expresses itself in the ideals of chivalry and courtesy.

In these three passages there can thus be glimpsed something of the range of responses Chaucer's use of the imagery of the religion of love prompted in his audience. On the one hand, the lusts of the flesh could be seen as dangerous and to be eschewed during our brief sojourn in a wicked world. Conversely, and under the broadening influence of the twelfth-century renaissance especially, they could be perceived as potentially dangerous but also as a means of leading man to religious truth and social excellence when controlled by reason. In the words of St Thomas Aquinas: 'The passions of the soul, in so far as they are contrary to the order of reason, incline us to sin: but in so far as they are controlled by reason, they pertain to virtue.' It is precisely within this orbit that *Troilus and Criseyde* may be seen to operate. The love of the hero and heroine is indeed beautiful and ennobling. It has indeed the power to raise the hero to those heights of vision a virtuous pagan may obtain. But excessive human passion is also seen as finite and tragically destructive, a mere nothing in comparison with the 'pleyn felicitee' that is above. For the moment, however, we must stay with this world.

As Troilus's eye pierces the congregation, he first glimpses the 'wommanly noblesse' of the attractive and knowing Criseyde. In strict theological terms, he has received that 'suggestion' which may well lead to 'delectation' and the sins of the flesh. In Dante's image, her 'depe impressioun' has begun to 'stiken' in the wax of his heart. This development may or may not lead to God. In terms of romance, however, 'affecioun' now flushes Troilus's boyish heart which is thus made ready for the refining passion of *fine amour*.

Such images of the heart as these last are entirely conventional, even commonplace, but we should know that they are a medieval common-place and not a modern cliché if we wish to criticize them. In *Troilus and Criseyde*, the heart is a frequently discussed object and is not some vague euphuism for sex and the feelings. It has an exact if not undis-puted scientific meaning derived from Empedocles and Aristotle. As in *The Knight's Tale* where we are told of the young Arcite that 'the intellect . . . dwelled in his herte', so it is with the equally tragic Troilus. His affair is not just a matter of his emotions. It is – according to our point of view – both a conversion and a perversion of man's highest capacity: his reason dwelling in his heart. We shall return to elaborate on this central point, but should here recall the sensible, kindly advice Reason herself gives Amant in the *Roman de la Rose* when she explains the true purpose of sexual attraction as the limited, pardonable desire to procreate and urges him to follow her superior guidance. In addition, we should also recall the conventional theology of *The Parson's Tale* where it is sug-gested that every man who abandons reason repeats Adam's fall when-ever 'he hath desired agayn the lawe of God with perfit consentynge of his resoun; for therof is no doute, that it is deedly synne'. To abandon reason for desire is thus a deadly sin, and deadly sin, we may remember, is a precise theological category. The Parson, allegedly quoting St Augustine, defines it as 'whan a man turneth his herte fro God, which that is verray sovereyn bountee, that may nat chaunge, and yeveth his herte to thyng that may chaunge and flitte'. This, of course, is exactly what happens to Troilus in the temple. He surrenders his heart or reason to an image of changeable and fleeting worldly beauty.

Troilus's 'delectation' – his surrender of his reason to the changing and fleeting Criseyde – takes the form of a prostrate devotion, the abject supplication of his free-will implied by *fine amour*. The newly converted youth hurries from the temple. While publicly showing his old attitude to love, he seeks the privacy of his bedroom – a purely aristocratic prerogative – and falls to his knees. He at once practises the intensely emotional and imaginative recreation of passion (his own rather than Christ's) recommended by teachers of the *devotio moderna* such as St Anselm when he advised the sinner to enter into the chamber of his own mind and exclude everything but God and the things which help in finding him. It is, of course, Criseyde who is the idol of

Troilus's devotion, and his 'excessive meditation' or 'delectation' now begins.

The intense, painful idealism of a boy's first love is characterized throughout by those 'medievalizing' qualities that are Chaucer's special addition to his source, additions sometimes as small as a phrase and sometimes extending to many stanzas, which profoundly change the register of the original. As Troilus takes purpose 'loves craft to suwe', his writhing anguish emphasizes the passivity and 'gentilesse' of the feudal rites that constitute the pagan religion of love. In secret and repentant humility he offers his spirit to Cupid and his service to his lady or saint, praying for her grace and mercy to release him from pain. In the extremity of his ardour he wills Criseyde into divinity, and, in the very intensity of his passion, becomes the true type of male *fine amour*.

We who know the inevitable outcome can see the ludicrousness and pathos of all this. But we should also recognize that it is in just such ways that the English Troilus is revealed as more innocent, more prayerful and more poignant than his Italian counterpart. He is also more acutely aware of God, Fortune and death. The English Troilus is, in short, a more thoroughly devout member of the heretical Church of Love than his Italian cousin. The intensity of the images and attitudes he strikes are of great significance to the religious and philosophical context of the poem as a whole.

We have seen how from the start Chaucer creates a subtle counterpoint between the liturgies of Christ and Cupid. While this is a conventional aspect of romance poetry, Chaucer here investigates its more profound aspects as nowhere else. Troilus's passion is indeed placed in a genuinely theological perspective. It really does concern sin, death and salvation. The very completeness with which the ecstatic religion of secular love mirrors ecclesiastical forms is a measure of Troilus's all too human plight. His whole being and reason are given to things we as Christians know to be worldly and transitory – to Criseyde, in fact. He has turned his heart from the true God. As we watch him do so, however – deeply sympathetic, our emotions kindled by the contagious energy of his – we should also remember that 'all who desert you and set themselves up against you merely copy you in a perverse way'. This passage from the *Confessions* of St Augustine again provides an essential perspective on the all-pervading element of religious allusion in Troilus's love. Sin of itself can create nothing and so can only manifest itself as a parody of the divine. It is so here. Troilus's breathless adoration of Criseyde is an exact and passionate reversal of the true faith which he cannot know. It is both religious and sacrilegious, a faith and a heresy. Furthermore, the passage from St Augustine we have just quoted concludes with a phrase that points to the end of the whole poem: 'by this very act of imitation they [i.e. sinners] only show that you are the Creator of all nature and, consequently, that there is no place whatever where man may hide from you'. The parody religion of love reveals the existence of the true. God is everywhere – even in pagan Troy.

Chaucer investigates Troilus's moving but unreasonable passion not only in terms of love itself but also in the context of the second great theme of romance – chivalry.

Such is the intense elaboration of the way the love affair is presented that it is sometimes possible to forget that Troilus is a prince from an earthly and pagan city involved on the wrong side of a just war. He has social and political responsibilities. These are emphasized by the narrator's comparing him with Hector, one of the Nine Worthies. He thereby stresses the values John of Salisbury had shown pertain to knighthood. These too become wrenched from their proper sphere. In the torrent of his love, Troilus's two cardinal duties to 'th'assege and his salvaccioun' get swept aside; or, more accurately, transformed into idolatrous passion on the one hand and the desire to be seen to act bravely by Criseyde (solely 'to liken him the bet for his renoun') on the other. In the heat of battle he is not – and, indeed, cannot be – the true Christian knight involved in spiritual warfare against the lusts of the world. He has not put on what St Paul calls 'the whole armour of God' in order to be 'strong in the Lord and the strength of his might'. Nor is his outstanding bravery a result of patriotism, the limited ideal of the worthy pagan. Instead, it is a public expression of social qualities made to serve an exclusively private aim – the winning of Criseyde's favour. The end of Troilus's chivalry is thus a limited but very precious worldly recognition. In the words of the Evangelist, Troilus loves 'the glory of man rather than the glory of God', and in winning the favour of Criseyde he will have 'received his reward in full'. The irony lies in the fact that just as through his illicit passion Troilus matures into an intensely human lover, so his ill-rooted chivalry makes him a hero second only to Hector. The deceptive things of this world are not without some value and beauty. Once again, a partial good is still a good. However, Troilus needs a figure to draw him away from his sorrowing isolation.

The first speech Pandarus makes on his sudden entry into the poem combines the themes of chivalry and the religion of love. It does so in a manner that also suggests much about the speaker's nature. Pandarus jokingly asks Troilus if he is frightened of the Greeks or if he has fallen into some 'devocioun'. His purpose is to make the young hero angry and so forget his evident sorrow. This is a kindly deed of friendship perhaps, but it suggests a light, worldly cynicism which places Pandarus in a comic scale that is inevitably vulgar when compared with Troilus's intense idealism. Indeed, we can begin to characterize the relationship between the two as a contrast between a romantic idealism so strong that it absorbs the individual into the very type of the aristocratic lover, and a comic mode which decorously allows for incidental and specific detail. It is as if Arcite had met the Wife of Bath. Troilus and Pandarus are thus two rhetorical types. They are also very much more.

For example, as Pandarus slowly brings Troilus to the point where he confesses his love for his niece, we can see him approaching a state highly regarded in the Middle Ages and Renaissance: *amicitia*, the non-physical and charitable love between friends which mirrors the ideal of all human relations. With this in mind, we can acknowledge that Pandarus's concern for Troilus's suffering is perfectly genuine, if far from simple. He is moved, he is sympathetic to the point of tears, but he places a comic slur on the ideal by being both a busybody and a false counsellor. He does not guide his friend in the paths of reason and God but towards a very beautiful and limited human love. If he partly personifies *amicitia*, he is also partly Ami from the *Roman de la Rose*, a cynic who, appearing to Amant after the overthrow of Reason, speaks 'like one well taught, for he had learned a great deal about love'. The greater richness of Chaucer's creation lies in the fact that Pandarus is a far warmer and more various figure than Ami, while his authority on love, though so freely given, derives from some singularly unsuccessful personal experiences:

> 'How hastow thus unkyndely and longe
> Hid this fro me, thow fol?' quod Pandarus.
> 'Paraunter thow myghte after swich oon longe,
> That myn avys anoon may helpen us.'
> 'This were a wonder thing,' quod Troilus.
> 'Thou koudest nevere in love thiselven wisse:
> How devel maistow brynge me to blisse?'

paraunter: perhaps

This brilliant use of a colloquial tone is not the only mode adopted in this passage. Memorable though it is, it is used infrequently. Pandarus is a focus for a far wider range of concerns. He is, for example, a source of *sententiae*, of received wisdom he somehow manages to reduce to platitude. His long speech (ll. 624–721) is full of wise saws and *exempla* within *exempla*. In recital, this almost certainly produces a comic effect, while the enforced silence of Troilus suggests the privacy of his suffering and so points to a central theme of this and all courtly passion – secrecy.

In addition to being a source of comic rhetoric, Pandarus is necessarily drawn into the imagery of the religion of love. He is, in this section, Troilus's confessor. As such, it is his responsibility to rouse the despairing and suicidal boy from the sin that knows no forgiveness and to urge him to look to the mercy of his beloved and so attain a state of grace with Cupid. Pandarus does so by showing Troilus the foolishness of his inactivity: 'unknowe, unkist, and lost that is unsought'. Pandarus's worldly common-sense here reveals Troilus's idealism in a mildly comic light – a particularly interesting perspective. But in urging action, Pandarus also points ironically to an important aspect of the Christian theology of the poem: the degree to which a man can and ought to participate in his own salvation, and how far this is a matter for an inscrutable God. The question of whether a man was redeemed by grace alone or whether his faculties could make him lead a life that merited such forgiveness was, we shall see, a central feature of English theological discussion in the 1380s. As Pandarus here urges action and forbids a despairing passivity in the face of Fortune, so this theme of personal responsibility for salvation is first mentioned in the parody religion of love. When Troilus, roused to speech, finally confesses that his 'swete fo' is Criseyde, Pandarus exalts her worth, and in showing his friend that he has fallen for a truly worthy woman – which, at this point, Criseyde undoubtedly is – he also reveals the beneficent mercy of Cupid in terms that again borrow from the language of Christian devotion:

> for nought but good it is
> To loven wel, and in a worthy place;
> The oughte nat to clepe it hap, but grace.

hap: chance

However, just as to attain peace with the true God, contrition, repentance and making satisfaction are necessary, so here Pandarus taunts Troilus with his old 'sinful' attitudes until the boy begs Cupid to forgive his 'japes'. Confession, contrition and atonement are made and, newly in harmony with his god, Troilus is offered advice on how to behave as a virtuous member of his church – in other words, as a courtly lover.

When the parody is complete, Pandarus then agrees to act as a go-between. He quietly dismisses both his widowed niece's responsibilities to 'celestial' love and Troilus's naive but no doubt sincere protestations of his pure intentions. The mechanism of the secret affair is put in motion, and the first book ends with three beautiful stanzas describing the re-born lover and civic hero:

> But Troilus lay tho no lenger down,
> But up anon upon his stede bay,
> And in the feld he pleyde the leoun;
> Wo was that Grek that with hym mette a-day!
> And in the town his manere tho forth ay
> Soo goodly was, and gat hym so in grace,
> That ecch hym loved that loked on his face.
>
> For he bicom the frendlieste wight,
> The gentilest, and ek the mooste fre,
> The thriftiest and oon the beste knyght,
> That in his tyme was or myghte be,
> Dede were his japes and his cruelte,
> His heighe port and his manere estraunge,
> And ecch of tho gan for a vertu chaunge.
>
> Now lat us stynte of Troilus a stounde,
> That fareth lik a man that hurt is soore,
> And is somdeel of akyngge of his wownde
> Ylissed wel, but heeled no deel moore,
> And, as an esy pacyent, the loore
> Abit of hym that gooth aboute his cure;
> And thus he dryeth forth his aventure.

thriftiest: most serviceable *japes:* jokes *heighe port:* haughtiness *ylissed:* eased
hym: i.e. Pandarus *dryeth forth his aventure:* pursued his destiny

The hell of love's despair has now been passed, and our relief is expressed by a humane ideal of courtly and chivalric refinement. We are led properly to delight in our own world. Troilus is both the fierce soldier and the gentleman whose *caritas* takes the form of graceful and easy good manners. From the intense secrecy of his emotions has sprung a resounding public excellence. There remains, however, the inner ache of unrequited love.

15

It is worth dwelling on the closing stanzas of Book I since they are crucial to the poem in several ways. They provide, first of all, a radiant image of human potential. Yet surely we must not give this a merely sentimental acquiescence. At the close of the twentieth century, and in a democratic and largely proletarian culture, what does it mean to admire a warrior prince and declare that a way of loving open only to the smallest of elites is an ideal?

At this point I must briefly step out of my role as literary historian trying to give an objective account of the works of a culture so different to my own. I must do so because Chaucer suggests that I should. It is part of his concern with subjectivity. In the remarkable Proem to Book II, Chaucer urges us to take a critical attitude to his entire history. Would we 'purchase' love at this price? Would we talk like this, behave like this? Could we even if we wanted to? It is for each of us to decide and, in deciding, to be aware of how we answer a question it is remarkable should have been raised at all. Through the medium first of the written word and now of the printed edition (mine lies propped open on a desk in a house that stands some twenty minutes from the Westminster where Chaucer spoke six centuries ago), I hear his words and become a part of his audience, not his fourteenth-century audience to be sure, for no amount of study can make me a medieval courtier, but of the posterity imagined by his text, by the act of writing down the spoken word. I have become a function of a poem written in a language very different from my own and concerning events in a long-dead culture. Language, love and manners – man's things – exist in man's element, which is time. With time comes change, the transitoriness of worldly matters which is the subject of the poem. When we then measure the historical events against our own contemporary experience, as Chaucer asks us to, we may admire or disapprove: 'this may liken the, and the right nought'. We might admire – perhaps with secret envy – a culture that can invest human emotion with the richness of poetry, or we might despise it for being based around bloodshed and the refusal to treat women as equals. In either case we are assuming a complete and objective understanding of how the poem works in its historical context and then using this to explore our own feelings. Chaucer requires us to do so, but we should recognize that in following him we have moved from literary and historical analysis to autobiography and polemic – and this book does not claim to go that far. I do not know how your experiences compare with those of Troilus and Criseyde, and I do not propose to tell you in what ways mine are different. I do not know if you revel in contemporary culture or find it lacking in nourishment, and I cannot discuss the state of the world with you. I am assuming that you are reading this book to find out about the literature of the 1380s and not the life of the 1980s. My text – as opposed to the endless vistas opened up by Chaucer's – is nothing more than a preparation for further study:

> Wherfore I nyl have neither thank ne blame
> Of al this werk, but prey yow mekely,
> Disblameth me, if any word be lame,
> For as myn auctor seyde, so sey I.

Or, at least, I hope I do.

16

We must now return to Chaucer the narrator – an imagined figure wholly different from Chaucer the poet – and see how he takes the attitude to his alleged text that any honest historian must. He is apparently the humble but alert *compilator* and *commentator*. In a narrative whose tone the poet has so largely created, the narrator claims to tell the truth as another has set it down. In a poem that does indeed contain a very large element of translation, the narrator asserts his objectivity and lack of responsibility for a work the poet has profoundly modified. Such ambivalence is wholly characteristic of Chaucer's genius.

The narrator of the second Proem rightly suggests that to study the past is to be aware of diversity: our own and that of other cultures. Such is the discipline of history and it is why Clio is the muse of the second book. But if Clio is Chaucer's inspiration, she speaks the language of Dante. As part of the attempt to understand the sundry 'usages' of the English Middle Ages it is necessary that we recognize both the opening allusion to the *Purgatorio* and its implications.

Chaucer's image of a storm-tossed boat corresponds exactly to the *navicella* of Dante's wit at the opening of his second *cantica*. In terms of the poem's sustained religious imagery, we have moved from the hell of love's despair to the inwardly wounded Troilus's spiritual healing in purgatory. This is an important development and one that will lead to the lovers' brief, ecstatic sojourn in the Earthly Paradise – for Dante the place of unenlightened human excellence – at the end of Book III. Before this can come about, however, Criseyde must be wooed and won.

Pandarus, the go-between and unsuccessful lover, makes his way to Criseyde's house where he finds his niece in her widow's garb enjoying an appropriate, civilized retirement. Yet even here we cannot escape destruction. Criseyde is listening to the tale of Thebes, another story of treachery and the sacking of a city – and one in which, through Diomede, she will later play a small and pathetic part. Criseyde is nonetheless revealed here as a witty, sociable woman of well-bred ease, concerned about the war and trying honestly to fulfil her widow's duties. But Pandarus's sly mention of a 'thing' he has to tell her wakes her curiosity. He then proceeds to the seemingly incidental praise of Troilus's military and social virtues and to what Criseyde will later call his 'peynted process': the speech (full of circumlocution, *sententiae* and a form of high emotionalism which slides easily into blackmail) by which he wakes her compassion for his supposedly dying friend. If she fails to show him her mercy she will be responsible for the death of both Troilus and Pandarus. She will be too cruel and her beauty worthless. If Pandarus has been partly Ami in respect of Troilus, he is here partly La Veille in respect of Criseyde. But his hectoring tone is singularly unpleasant, while his abuse of his position as Criseyde's guardian (comparable with his abuse of his relationship of *amicitia* with Troilus) is made the worse by his lying insistence that he 'never othere mente' than that Criseyde's interest in Troilus should be discreetly platonic.

Criseyde is initially outraged by Pandarus's suggestions. She does not yet have a harlot's heart and she knows that her uncle and adviser is urging an evil course on her widowed life. Before the affair has even commenced, she sees that 'of this world the feithe is al agoon'. Like us all, and from the very start, Criseyde is adrift in a world where 'feithe' and 'trouthe' – the very qualities that Troilus will so wholly embody – are rare in the extreme. She has only her own moral strength to rely on, but, as she is 'the ferfulleste wight', caught between the duties of her widowed state and saving the life of her mentor and his friend, a lonely woman faced with the ruthless subtlety of her uncle, she opts for faith and compromise.

When Pandarus has wrung from Criseyde her statement that she will do what she can for Troilus short of threatening her honour and – with a further irony – she has given her promise to be true to her word, the subject of their conversation changes to 'othere tales glade'. But the seed of curiosity, if not of love, has been planted. Criseyde wants to know how Troilus came to admire her. She at once becomes vividly sympathetic to the audience, and Pandarus obliges her with two lively descriptions of Troilus's thwarted passion. One is an account of the scene in the hero's bedroom; the other (an earlier occasion we have not heard about before) concerns Pandarus's view of Troilus when the lover, thinking he was alone, offered an anguished prayer to Cupid. Has Pandarus made this up, or more subtly, has Chaucer deliberately kept this information secret until now so that, as we think back over the bedroom scene in Book I, it is only here that we realize how much the seemingly innocent Pandarus knew, how wrong we were to assume that we were in possession of the whole truth? The latter is perhaps more likely. It points to the uncertainty of all human knowledge and makes us dupes of the narrator just as his characters are the dupes of Fortune. It also greatly enhances our sense of Pandarus as a manipulator.

That Pandarus does indeed exist as a manipulator of men and women is, of course, of the greatest importance. We have just seen how skilful his ruthless worldly wisdom is when he wants to get his way. Troilus and Criseyde do indeed appear to be his puppets – or, at least, he is confident that this is so. But is it? Surely Fortune, working under the sway of Providence, is the real 'executrice of wyrdes'. In bringing the hero and the heroine together Pandarus may well think he can control people's lives, but in reality he is neither Fortune nor Providence. He is a bawd. The narrative of the second book is shrewdly constructed to illustrate this, to illustrate that the great manipulator is not the only force in the universe and that men alone are not entirely responsible for shaping their lives.

As far as Pandarus is concerned, the narrative – *his* plot – consists of his returning to Troilus's palace. Here, with a deal of comic cynicism, he eventually reports his success and instructs his friend to write a love letter which he will then deliver at such a time as to guarantee Criseyde will read it when sitting by a window from which she will watch the hero ride past. It is a very clever stratagem – so clever, in fact, that Fortune has already thought of it. Her manipulations, casting an ironic light on the freedom of Troilus and Pandarus to shape the hero's destiny, result in one of the loveliest passages in the whole poem.

Left alone after the departure of her uncle, Criseyde sits by her window:

> But as she sat allone and thoughte thus,
> A cry aros at scarmuch al withoute,
> And men cride in the strete, 'Se, Troilus
> Hath right now put to flighte the Grekes route!'
> With that gan al hire meyne for to shoute,
> 'A, go we se! cast up the yates wyde!
> For thorwgh this strete he moot to paleys ride;
>
> 'For other wey is fro the yate noon
> Of Dardanus, there opyn is the cheyne.'
> With that com he and al his folk anoon
> An esy pas rydyng, in routes tweyne,
> Right as his happy day was, sooth to seyne,
> For which, men seyn, may nought destourbed be
> That shal bityden of necessitee.

This Troilus sat on his baye steede,
Al armed, save his hed, ful richely;
And wownded was his hors, and gan to blede,
On which he rood a pas ful softely.
But swich a knyghtly sighte, trewely,
As was on hym, was nought, withouten faille,
To loke on Mars, that god is of bataille.

So lik a man of armes and a knyght
He was to seen, fulfilled of heigh prowesse;
For bothe he hadde a body and a myght
To don that thing, as wel as hardynesse;
And ek to seen hym in his gere hym dresse,
So fressh, so yong, so weldy semed he,
It was an heven upon hym for to see.

His helm tohewen was in twenty places,
That by a tyssew heng his bak byhynde;
His sheeld todasshed was with swerdes and maces,
In which men myght many an arwe fynde
That thirled hadde horn and nerf and rynde;
And ay the peple cryde, 'Here cometh oure joye,
And, next his brother, holder up of Troye!'

For which he wex a litel reed for shame,
Whan he the peple upon hym herde cryen,
That to byholde it was a noble game,
How sobrelich he caste down his yen.
Criseyda gan al his chere aspien,
And leet it so softe in hire herte synke,
That to hireself she seyde, 'Who yaf me drynke?'

scarmuch: skirmish   *meyne:* household   *yates:* gates   *weldy:* wieldy, active
tyssew: tissue   *thirled, etc.:* pierced through the layers of his shield   *yaf:* gave

Of all the vignettes of love and chivalry Middle English romance has to offer, this is perhaps the loveliest and most subtle. It is both a narrative moment and an emblem: a visual representation of moral ideas.

The unseen observer stares distractedly down into the street. The quiet withdrawal of her young and widowed life has been made turbulent by her uncle's revelations. She is beloved and, in turn, must exercise compassion. She has been told by her deceiving mentor to render *caritas* for *cupiditas*. In her favour lies the power of life and death. Now, as she begins to weigh the consequences of her situation, Fortune so contrives events that the youth who loves her enters at the city gate. He cannot see her and does not know she is watching. He is ignorant of Pandarus's success. But to all who look on him, Troilus is the image of their ideal and a cause of joy: brave, strong, demure, 'so fressh, so yong', their saviour and protector in his battered armour. He is Mars, the god of war.

But as we read or hear these lines (which are Chaucer's invention) and as we watch the Trojans greeting their hero, a range of associations they could not possibly know come before our mind's eye. As Christians, we think of another hero's entry into another city. The people call for the portcullis to be raised, Troilus rides through the Dardan Gate, and we remember the Psalms:

> Lift up your heads, O gates!
>   and be lifted up, O ancient doors!
>   that the King of Glory may come in.
> Who is the King of glory?
>   The Lord, strong and mighty,
>   the Lord, mighty in battle!

As we think of Criseyde, we remember the prophecy of Isaiah:

> Behold, the Lord has proclaimed
>   to the end of the earth:
> Say to the daughter of Zion,
>   'Behold, your salvation comes;
> behold, his reward is with him,
>   and his recompense before him.'

And finally we think how, in the gospels of Matthew and John especially, Christ's entry into Jerusalem was seen as a fulfilment of these Old Testament words. As such references cluster around the imagined pagan scene, so they distance and circumscribe it in terms of the poem's explicit Christian purpose, while at the same time greatly enriching the imagery of the religion of love.

Let us take the Christian purpose first. Christ's riding on an ass into Jerusalem was the humble entry of the God of Love into the earthly city. Here he would, as he knew, eventually be killed, only to rise again. Breaking the bondage of sin and death, Christ would allow believing souls into the other-worldly order of the New Jerusalem. The earthly city itself would be destroyed:

> Would that even today you knew the things that make for peace! But now they are hid from your eyes. For the days shall come upon you, when your enemies will cast up a bank about you and surround you, and hem you in on every side, and dash you to the ground, you and your children within you, and they will not leave one stone upon another . . .

The enemies of worldly Troy will also leave not one stone standing upon another, yet the entry of this hero is proudly beautiful and not salvational. Troilus is the incarnation of war and his love is private, sexual, cupidinous. In his inner soul he rather seeks salvation than offers it. He does not know that he is entering the city in whose limited cause he will die. He has put on the bondage of sin and death, and is unaware of the mercy that will break through this coil and lead his soul to another-worldly order. When, for St Bernard and the author of *The Ancrene Riwle*, Christ came as a knightly lover to the soul, it was to die for her and so save her. Troilus also comes as a knightly lover and will die. He, however, must be offered salvation. As he enters the Dardan Gate he is both the very image or type of human excellence unenlightened by faith and the antitype of Christ. The vocabularies of human and divine love – the two languages of the poem – are brought exactly and revealingly together.

While Criseyde watches the triumphal entry of her lord of love, neither the man nor the woman is condemned outright. The Christian imagery we bring to their situation does not necessarily damn them – rather, it places them. As we have mentioned, Troilus is slowly becoming an embodiment of the very best an unenlightened pagan can attain, and that, as we shall see, is a great deal. The grandeur and pathos of Criseyde's love and treachery lie in the fact that she recognizes this excellence but betrays it. Now as she looks on her knight, however, the impulse to love is stirred as it was in Troilus himself. 'The mind,' we may recall, 'created quick to love, is readily moved towards everything that pleases, as soon as by pleasure it is aroused to action.'

What pleases Criseyde as she slowly inclines to love are not simply the obvious, wholesome attractions of a virile young prince of the royal blood. Criseyde is not a schoolgirl nurturing a crush on some doe-eyed rock star. She is a Trojan lady, a courteous and intelligent woman capable of a refined and noble intuition of the best values of her society. She herself later tells us exactly what these are, what pleases her. The tragedy lies in the fact that this is the last speech she will ever address to Troilus:

> 'For trusteth wel, that youre estat roial,
> Ne veyn delit, nor only worthinesse
> Of yow in werre or torney marcial,
> Ne pompe, array, nobleye, or ek richesse
> Ne made me to rewe on youre destresse;
> But moral vertu, grounded upon trouthe,
> That was the cause I first hadde on yow routhe!

'Eke gentil herte and manhod that ye hadde,
And that ye hadde, as me thoughte, in despit
Every thyng that souned into badde,
As rudenesse and poeplissh appetit,
And that youre resoun bridlede youre delit;
This made, aboven every creature,
That I was youre, and shal while I may dure.

'And this may lengthe of yeres naught fordo,
Ne remuable Fortune deface . . .'

routhe: pity   *remuable:* changeable

In this deeply touching but ironic statement – made all the more so by
its place in the narrative – we see both the stature the virtuous pagan can
attain and how these qualities rouse love. Since the passage also draws
to itself many of the central issues of the poem – the range, value and
nature of the hero's excellence and the heroine's perception especially –
it is worth examining in detail. To do so here is in some respects to put
the cart before the horse, to discuss the heights of love before describing
the long haul by which they are scaled, but to have an idea of what the
ideal is will inevitably enrich our view of its attainment.

Criseyde's low valuation of both the 'veyn delyt' roused by Troilus's
beauty as well as his obvious worldly attributes – his inherited rank, his
prowess and wealth – suggests that she values qualities below the glit-
tering surface of life. She can see beneath the alluring but accidental gifts
of Fortune. And the fact that she can do so measures the depth of her
fall. She here rejects the idea that what is truly valuable lies in the chance
gifts of inheritance and worldly possession. Like Dante in *Le dolce rime
d'amore*, she realizes that true nobility stems from innate virtue in a man.
Dante would say that this quality was planted by God. Criseyde herself
describes it as 'moral vertue, grounded upon trouthe'.

This first term means far more than churchwardenly rectitude, though
it includes avoidance of 'dissensioun', 'lak of stedfastnesse' and what
Chaucer memorably describes in his ballade of that name as 'wilful
wrecchednesse'. It suggests rather the exercise of what we now call heart,
mind and spirit – in other words, unaided human excellence, the qualities
that make us instinctively admire the 'good' man. These qualities are
'grounded', to use Criseyde's word, on one of Chaucer's most revered
terms: 'trouthe'.

To those for whom number of itself is impressive, there are slightly
over 140 uses of 'trouthe', 'trewe' and 'trewely' in *Troilus and Criseyde*,
while the full significance of this many-layered noun and its derivatives

colours the entire action. To itemize the various implications of 'trouthe' is thus a necessary activity, but we should realize that in so doing we are putting asunder a union of ideas that Chaucer and the tradition in which he worked had very carefully joined.

The simplest meaning of 'trouthe' is that something is correct, as when in Book IV Fame is said to report 'false thynges' and 'thynges trewe'. There are, however, two further and related layers of meaning. These refer to a man's 'trouthe' – his pledged word, his personal integrity, his loyal, dependent relation to his society – and to God's truth. The first is a measure of moral worth, the latter is to be understood both as the constancy of the Creator by which he maintains the cycle of the physical world and his embodiment as Christ, the 'way, the truth and the life', whose doctrine for believers is such that 'if you continue in my word, you are truly my disciple, and you will know the truth, and the truth will make you free'. The concept of truth thus rises in a seamless progression from statements about the real nature of things, through an individual's integrity which is, in its turn, an aspect of God's control of the world, and so to the loving sacrifice God himself made to save that world. We shall see that all these meanings apply to the poem and are, indeed, central to much of the finest Middle English literature, but we should concentrate for the moment on how the love of Troilus and Criseyde develops so that the hero shows those values of personal integrity or 'trouthe' to his pledged word, qualities which reveal themselves as he comes to personify the ideal courtly lover.

Troilus develops to be the 'gentil', manly figure, eschewing 'rudenesse and poeplish appetit'. He seems to Criseyde at least to be ruled by reason rather than pleasure and so to be the ideal of the virtuous pagan. It is only by her being won to his love, however, that these virtues can flower, but by bestowing her 'mercy' on her abject lover she really does bring Troilus to that state of worldly excellence a heathen can attain.

She does not surrender at once. We should note two points here. The first is the narrator's sly personal intrusion in ll. 665–72 where he mentions (and so asks us to imagine) the subtle processes of Criseyde's thought as her love begins to blossom. Since Chaucer does not present these in their entirety, it is we who have partly to reconstruct them, we who have to create the non-textual narrative. This we have seen is a technique Chaucer will frequently call on his audience of initiates to employ. Secondly, we should note that the way in which Chaucer does present what he shows us of Criseyde's state of mind is wholly medieval and completely different from what we have come to expect from the novel.

As the planet Venus sets her determining course, Criseyde tries to solve her perplexities through an act of apparently free intelligence. She thinks, and her thinking in her long soliloquy (ll. 693–805) takes a precise medieval form. It is not a random flow of associations – a psychological process – but a series of arguments ranged for and against, *sic et non* in the proper medieval manner. On the one side, love for Troilus would be an honourable and safe *aventure*, flattering to Criseyde and to her beauty. It would certainly be far freer than the restraints of marriage. On the other hand, there would necessarily be some restrictions and pain. There are also the dangers of gossip and threats to her reputation. Criseyde's soliloquy is thus a *contentio*, and for the moment she cannot resolve it. Instead, she descends to her garden (always a significant location in romance) and listens to Antigone's praise of love. She learns, seemingly for the first time, that love is a divine power and the seat of earthly virtue. She then retires to bed and, in her prefiguring dream, her heart, the seat of her moral worth and identity, is torn out by a white eagle and changed for Troilus's.

This last is a memorable image, suggesting that complete identity with the other which is love. It at once reveals the mysterious inwardness of the emotions and relates these to the religious imagery of the poem. The idea that the human heart is movable, for example – that it can follow Christ's to Heaven – is as old as St Gregory and is mentioned by Cynewulf. In the biography of St Catherine of Siena (a work contemporary with *Troilus and Criseyde*) the story is told of how Christ appeared to the saint, removed her heart and replaced it with his own. Many, it was said, were witnesses to the scar that remained.

Criseyde is thus being won to love, and her emotions are naturally presented in terms of religious imagery. However, we must now return to Troilus and see how the developing imagery of the religion of love also applies to him.

For the moment, Troilus is ardently pursuing Criseyde's 'grace' through his excellence as a soldier and courtly lover. The repeated fever imagery by which he is described conventionally suggests the element of 'sin' that must be purged before he is whole. Pandarus meanwhile, having significantly promised that 'thou shalt be saved by thy feyth, in trouthe', sets about enabling the mechanism of his 'redemption'.

The latter half of Book II shows this process with particular subtlety. There is, first of all, the excellent sense of social realism, the recreation of the texture of courtly life. Pandarus, trudging to and fro, invents the straw figure of Poliphete who is apparently threatening Criseyde's welfare. He organizes the royal family against him, and so manipulates

Troilus towards his feigned sickness at his brother Deiphebus's palace where Criseyde, by another arranged coincidence, will meet him in the privacy of his sickroom. Here, with a subtle narrative irony, she will beg the help of the man to whom she alone can offer saving mercy in this world. Such a complex of manipulation conveys the intense secrecy necessary to *fine amour* and provides an element of intrigue. Against this somewhat vulgar pattern of worldly contrivance, however, are set first our glimpses of Criseyde's blossoming passion – again, we are invited to imagine her thoughts rather more than we are told them – and secondly, the all-embracing imagery of the religion of love.

We have already heard Pandarus utter one phrase of crucial significance. In the heretical church of love, Troilus will be saved by faith: 'thou shalt be saved by thy feyth, in trouthe'. Now, at the close of Book II, as Troilus writhes in the breathless anguish of young love's expectancy, there plays over his near delirium a whole range of associations derived from theology and translated into the language of the religion of love. To appreciate these, we need to view the construction of the poem in its broadest perspective.

We have mentioned that the first book of *Troilus and Criseyde* was the hero's *Inferno*, the place where he learned of his sin against Cupid and suffered in what seemed a hopeless despair. It follows that the second book and most of the third are his *Purgatorio*, the place where, first under Pandarus's ministrations and then under the sway of Criseyde, his lover's soul will be purged by a refining penance willingly undergone in the hope of bliss. This bliss will be reached in the Earthly Paradise – the symbolic location of unenlightened human excellence – that Troilus attains at the close of Book III.

Since the preparations for this climax require Troilus to be largely passive, by far the greater part of the action of the second book belongs to Pandarus and Criseyde. Troilus when we glimpse him is either the perfect example of chivalry (the active life) or the sick and suffering lover bewailing his anguish, sending petitions of hope, and following the penitent or contemplative existence. Both aspects of his behaviour witness to the utter sincerity of his love, the fixity of the 'trouthe' with which he has plighted his heart. His 'feyth' in the redemption Criseyde can offer is absolute, and from it flows a refining excellence which does indeed begin to move her pity. In terms of the religion of love, his faith will in truth win his salvation. He will traverse Hell, ascend Purgatory and then enter the delights of the Earthly Paradise.

The correspondence to the broad structure of the *Purgatorio*, to Dante's observation of and participation in the processes of penance and his eventual view of the Earthly Paradise, that Chaucer's poem here reveals is important. A necessarily brief account of Dante's second *cantica* will begin to make clear the exceptional completeness of the English poet's exploration of the imagery of the religion of love.

In the Italian poem, when Dante and Virgil have emerged from Hell, they arrive at the foot of Mount Purgatory. They first meet those who have made only a deathbed repentance of their sin (we may here care to think of Troilus's confession) and then proceed up the spiralling path on whose seven stages hopeful souls are expiating the Seven Deadly Sins. When Dante has passed through the refining fire, had his dream of the ideals of the active and contemplative life, and found his will 'free, upright and healthy', he has a changed and more subtle understanding of what before seemed confused. He can make his confession to Beatrice, be immersed in the restoring innocence of Lethe, and enter the Earthly Paradise – a place which we have seen suggests the beatitude and inno- cence attained by the full exercise of the virtues accessible to men without Christian revelation. This development compares with the theological framework of the religion of love underlying the structure of Books II and III of *Troilus and Criseyde*. In these two books, Chaucer's hero also undergoes his purgation, professes his absolute devotion to Criseyde and then, fainting after recognizing his sins, is restored to consciousness in the rapture of passion. He then comes to appreciate as he never had before the beauty of the world available to the virtuous pagan. This he expresses in his hymn (Book III, ll. 1744–71). By the close of the third book, Troilus's passion has indeed made him a model of worldly excel- lence. In the exultation of his love he becomes aware of the grandeur of God in His creation and is purged of the Deadly Sins:

> And though that he be come of blood roial,
> Hym liste of pride at no wight for to chace;
> Benigne he was to ech in general,
> For which he gat hym thank in every place.
> Thus wolde Love, yheried be his grace,
> That Pride, Envye, and Ire, and Avarice
> He gan to fle, and everich other vice.

yheried: praised

We should now trace how he arrives at this state. To do so, we must show how the religious imagery already outlined combines with that of astronomy, astrology and myth to place Troilus's love in a truly cosmic setting.

17

The third book of *Troilus and Criseyde* is perhaps the greatest sustained narrative of erotic joy in English literature. So large a claim is justified by the excellence of the construction and the power of the new vision which sustains it. Here is a rapture that at once absolves the preceding anguish and points to the tragedy to come. Taking up themes that complement and hugely develop the earlier chains of religious imagery, we move from sickness and despair into the radiance of a new presiding deity – celestial and natural Venus.

It is profoundly suggestive that Venus in her two forms should be the inspiration of Book III, but, as we have mentioned, a diversion along the triple medieval paths of astronomy, astrology and myth is necessary to see why. Happily, this will also give some indication of the scale on which the poem operates.

When Troilus rode in through the Dardan Gate, the very image of the virtuous pagan yet unaware of his observing and thoughtful beloved, we saw that 'blisful Venus' was looking favourably down from her seventh sphere. Once again, the medieval scientific reference has a precise meaning and one devoid of both the cold impersonality of modern astrophysics and the wishful thinking of a contemporary horoscope. It takes us rather into a universe conceived of as purposeful, loving and serenely organized, a cosmos envisaged in a now abandoned model that we can perhaps think of as being among mankind's happier inventions, but one which for the medieval mind was the work of God.

God – the ultimate source of love – is in that Heaven for which Dante at his most intense is the best cartographer, since he knows that there, where all is *pura luce, luce inteletual, plena d'amore* ('pure and intellectual light and full of love'), the normal categories of time and space break down. This is the realm of the 'unmoved Mover', the motionless initiator of movement in the planets and their crystalline spheres which revolve in their courses above 'this litel spot of erthe'. They revolve above Troilus and us all, not because they are automata set in motion by the divine toy, man (God would not be infinite and transcendent if He were this), but because they themselves desire his love. It is their natural impulse or 'kindly enclyning' to move in such a way. Just as the human mind 'created quick to love, is readily moved towards everything that pleases, as soon as by pleasure it is moved to action', so it is with the planets. Rapturous in the love of their Creator, the great cycles of the cosmos dance their round as an expression of their spiritual love, and do so in circles whose form imitates the perfect form of God. Such is cosmic, spiritual love. Since it profoundly affects the human passion of Troilus and Criseyde, it is necessary to examine it closely.

The first of the revolving spheres, invisible to the mortal eye and yet the largest object in created existence, is the *primum mobile*. This revolves from east to west in a vast circuit lasting twenty-four hours. Beneath it, and retarded by its wake as they follow their slow east–west course, are the hollow transparent globes in which the planets reside. The first of these is the *stellatum*, the sphere of those stars whose positions relative to each other are fixed. Then come the seven planets: Saturn, Jupiter, Mars, the sun, Venus, Mercury and the moon. As each revolves in its sphere because of its 'kindly enclyning' towards God, it moves neither in darkness nor in silence but amid the light of the sun and 'sownes ful of hevenyssh melodie'. This is indeed a vision of the greatest beauty, both stately and conscious. It is conscious because, appertaining to each planet, is its intelligence (known as its 'soul') whose nature it is to be moved by the intellectual love of God and so cause both the planet and its sphere to revolve.

But what of existence below the moon, in other words life in our own and Troilus's sublunary world? This – and the distinction is fundamental – is the realm of Nature and demons, of 'visible and invisible foon', of the corruptible, contingent and mutable. It is also the realm of Fortune who, for Dante at least, was the earth's intelligence. The earth, it should be noted, was considered to be spherical and not flat.

This mutable, sublunary world is also the region of the Four Elements which are made up in their turn from the Four Contraries: hot, cold, moist and dry. In *The House of Fame*, Chaucer adds 'heavy' and 'light' to these. Hot and dry produce fire, the lightest of the elements and the one that has risen to the outer limit of Nature's realm to a sphere beneath the moon. Below fire is the air, which is both hot and moist. Supporting the waters of the seas – themselves made up of cold and moist – lies the cold, dry earth, insignificant in size relative to the cosmos of which it is both the centre and lowest point to which all descends, the influence of the planets especially.

Man, who struts his proud way across this earth, is also (in his physical and emotional existence at least) made up from the Four Contraries. Hot and dry, which constitute fire in the greater world, make choler in the little world of man whose 'choleric complexion' or 'humour' is unsociable, vindictive, highly-strung. Hot and moist – the contraries of air – make blood in a man and lead to the 'sanguine complexion' which is basically cheerful, if capable of short-lived anger. Cold and moist – the contraries which make up water – lead to the 'phlegmatic complexion' which is dull and sluggish. Finally, cold and dry make the 'melancholy humour' which causes people to be intransigent, to nurture long and fretful hatreds and to behave in what we now call a neurotic way. And just as the earth itself is subject to the sway of the planets, so is this world of physical man. The influence of the planets changes both his nature and his fortune.

At this point we move from astronomy to astrology, and, in particular, to the planet Venus. The influence of Venus produces – as we might expect – amorousness and beauty. As a beneficent planet second only to Jupiter, she causes happy events in her role as *Fortuna Minor*, while, as the most beautiful of the astral deities, it is in her power to enhance rhetoric: *soavissima di tutte le altre scienze*, as Dante calls it, 'the loveliest of all the other disciplines' of the *trivium* and *quadrivium*. Venus is the planet of both lovers and love poets – of Troilus, Criseyde and the narrator.

Celestial influence is disseminated through the air and helps to determine a person's life both from the position of the planets at his birth – Venus, the narrator tells us, 'was nat al a foo to Troilus in his nativitee' – as well as at particular moments in his existence, such as when Troilus rode through the Dardan Gate. These concepts raise a number of problems, in particular how influences from the pure and superlunary world can be bad for man and, secondly, how completely the planets really determine the course of his life.

The answer to both questions once again centres around the moral and intellectual qualities a person may possess. Thus while the temperament and fortune a planet sets for a man at his birth can well seem to determine his nature, the exercise of reason should allow him to rise above it. The Church readily accepted that the planets could indeed influence physical properties – the complexions – but, in her attempt to assert the freedom of the will, she suggested that such influences could only motivate a propensity to act, a propensity which, if it clearly inclined to evil, should be resisted. Similarly, the reason why the planets can cause bad effects in the broader social sphere lies in ourselves and not in the stars. We live in a fallen world and so cannot always make proper use of influences that in themselves are good. They become perverted by our own nature. However, while a wise man will always be stronger than the stars, in the third book of *Troilus and Criseyde* celestial Venus is essentially beneficent and her influence is such that it helps to bring the hero to the Earthly Paradise.

It is thus possible to see Venus in her planetary aspect profoundly shaping the destinies of both Troilus and Criseyde, influencing these for temporary good and in a way that relates the lovers to their entire cosmos. Troilus in particular will rise to feel love binding the universe together in the fair golden chain of cause and effect (Book III, ll. 1744–71). There will be aspects of his passion that are indeed good, wholesome and natural.

But we have also seen that Troilus partly surrenders his reason to cupidity and, in so doing, falls into the worship of the goddess Venus – *Venus Naturalis* rather that *Venus Coelestis*. That this worship relates to the blasphemous, parodic imagery of the religion of love is made clear by the Proem to Book III which is, in effect, a eulogy to Venus couched in the language of an invocation to the Virgin.

We have met *Venus Naturalis* twice before: briefly in Book I of *The House of Fame* and again in *The Parliament of Fowls*. In the last she was, as Professor Brewer describes her, 'a moral allegory, signifying selfish, lustful, illicit, disastrous love'. Much of the ingenuity of the medieval mythographers had been expended on her from the time of Fulgentius in the sixth century who had made Venus represent the lust that rises from excess, through Alanus in *De Planctu Naturae* where Venus is an apostate to Nature, revelling with Antigamus or 'Anti-marriage' instead of directing sex to its proper end of wedlock and childbearing, and so to Boccaccio whose *Teseida* is a source for both *The Parliament of Fowls* and *Troilus and Criseyde*. Boccaccio's earthly Venus, like Chaucer's, is associated with the relatively innocent delights of Cupid, then with sighs of frustrated sexual passion, with Priapus, with the loss of chastity, and finally with wealth and voluptuousness. In the *Teseida* she holds Lasci-viousness by the hand, while in the other she displays the apple given to her by Paris. *Venus Naturalis* in her self-indulgent destructiveness is thus clearly associated with the fall of Troy. To apostrophize her in the Proem to Book III is suggestively ironic, and at this point we may remember that on the walls of her temple in *The Parliament of Fowls* were portrayed images of tragic and cupidinous lovers. Among Chaucer's additions to these are

> Tristram, Isaude, Paris, and Achilles,
> Eleyne, Cleopatre, and Troylus.

There can thus be little question that Chaucer followed the tradition which associated the fall of Troy with the vices of *Venus Naturalis*; but, by presenting her alongside her heavenly embodiment, he achieves a broadness and subtlety beyond the reach of a mere moralizer.

18

Having suggested something of the cosmic forces that shape the hero's destiny, we must now examine how that destiny works itself out and then connect Troilus's fate once again to the imagery of the religion of love.

We have seen that the narrative of the third book opens with Troilus lying in breathless expectation of Criseyde. As with the declarations made when she finally arrives, there is a combination here of the most refined, beautifully courteous ardour and the vulgar, almost farcical elements provided by Pandarus's manipulations. Such is the sublunary world. It is Pandarus who has schemed for and partly guided this first encounter, however, and he who now weeps at its beauty. But it is the lovers themselves who provide the solemn and charitable tone. What immediately moves us is the utter sincerity of the hero and the perfection of Criseyde's response (ll. 50–182). For Pandarus, this perfect *exemplum* of a central moment from *fine amour* is nothing less than a miracle. *His* rapture is inevitably comic:

> Fil Pandarus on knees, and up his eyen
> To heven threw, and held his hondes highe,
> 'Immortal god,' quod he, 'that mayst nought deyen,
> Cupid I mene, of this mayst glorifie;
> And Venus, thow mayst maken melodie!
> Withouten hond, me semeth that in towne,
> For this merveille, ich here ech belle sowne . . .'

withouten hond, etc.: 'it seems to me that, because of this miracle, all the bells in the town are pealing without being rung by hand' (i.e. of their own accord)

In its combination of vicarious manipulation, ardour and comedy, this scene of first meeting brings into focus many of the main narrative elements of the poem. Fully to appreciate the handling of the *matière* in *Troilus and Criseyde*, however (the formal control of which is surely one of the supreme intellectual achievements of Middle English literature), we must try to see these elements in the full range of their dramatic and rhetorical relationships.

For example, just as the scene of the confession of love prefigures both the manipulation and the solemn, joyous ecstasy of the later scene of love-making itself, so the confession Pandarus now makes, his admission of the guilt he feels in being a bawd under the guise of *amicitia*, his urging of secrecy and his concern with the perils of a lost reputation, in turn prefigure the characters' later moral anguish. Pandarus's worst fears will be justified. His confession of guilt after Troilus's confession of love points to the fate that is present even in the birth of joy. It challenges the audience to remember what the characters cannot know and reveals an often-used principle of romance: the idea that the narrative, while conceived as a story moving forward in time, is also constructed as a series of incidents in which motifs are repeated with ever greater intensity until all their implications are fully worked out. If the plot is a linear tale, it is also – like the ripples of a stone thrown into a pool – a series of ever expanding concentric circles in which individual themes are repeated and their ever broader implications revealed.

Two consequences follow from this. First, while suggestions of the whole are implicit in any of the parts, that whole cannot be seen until the poem reaches its close – 'th'ende is every tales strengthe'. Secondly, that whole can only be seen from a point outside the circles themselves – by the boy who threw the stone, if you like, but not by the stone itself. This has obvious and important repercussions on the construction of *Troilus and Criseyde*, since it obliges us to view each major element in terms of both the known end of the narrative and the divine surprise of Troilus's redemption. All that precedes it leads inevitably to his death, but, after his demise, we can share with him his view of his destiny. We stand with the hero on the banks of Heaven looking down on events in which we were involved but are now no longer a part. In terms of Book III, the most dramatic use of what we may call this structural and prefigurative irony is seen in Pandarus's supper-party and its aftermath.

Though aware of his guilty and ambivalent position, Pandarus is determined that Troilus (who has forgiven his friend in a torrent of youthful gratitude) shall consummate his love. Occasional meetings have left the young man burning 'for sharp desir of hope and of pleasaunce', but his reason, though wrenched from the proper worship of his Maker, is still strong enough to bridle any need to gossip about his feelings. He lets no one know of his love save Pandarus and Criseyde. In his secrecy lies both a part of his perfection as an exemplar of *fine amour* and the seeds of his later tragedy. In purely social terms, Troilus is an excellent man. He maintains the necessary discretion and so reveals his 'trouthe' to Criseyde. She, greatly pleased, is won ever closer to his love.

Pandarus now casts himself once again as the bawd in the guise of Fortune. Through his 'purveyaunce' – his foresight and willingness to make preparations – he arranges a supper-party at which Criseyde will be present. Troilus easily falls in with his plans to surprise her when this is over. As for Criseyde, it is left for us to decide what she thinks. Pandarus tells her that Troilus will not be at the soirée, but:

> Nought list myn auctour fully to declare
> What that she thoughte whan he seyde so,
> That Troilus was out of towne yfare,
> As if he seyde therof soth or no;
> But that, withowten await, with hym to go,
> She graunted hym, sith he hire that bisoughte,
> And, as his nece, obeyed as hire oughte.

> *list:* pleases   *yfare:* gone   *soth:* truth

To plant the seed of doubt is once more to invite intuition outside the text.

The guests arrive. Troilus, we are told, has been confined in a 'stewe', or small room, since midnight. It is he who is the unseen observer this time. His submission to such a low contrivance is perhaps its own critical comment. Now, however, as the party ends, the real goddess, 'Fortune, executrice of wirdes', supervenes. Under her influence the planets cause a torrential downpour. Pandarus deftly persuades Criseyde to shelter in his house out of the 'smoky rain'. This is at once a delightful social detail and a trap. Like the Wife of Bath, Pandarus is master of the 'olde daunce'. When Criseyde, separated from her ladies, is in bed, Pandarus releases Troilus from the 'stewe' with the promise that 'thou shalt into hevene blisse wende'. The ardent boy prays to Venus and cites (with an unconscious irony we must appreciate) classical precedents of disastrous love as examples of erotic fulfilment. Pandarus, meanwhile, goes to Criseyde.

In terms of both *matière* and *sens*, we have suggested that the scenes which follow are a recapitulation of themes glanced at in the earlier confession of love but now raised to a higher power. They also prefigure the tragedy to come. Let us examine this in more detail.

Pandarus's contrivances and plausible excuses as he tells Criseyde of Troilus's presence in the house have about them those simultaneous elements of vulgar comedy and worldly ruthlessness that were present in the first two books. They suggest the urgent secrecy of *fine amour* but also reveal its perils. Again, there is the hectoring tone familiar from Book I, although this time it is more insistent, more openly sexual. But the true narrative greatness lies in the consequences drawn from the creation of another straw man (Horaste, this time) whom, Pandarus suggests, it is rumoured Criseyde favours. These entirely false tales have supposedly come to Troilus's ears, and so a love that is indeed to be terribly betrayed is brought to its consummation by a lying rumour of an alleged deceit. Criseyde, wholly true for the moment and chaste in her desires, is being willed by her uncle to surrender herself in order to dispel lying rumours of her 'untrouthe'. Trapped by falsehoods that prefigure her own later and all too real betrayal, Criseyde inveighs against the instability of earthly happiness in lines that derive from Boethius. Their formal, non-naturalistic beauty rings out as a comment on the whole poem and on all worldly joy – the very joy that is about to be rapturously experienced (ll. 813–90). 'O brotel wele of mannes joie unstable!' Criseyde's valuation of worldly happiness is horribly, terribly true, yet its full measure can only be appreciated after the ecstasy she and Troilus are about to experience.

All Criseyde's attempts to preserve her chastity, to reassure Troilus of her good faith first by messages and then with a ring set with a blue stone (blue is the colour of fidelity), are to no avail. Above her, the mighty cycles of the planets rain down their influences. Fortune, her victim failing to rise above her, exerts her power. To Criseyde, who we know as a matter of historic fact will be the falsest of women, the world is a sliding and dangerous place where even her purest intentions become smirched with jealousy and rumour. She knows her duties to her honour and her widowed state. She knows the tenderness of her feelings for Troilus. Her heart is moved with genuine charity for his suffering. Her plight is real and pitiable – and false. Pandarus's urgency, however, his reports that seem 'so lyk a sooth' as he tells her of an anguished Troilus on the point of death, the romantic fable (its lies undetected) which he then spins about Troilus coming through the rain to his house, the safety of the house itself and her own desire to do 'al for gode', begin to persuade her. Criseyde is a woman alone and she relies on her only relative to advise her. Pandarus, 'that could so wel fele in every thing', now judges that it is time to bring Troilus on to his created scene. As the boy falls to his knees, so we are again left to imagine the inner secrets of Criseyde's mind for ourselves:

> Kan I naught seyn, for she bad hym nought rise,
> If sorwe it putte out of hire remembraunce,
> Or elles that she took it in the wise
> Of dewete, as for his observaunce;
> But wel fynde I she dede hym this plesaunce,
> That she hym kiste, although she siked sore,
> And bad hym sitte adown withouten more.

observaunce: homage   *siked:* sighed

As Criseyde then makes the great and moving profession of her 'trouthe', the depth of her sincerity points ironically to her later deceit.

We can see her in the full cycle of the story. Troilus, however, can only experience what he sees and hears in this present moment. What he recognizes is the pain the devices of Pandarus have inflicted on his mistress. He is so deeply ashamed, so utterly repentant, that

> ... he felt aboute his herte crepe,
> For everi tere which that Criseyde asterte,
> The crampe of deth, to streyne hym by the herte.

asterte: let fall

Troilus faints in anguish. This is the very image of death, and just as at the close of the poem Troilus will die indeed and his soul be taken up to Heaven, absolved of its sin through the loving mercy of God, so here, after this metaphorical death, Troilus will be revived by the love and mercy of his mistress and enter the Earthly Paradise. Mental anguish and physical collapse will be restored to mental rapture and physical delight. Both will help the hero to perceive a great but limited metaphysical truth – the glory of God in the finite, created world. If we are to appreciate this fully, however, we must return to our model of the medieval universe and in particular to its concept of the little world of man.

Chaucer provides us with an account of Troilus's fainting that is entirely accurate in terms of medieval physiology. He tells us that his spirits were so oppressed by his sorrow that they gathered together and ceased to drive the mechanisms of his body. This means far more than that the lover was in what we now call 'low spirits' – after all, he was despairing. Just as it was necessary to outline the construction of the cosmos to understand how the planets came to influence Troilus's fate, so it is necessary now to describe the physiological model of medieval man to explain Troilus's collapse. In so doing we shall begin to complete our picture of the medieval universe and acquire a vocabulary which is the fundamental language of medieval thought. To use any other is to make Troilus a mirror of ourselves rather than the construction of the poet.

Since the best place to look for such basic information on physiology is an encyclopedia, we should turn to a medieval one – the *De Proprietatibus Rerum* of Bartholomaeus Anglicus. This was helpfully translated by Trevisa and was one of Shakespeare's reference books as well.

We can begin with the contraries of hot and moist that make up a man's blood. This, Bartholomaeus tells us, lies seething in the liver, from whence arises a smoke that becomes refined into the 'natural spirit' which propels the blood through the limbs. Further refined into 'vital spirit' as it enters the head, those parts of the vital spirit that then go to the brain are purified once more into 'animal spirit' of which a quantity motivates the organs of sensation. Those portions of animal spirit left over, however, have two further and crucially important functions. Of an almost immaterial purity, they connect a man's body to his higher faculties. They are, in the noble Elizabethan phrase, 'a true love knot to couple heaven and earth'. Just as the cruder spirits 'worketh in the artery veins and pulses of life', attending to those functions of growth, movement and so on which man's so-called 'vegetable soul' shares with the plants and all living things, so his animal spirits move his 'sensitive' and 'rational' souls – the seats respectively of his 'wits' and his reason. It is these parts of his soul that are blanked out when Troilus faints.

That man has a single, immaterial and immortal soul divided into vegetable, sensitive and rational parts was a long-held and commonplace assumption of the greatest importance. It is found in antiquity and in the Church Fathers. It is central to the Middle Ages, necessary to an understanding of the lyrics of Donne, and recognized by Milton's Satan as he stares in anguished wonder about Eden and glimpses the pristine beauty of a world of 'growth, sense, reason, all summed up in man'. As St Gregory had declared a thousand years before, because man has these all-embracing faculties, 'he is rightly called by the name of the world'. Alanus, Jean de Meung and Gower say the same. Chaucer's Troilus is similarly an epitome of his cosmos and has, therefore, certain responsibilities towards his tripartite soul.

The Parson tells us what these are: 'God sholde have lordshipe over resoun, and resoun over sensualitee, and sensualitee over the body of man.' For the moment, Troilus's manly body is in a dead faint. It will be revived, along with his 'resoun' and 'sensualitee', to rejoice in new, unguessed perspectives of delight. To appreciate what these are, however – to understand the glory of the Earthly Paradise he is about to enter – it is necessary to appreciate his position before he arrives there.

We should begin with his rational soul. This, as man's most exalted gift, the immediate creation of God and wholly independent of the physical world, should, as the Parson says, be ruled by the God who made it. Its true home is above the sphere of the moon. In the strictest philosophical terms – Boethius's terms, in fact – the rational soul has two properties that help it perceive these duties of obedience and aspiration in a fallen world. The first is *ratio*, which is the ability to arrive at the truth by the process of logical argument. The second is *intellectus*, which is the ability to see self-evident truths and grasp them intuitively. Such self-evident and intellectual truths are essentially moral and are therefore concerned with right action. To perceive them – to know the truth – is to recognize a duty that must be obeyed. In the words of the great Elizabethan divine, Hooker: 'Reason is the director of man's will, discovering in action what is good.'

As a sequence of ideas, this is perhaps not difficult to understand. We have *ratio* enough for that. What is much harder is to bring such notions back to life, to understand them as felt and even commonplace experiences. Probably we can never finally do so. We cannot for long disencumber ourselves of what we are. What we can do, however, is to see in what ways we are different. A few moments considering the dark, shapeless mass of repressions, fears and instincts with which contemporary man's model has saddled him should show this. Our heart is full of fear and mixed intentions. Metaphorically it is a place of feeling and physically it is a pump. For Chaucer – and so for Troilus – it was the seat of reason and thus of the divine.

At this point it may be reasonably objected that however good a man Troilus might be and however ardent his 'trouthe', his *intellectus* cannot fully appreciate the divine since he is a pagan (albeit a righteous one) living in the time before Christ. He is necessarily ignorant of the New Testament and revealed truth. This is a profound and important objection, and one which, as we shall see, is fundamental to Chaucer's purpose. The salvation of the 'righteous pagan' was a central problem of medieval English theologians. It absorbed some of the best energies of Langland, the author of *St Erkenwald* (who may have been the Gawain-poet himself), Chaucer, and, among the theologians, Wyclif, Holcot and Bishop Bradwardine. It concerned no less an issue than the power of God's grace, his power to save any sinner. As such, the matter should be approached warily and by way of St Paul, for whom the matter was a problem of practical and immediate importance.

In his Epistle to the Romans, St Paul declares that 'ever since the creation of the world his invisible nature [i.e. God's], namely his eternal power and deity, has been clearly perceived in the things that have been made'. This is magnificently exemplified in Psalm 19, for which only Haydn and the Authorized Version can provide a sufficient music:

The heavens declare the glory of God; and the firmament sheweth his handiwork.

Day unto day uttereth speech, and night unto night sheweth knowledge.

There is no speech nor language, where their voice is not heard.

Their line is gone out through all the earth, and their words to the end of the world. In them hath he set a tabernacle for the sun,

Which is as a bridegroom coming out of his chamber, and rejoiceth as a strong man to run a race.

His going forth is from the end of the heaven, and his circuit unto the ends of it: and there is nothing hid from the heat thereof.

The law of the Lord is perfect, converting the soul: the testimony of the Lord is sure, making wise the simple.

For St Paul, such knowledge of God is innate and written on the hearts of all men. In other words, they can come to it by the exercise of reason or *intellectus*. For those living before the time of Christ, obeying or refusing such law after reason had glimpsed it was a matter of choice or free-will. This is made clear in the rousing challenge of Joshua, who was often considered a 'type' or Old Testament prefiguration of Christ. Among other reasons for this, his name – given to him by Moses – means 'God is salvation'. Joshua is also the Septuagint version of Jesus:

Now therefore fear the Lord, and serve him in sincerity and faithfulness; put away the gods which your fathers served beyond the River, and in Egypt, and serve the Lord. And if you be unwilling to serve the Lord, choose this day whom you will serve, whether the gods your fathers served in the region beyond the River, or the gods of the Amorites in whose land you dwell; but as for me and my house, we will serve the Lord.

It was St Paul's view, however, that instead of following the dictates of reason and so enlightening their souls, most pagans had preferred the gods on the wrong side of the river. The Epistle to the Romans must serve as a partial gloss for Troilus's love:

. . . Therefore God gave them up in the lusts of their hearts to impurity, to the dishonouring of their bodies among themselves, because they exchanged the truth about God for a lie and worshipped and served the creature rather than the Creator, who is blessed for ever! Amen.

In abandoning reason, these people have fallen into sensuality, the lower realm of the sensitive soul. How does this operate?

Just as the rational soul has two faculties, so has its sensitive compeer. Half of these are what we still call the five senses – touch, taste, sight, smell and hearing. The rest are the five 'inward wits'. Of these, memory is the most readily understood today, and it is of course the memory of Criseyde that Troilus carries with him from the temple. That he was immediately attracted to her was a function of the *vis aestimativa*. This is 'estimation', or, more easily, 'instinct'. It is the 'lawe of kynde' and the drive which causes Chauntecleer 'naturelly' to flee his enemy the fox. When Criseyde becomes 'this in blak, lykinge to Troilus', that is, when he recognizes her superiority to other women, he is using what the medieval period described as 'common-sense'. This is a concept quite different from that implied by our own use of the term. Medieval common-sense is the knowledge that the five senses are working properly and the subsequent ability to make distinctions based on the information they provide. Lastly, when Troilus makes 'a mirour of his minde' in which he sees his beloved 'al holly hir figure', he is being first of all 'imaginatif' – in other words, he is constantly thinking about her – and secondly, when considering her several excellences, separating and uniting them, he is using his *vis phantastica* – his 'fantasy'. This is a word which, like 'imagination' and 'common-sense', remains in the language to denote a wholly different set of values and concepts. But in all the uses of the sensitive soul – and in strictly theological terms – what Troilus is doing here is moving towards sin. His thoughts are that 'delectation' which leads the will to consent to error.

We have seen that it was St Paul's view that while the rational pagan could indeed glimpse a portion of the truth through his reason, he was not strong enough to live by his rational soul alone. Paul's description of the general run of fallen pagans who have lapsed into the realm of the sensitive soul is particularly abrasive:

They were filled with all manner of wickedness, evil, covetousness, malice. Full of envy, murder, strife, deceit, malignity, they are gossips, slanderers, haters of God, insolent, haughty, boastful, inventors of evil, disobedient to parents, foolish, faithless, heartless, ruthless.

The greater cycle of the Troy story can perhaps be seen in these terms, but surely they are too harsh for the Troilus of Book III. The difference derives from Chaucer's use of the two other traditions which he then skilfully merged. The first of these is the limited but very real excellence that the code of behaviour demanded by *fine amour* placed on a man. Criseyde, as we have seen, provides perhaps the best description of this, recognizing that it goes far beyond a disdain for 'rudeness and poeplish appetite' to embrace the philosophical qualities of 'moral vertu, grounded upon trouthe'. These values should then be seen as an expression of that unenlightened excellence which can lead a virtuous pagan to the Earthly Paradise. This, as we have seen, is a place which prefigures Heaven and expresses that beatitude and innocence available to men unenlightened by Christian revelation. An important passage from Dante's *De Monarchia* describes the position exactly:

Ineffable Providence has set two ends for men to strive towards: the beatitude of this life, which consists in the operation of his own virtue and is figured in the Earthly Paradise, and the beatitude of eternal life, which consists in the enjoyment of the vision of God, to which man's own virtue cannot ascend unless assisted by divine light, which is to be understood by the Heavenly Paradise . . . We come to the first by the teaching of philosophy, if we follow it by exercising the moral and intellectual virtues; to the second by spiritual teaching, which transcends human reason, if we follow it by exercising the theological virtues, faith, hope and charity.

It is precisely this Earthly Paradise Troilus is to enter in Book III. Through the exercise of his secular moral qualities his *intellectus* will discover the beatitude of this life. Then, through the operation of Fortune, he will lose it. There will be the suffering of the later books. Finally, through the unexpected mercy of God, the Heavenly Paradise will be opened to him at the end of Book V. He will be saved by forces greater than human reason. The circular construction of the plot is again its own perfect comment. To appreciate the Heavenly Paradise of the last book, however, we shall have to look more closely at the Earthly Paradise of the third.

19

Troilus is roused from his faint by that combination of worldly comedy and true compassion which characterizes the central sections of the poem. We laugh as we are deeply moved, and the paradox makes us aware of life in the sublunary world. The body and exhilarating physical touch are now, with the intense idealism built around such things, the great matter of the narrative.

To the followers of *fine amour*, the body is a tabernacle. To the worldly, the practical and the necessarily more cynical, it is here an object for first aid. Pandarus pulls off most of Troilus's clothes and throws him into Criseyde's bed. The faintingly physical must be restored through 'divine' and merciful touch. Criseyde kisses Troilus into consciousness, and Pandarus – irrelevant now – moves aside as the heroine hears Troilus's full 'confession'. The level of *matière* is excellently wrought, and yet, beneath its farce and charity, lies the serious and commenting level of *sens* – the imagery of extreme idealism. Like Dante on the highest levels of Purgatory, Troilus has been purged of the Seven Deadly Sins and has glimpsed the possibility of the Earthly Paradise. It is only after his loss of consciousness, his immersion in Lethe and subsequent confession, however, that he can enter it. And, just as Dante emerges into that realm of unenlightened human perfection with a new guide – the Beatrice who shrives him and leads him upwards – so Troilus is no longer under the sway of Pandarus but offers 'al in goddes hand', and surrenders to Criseyde and the first encounters of a bliss through which he will perceive the full 'trouthe' and glory of the world as men without Christianity can perceive it. All the great forces in the poem have led to this: the 'lawe of kynde', the manipulation of Pandarus, Troilus's desire, Fortune, the stars, and, most movingly of all, Criseyde's own choice:

> 'Ne hadde I er now, my swete herte deere,
> Ben yold, ywis, I were now nought heere!'

yold: yielded

Chaucer's description of the love-making is a supreme creation of art and is achieved in a number of ways. The suggestion of a multiple consciousness again reflects the fallen world with a generous, wise complexity. There is, first of all, the sense of sheer release offered by the plot and the power of the narrator's sensuality. More subtly, there is the appeal to the 'experience' of the audience – the imagined group of initiates in love – which is couched in terms of the assertion that physical bliss is indeed a righteous thing, a beauty that the narrator in his in-experienced state cannot fully express. It is left to us, the allegedly wiser, to recreate the love-making out of our own memories. We must evaluate it by what *we* know and recreate the ardour by our own. Inspired by the narrator, we are asked to recall our experiences of bliss. Perhaps, in view of the constant, monitory ground-bass of disillusion, we are also asked to remember our experience of those who, greatly loved, faded into the deceitful light of common day. A technique of suggestion that through-out has lent the greatest subtlety to the characterization is here perfectly adapted to one of the central problems of literature – the depiction of sexual ecstasy. By referring this to ourselves, the narrator asks us to recreate the joy with an authority only we can judge. He thereby absolves himself from any charges of prurience or vulgar effect. And the love-making eventually ends, as it must, with gentle humour and quiet praise:

> Resoun wol nought that I speke of slep,
> For it acordeth nought to my matere.
> God woot, they took of that ful litel kep!
> But lest this nyght, that was to hem so deere,
> Ne sholde in veyn escape in no manere,
> It was byset in joie and bisynesse
> Of al that souneth into gentilesse.

We have given our experience to others. Now, as morning steals across Troy, the two lovers utter their *aubades* or songs of dawn parting. Each is a perfect lyric, and intermingles the memory of joy (all worldly pleasure is transitory) and a hatred of the day (all courtly love is secret). These

speeches, non-naturalistic, conventional yet true to experience, are
celebrations of a rapture that is already the victim of time and subject
to separation. Each aspect of these lovers' ecstasy prefigures its destruction. Nowhere is this more plangently expressed than as each
plights 'trouthe': the woman with a passionate sincerity it will be
beyond her strength to maintain, the man with an integrity it will be
his tragic glory to keep.

Yet eventually they are obliged to part, and, with the vulgar sun, comes
Pandarus, intruding his near fabliau presence into the romance. He
embraces Criseyde – an extraordinary moment – and then, receiving
Troilus's rapturous thanks, admonishes him with words made the more
dreadful by their source:

> 'For of fortunes sharpe adversitee
> The worst kynde of infortune is this,
> A man to han ben in prosperitee,
> And it remembren, whan it passed is . . .'

As Paolo and Francesca, the damned yet sublime lovers of the *Inferno*,
reflecting the words of Boethius, declare:

> 'Nessun maggior dolore
> che ricordarsi del tempo felice
> nella miseria.'

Yet, for all these suggestions of future woe, the overwhelming impression achieved amid the irony is of a shared and all but inexpressible
rapture of trust and beauty. Finally, crucially, there is also the expression
of a joy that approaches mystical intuition. In the sublimity of his loving
ardour, Troilus the virtuous pagan perceives the working of a God
whose mercy, unknown to him, will save his soul after its loss of fleeting,
worldly pleasure:

> 'Love, that of erthe and se hath governaunce,
> Love, that his hestes hath in hevenes hye,
> Love, that with an holsom alliaunce
> Halt peples joyned, as hym lest hem gye,
> Love, that knetteth lawe of compaignie,
> And couples doth in vertu for to dwelle,
> Bynd this acord, that I have told and telle.
>
> 'That that the world with feith, which that is stable,
> Diverseth so his stowndes concordynge,
> That elementz that ben so discordable
> Holden a bond perpetuely durynge,

That Phebus mote his rosy day forth brynge,
And that the mone hath lordshipe over the nyghtes, –
Al this doth Love, ay heried be his myghtes!

'That that the se, that gredy is to flowen
Constreyneth to a certeyn ende so
His flodes that so fiersly they ne growen
To drenchen erthe and al for evere mo;
And if that Love aught lete his bridle go,
Al that now loveth asondre sholde lepe,
And lost were al that Love halt now to-hepe.

'So wolde God, that auctour is of kynde,
That with his bond Love of his vertu liste
To cerclen hertes alle, and faste bynde,
That from his bond no wight the wey out wiste;
And hertes colde, hem wolde I that he twiste
To make hem love, and that hem liste ay rewe
On hertes sore, and kepe hem that ben trewe!'

hestes: decrees   *gye:* direct, control   *heried:* praised   *rewe:* pity

By virtue of its quality, position and content, this lyric is of great importance to Book III and to *Troilus and Criseyde* as a whole. Editors usually and rightly comment that since Chaucer had already used the praise of Venus that Boccaccio's hero utters at this point, he substituted for it a lyric based on ideas derived from *The Consolation of Philosophy*, in particular the eighth metrum of the second book and sixth prose of the fourth. However, this substitution is far more than an example of skilful invisible mending, the idea that 'your old smock brings forth a new petticoat'. At the pinnacle of his worldly fortunes, Troilus's *intellectus* perceives and praises the great, self-evident truth that a single God orders the universe through love. He has approached that state where, in St Augustine's words, the soul moves 'towards the enjoyment of God for its own sake'. This is true *caritas*. In achieving this, Troilus has advanced as far as the virtuous pagan may and so earned his sojourn in the Earthly Paradise. Dante, it will be recalled, had defined this state as 'the beatitude of this life', one which was achieved by exercising the moral and intellectual virtues. It was a limited but very real excellence. It is part of Chaucer's vision to see that its pursuit was not incompatible with the practice of *fine amour*. Indeed, this is the core of his praise of human love. At its height, human love really can lead to a genuine intuition of the divine. This is just the conception which the final lyric of Book III expresses. Since its philosophical content is modelled on Boethius, we should turn to him (or, more precisely, to his mentor Philosophy) whose teaching inspires the moral and intellectual virtues. In the fourth book of the *Consolation*, Philosophy is concerned as part of her treatment of Boethius's human unhappiness to explain to him 'the oneness of Providence, the course of Fate, the haphazard nature of the random events of chance, divine knowledge and predestination, and the freedom of the will'. In other words, she wants to explain to him the fundamental truths of existence.

We have recognized that the proper starting-place for such a discussion is the distinction Philosophy draws between Providence and Fortune or Fate. As Philosophy says, 'the order of Fate is derived from the simplicity of Providence'. It follows from this that, in the mutable, sublunary world:

> The course of Fate moves the sky and the stars, governs the relationship between the elements and transforms them through reciprocal variations; it renews all things as they come to birth and die away by like generations of offspring and seed. It holds sway, too, over the acts and fortunes of men through the indissoluble chain of causes; and since it takes its origins from unchanging Providence, it follows that these causes, too, are unchanging. For the best way of controlling the universe is if the simplicity immanent in the divine mind produces an unchanging order of causes to govern by its own incommutability everything that is subject to change, and which will otherwise fluctuate at random.

It is this heroic perception of divine and loving constancy that Troilus achieves in the Earthly Paradise of Book III and expresses in his lyric. In technical terms, as a pagan schooled by virtue or human 'trouthe', his *intellectus* has briefly advanced beyond the fallacious deities of Trojan belief to the self-evident truths of monotheism and divine love. He has realized 'the beatitude of this life' and perceived a portion of the divine truth written in his heart. We might say he has made the choice of Joshua and achieved the knowledge of David. It is of the greatest moment that at this, the happiest period of his mortal existence, the lover offers us neither an invocation of pagan deities nor a ballade in praise of his mistress. Instead, he sings a philosophical lyric than may properly be called a psalm or hymn. This is at once the highest moment of earthly achievement and a prefiguration of the 'pleyn felicitee' that Troilus will know when, after his death and the benevolent intervention of God, he is brought to the Heavenly Paradise. Such beatitude, however, can only be realized by forces beyond *intellectus*, by what Dante calls that 'spiritual teaching, which transcends human reason'.

20

In the *Divine Comedy*, Beatrice is an aspect of God's grace who leads Dante beyond the Earthly Paradise to Heaven itself. He enters that region where human thought eventually pales before revealed truth. In Chaucer's poem, Criseyde is both an embodiment of the limited 'grace' offered by the religion of love and the very human victim of politics and her own weakness. She personifies the world. She cannot be a guide to Heaven. Rather, she is separated from Troilus and then abandons him. He is obliged to descend from the Earthly Paradise and return to despair, to an earthly region where the workings of human reason are clogged with misery.

The public events of Book IV are brief and brutal. The war is now going against the Trojans and we should note how its worsening measures the ever greater distance between Troilus and Criseyde. In a time of truce, Calkas, once again assuring the Greeks of the city's inevitable destruction, begs them to 'rewe on this olde catif in distresse' and arrange that the one real treasure of his life be exchanged for Antenor. The Trojan parliament, in the anguished, silent presence of Troilus, bows to this under pressure from the people. They are unwitting fools who are not only destroying the secret happiness of their hero but blindly willing their own destruction. A ruthless public ignorance thus leads to the destruction of both Troilus and Troy. Such is the public action of the fourth book. The poetic greatness lies in the long and various expressions of despair, the hopeless ways in which the characters try to influence the *matière* of the work, and in the sad commentating level of *sens*.

The decisions of the Greek and Trojan parliaments emphasize both the secrecy and the fragility of *fine amour*. Without the public vow of marriage, the relationship between Troilus and Criseyde offers no defence against the rough uses of the world. And marriage is out of the question. In the happy stage of their love, marriage was never an issue; now it is impossible. Troilus knows full well that it would be pointless to ask his father for Criseyde's hand. Priam has made a decision in parliament that he cannot revoke. Besides, such a request would inevitably seem strange, while the asking of questions would reveal secrets discreditable to Criseyde. For the moment, an elopement is out of the question too. First of all, the Trojan War itself is the result of 'ravysshing of wommen so by myght', and, particularly since it is now going so badly, for Troilus to 'erre' in this way would seem singularly reprehensible. But the chief argument against an elopement is that it would distress Criseyde by bringing 'disclauendre too hire name'. Ironically, the all important theme of reputation, which was not a problem in more prosperous times, is now sounded. The 'gentil' behaviour that was the ground of the affair must at all costs be maintained. Tragically, it offers no escape:

> 'Thus am I lost, for aught that I´kan see.
> For certeyn is, syn that I am hire knyght,
> I moste hire honour levere han than me
> In every cas, as lovere ought of right.
> Thus am I with desir and reson twight:
> Desir for to destourben hire me redeth,
> And reson nyl nat, so myn herte dredeth.'

levere: rather   *twight:* drawn

From the heights of understanding a virtuous pagan can achieve in the Earthly Paradise, Troilus rapidly descends into despair. After his vision of an orderly world thrilling with the love of God, there is now only the false, anguished view of a universe under the sway of the blind goddess. Fortune – *imperatrix mundi* – is the muse of Book IV, and Troilus's complaint to her is one of the most moving of the formal and non-naturalistic speeches in the poem. Fortune's deceitfulness after his service horribly prefigures Criseyde's treachery; while, as Troilus invokes his own soul, his eyes that delighted in Criseyde's presence, and his mistress herself, the utter 'trouthe' of his devotion is assured. He is bound wholly to 'the creature rather than the Creator'. Our sympathies are deeply roused, and our awareness of Troilus's plight is made the more painful as we measure its very real human suffering against what is – in philosophical terms – its folly.

Troilus had once a sure understanding of the universe. Now, at the start of Book IV, he can be likened to the dismayed Boethius at the opening of the *Consolation*. There, Boethius is questioned by Philosophy:

'Tell me, then, since you have no doubts that the world is governed by God, what are the means by which you think He guides it?'

'I can't answer the question,' I replied, 'because I don't understand what it means.'

'I was right, then,' she said, 'in thinking that something was missing. Your defences have been breached and your mind has been infiltrated by the fever of emotional distraction. So tell me, do you remember what is the end and purpose of things and the goal to which the whole of Nature is directed?'

'I did hear it once,' I said, 'but my memory has been blunted by grief.'

So has Troilus's. It is not Philosophy who comes to him now, however, but Pandarus.

Once again Pandarus sees his friend longing for death and is deeply moved. But this time he is all but powerless. There are the same tearful sentiments of *amicitia* we saw in Book I, but the offered advice is glib. The idea that Troilus has had his full measure of delight, that there are other girls and new loves to chase, is particularly flat and degrading. To be fair, Pandarus 'roughte not what unthrift that he seyde', but his 'lechecraft' is very far from the medicine offered by Boethius's mentor. In his own mind, Troilus is bound for death (he does not know how true this is), but the ironies of the circular construction of the narrative are particularly exact when Pandarus asks if Criseyde knows of Troilus's pain, finds that she does not, and arranges a night-time meeting between them. The action of the poem up to the early stages of Book III – an action that has led to the greatest joy – is now recapitulated in a way that can only lead to sorrow. The tearful meeting of the lovers in the fourth book should be compared with their ecstasies in the third. First, however, Criseyde has to be brought to her lover.

As she sits among her cloying, sentimental friends, the purity of Criseyde's 'trouthe' is strongly reinforced; but it is only when she can be alone that the fullness of her passion expresses itself. In the church of love, her 'trouthe' is such that she is prepared to be one of love's martyrs. She hopes to be renowned for her faithfulness. The tragic irony of this is intense, while the narrator's commentary again heightens its dignity by the suggestion of his own defects:

> How myghte it evere yred ben or ysonge,
> The pleynte that she made in hire destresse?
> I not; but, as for me, my litel tonge,
> If I discryven wolde hire hevynesse,
> It sholde make hire sorwe seme lesse
> Than that it was, and childisshly deface
> Hire heigh compleynte, and therfore ich it pace.

pace: let it pass

Once more, it is Criseyde's pity for Troilus's distress that results in their meeting, their last intimate embrace. The narrative motifs that led to joy and human excellence now lead to despair.

The section that follows, Troilus's soliloquizing debate on the nature of Fortune, is one of the most difficult in the entire poem, and was almost certainly a later addition. If we interpret it as being either the moral of the work or an expression of Chaucer's own philosophy, we shall go badly astray. It is a dramatic moment, and, in line with the rhetorical tradition, we should take Milton's advice and consider 'not so much what the poet says, as who in the poem says it'. The speaker here, of course, is an anguished boy on the point of suicide. His lost joy and insight are based on a secret, worldly love that is left quite defenceless when threatened by the public world. At the height of rapture, joy led to an insight into human excellence. An overwhelming sense of bliss resulted in Troilus's rational soul – his *intellectus* – perceiving the excellence of a loving God. Now, in his despair, Troilus can no longer grasp such great and self-evident truths. There is only his *ratio*, its workings impeded by wretchedness, to guide him into logical error. For Troilus, the great truth is now his despair. He can only envisage himself as a victim. He utterly surrenders one of his noblest human attributes: his free-will. He can see himself only as Fortune's slave, the victim of powers beyond his control. His agile, erring mind tries to prove this in a dozen ways. His arguments, like those in his hymn at the end of the third book, derive from Boethius. Now, however, instead of allowing him to see great if limited truths, Troilus can only demean his own nature and, in so doing, win our pity. We know he is suffering and we know his reasoning is wrong. His God is no longer a source of cosmic love but an inert proposition in a false argument. As the soaring eagle of the *Paradiso* tells Dante, whose vision at this time is similarly clogged with human error: 'You are like one who knows a thing well by its name but cannot perceive its quiddity [its true essence] unless someone sets it forth.' But there is no one to set forth the true nature of God for Troilus. Once he perceived it in his joy, now he is blind with grief. He is lost in the wandering maze of false speculation and the effect is both painful and comic. We are moved by the anguish, saddened by the falsity of the argument, and amused by the would-be philosopher's tongue-tied, desperate stumbling:

> 'And over al this, yet sey I more herto,
> That right as whan I wot ther is a thyng,
> Iwys, that thyng moot nedfully be so;
> Ek right so, whan I woot a thyng comyng,
> So mot it come; and thus the bifallyng
> Of thynges that ben wist bifore the tyde,
> They mowe nat ben eschued on no syde.'

This is unenlightened human reason, and

> 'Io veggio ben che già mai non si sazia
>   nostro intelletto, se 'l ver non lo illustra
>   di fuor dal qual nessun vero si spazia.'

(*I see well that there can be no satisfaction for our intellect unless illuminated by that truth beyond which no truth ranges.*')

In the Earthly Paradise, Troilus had glimpsed that light. Now it is extinguished. Human reason is not the final answer to human problems.

In terms of a fourteenth-century audience, Troilus's grappling with free-will and predestination as part of the larger range of issues concerning Fortune, Providence, faith and salvation suggest the very considerable degree to which these issues had become matters of debate among well-informed laymen. Chaucer's own translation of Boethius and much of the content of *Piers Ploughman* witness to this, and it is right to see the Oxford theologians especially as the originators of it. Duns Scotus (*c.* 1265–1308) and his school, for instance, bringing to theology the rigour of the geometer, had set out to demonstrate the logical properties of theological terms. However, the nature of God cannot be a distinct object of knowledge dependent on man's description. Extreme rationalism came, therefore, to be regarded with suspicion. In particular, the condemnation in 1277 of over 200 theological propositions based purely on rationalism and put forward by the Arts Faculty in Paris resulted in those theologians who wished to remain orthodox being obliged to consider the truths of revelation quite as much as those of deduction. It was now held that natural reason could deduce only what were seen as being probable truths. In other words, there was a sphere in which man's natural intellectual abilities could provide likely guidance. Beyond and above this, however, were the inscrutable workings of God and the need for faith. It is with these that the bewildered Troilus ends his lament. He surrenders – finally and properly – not to Fortune but to Providence.

The intrusion of the worldly Pandarus at this point is a brilliantly contrived effect. Just as in the first book, when he interrupted Troilus's abject misery and suggested that the boy should make some positive effort to win his own redemption, so here Pandarus's vulgar commonsense as he tells the lover that Criseyde has not yet gone casts an ironic light on Troilus's grief. Besides, according to Pandarus, Criseyde 'hath som-what in hir hertes privetee' that might 'distorbe' their apparently inescapable separation. Troilus should go to her to find out what this is. Once again, the young lover is being urged to take the initiative over his fate.

The last intimate meeting of the two lovers takes up the remainder of Book IV and is one of Chaucer's most sustained passages of high sentiment. It is also constructed with that continuous irony, both tragic and prefigurative, that is the very nature of the whole poem.

The lovers come together in shared and fainting grief. Troilus genuinely believes that Criseyde is dead and begins to lay out her body in preparation for her funeral. This is no oblivion before being raised into the Earthly Paradise through a lover's 'grace', however. The metaphors of the worldly religion of love have evaporated. Instead of salvation there is only hatred of Fortune and 'Jove'. Suicide is the one possible release. In terms of Christian religion there is only the ultimate sin of despair which ensures damnation. But Troilus is saved by Criseyde's recovery. Just as she had kissed him back into life after his faint, so he

> Took hire in armes two, and kiste hire ofte,
> And hire to glade he did al his entente;
> For which hire goost, that flikered ay on lofte,
> Into hire woful herte ayeyn it wente.

For the horrified Criseyde it is 'grace' indeed that she stirred. She then declares:

> '. . . lat us rise, and streght to bedde go,
> And there lat us speken of oure wo.
> For, by the morter which that I se brenne,
> Knowe I ful wel that day is nat far henne.'

morter: candle used as a clock

This is one of the most moving moments in the whole poem. Having been roused from a dead faint and thoughts of death, the two lovers once again share the same bed. But the inevitable contrast with Book III shows to what state they have come. Instead of rapture leading to divine insight, there is exhausting pain and the simple, human truth that they have only each other, only their little plans and contrivances against fate. These they discuss as the dawn threatens their intimacy.

The only hope that is left to them is Criseyde's 'trouthe' – the very virtue we know she will destroy. She insists throughout that her integrity is constant. She promises that Troilus will see her again – within ten days. They have often been parted for longer. Besides, there is, she believes, the possibility of peace between the Greeks and the Trojans. They are now talking as if the war will soon be over. Of course it will be, but in ways that Criseyde cannot foresee. For the brief, pathetic present she is adamant that things will get better. Above all, she insists that she can be trusted:

> And treweliche, as writen wel I fynde,
> That al this thyng was seyd of good entente;
> And that hire herte trewe was and kynde
> Towardes hym, and spak right as she mente,

And that she starf for wo neigh, whan she wente,
And was in purpos evere to be trewe:
Thus writen they that of hire werkes knewe.

starf: died

There is no apparent reason to doubt this, yet Troilus is uneasy. He fears Calkas's influence over his daughter once she is outside the city walls. He is afraid of the worldly, lusty Greek knights. In the face of Criseyde's absolute protestations of devotion, he doubts her and suggests they elope. Criseyde again summons her 'trouthe' and counters Troilus's proposal with strong arguments. Troy needs her hero. If peace were achieved, Troilus would not be able to return to his own city for very shame. By eloping, he will lose his honour and the people will condemn him for 'lust voluptuous and coward drede'. Criseyde's own name besides – and this is perhaps the cruellest irony – would become 'spotted' by her agreeing to the elopement. She urges that the only thing left to them is that they make a virtue of necessity and trust each other. Still Troilus is not reassured. Finally Criseyde rounds on him – it is the first and only argument we see them have – and berates Troilus's lack of trust. She insists again and again on her fidelity, on her ability to contrive things so that they will meet once more. With the greatest irony, she even commands that Troilus be faithful to her while she is away. At last he vows the fidelity it will be his tragedy to keep, and she, reassured, provides that beautiful description of the reasons why she first gave him her love. At the very moment of their parting, confident in a faith we know she will break, Criseyde rises to her supreme moment of moral value in the poem. She knows that it has been her great good fortune to love and be loved by the very embodiment of human excellence. She knows what such excellence is and she knows its worth. In their last private moments together, Criseyde reveals the value of the whole affair, her own perception of 'moral vertue, grounded upon trouthe'. The lovers kiss, and then, as the sun rises, they part.

21

The last book of *Troilus and Criseyde* is an almost unbearable picture of an ever deepening grief. Only at the end – and in a quite unexpected manner – will this anguish be assuaged through the mercy of God and in a way that brings to a conclusion the entire import of the poem.

We are presented at the start with the sudden appearance of Diomede as he comes to lead Criseyde to both her traitor father in the Greek camp and her betrayal of her lover. Troilus is part of the attendant company. Patiently suppressing his grief, he is yet sure, despite all his beloved's promises, that she will betray him: 'He hadde in herte alweyes a manere drede'. For the moment, however, her grief seems to equal his. She is silent, and Troilus's only words are addressed to her: 'now holde youre day, and do me nat to deye'. We are reminded – if we need to be – that Criseyde has promised they will meet again in ten days' time.

When Troilus has gone, Diomede symbolically takes the bridle of Criseyde's horse and leads her towards her destiny. Where Troilus in his purity and innocence had hidden his love, seeing no way to bring it to its consummation, Diomede at once schemes to make himself acceptable. His guile and suddenness are both in vulgar contrast to Troilus's courtship. As Diomede plays on Criseyde's isolation, swears on his truth as a knight, and promises that his intentions are chaste and fraternal, so we are instantly revolted by him. Where Troilus was virginal and idealistic, this man, we feel, is an experienced player of the game. His whole self-presentation is a grotesque parody of what we have seen in the last four books:

> 'Thus seyde I nevere er now to womman born;
> For, God myn herte as wisly glade so,
> I loved never womman here-biforn
> As paramours, ne nevere shal no mo.
> And, for the love of God, beth nat my fo,
> Al kan I naught to yow, my lady deere,
> Compleyne aright, for I am yet to leere.

> 'And wondreth nought, myn owen lady bright,
> Though that I speke of love to yow thus blyve;
> For I have herd er this of many a wight,
> Hath loved thyng he nevere saigh his lyve.
> Ek I am nat of power for to stryve
> Ayeyns the god of Love, but hym obeye
> I wole alwey; and mercy I yow preye ...'

paramours: mistress   *leere:* learn

Criseyde's answer is merely courteous. Her sorrow still oppresses her as she enters the Greek camp and is embraced by her treacherous father. For the moment, we leave her in her misery.

Back in Troy, the long process of Troilus's anguish begins. It is something Chaucer will present with a numbing insistence and a carefully, cruelly, contrived series of variations. At times the suffering will be almost too intense. Again, it is we who are required to validate the experience by reference to those times in our own lives when we have known the intense isolation of the betrayed. Though Pandarus inevitably intrudes on the woe and – as in the first and fourth books – tries to show Troilus the absurdity of this prostrate grief, his apparent common-sense rings singularly hollow. He dismisses the prefigurative dreams the lover has been having as old wives' tales. Like Pertelote in *The Nun's Priest's Tale*, he thinks that dreams are nothing more than illusions rising from an excess of melancholy humour. Though we know that Troilus's dreams have indeed foretold the truth, for Pandarus dependence on such things ill becomes a man's dignity:

> 'Allas, allas, so noble a creature
> As is a man shal dreden swich ordure!'

Coming from Pandarus, this is a profoundly ironic comment.

In the attempt to rouse Troilus from his evident distress, Pandarus, as always, suggests action. The couple make their visit to Sarpedoun, amid whose astonishing wealth (something the period would have seen as among the joyful if impermanent gifts of Fortune) the young lover feels desperately unhappy. He too once revelled in the gifts that Fortune can give. His whole being was centred around the happiness that goddess could supply. Now Troilus exists as the antithesis of Sarpedoun and is anxious that he and Pandarus should depart.

There follows another view of the anguished waiting in Troy – Chaucer's picture of the doomed lover in the doomed city. Pandarus knows in his heart that all hope is hopeless now, yet he silently attends on his friend and listens to what is one of the most beautiful of the formal and non-naturalistic speeches in the poem: Troilus's lament before Criseyde's deserted palace. Instance by instance, the anguished boy remembers the details of his lost delight. Far from his vision of the whole world thrilling and united in the love of God, he now dwells among broken things, the jagged edges of memory. The songs he writes are short and self-pitying. There are no more joyous hymns, only wretched expressions of despair.

So time passes until the ninth night after Criseyde's departure and the coming day of her supposed return. We have watched the period of Troilus's separation and anguish. We come now to the moment of promised reunion. As we do so, the focus of the narrative is turned on Criseyde. It will remain on her for a long time and we will watch her pass from a longing for death, to her ardent memories of Troilus, her hopes of returning to Troy, and her subsequent fears about stealing away from the Greek camp. In other words, we watch the gradual process of her deceit. At first Criseyde tries to tell herself that she will indeed find the courage to leave the camp, but, as we are shown this, so the narrator suddenly makes us aware of the cruel passing of time. We have watched Troilus counting the hours of separation; we are shown Criseyde summoning up her resolve. We are then told:

> But God it wot, er fully monthes two,
> She was ful fer fro that entencioun!
> For bothe Troilus and Troie town
> Shal knotteles thoroughout hire herte slide;
> For she wol take a purpos for t'abyde.

The sickening cruelty of such weakness prepares us for Diomede's courtship and Criseyde's all but unforgivable deceptions.

Diomede's motives are precisely defined:

> This Diomede, of whom yow telle I gan,
> Goth now withinne hymself ay arguynge
> With al the sleghte, and al that evere he kan,
> How he may best, with shortest taryinge,
> Into his net Criseydes herte brynge.
> To this entent he koude nevere fyne;
> To fisshe hire, he leyde out hook and lyne.

fyne: bring to a conclusion

Where Troilus languished, Diomede is out for the main chance. He sets about his task with callous subtlety. He appears genuinely interested in his prey, and courteous towards her. He is apparently concerned about Troy and Criseyde's unwedded, unhappy state. It 'semed', however, that at first she took no notice. Diomede then increases the pressure. The 'gentilesse' of Troilus is replaced by cynical interest and a mere show of courtly manners. Diomede paints for Criseyde a vivid picture of the fall and destruction of her city. We have moved from the apparent equal combat of the first book to the assurance of imminent destruction. Once again the state of the war measures the state of the lovers.

The lascivious Diomede continues throughout to present himself in what he hopes is his most attractive light. He is, he says, kind, courteous and loyal. He even manages a blush and a stammer – feeble signs of love when compared with Troilus's faint. He also tells Criseyde of his social status. He too is a king's son, and he seems to believe that such gifts of Fortune are to be preferred to the inward excellence of Troilus the virtuous pagan. At last his meretricious pleading begins to have its effect. At their subsequent interview, quite without preparing us, the narrator has Criseyde declare:

> 'But as to speke of love, ywis,' she seyde,
> 'I hadde a lord, to whom I wedded was,
> The whos myn herte al was, til that he deyde;
> And other love, as help me now Pallas,
> Ther in myn herte nys, ne nevere was.
> And that ye ben of noble and heigh kynrede,
> I have wel herd it tellen, out of drede.'

Utter hypocrisy here masquerades as virtuous widowhood. Troilus is not allowed even to exist. Diomede, much encouraged, presses his suit. Criseyde's perception of real human values, the 'moral vertu, grounded upon trouthe' she relished in her true lover, is suddenly replaced by degrading, temporary values snatched from circumstance.

The whole process of Criseyde's deception is superbly achieved. We have known all along it will happen, yet up to this point the narrative register has given every indication that Criseyde will be true. All the workings of her mind we have seen so far have been anguished proofs of her fidelity. The motivation behind her sudden, dire deceit is barely shown to us. Indeed, there is only the one stanza quoted above to set against all that has gone before. By refusing fully to explain her treachery, Chaucer suggests the unfathomable, unknowable quality of other people's minds and emotions. As a result, we are profoundly shocked, deeply hurt and resentful – yet we have known all along that this betrayal will take place. To make the inevitable so shocking is a profound artistic achievement.

The narrator meanwhile retreats behind his sources as if to make sure of his own lack of responsibility for the treachery he has just presented. 'The storie telleth us', 'I fynde ek in the stories elleswhere', he declares as he concentrates our resentment at Criseyde's behaviour on the slight and brutal detail of her offering Diomede a brooch that Troilus had once given her as a love token. The gift of this brooch is a tiny act of pure and gratuitous treachery – and Criseyde knows it is. While she cannot imagine the appalling consequences this wretched action will have, her lament for her lost reputation which follows is deeply and immediately moving. Criseyde knows her own depravity and weakness, and she knows that she cannot rise above them:

> 'But, Troilus, syn I no bettre may,
> And syn that thus departen ye and I,
> Yet prey I God, so yeve yow right good day,

> As for the gentileste, trewely,
> That evere I say, to serven feythfully,
> And best kan ay his lady honour kepe'; –
> And with that word she brast anon to wepe.

When her lament is over and we have been genuinely moved by the plight of the woman we came so suddenly to despise, the narrator offers us two further stanzas. Both raise to new heights techniques we have seen him use before. In the first of these stanzas he shows his ignorance of the full processes behind Criseyde's motivation:

> But trewely, how longe it was bytwene
> That she forsok hym for this Diomede,
> Ther is non auctour telleth it, I wene,
> Take every man now to his bokes heede;
> He shal no terme fynden, out of drede.
> For though that he bigan to wowe hire soone,
> Er he hire wan, yet was ther more to doone.

wowe: woo

The betrayal is both a mystery and a truth. Further, its very wretchedness is a call to *caritas*, a cause for Christian forgiveness. In the power of the narrator's delicate compassion, our own is kindled:

> Ne me ne list this sely womman chyde
> Forther than the storye wol devyse.
> Hire name, allas! is punysshed so wide,
> That for hire gilt it oughte ynough suffise.
> And if I myghte excuse hire any wise,
> For she so sory was for hire untrouthe,
> Iwis, I wolde excuse hire yet for routhe.

routhe: pity

Only when we have witnessed the betrayal, felt anger, and been urged to forgiveness are we returned to the expectant Troilus and the end of the ten-day period of parting.

Troilus goes out to await the return of his beloved. She does not come. It is crushingly, humiliatingly simple. While we know the reasons for it, Troilus does not. Pandarus guesses the truth, however.

Only after six further days does Troilus abandon hope and, in a wild anguish, prepare himself for death. He also has another prefigurative dream, this time of Diomede as a white boar. Pandarus once again denies the validity of dreams and urges instead that Troilus should write to Criseyde. The beautiful but pathetic letter is sent. An ambiguous answer is returned. All that Troilus seems to have now is his dream of the wild boar. He consults his sister Cassandra about it. She tells her brother the truth: the boar is Diomede. As she reveals this, so Cassandra places Diomede's story in the context of the brutal tale of the fall of Thebes that, we may remember, Criseyde was reading in Book I. It seems as if the whole universe is in a state of constant, mad destruction, an unending cycle of woe and bloodshed. This feeling is reinforced when we hear of the death of Hector, which is, of course, a prefiguration of the death of Troilus himself. He, meanwhile, angrily refuses to believe Cassandra's interpretation of his dream. It is the first and only time we have seen him behave with a cruel lack of good manners. His discourtesy is a measure of his anguish. Above all, Troilus is confused by the vagueness of the letter he has received from Criseyde. Then, finally, he has proof of her deceit. The little brooch, so wretchedly given to Diomede, is discovered on Diomede's captured armour. It tells the whole story.

The lover retreats to the privacy of his chamber for the last time. Once more his thoughts are concerned with death. Again, and in the established pattern, Pandarus comes to him. But this time he is truly powerless: 'A word ne coude he seye.' All that remains are the traces of their friendship and, finally, their shared bitter thoughts of Criseyde.

On the previous occasions when Pandarus had come to the sorrowing Troilus, he had roused him from thoughts of death by plans for action. The only action now is the savage pursuit of death itself. But even here Troilus is for a long time cheated. The last cruel twist of Fortune is that she does not wish Troilus to revenge himself on Diomede by killing his Grecian rival.

The complex conclusion to this great poem now begins. For five stanzas the narrator speaks out in his own voice. He will not tell of Troilus's heroism; his purpose is to speak of his love. He then begs the women in the audience to forgive him if they are angered by his presentation of Criseyde's deceit. He promises them stories of virtuous women, a promise he was partly to keep with the incomplete *Legend of Good Women*. He then warns women to beware of men's deceit. Finally he turns to his own book. At the end of his poem, he addresses his monumental work. Like Dante amongst the shades of the ancient poets, Chaucer knows that he also is part of their company. He knows too that in a mutable world, the very world of his poem, even language is changing and uncertain. He craves above all to be understood.

Then, at what seems to be the end, comes Troilus's death. It is a matter of a single line: 'dispitously him slough the fiers Achille'. We have known all along that we would come to this point – from the very start of the poem the predetermined pattern had been set before us. There is no freedom in the sliding and deceptive world of Fortune. The only true freedom is the truth of God in the permanence of the heavens, and it is into these regions that Troilus now journeys. We are concerned, finally, with his immortal soul. Throughout the poem he had revealed himself as the very model of the virtuous pagan. He had followed human 'trouthe' with utter integrity. At the height of his ardour, his *intellectus* allowed him to glimpse the truth of God written on his heart. Yet this alone could not save him. The foundation of his love was worldly appetite – beautiful, treacherously insecure and ultimately the plaything of Fortune. But he is saved. The excellence he has achieved does not go unrewarded. With the blissful surprise of divine charity, Troilus's soul is freed from the determinist world and its appetites, freed from pain. Amid the harmony of the circling spheres, he learns true felicity and can see the little spot of earth for what it is: a place which, for all the ardour and excellence of the life lived there, is a mere point in the vastness of the cosmos, a place of insecurity, woe and fleeting joy that cannot compare with heavenly bliss. The litany of Cupid that brought him to the Earthly Paradise evaporates in the face of true religion. Just as Troilus went through a metaphorical death to rise to the heights of worldly happiness a virtuous pagan could achieve, so now, with his real death, he enters the Heavenly Paradise through the mercy of God. He finally knows truth indeed.

And it is this perception of the power of the living God that allows Chaucer the narrator to turn to his audience at the close of his work and urge on them the precepts of St Paul. Though descendants of the Trojans and a group of initiates in the fine arts of love, these young people are blessed with a revelation of the divine infinitely more powerful than that available to Troilus. They are Christians. For them there is a higher, surer and more glorious love than *fine amour* – the love of God:

> O yonge, fresshe folkes, he or she,
> In which that love up groweth with youre age,
> Repeyreth hom fro worldly vanyte,
> And of youre herte up casteth the visage
> To thilke God that after his ymage
> Yow made, and thynketh al nys but a faire
> This world, that passeth soone as floures faire.

> And loveth hym, the which that right for love
> Upon a crois, oure soules for to beye,
> First starf, and roos, and sit in hevene above;
> For he nyhl falsen no wight, dar I seye,
> That wol his herte al holly on hym leye.

And syn he best to love is, and most meke,
What nedeth feynede loves for to seke?

Lo here, of payens corsed olde rites,
Lo here, what alle hire goddes may availle;
Lo here, thise wrecched worldes appetites;
Lo here, the fyn and guerdoun for travaille
Of Jove, Apollo, of Mars, of swich rascaille!
Lo here, the forme of olde clerkis speche
In poetrie, if ye hire bokes seche.

repeyreth: return   *faire:* market   *payens:* pagans   *guerdoun:* reward   *rascaille:* mob

And so the poem comes to its end with a prayer which, as we have
seen, derives from Dante. Just as Chaucer showed his hero traversing his
Inferno and *Purgatorio* of love to reach the Earthly Paradise, and then,
through the exercise of God's mercy, revealed his unexpected salvation in
the Heavenly Paradise, so now the earthbound poet and his audience of
lovers look up to those regions where the soul of Troilus is already
saved. Not for them – as yet – is this place of bliss. Rather, as they draw
aside the veils of poetic beauty, listen to the narrator, analyse the subtle
handling of *matière* and the widely ranging concerns of the *sens*, so they
come to appreciate a matured understanding of the glory and limitations
of this world, and relish the hope of mercy and their own salvation. This
great poem, in the authentic medieval manner, speaks finally of God.

THE CANTERBURY TALES

22

Troilus and Criseyde is Chaucer's finest complete achievement, but in
their inexhaustible variety *The Canterbury Tales* (1386/7–1400) contain
the widest range of his poetry. They offer now the heroic, tragic or
pious, now the humorous and downright bawdy. It was probably these
possibilities that caused Chaucer to abandon the earlier *Legend of Good
Women* (a series of narratives based on amatory heroines and parodying
a compilation of saints' legends), well told and technically experimental
though many of these stories are. The ten extensive fragments that make
up the uncompleted *Canterbury Tales* also suggest the encyclopedic
breadth of interests, the awareness of a range of responses, that had
characterized Chaucer's earlier work. It is this wealth of attitudes which
has always been most appealing (fifty-eight substantial medieval manuscripts of *The Canterbury Tales* survive) and which prompted the seven-
teenth-century poet John Dryden to declare: 'Here is God's plenty!' *The*

Canterbury Tales have long established themselves as Chaucer's most popular achievement.

Despite the incomplete and partially unrevised state of the text, it will be useful to start by considering the twenty-four finished or abandoned narratives as a whole. If we ask how the collection might have been perceived by contemporaries, then both the format of some of the manuscripts in which it is preserved, as well as certain aspects of various tales themselves, show that we are dealing not simply with a selection of stories assembled for their own sake, but with a special type of literary compilation that was widely popular in the Middle Ages and was designed to appeal to an audience who sought both 'solas' or mirth as well as that teaching or 'sentence' which was the fruit of a careful interpretation of the text. *The Canterbury Tales* were meant to divert and raise fundamental questions in the minds of their audience. Hence the juxtaposition of fabliaux and other comedy with narratives more obviously serious in intention.

One important element in these last tales especially was the handing on of the wisdom of the past, something we have seen was a major responsibility of all medieval poets. Much of this learning or 'auctoritee' concerns themes that had always been of great interest to Chaucer: Fortune, dreams, married love, sin, and the nature of desire, for example, and it is this that partly explains the disquisitions on philosophy and ethics placed on the lips of the pilgrims and the characters which – imagined characters themselves – they seem to have created. In the margins of the colourfully illuminated Ellesmere manuscript there are even headings to indicate who some of the authorities cited on these topics are. Thus in certain respects *The Canterbury Tales* were perceived by their original audience as a *compilatio*, a collection of wit and wisdom, philosophy and précis, with which preachers and, increasingly, educated members of the laity would also be familiar.

As we might now expect, Chaucer's shrewd and vigorous intellect ensured that such literary imitation was no straightforward matter. *The Canterbury Tales* are not a simple encyclopedia of received ideas. Though the individual works contain digests of Boethius and the Church Fathers, parts of the Bible and the lives of the saints, we should always be aware of who is offering this information and under what circumstances. We saw in our discussion of the *Roman de la Rose* that this was a standard rhetorical requirement. In addition, the humorous and lively context in which much of this material is set nearly always prevents it from being dry or merely didactic. In *The Merchant's Tale*, for example, the great commonplaces of desire and marriage are rehearsed by a lecherous old man and his sycophantic friends. In *The Nun's Priest's Tale*, dream theory is discussed by a couple of chickens. The Wife of Bath – that self-confessed expert on textual interpretation – provides us with truths which she humorously fails to understand. If a medieval encyclopedia was a summa of wisdom, a *speculum* or mirror of truth, *The Canterbury Tales*, summarizing knowledge and reflecting the world, show us how *sentence* is a problematic issue.

An essential aspect of this diversity is Chaucer's vivacious delight in character, detail and incident. The depiction of a pilgrimage was exactly suited to this. Pilgrimage was, first of all, an abiding image in the medieval mind. As the journey of the devout towards some distant shrine enhanced their faith and could bind them together in that state of charity or loving social integration which was the perfect expression of earthly life, so the serious purpose of all existence was reflected in the image of mankind's journey from the city of this world towards the New Jerusalem of the next. The parallel was both very serious and commonplace. Deguileville's *Pèlerinage de la Vie Humaine* was widely known in Lydgate's translation: *The Pilgrimage of the Life of Man*. Chaucer, with far wiser insight, preserved the allegory but revealed how abiding truths are often filtered through the individuals who express them. The timeless reality of man's pilgrimage to God is the *sentence* underlying the work; vivid incident, however, is its *matière*. Hence the snobberies and outbreaks of bickering, the retorts and ripostes that enliven the journey from London to Canterbury. The ideal of pilgrimage quietly informs the whole procession, giving a grander purpose to the noisy expression of daily life, but, by showing the people of fourteenth-century England brought together for the purpose of devotion, it suggests at one and the same time the divine comedy of salvation and the human comedy of earthly existence.

The device also had many literary advantages. First of all it allowed Chaucer to break free from the exclusive world of courtly romance and explore other genres and poetic forms. This in itself was an important artistic step, and his success is a mark of the plenitude of his genius. Because of the wide social sweep that his pilgrims embrace, Chaucer could also give to appropriate figures narratives as different as romance, fabliau, saint's legend, exemplary stories and sermons. Secondly, the pilgrimage was also a most convincing way of binding together such a group of characters. By the apparently simple technique of gathering a heterogeneous collection of men and women in a public house and having them agree to tell what seems originally to have been planned as two stories each both on their way to Canterbury and on their return journey,

Chaucer could develop the diversity of his art to its furthest extent.

The pilgrims themselves are introduced in the General Prologue, and the opening at once reveals Chaucer's mastery. In two verse paragraphs he moves from a grand but precisely evocative picture of spring and potency revived to his own humble faith, from the magisterial sweep of the zodiac to details of the Tabard inn. He pictures the awakening of the whole medieval world, for, while reminiscences of the budding gardens of dream poetry and romance suggest the rousing of human desire, the more earthy feeling of wholesome beauty in these descriptions suggests that experience of God's benevolence and Nature's loving plenitude which we encountered in some Latin philosophical works of the early Middle Ages. Finally, and as an intimate part of this, we see men waking to a new enjoyment of the spirit, a budding of religious devotion after the desolation of winter. It is against such a background of piety, gratitude and renewed feeling that Chaucer describes his pilgrims.

The portraits are extremely vivid. Their informality is also exceptionally subtle. The narrator, for example – Chaucer's image of himself in his own work – is reserved and lacking in self-confidence, as always. Once again, his is evidently to be no authoritative voice, ordering, explaining and telling us what is what. Rather he points to his own deficiencies, his little wit and the chance that he has made mistakes. Chaucer the poet looks on Chaucer the narrator with an eye that bids us correct and interpret what we are shown. He is, for instance, confused by social rank. He does not describe his pilgrims in what some believed was the strict hierarchy of feudalism. Nor is he a polished rhetorician, providing for each of his characters a well-ordered formal portrait. He sees vividly but confusedly, as we all do in a company of strangers. He senses the little groups into which the party gathers and glimpses an embroidered coat, a golden brooch, a wart, an ulcered shin. He is also aware of individual characteristics: ardour, bragging, the open hand, the purse-proud and the devious. We feel his affection or amused contempt as he constantly invites us to interpret, sometimes to judge, but rarely to condemn outright. His ideal characters are, besides, wholly convincing and presented quite without satire or ambiguity. If Chaucer sees detail, he also glimpses something more permanent in the medieval view of mankind, for a background of 'estates' literature with its conventional notions about how members of the social order should be portrayed allowed him to present such model types as the Knight, the Parson and his brother the Ploughman in the familiar feudal terms of those who fight, those who pray and those who work the land. All three are men of deep and attractive integrity, perfectly adjusted to their faith and the world in which they live. Chaucer also shows his affection for the amorous and dutiful young squire and for the Clerk of Oxford – a representative of the contemplative ideal – who is devoted to the unprofitable pursuit of scholarship. Such quiet comparisons and contrasts between the pilgrims are one of the greatest pleasures the General Prologue has to offer.

The portrait of the Franklin with his splendid white beard, love of good living and active interest in social responsibilities suggests Chaucer's qualified admiration for the landed gentry. He is also fascinated by professional skills, whether these are honestly practised, like those of the Yeoman and the Manciple, or practised with varying degrees of deceit, such as are revealed by the Sergeant-of-the-Law, the Shipman and the expensively dressed Doctor. Indeed, Chaucer's knowledge of a wide variety of callings shows his interest in the specialized, individualizing world of work. This is an important and novel aspect of an art so sure of its power that Chaucer can, as we have seen, frequently break the traditional patterns of rhetorical description and, with a deft suggestion of subjectivity, present what seems like life itself.

One result of Chaucer's refusal to conform to the strict rules of type and appearance demanded by the rhetoricians is that he can show his fascination with the ways in which people earn and spend their money. The smug, anonymous Merchant, for example, is characterized largely by his business concerns, whether these are legal or not. The Guildsmen, banded together in a fraternity yet having as little as possible to do with the other pilgrims, also care greatly about revealing the prestige their money brings them. Wealth and social status are again major interests of that most glorious and subtly created character, the Wife of Bath. She too has her skilled trade. She is a weaver. Above all, however, she is gaudy, gregarious and sensual. Five times married and no better than she should be, through what she later shows us of her bursts of laughter and anger, her sheer raucous physical presence, we sense how thoroughly this complex literary creation – part La Veille from the *Roman de la Rose* and part West Country bourgeoise – seems to relish her earthy but monitory existence.

It is an important aspect of Chaucer's artistry that the Wife of Bath makes an effective contrast to the portrait of the Parson which follows. The Parson and his brother the Ploughman vigorously pursue a life of honest poverty and so are truly Christian. But many others who are attached to the Church have been led astray by riches and the delights of the world. In their individuality they fail to conform to the approved type. Through a triumph of daring rhetoric and human sympathy, they blossom as individual characters while their shortcomings are gently exposed. The refined Prioress, for example, has her worldly vanities, while the Monk and the Friar – men supposedly given over to poverty, chastity and obedience – show Chaucer's critical but well-mannered response to abuses in the Church of his day. This was a rare achievement in an age of virulently anti-clerical satire.

Chaucer presents the Reeve (the man who managed the estates of a large landowner) as corrupt and forbidding, while the Reeve's enemy the Miller is vividly characterized through his physical attributes: his oafish strength, red beard, wart and huge mouth. Then come the Summoner and the Pardoner, men who brought people before ecclesiastical courts or who sold forgiveness of sin for cash. Both are sinister and physically repulsive. However, while we are beguiled by their roguery, we should also notice how exaggerated, almost cartoon-like elements mingle here with anti-clericalism and the characters' own perverse or inappropriate interest in dress, money and sex. It is an engaging irony that the occupations of these men of little faith carry with them suggestions of the Last Judgement. The underlying seriousness of the religious life is thus reinforced.

Finally, we are introduced to the Host, Harry Bailey, the genially domineering landlord of the Tabard inn. When the pilgrims have paid their bills, he declares that he will join them on their journey. It is Harry Bailey – a figure somewhat like a Lord of Misrule and almost certainly derived from a living character – who suggests that the pilgrims beguile their time with a story-telling competition, who has himself appointed umpire, and who recommends that the prize for the best tale should be supper at the Tabard paid for at the pilgrims' common expense. Harry Bailey is a remarkable comic invention, and it is his extrovert nature rather than his social rank that makes him the ideal, if not always successful, leader of this lively group. He rouses them all the following morning and organizes the drawing of straws which results, by chance or design (Chaucer's ambiguity about his theme of Fortune is typical), in the Knight telling the first tale.

23

Fortune is again one of the major subjects of this great romance. The poem was a long time in the making, for Chaucer appears to have worked on his narrative 'Palamon and Arcite' and to have abandoned a draft called 'Anelida and Arcite' before he finally decided that the story should become *The Knight's Tale*. Once more the work is modelled on Boccaccio, whose *Teseida*, employing the structure of Latin epic,

Chaucer here greatly reduces in length and also thoroughly medievalizes. Written during the same period as *Troilus and Criseyde*, the poem is similarly concerned with love and war in a non-Christian society and with the philosophy of Boethius. *The Knight's Tale* is, besides, a work of magnificent stateliness and a high degree of formal organization. These qualities contrast strongly with the poet's sombre revelation of the world's violence and uncertainty.

The narrative of *The Knight's Tale* is clearly not original. Boccaccio himself derived much of his material from the Latin poet Statius, and such borrowing – the sense that 'olde stories' are part of received wisdom – is, as we have seen, of great significance to our understanding of much medieval literature in general and *The Canterbury Tales* in particular. It follows that narrative invention was not a principal concern of medieval writers. A poet's interest – and that of his audience – lay partly in how he refashioned received material. Such a procedure makes technique a matter of major importance, and to appreciate what Chaucer is doing in *The Knight's Tale* we need to recover something of his delight in the amplification of detail and description, formal apostrophes and exclamations, laments, set-piece speeches and other devices learned from handbooks on rhetoric such as that by Geoffrey de Vinsauf. Although Chaucer was to satirize the excesses of this work in *The Nun's Priest's Tale*, successful parody relies on a thorough knowledge of the original; in *The Knight's Tale*, an appreciation of Chaucer's rhetoric is fundamental to our response. If we read the work as a novel we shall be disappointed. If we appreciate it as a medieval romance – a slow, gorgeous and serious description of the noble life – then we shall begin to see its mastery.

An account of the plot of *The Knight's Tale* will reveal both its symmetry and its concern with intrusive violence. Once more, the way in which the work is constructed is a special aspect of its meaning. The poem opens with the triumphal return of Theseus and his new bride to Athens, and this delight in lengthy descriptions of pageantry partly sets the tone of the work. However, we should also recognize the concern to present Theseus as a virtuous pagan and an ideal ruler embodying 'gentilesse' and 'pitee' – the medieval aristocratic virtues of courteous and charitable concern. These are revealed particularly when Theseus at once agrees to ride out and avenge a party of Theban widows – noble victims of a gratuitous cruelty – who greet his procession and beg his aid. The best human values and the extremes of fortune are here exemplified, while an accurate picture of medieval warfare is provided when, after Theseus's sack of Thebes, two young and all but identical nobles are found lying together 'nat fully quyke, ne fully dede' in a pile of enemy corpses. This similarity between Palamon and Arcite – for such the two knights are called – is important. Idiosyncrasies of character are not a major element in *The Knight's Tale*, and the close resemblance of Palamon and Arcite – a bond made all the firmer by their sworn and valued friendship – suggests that they are representative figures, part of Chaucer's concern with love and war, Mars and Venus, the presiding deities of courtly man. Like the Parson, the Ploughman and the Knight himself, Palamon and Arcite are easily recognizable types. This is again emphasized when both youths receive the same treatment at Theseus's hand. They are imprisoned without hope of ransom or release. Henceforth, prisons become an image of the human condition in the poem, its benighted suffering and apparent arbitrariness.

We have seen that, besides warfare, a central aspect of the life of courtly man was courtly love. *The Knight's Tale* provides a telling analysis of its nobility and latent absurdity, while also fully recognizing the tragic potential of extreme emotion. At the close of the first part, the poet contrasts his picture of the young knights' prison with the spring garden below, in which the beautiful Emelye is gathering flowers to celebrate May. Throughout the poem, Emelye remains a distant, conventional ideal of virgin loveliness. She is the perfect type of the courtly lady. The narrative irony lies in the fact that she is wholly unaware she has been glimpsed first by Palamon – who is unsure whether she is a woman or a goddess – and then by Arcite. The youths immediately begin to quarrel over a girl it seems unlikely either will ever meet, let alone possess. In the prison of their earthly existence they had once comforted each other with that charitable friendship or *amicitia* which was to be preferred to cupidity. But sexual passion, an irresistible intrusion of violent emotion, has now threatened their affection, and each submits, sighing, to the role of the courtly lover. The content and structure of their laments again show the rhetorical nature of the poem and reveals subtle variations within the conventions of *fine amour*. Arcite's passion is the more physical, while Palamon – in images that conventionally parody the language of Christian faith – declares that to be deprived of Emelye's sight is to die. For him, she is wholly divine.

The Knight's Tale closely examines the relationship between passion and death, and, as we have also mentioned, the arbitrary nature of fortune. This last idea is reinforced when Arcite is suddenly released from Theseus's prison at the request of a mutual friend. There follows an elegant *demande d'amour* as the narrator asks with gentle irony who was the more happy: Arcite free but unable to glimpse Emelye, or the imprisoned Palamon who may at least have a chance to see his love. The underlying seriousness of the poem is also made clear when both young men lament the instability of earthly fortune in carefully patterned speeches that derive from *The Consolation of Philosophy*. Once more, rhetoric is a prime concern.

Symmetry of construction in *The Knight's Tale* is achieved not just by Palamon and Arcite's complementary laments but by the time-scheme as well. The lovers first saw Emelye in May, and it is in May – the month of lovers – that the two young men meet again. In the intervening time Arcite had suffered the lover's conventional torments and had then spent several years disguised as a serving-man in Theseus's court. His voluntary humiliation had been rewarded with occasional glimpses of Emelye. After seven years of imprisonment, Palamon decides to make his escape. The rivals finally encounter one another in a wood where Arcite has gone maying. They agree to fight the following day when Arcite has brought Palamon some armour. The merciless Cupid here makes even his own festival a time of bloodshed. Further, the courtesy of the two youths is offset by the animal imagery with which their fighting is described. As Boethius had shown, under the influence of violent emotion even courtly man descends to the level of beasts.

Such formal and non-realistic patterning of the narrative as we find in *The Knight's Tale* makes clear an important feature of much medieval poetry and one we have already examined in the context of *Troilus and Criseyde*: the fact that narratives are often constructed in discrete units which relate to each other not simply through suspense and intrigue but by a formal design of comparison and contrast. As the parallels multiply, so differing and deeper viewpoints are achieved. Thus while the fight between Palamon and Arcite is a bloodthirsty one, a violent re-statement of the quarrel in the prison, it also has its place in the full development of Chaucer's interest in the relation of private passion to social order. This becomes clear when he begins to show us that humankind, though racked by emotion, can nonetheless try to impose harmony on the world.

The lovers' fight is interrupted by Theseus – the narrator sees his appearance in the wood as an act of 'destinee' – and, having heard the young men's confessions, he at once determines on their deaths. An appeal from the ladies of the court succeeds in tempering such justice with mercy and, in a long speech, Theseus recognizes the ruthless, arbitrary power of love and the follies that service to Cupid has forced Palamon and Arcite to commit. Theseus then asserts his role as the benevolent source of human law. He declares that to settle the young men's conflict a splendid tournament will be fought exactly one year hence and in the same spot where they have all met. In this way the noble ruler tries to convert private violence into public ceremony. This is at best an ambiguous solution, for it will reinforce the cruelty of love and the arbitrariness of fortune even while it seeks to contain them. The place, the date and the issue to be fought all recapitulate previous issues and point to further developments and new viewpoints.

Man proposes, but the gods in *The Knight's Tale* dispose with great cruelty. The third part of the poem broadens its concerns by analysing events from a cosmic perspective. It is largely given over to the descriptions of the temples Theseus builds to Venus, Mars and Diana, at once classical gods and the planets of astrology to whom Palamon, Arcite and Emelye respectively pray. The descriptions of the three temples again show the importance of rhetorical ornament in the poem and convey an impression of the universal violence embodied in each god, whether this is revealed through anguished sexual passion, warfare, or the interesting combination of chastity and destructiveness personified by Diana. We are indeed made vividly aware of the gods' power and, when we eavesdrop on the quarrel of the deities themselves, of their ruthless petulance. Venus has promised that Palamon shall possess Emelye, Mars that Arcite shall be victorious in the tournament. The issue is resolved by Saturn, the oldest of the gods and Chaucer's awesome presentation of primordial chaos. When the tournament has been fought – and its lengthy description shows Chaucer's language at its most magnificent – a fury sent by Saturn causes the death of the victorious Arcite. He wins the tournament but loses the girl. Saturn thus provides a legalistic if dreadful solution to the dilemma, and a supreme example of intrusive violence. Arcite's passing is described with great pathos and realism, while the account of his cremation is both a display of rhetoric and an exposition of the way in which ceremony can allay the brutalities of existence. The latter must now be further resolved. Palamon eventually wins his promised bride – the match, despite the ardour that precedes it, results from a purely political initiative – but, for all its final happiness and Theseus's noble attempts to explain man's place in what he, as a virtuous pagan and student of Boethius, sees as a benevolent universe ruled by powers beyond fortune and the gods, the abiding impression left by *The Knight's Tale* is of the medieval pageants of love and death moving closely side by side:

> What is this world? what asketh man to have?
> Now with his love, now in his colde grave
> Allone, withouten any compaignye.

24

The whole party, the 'gentils' in particular, are impressed by the Knight's philosophical romance. The Host then turns to the Monk for a tale, presumably hoping for a narrative from a member of the Church, or the second of the three estates. He is interrupted by the Miller, however, whose drunken boast that he will tell just as good a story as the Knight – a narrative which he intends partly as an insult to his enemy the Reeve – shows how vivid the 'link' passages between the tales can be. Through them, the imagined pilgrimage takes on its own life. The Miller eventually gets his way (despite Harry Bailey's rebuff and the Reeve's angry murmurings) and his 'cherles tale' reintroduces us to fabliau: the comic, concretely observed and bawdy story of low-life characters, extramarital intrigue and coarse revenge. Such a tone is appropriate to the Miller, but we should also recognize that his tale is not a slice of everyday medieval life – the true voice of the people – but a literary contrivance every bit as sophisticated as *The Knight's Tale*, to which, indeed, it forms an excellent and telling complement.

This is clear even from its plot. We move from Athens to medieval Oxford, where two local youths – very different figures from Palamon and Arcite – pursue Alisoun, the alluring wife of an elderly, possessive carpenter who is then cuckolded and tricked into contriving his own come-uppance. Such a bare outline perhaps indicates the conventional nature of the characters and incidents – the tale has a number of European analogues – but it can suggest neither how Chaucer refashioned his material to convey an impression of youngsters in the first flush of sex nor the precise physical description by which he makes their outrageous trickery possible. It also neglects two further qualities: first the untroubled bawdy of a tale about swiving, farting and branding bare arses, and secondly the fact that all this is contrasted with some deeply serious religious metaphors.

The skills of John, the ageing cuckold of the story, are exploited by Nicholas, his young student lodger, to gain a night with Alisoun. Nicholas convinces John that he has discovered a second flood is imminent and that the three alone will be saved as long as they hide separately in barrels suspended from the eaves. Old John, despite knowing that men should not peer into the future (the theme of predestination is amusingly caricatured here), is easily convinced. In his simplicity and touching, foolish concern for his wife, he does not pause to ask why he of all people should be singled out for rescue from divine wrath. Instead, he becomes a grotesque parody of the original Noah whom God preserved when the world was drowned to punish its sexual sins. As John waits in his tub – a comic inversion of Noah's ark which was a vessel the Middle Ages, ever apt to find symbolic significance, saw as an image of the Church and salvation – his wife and lodger take advantage of the supposed avenging flood to enjoy their youthful lust. Nicholas has secured their pleasure through a daring travesty of Scripture.

But the couple are interrupted. Absalom, a shrewdly portrayed, squeamish dandy, comes courting Alisoun with somewhat old-fashioned, provincial phrases of courtly love based partly on the Song of Songs. That a lowly clerk should use them at all would have amused Chaucer's audience, but Absalom's pestering suit is horribly punished when Alisoun sticks her bare bottom out of the window for Absolom's passionate night-time kiss. Something of the range of poetic styles in *The Canterbury Tales* is suggested by a comparison between the magisterial philosophic pessimism of the lines we have quoted from *The Knight's Tale* and this passage with its swift juxtaposition of the language of courtly lyric, colloquial speech and description:

> This Absolon doun sette hym on his knees
> And seyde, 'I am a lord at alle degrees;
> For after this I hope ther cometh moore.
> Lemman, thy grace, and sweete bryd, thyn oore!'
> The wyndow she undoth, and that in haste.
> 'Have do,' quod she, 'com of, and speed the faste,
> Lest that oure neighebores thee espie.'
> This Absolon gan wype his mouth ful drie.
> Derk was the nyght as pich, or as the cole,
> And at the wyndow out she putte hir hole,
> And Absolon, hym fil no bet ne wers,
> But with his mouth he kiste hir naked ers
> Ful savourly, er he were war of this.
> Abak he stirte, and thoughte it was amys,
> For wel he wiste a womman hath no berd.
> He felte a thyng al rough and long yherd,
> And seyde, 'Fy! allas! what have I do?'
>   'Tehee!' quod she, and clapte the wyndow to,
> And Absolon gooth forth a sory pas.

lemman: beloved   *thyn oore:* have mercy

Absalom's fantasies crumble under the weight of his disgust and he returns with a red-hot coulter. This time it is Nicholas who, in response to Absalom's pleas, sticks his bottom out of the window, farting dreadfully before being branded. As Nicholas shouts for water to douse his pain, so John thinks the flood has come, severs the ropes on his barrel, hurtles to the ground and breaks his arm. So much for salvation from a wicked world. Alisoun and Nicholas, with the comic cruelty of fabliau, convince the neighbours John is mad. The result is timeless farce and not eternal scriptural truth.

The Miller's Tale takes its place in the unfolding narrative of *The Canterbury Tales* and enriches the possibilities of fabliau through the individualizing of stock characters and a daring use of religious analogy. It also sets learned clerk against untutored craftsman. *The Reeve's Tale* furthers these possibilities. Just as the Miller has told a tale against a carpenter, so Oswald the Reeve – who has been an apprentice carpenter in his youth – tells a tale in which John and Alan, two Cambridge scholars characterized by the first comic use of a northern accent in English literature, gain their revenge on the conventional chicanery of a miller by lying with his wife and daughter. But if there is similarity here, there is also contrast. Although the bedroom farce, its stumblings in the dark and its cruel, crazy logic, is perhaps even more vivid than comparable events in *The Miller's Tale*, the Reeve permeates his fabliau with his own sourness. His Prologue presents him as an ageing, bitter but impotent lecher, while his picture of the miller's village of Trumpington offers a view of a sinful and squalid place. The events that occur there – the theft of the students' corn while they are forced to chase their horses which the miller has freed, the subsequent seduction of his proud wife and spinster daughter when the scholars are obliged to spend the night in his mill – are assuredly very funny, but they lack the underlying wholesomeness of the events in *The Miller's Tale*. Human coupling is likened to rearing horses and therefore suggests desire out of control, while the grinding mill is both a sexual metaphor and an image of the mills of justice grinding fine and ensuring that revenge is extracted, measure for measure. The Reeve's own vindictiveness is emphasized when, his story and concluding prayer complete, he declares: 'Thus have I quyt the Millere in my tale.'

The Reeve's Tale is keenly enjoyed by Roger the Cook, one of a number of figures who come vividly to life, particularly in the link passages. After some professional badinage between him and the Host, the Cook begins his tale, a narrative apparently centring around the lively Perkin Revelour and probably designed as the story of a medieval idle apprentice. The poem might have given us a rare glimpse of medieval city life, but unfortunately it is incomplete.

The incomplete *Cook's Tale* is usually seen as ending the first fragment of *The Canterbury Tales*, but Chaucer's interest in fabliau is developed in the narratives of other pilgrims, notably that of the Merchant. Some see *The Merchant's Tale* as taking a penultimate place beside the stories of the Wife of Bath, the Clerk and the Franklin and so forming part of a debate on marriage. This may be so. It is also useful to see this narrative from a newly and unhappily married man as an example of the exuberance of invention which Chaucer brought to genre and received material. The core of the tale is pure fabliau. A repulsive old man weds a young bride who turns with relief to the attentions of his squire. The husband then goes blind and, by a comic ruse, the wife and her paramour make love in a pear tree in the husband's secret garden, the wife standing on her spouse's shoulders. To this grotesque situation Chaucer brings a wealth of debate, pageantry, evocative allusion, magic and humour which both enrich the poem and supply its comic conclusion. Strong visual images developing the poem's consistent irony also reinforce its moral interest.

The poem opens with the ancient January's praise of marriage, a description of the perils of bachelorhood, and the theologically proper view of a wife as a helpmate. These notions – contributing to *The Canterbury Tales* as a *compilatio* – will be ironically justified later. But even before his two brothers' learned confrontation on the joys and woes of marriage (another standard medieval theme developed here with encyclopedic amplitude) it is clear that January's object is not morality but lust. He marries the beautiful May in a ceremony of great splendour at which Venus dances with her torch. The ensuing bedroom scene forms a grotesque contrast. January, the fabliau hero, then begins to work his own destruction. He sends May to comfort Damyan, the squire who is sickening for her as a courtly lover should. Criticism of such conventional adultery is implied through the mock-serious tone of the rhetoric and the scene where May is forced to destroy her love letters in the privy. But the final moment in the garden is comprehensively ironic. The garden is now the blind and jealous husband's one place of supposed security, his Earthly Paradise where he woos May with unintentionally ironic allusions to the Song of Songs, a work whose sensuous imagery the Middle Ages read as an allegory of Christ's love for the faithful. Viewed also as a garden from the *Roman de la Rose* – a place where the *vieux jaloux* is equally inappropriate – January's Eden is a proper locale for Damyan, the snake who has been smuggled into it. May now fakes a pregnant woman's longing for pears and climbs the tree beneath which she and January are sitting. The branches suggest January's cuckold's horns as May and Damyan fornicate in a situation that is neither courtly nor loving. But the absurdity and humiliation of all three characters has been watched by others. The lovely garden has for some long time been an extension of fairyland. Pluto, the horrified fairy king, restores January's sight, but Proserpine gives May the wit to calm her husband's anguish by declaring that this tussle in a tree has been designed to cure his blindness. Caught *in flagrante*, she presents herself as a virtuous helpmate. The opening assertions of the poem are ironically proven. Finally the Merchant, hoping to tell a tale against the fecklessness of young wives, really reflects in himself the absurdity of the old man, the *vieux jaloux*. This ironic relationship between teller and tale, developed with remarkable virtuosity throughout *The Canterbury Tales*, is again part of the work's abiding fascination.

The Merchant's witty use of visual images is less characteristic of the tales of the Shipman, the Summoner and the Friar. What these stories do share (along with *The Canon's Yeoman's Tale*) is a marked anti-clerical theme. The Shipman's fabliau, which was clearly not meant for him since the narrator is female, is nonetheless an amusing story of a monk's adultery with a merchant's wife and uses the common folk-lore motif of a debt – financial and sexual – cunningly repaid. *The Friar's Tale* and the Summoner's riposte stem from personal and professional rivalry. In the first, a summoner falls in with a fiend, torments a poor widow and, when she tells him to go to the devil, is snatched away by his companion. *The Summoner's Tale* opens with a Prologue in which hordes of damned friars are shown living in Satan's anus – the pit of hell. This scatalogical theme is continued in a story in which a hypocritical friar is rewarded with a fart whose sound and savour he must divide among his twelve brothers. A squire provides an amusing solution.

25

The link passages constantly refresh our idea of the pilgrimage as an imagined journey. When, somewhat late in the day, the pilgrims are joined by a sweating and duplicitous Canon who departs as his Yeoman begins to reveal too much, the party is built up to thirty-three members – a number whose mystical significance relates to Christ's years on earth – and treated to a tale of alchemy, a false science the Church had recently condemned. Perhaps because of the departure of his master, the Canon's Yeoman allies himself to the 'trouthe' of the Christian faith rather than the endless, deceptive mazes of his 'craft' – the pursuit of illusory gold. This last he describes both from his own experience and in a tale in which a canon, by transmuting base metals through a device which some see as a black, comic parody of the eucharist, tricks a greedy cleric. *The Canon's Yeoman's Tale* and its Prologue are thus lively, serious accounts of alchemy and of intellectual and moral illusion.

26

There is evidence to suggest that among Chaucer's contemporaries the Wife of Bath was one of the most popular of the pilgrims. She has never really been dislodged from this position. However, enriched by experience of the novel, it is too easy to see the strident, middle-aged Alisoun merely as a marvellous personality – which she certainly is – while she garrulously exposes the miseries she has inflicted on her five husbands. Such surface realism is a literary mode rather than an end in itself, and the realism of the Wife of Bath is partly that of fabliau which, as we have seen, is a special type of poetic contrivance. Further, the wonderful raciness of her language is contained in Chaucer's couplets and so should prompt us to think of it as a vindication of the rhetorical rule that poetic comedy is best achieved through a 'low' style. If we are seeking analogues for the Wife of Bath, then, as has been mentioned, they are to be found in such explicitly didactic but erring figures as La Veille in Jean de Meung's earthy vision of sexuality in the second part of the *Roman de la Rose*, or the 'bad wife' of the sermons. Chaucer's special contribution to this tradition was to combine in one character the opposing sides of a debate on women and marriage and so fashion both a lively figure and a compendium of received views.

The Wife of Bath's knowledge – like her tale – involves continuous paradox, raising to a high level Chaucer's fascination with the problem of interpreting texts. In the superbly garrulous length of her Prologue the Wife pits exuberant personal experience against received authority and, by paraphrasing conventional anti-feminist views in marital harangues, exposes the bigotry that underlies them. At the same time, she implicitly suggests that such attitudes may well be justified. After all, though she argues for personal freedom, some of our sympathy goes to her poor husbands. But the Wife is particularly interesting when, viewing her as a literate layperson, we see her set about the interpretation of Scripture and the Fathers. For the Church this was a profoundly worrying problem in an age of many heresies, and Gower had inveighed against those who read their Bible *simpliciter* – naively, that is, or without respecting the gloss. The Wife provides her own gloss, however, from the raucous voice of common experience. The personal becomes the measure of her values. Hers is thus no pious reading guided by tradition, but an exuberance of subjectivity and quick-witted intellect. For example, the Wife can reveal the contradictions in Scripture with the niceness of a scholiast and she disputes a canon law ruling that second marriages were bigamous. But perhaps most interesting is her attack on virginity – the highest position on a conventional scale that descended through widowhood to that married state which, for St Paul, was better than burning with unsatisfied lust. Jerome too had discussed virginity, suggesting the great prize that rewarded chastity and those able to sustain it. The Wife agrees, but stands Jerome's argument on its head. Virginity, she declares, is indeed a worthy state for those who can endure it. Quite simply, she cannot:

> Virginitee is greet perfeccion,
> And continence eek with devocion,
> But Crist, that of perfeccion is welle,
> Bid nat every wight he sholde go selle
> Al that he hadde, and gyve it to the poore
> And in swich wise folwe hym and his foore.
> He spak to hem that wolde lyve parfitly;
> And lordynges, by youre leve, that am nat I.
> I wol bistowe the flour of al myn age
> In the actes and in fruyt of mariage.

welle: source   *foore:* path

Her statement, expressed with a colloquial energy that is a distinct quality of Chaucer's comic style, is seemingly irrefutable, and should be seen as part of the Wife's wider attempt to prove that sexual organs were given us both for excretion and to use abundantly for 'engendrure', a matter she can 'wel understonde'. Nonetheless, and contrary again to the teachings of the Church, the Wife is more interested in the means of procreation than in its ends. We hear of no children. Her apparent object in marriage is 'maistrie', the assumption of a forbidden dominant female role, and a matter that greatly interested Chaucer. At this point we move from the interpretation of texts to life – from words to deeds.

The Wife reveals her pursuit of 'maistrie' in a series of vivid private anecdotes supposedly designed, like the lists of monstrous wives read out to her by the comely young Jankyn, her last and most favoured husband, as *exempla*, stories illustrating a general moral truth. Underlying them is the fascination of intimate gossip and a seeming self-knowledge. With a rich final irony however, when Alisoun has burned Jankyn's book of authorities, been struck and then fearfully revived with the offer of 'maistrie', she unwittingly challenges her own doctrines by being true and kind, and living with Jankyn without 'debaat'. Despite her outrageously energetic attempts to misinterpret the *sens* of holy texts, their true *sentence* is revealed in her own life, in her 'experience'. Such contradictions serve to deepen her raucous and representative humanity and reveal the subtlety with which Chaucer exposed the relationship between individuals and received ideas.

The Wife of Bath's Tale is Chaucer's only approach to the vast body of medieval Arthurian legend and concerns similar matters to those raised in her Prologue. It begins with a squire's trial for rape. Such an act is a supreme expression of inhuman and uncourtly lust. It shows mere selfish cupidity untouched by 'gentil' behaviour. Justice demands the squire's execution. At his trial, however, the queen successfully pleads for clemency, and what in the king's court of law is seen as a clear case for the death penalty is converted in the queen's court of love to a problematic *demande d'amour*. The squire is given a year and a day to discover the thing that women most desire. Guilty of extreme male aggression, the squire is sent out on a romance quest which will eventually result in his discovery not just of love but of the true meaning of courtly existence.

The anonymous young man – he is a representative figure rather than a character and so does not need a name – eventually receives what appears to be an answer to the queen's question from one of the great figures of romance: the loathly lady. In return for a promise of marriage, the loathly lady says that what women desire is 'maistrie'. The queen's courtiers agree with this and the squire's life is saved. However, the horrified young man now has to honour his promise and marry his rescuer.

Once in their bedroom, the loathly lady uses arguments from the Bible, from Dante and Boethius to convince the squire by the force of her eloquence that true gentility does not lie in beauty, wealth and social position – those gifts of Fortune he so values and she so lacks. True human value lies in innate moral worth, in that form of love and 'gentilesse' which rejects the lascivious and the socially exclusive for a concern with true goodness, honest poverty and worthy old age. The cupidity the young squire has so relished must be replaced by charity and what we have seen Criseyde define as 'moral vertue, grounded upon trouthe'. Only then will he find real love. The sometime rapist at last submits to his wife's superior knowledge. He kisses her and – of course – she is at once transformed into a beautiful princess. Having learnt the moral values on which relationships are based, the squire is rewarded with the chance of physical pleasure. His wife then lovingly submits to him. In other words, she abandons the 'maistrie' she once professed and so preserves decorum. Despite the proven dangers of youth and beauty, the couple then spend the rest of their lives in 'parfit joy'. By realizing the proper values on which human worth and marriage are based, the pleasures of courtly love are placed on a true moral foundation.

The Wife of Bath's Tale is thus a sophisticated little parable and, like all such pieces, it calls for interpretation. Not surprisingly, the Wife herself willingly sets about the task. As we might expect, she gloriously misinterprets her text. She sees it as an expression of the triumph of 'maistrie', concluding her exegesis with a wistful look at the loathly lady's conversion to beauty and expressing her own wish for more sensuous and easily dominated young squires with their transforming kisses. The fact that the Wife of Bath misapplies her own tale illustrates perfectly the fascination Chaucer reveals throughout *The Canterbury Tales* with text and interpretation, authority and experience.

27

The incomplete *Squire's Tale*, with its delight in courtly entertainment and such 'mervailles' as flying horses and a ring that allows its wearer to understand the language of birds, suggests that the whole was probably intended as one of the long – sometimes very long – tales of delight that constitute much medieval romance. The figure of the Squire himself is certainly made to find the fertility of his own invention somewhat bewildering and there may be an element of satire on excessive narrative complexity here. Such prolixity, as well as the incest motif in the original of this tale, were both alien to Chaucer, and the ensuing narrative from the Franklin is a masterly example of concise yet intricate and ambiguous story-telling.

The tone of the Franklin's opening words to the Squire and the resolutely down-to-earth Harry Bailey at once reveal this rich commoner's concern with a central theme in many of Chaucer's mature works: 'gentilesse'. This is a quality which is reflected in the aristocratic ethos at its most perfect, but one which we have seen is really an innate virtue planted in man by God and so is essentially independent of class. It is a form of moral worthiness or true nobility which has nothing to do with Fortune's gifts of money, birth and status, and which all – even a Franklin mildly uncomfortable about his social standing – may aspire to. *The Franklin's Tale* itself is modelled on the once fashionable Breton *lai*, and exemplifies 'gentilesse' by exploring the implications of two qualities closely associated with such behaviour. First comes 'fredom' or that liberality of manner which is an ideal particularly appropriate to a

Franklin or 'freeman' who was literally one whose life was not proscribed by rigid feudal duties. Secondly, and perhaps more importantly, *The Franklin's Tale* also examines a further aspect of the 'gentil' ideal which is open to all: 'trouthe'. 'Trouthe', the hero of the tale sententiously declares, 'is the heyeste thyng that man may kepe', and our discussion of this quality in *Troilus and Criseyde* revealed how central it was to Chaucer's thinking. We saw there that truth is not simply the opposite of lying, but is an aspect of personal integrity, of keeping one's word. In Chaucer's ballade *Truth*, it is just this virtue that keeps the bonds of society tightly knit. But truth is also shown as an aspect of divine love or the 'stable faith' with which God, in the opinion of Boethius, preserves the great cycle of the planets, the seasons and the tides. To be apart from this cosmic truth is to be apart from God, but to love God heartily is to know the truth 'and the truth', as St John declared, 'shall make you free'. Truth thus develops from factual accuracy, through personal integrity to salvation. Preserving truth preserves man's ideal relation to his universe. To lose truth is to fall into error and illusion.

Such moral intricacy is expressed through an equally intricate tale in which interpretation – the requirement to look beneath the *sens* for the *sentence* – is particularly engaging. Dorigen, a lady of high birth, marries Arveragus, and it is agreed that their private life should be led on equal terms while in public they preserve the decorous relation of man to wife. As lovers, they have exchanged both the freedom of friends and the vows of marriage. However, during Arveragus's enforced absence Dorigen rashly promises her love to a mere squire, on condition he perform the seemingly impossible task of removing the coastal rocks which Dorigen sees as a threat to her husband's safe return. She thereby puts in danger the vow she swore at her marriage and so threatens her truth to her plighted word. In her loneliness and unhappiness she cannot understand the *stabilis fides* or 'fixed faith' and truth by which a benign Creator maintains the world's harmonious round. By seeking the illusory disappearance of the rocks, Dorigen has put both her integrity and her faith in peril. Nonetheless, we should note that in her foolish weakness she has also mortgaged her freedom by binding herself to an oath which, while its terms seem unlikely ever to be fulfilled, her 'gentilesse' will oblige her to honour if she is ever required to prove her 'trouthe'.

The adulterous squire (his name is Aurelius) then sickens as a conventional courtly lover should, but eventually he promises all his wealth to a 'clerk' who agrees to make the rocks disappear by magic. In other words, diabolic illusions are set against divine truth. *The Canon's Yeoman's Tale* has already shown how profoundly evil the illusions of magic are, but that the feat is indeed achieved suggests the delicate symbolism with which the rocks have become veiled. First viewed by Dorigen as a cruel, inexplicable threat to her marriage, they have now become a token of its enduring 'trouthe' – the rock, indeed, on which her marriage is built. It is only by an illusion that they have been spirited away, and it is Aurelius's adulterous passion that is the real threat. Dorigen's consequent anguish causes her to contemplate suicide – her lament is a long, encyclopedic yet somewhat hysterical list of precedents for this – but, rather than commit what was regarded as the gravest of sins, she movingly confronts her husband and submits to his ruling. Despite his misery, Arveragus declares with that sententious rhetoric the Franklin so relishes: 'Trouthe is the heyeste thyng that man may kepe', and tearfully asserts his 'maistrie' by sending his wife to honour her promise.

Where spells can create an illusion, the sanctified vows of marriage reveal the 'trouthe', and this as we have seen goes straight to the heart. Aurelius is so touched by the 'gentil' action – the integrity of these married lovers – that he frees Dorigen from her promise to him. He abandons both his illicit desire and his hopes of obtaining it through an illusory reshaping of God's true pattern for the real world. The clerk, also moved by the scene he has witnessed, cancels Aurelius's debt and so proves that a mere scholar can be as 'gentil' as a knight or a squire. 'Gentilesse', it is shown, is not dependent on social status. It is a moral value that has united man and wife, squire and clerk in an honourable 'freedom', an equality of 'gentilesse'. The final literary gambit can now be played. The Franklin ends his aristocratic *lai* with a conventional *demande d'amour*. Which of his characters, he asks, was the most free? In other words, who best exhibited 'franchise', that open-minded element of true 'gentilesse' that has no necessary connection with noble birth? The answer is that there is no answer. The question is insoluble.

28

Chaucer derived *The Clerk's Tale* from Petrarch's expanded Latin version of the last narrative in the *Decameron* and a French re-telling of what was already a popular story, altering his sources with that scholarly and artistic care we have seen to be typical of him, and also with economical yet radical effect. His final narrative is particularly subtle, especially when we consider its position beside *The Merchant's Tale*, but at first it may be difficult to see why.

On the level of plot, *The Clerk's Tale* appears merely an exercise in melodrama. Walter, the Marquis of Saluzzo, is obliged to marry and chooses the poorest serf in his village with the proviso that she must accept all his acts with patience. Griselda becomes famous as a perfect wife, but her trials begin when her lord first snatches away her children to apparent death, returns her to her father, and then recalls her to act as his servant at his second marriage. She even has to praise the beauty of the new bride. Griselda willingly endures such sufferings, but her humble patience is rewarded when the supposed second wife is revealed as none other than her own daughter. An emotional reunion leads to happiness ever after.

That Chaucer should treat such material – and the French version can countenance it only because it is part of unquestionable 'auctoritee' – confirms the importance of a number of factors central to our understanding of medieval literature and Chaucer's particular sophistication. For instance, we have seen that originality of plot was a matter of small concern to a contemporary audience, and that the story-line itself (and hence the audience's response to the literal sequence of events) was nearly always but one aspect of their appreciation. They knew from sermons and biblical parables, if not from critical theory, that many narratives could support an allegorical interpretation which stressed matters of faith and doctrine, while they could also read these pieces on what was called a tropological level for their moral insight. Thus if *The Clerk's Tale* is the story of a peasant's marriage to a great lord, then, recalling our analysis of *Erec and Enide*, we should remember that the supposed proper humility of a serf and wife to her master could be seen as an image of the soul's rightful humility before God. The Clerk himself suggests this interpretation when he declares that he has told his tale less to provide a picture of how virtuous wives should behave in real life than as an analogy of how the good Christian should be as constant and uncomplaining in adversity as Griselda proved to be. If we are thus prepared to see Griselda as an image or 'type' of the virtuous soul, a dignified, delicate web of allusion and refined sentiment wraps about her. She is a poor Christian, yet at times her modest acceptance of new-found glory is likened to that of the Virgin herself.

But we have seen that it is characteristic of Chaucer's genius to play daring games with received literary forms. If he presents this story partly as a conventional moral allegory, he also heightens the theatricality of his characters in a manner that both reflects the tastes of late Gothic art and threatens the validity of the parallel the tale supposedly has to offer. For example, Walter's social status may well suggest the power of God, but he is also far more of an ogre than he appeared in Chaucer's sources. Again, the refined and somewhat sentimental melodrama that clings to the 'real' as opposed to the allegorical Griselda seems to have appealed to a fourteenth-century audience rather as the tribulations of Esther Summerson did to Dickens's readership. It is with this heightened surface realism, however, that the problems begin. Our awakened human sympathies quite simply conflict with the 'sentence' the poem is proposing. Our response to the *matière* denies the lesson of the *sens*. As the Clerk himself realizes – developing once more that ambiguous relation between teller and tale that is so characteristic of these narratives – his story lives ambivalently in worlds at once literal and exemplary. Interpretation is again a debatable issue.

The interest in refined sentimentalism, morality, faith and extreme events apparent in *The Clerk's Tale* is also a characteristic of the narratives of several other pilgrims, and reaches an apogee in *The Prioress's Tale*. For example, the Physician's account of how her father slew the exemplary Virginia rather than deliver her into the hands of a lustful judge, who is in turn exposed and commits suicide, is an early work that derives from Livy via the *Roman de la Rose*, and is well received even by the worldly Harry Bailey. *The Man of Law's Tale*, however, is conceived on a much grander scale. On the literal, narrative level it is the story of Constance, the devout daughter of a Christian Roman emperor. We see her marriage first to a pagan who feigns conversion and is killed, her long sea voyages in a rudderless boat broken only by her marriage to an English king who is truly converted, and Constance's eventual reunion with her father and second husband followed by her death in Rome, the moral centre of the work. Probably coming after the fabliaux of the Miller and the Reeve, this narrative contributes to the variety of *The Canterbury Tales* by being deeply serious, full of pathos and fine philosophical exposition and, above all, by being an account of what was believed to be a true Christian history. Because of this latter fact, the deeper levels of interpretation that can be brought to the central images throw much light on how contemporaries interpreted many such works. A short digression on this important aspect of medieval critical theory may be useful.

We have noted a long tradition of allegorical interpretation of literary texts stemming from revisions made to classical rhetorical theory by St Augustine. Since serious secular work was often regarded as subject to theology, modern poets could also draw on these techniques. We have seen that the emphasis in all such interpretation was on encouraging the audience to go beneath the surface sense of the poem to extract its true *sentence*. *Sentence*, we have seen, was invariably an aspect of Christian teaching. When this approach was applied to the

Bible itself, many of the great exegetes – among them Bede, St Thomas Aquinas and Dante – believed that there were four levels on which a text could be studied. The first was the already familiar one of the literal meaning which tells through words of deeds and events. The second, which is variously named but which we may refer to as the allegorical level, concerned the life of Christ, the Creed and the sacraments. The moral or tropological sense concerned the proper ordering of life, while the fourth or anagogical level suggested the last great things: death, judgement, Heaven, Hell and the triumph of the Church in eternity. A medieval Latin mnemonic puts the matter succinctly:

> Littera gesta docet; quid credas, allegoria;
> Moralis, quid agas; quo tendas, anagogia.
>
> *(The letter tell us what was fact*
> *While faith to allegory tends;*
> *The moral tells us how to act*
> *And anagogy of our ends.)*

For a detailed illustration of how this form of reading can be applied to a Chaucerian text, we can return to *The Man of Law's Tale*.

In addition to the narrative level, we should note that what we have seen is properly termed the poem's allegorical concern with the Christian duties of conversion and the sacrament of baptism. Further, there is the poem's moral or tropological interest in the right conduct of life amid the stormy waves of fortune, and the way in which the sea journeys themselves and their eventual happy outcome may be compared in a mystical sense with the soul's final journey to the reunion of the blessed in paradise. We shall return often to such a characteristically fourfold interpretation of medieval religious texts, but should note here how the Man of Law's seemingly improbable, melodramatic tale is in fact a pious and sternly beautiful attempt to view supposed real history as an exemplary image of human life when it is lived with constancy and fortitude under divine Providence.

Both *The Second Nun's Tale* and the narrative told by her mistress are again saints' legends. Both also open with a conventional Prologue rich in that delicate yet magisterial rhetoric and theology so characteristic of Dante and the mature Chaucer, yet too often ignored in favour of the vivid realism of the comic tales. The Prologue to *The Second Nun's Tale* indeed contains a partial translation of what is perhaps the greatest of all the versified prayers from the Middle Ages – St Bernard's hymn to the Virgin in the *Paradiso*. The Prioress's own invocation to the Virgin and prayer for help once more suggest the refinement she brings to worship and the beauty of much medieval Marian devotion:

> My konnyng is so wayk, o blisful Queene,
> For to declare thy grete worthynesse
> That I ne may the weighte nat susteene;
> But as a child of twelf month oold, or lesse,
> That kan unnethes any word expresse,
> Right so fare I, and therfore I yow preye,
> Gydeth my song that I shal of yow seye.

konnyng: skill   *unnethes:* scarcely

The comparison suggested between this refined English lady and a child – each under the protection of the Virgin – is an important foretaste of that devotion to innocence which supports her tale.

The Prioress's narrative tells how a seven-year-old boy, having learned a Latin hymn to the Virgin, is murdered by the local Jews but continues singing until his body is found and buried. The combination of wonder, cruelty and purity raises this saint's legend to the highest levels of late Gothic art, while the charm of the setting and the divine rapture of the miracle are in stark contrast to the murder and the mother's grief. In its small yet exquisite compass, the tale is an image of Gothic piety and the concept of the Holy Innocents. As such, it is important to realize the true nature of the Prioress's savage hatred of the Jews. This is not a virulent outburst of anti-semitism, an expression of some latent sadism in the cloistered psyche of an over-refined gentlewoman – indeed, it is neither psychological nor social in origin at all. It is theological. The Jews in *The Prioress's Tale* are an allegorical and typological representation of devils and bogeymen, people without Christ.

29

When Harry Bailey breaks the sober wonder inspired by *The Prioress's Tale* and turns to Chaucer the pilgrim for a story, Chaucer the poet wittily exploits the ambiguity of this. Chaucer the poet – a man capable of the most sophisticated artifice, widely read in his classical and medieval forebears, and the creator of such searchingly sophisticated poetry as *The Canterbury Tales* themselves – has Chaucer the pilgrim tell the story of Sir Thopas.

This is a parody of native, stanzaic and tale-rhymed romances such as Chaucer himself had read in his youth. Eighteen such poems are preserved in the great Auchinleck Miscellany which some argue that Chaucer knew.

On one level his parody is a sharp exposure of the shortcomings of such old-fashioned works while on another it is a narrative as potentially tedious as the worst of its originals. In this way Chaucer at once suggests how far English poetry had grown from its vernacular origins while again presenting us with that naive persona whose incompetence had been so useful to him from the time of *The Book of the Duchess*. Chaucer the pilgrim's insistence on the verbal and narrative clichés of his work is a most entertaining example of Chaucer the poet's deft playfulness. However, Harry Bailey eventually calls a halt to his doggerel.

Chaucer's ensuing *Tale of Melibee* – which is far more to his audience's taste than it is to ours – is a serious piece of didactic prose given ironically to the greatest English poet of his age. It is an encyclopedic, secular homily in which Melibee's wife Prudence discusses the need to restrain violence, the idea that men should submit to the wise advice of their wives, and the forgiveness of enemies. In its depiction of sudden calamity and suffering, the work may well owe something to the Book of Job.

30

As we approach the sermon – the last major genre to be used in *The Canterbury Tales* – the often playful but always serious interest in interpretation Chaucer shows throughout his work reveals its most extensive development. To appreciate the background to this we should know that sermons and their rhetoric were of seminal importance to the culture of the Middle Ages and that, imitating Christ's own practice, they were seen as one of the noblest of the ecclesiastical functions. Parables or exemplary stories in particular, with their surface meaning and underlying moral purpose, are particularly relevant to *The Nun's Priest's Tale*. The narrator of this work also reveals himself as having that becoming humility, genuine knowledge and great technical ability which the ideal preacher was required to possess. These qualities allow the Nun's Priest to tell a tale of interest to both the intellectuals in the party as well as the less educated.

The story told by the Nun's Priest is dramatically situated in the seventh fragment of *The Canterbury Tales*, the section where the dynamic relations between the various narratives and their speakers is particularly lively. For some time the Monk has been wearying the company with a list of 'tragedies' recounting how Fortune topples the proud. When presented as a list of *exempla* in this way, the theme formed a rather monotonous genre of poetry, one made widely known in England, however, by the 36,000 or so lines of Lydgate's *Fall of Princes*.

The Monk's Tale is probably a fairly early working of this unpromising genre by Chaucer himself. Indeed, the poem may well date from the earliest period of his Italian influence. The story of Ugolino, for example, whose death by starvation alongside his children has always been one of the most popular passages in the *Inferno*, Chaucer here re-tells in a way that converts Dante's tragic horror into the pathos which is so characteristic of much late Gothic art. However, Chaucer evidently felt that the 'fall of princes' genre was unsatisfactory – the repeated short tales have little narrative interest – but with wise economy he preserved his attempt, finding it useful much later as a work to be told by a pompous and sinful cleric.

Far from fulfilling his duty of winning souls to salvation through charity and skilful narration, the Monk's tale bores both the Knight and Harry Bailey to such a degree that the Host eventually feels obliged to cut in and silence the speaker, satirizing his morals, his poetic language and, indeed, the whole idea of tragic destruction in a world that was seen ultimately in terms of salvation. Harry Bailey adds that it is only the clinking of the bells on the bridle of the Monk's mount that has stopped him from going to sleep and falling off his horse. This comment has a vivid comic realism, but it is also – and in a way we should be constantly aware of – a means of making a moral point. The bells are a symbol of the pride the Monk has been lamenting. He is guilty of the very sin he castigates. This is a fine example of the way in which Chaucer relates teller to tale in a particular context. The Monk's tinkling bridle declares his error to the world, for, in the words of the Parson, 'God seith by Zakarie the prophete, "I wol confounde the riders of swiche horses."' A medieval audience, more familiar with biblical texts than many of us, could hear allusions in *The Canterbury Tales* to which we may well be deaf.

It is now the Nun's Priest's turn to entertain the audience. When Harry Bailey turns from the Monk who, understandably enough, has retreated into silence after the onslaught on his tale, our impression of the Nun's Priest begins to fill out. When we first saw him in the General Prologue he was but one of three religious brothers, as alike as peas in a pod. Now we learn that, in contrast to the Monk, the Nun's Priest is not mounted on an expensive palfrey (such social details are again matters to which the medieval audience would have had a more immediate response than we can muster) but has to make do with a jade that is 'bothe foule and lene'. In other words the man is poor, the ill-provided servant of a great lady of the Church. We should also note his humble willingness to tell his tale, and should perhaps detect a quiet, engaging humour in his promise to be 'merie'. We have just seen Harry Bailey at his most overbearing, ridiculing the Monk for the boredom his tale has induced. The Nun's Priest's wry assessment of this suggests a certain tact on his part. Finally, to complete our initial impression and reinforce the contrast with the Monk, Chaucer calls his narrator 'this swete preest, this goodly man, Sir John'. Thus, poor and apparently reserved though he seems, we are told that the Nun's Priest is a fine individual who seems admirably to fulfil the requirements of his vocation. In such deft and various ways Chaucer conveys something of the complex privacy of inner and professional life. However, when at the close of the tale Harry Bailey tries to see the Nun's Priest himself as a parallel to Chauntecleer, the libidinous cockerel hero of his story, this subtle characterization is deepened by an awareness of a possible subjective relation between teller and tale. Perhaps the virile Nun's Priest is not as comfortably suited to his vocation as Chaucer the naive narrator assumed. But whatever we may choose to make of Harry Bailey's intuitions, it does seem that the Host himself believes that art can sometimes reveal the nature of the artist, that literature can be personal as well as rhetorical.

Such subtlety is matched by what is soon made to appear as the Nun's Priest's own literary sophistication. The Monk has bored the company with his dreary recital of instances exemplifying the fall of pride. The Nun's Priest, however, taking up the same theme, tells a tale in which an elderly widow's cockerel, beguiled by love of his wife, fails to take notice of dreams he believes are a warning from God and, revelling in his proudly sensual delights, shows off his glory. In the moment of his pride he falls victim to a fox which, when the widow has pursued with a marvellous hullabaloo, he then tricks into releasing him. The tale is thus a delightful and apparently simple animal fable. The story itself was also very well known, but it was not usually regarded as a natural vehicle for literary sophistication. Boccaccio, for example, dismissed such pieces as suitable only for children and old women. Certainly, few in Chaucer's contemporary audience would initially have suspected that *The Nun's Priest's Tale* is in fact hugely engaging, stylistically various, and a work that weaves dextrously together some of the most serious issues of the day. This it does in a manner that, far from exulting in fashionable new insights (and so perhaps falling into the error of intellectual pride) reveals a wryly mature and agile mind illuminated by that great gift, humour. As we shall see, the work is in fact one of the most searching products of Chaucer's lifelong involvement with the paradoxes and ambiguities of literary communication.

On the literal level, *The Nun's Priest's Tale* is an attractive and apparently straightforward piece. Indeed, the opening paragraph in which the poor widow's cottage is described is as beguiling as anything in all Middle English literature. It is not only a simple picture, however. A medieval audience would have at once begun to interpret it as an image of a poor and virtuous life led contentedly on the dunghill, earth. Familiar with the idea of animals being used as personifications of sin, they would also have been able to recognize the abundantly human and fleshly Chauntecleer as a 'type' of Pride, the chief of the Seven Deadly Sins. All this was conventional and straightforward, but no doubt the audience would have appreciated how infinitely more enjoyable all this is than the treatment of the same theme by the Monk.

It is a further delightful aspect of the work that Chauntecleer's pride expresses itself as a parody of the courtly world. Cooped up in a corner of the widow's narrow cottage, Chauntecleer is nevertheless as 'royal as a prince is in his halle'. We are amused by his vanity, but perhaps we also begin to think that life in the real and royal world, though thick with ceremony and brocade, was just as vainglorious as life in the widow's backyard.

A further parallel to human existence is offered by Chauntecleer's relations with his wife. Their marriage is at once a comic evocation of loving courtly refinement and a knockabout struggle for 'maistrie'. Two major themes in Chaucer's poetry are thus brought together in a way that is at once amusing and convincing. Nevertheless, since this tale is also a sermon we should examine the place of Chauntecleer's abundant sexuality in marriage. It is here that the interpretative problems become particularly fascinating.

What we may call the 'hard-line' approach to love and marriage required, as we have seen, a chaste recognition of sexuality as a natural desire for increase. This was common to all men and beasts – including cockerels. Excessive sexual indulgence, however, was regarded as sinful. This was true even in marriage, and uxoriousness – the too great loving of one's wife – was seen as recapitulating the original sin of Adam when he submitted to Eve's ruling rather than to God's. This hard-line approach allows us to see the libidinous Chauntecleer as a 'type' of Adam and thus of all sinners. In his desire to 'feather' Pertelote, he yields to the delight of both the senses and the heart. This leads, as with Adam, to a weakening of the will and a confusion of the intellect – in other words, to Chauntecleer's fall.

Chauntecleer has had a dream which he regards as a premonition that something dreadful is about to happen. As proud of his intellect as of his sexual prowess, he believes his dream to be nothing less than an *oraculum*, a divinely inspired vision of the truth. He tries to prove this interpretation at considerable length and with an amusing breadth of scholarship. His wife, keen to establish her 'maistrie' through a downright assertion of common-sense, declares that the dream is no wonder at all. It is merely the result of indigestion, and this she can easily purge. In the birds' raucous conversation, Chaucer combines a discussion of a favourite topic – the ambiguous nature of dreaming – with his interest in marriage and 'maistrie'. The chirping hens at one and the same time provide information for *The Canterbury Tales* both as a *compilatio* and a satire on intellectual pretension. But there are further layers of irony. First of all, despite the vivacious discussion of the nature of dreams, the valid warning contained in Chauntecleer's dream itself is soon forgotten by him in an access of sexual desire:

> 'Madame Pertelote, so have I blis,
> Of o thyng God hath sent me large grace;
> For whan I se the beautee of youre face,
> Ye been so scarlet reed aboute youre yen,
> It maketh al my drede for to dyen;
> For al so siker as *In principio,*
> *Mulier est hominis confusio,* –
> Madame, the sentence of this Latyn is,
> "Womman is mannes joye and al his blis."
> For whan I feele a-nyght your softe syde,
> Al be it that I may nat on yow ryde,
> For that oure perche is maad so nawe, allas!
> I am so ful of joye and of solas,
> That I diffye bothe sweven and dreem.'

o: one   *siker:* true
In principio, etc.: In the beginning the wife was the ruin of the man   *sweven:* dream

This is a delightfully subtle and ironic passage. Chauntecleer apostrophizes his wife as a courtly beauty, but her hen's features are, in fact, the very opposite of what was regarded as conventionally attractive. Chauntecleer also forgets what he believes to have been his divine dream-warning and, along with this, his Latin. Quoting a text which means that women are the cause of man's fall, he interprets it to mean that sexual love is the highest bliss a man can know. Such an error is profoundly suggestive. On the one hand it prompts thoughts of the hard-line approach to the place of sex within marriage and so identifies Chauntecleer as a 'type' of Adam. On the other hand it brings to a head what has been implicit throughout the Nun's Priest's description of married life: the fact that sexual pleasure may indeed be the greatest delight many of fallen humankind can experience. Chauntecleer's confusion points humanely to what may also be our own. Further, just as our feelings about sexuality may be ambivalent, so, as we see Chauntecleer picking his royal progress across the widow's yard, we may also be torn between conventional attitudes of contempt for the dunghill earth and delight in its beauties, its flowers and the song of the 'blisful briddes'. Needless to say, Chauntecleer feels himself vastly superior to these last. In this passage we can thus see how the humane energies of the narrator are perhaps in conflict with the conservative 'sentence' required by his tale. Such ambivalence is deeply suggestive.

Unlike the Monk, the Nun's Priest also refuses to see the fall of his proud prince as necessarily a total annihilation. He does not subscribe to the lugubrious pessimism of the 'fall of princes' genre. Though the proud Chauntecleer indeed struts his way into the very jaws of the fox – there is little difficulty in interpreting these as the jaws of Hell – he also tricks his way out of them again. He escapes. The devilish foe fails to get his way. But while we laugh with comic relief, we should also realize that Chauntecleer's salvation is, in fact, profoundly Christian – far more so indeed than the Monk's pessimism. As the Parson declares, though the devil may work through 'queyntise' or that cunning with which Russell the fox lures Chauntecleer to apparent death, men and even chickens 'shal withstonden him by wit and by resoun and by discrecioun'. There is hope even to the last.

The ironies of narrative, characterization and theme in *The Nun's Priest's Tale* are matched by an equal subtlety of styles. We have seen, first of all, that the work is a riposte to the tedium of the Monk's attempt at the 'fall of princes' genre. In place of that work's often lugubrious rhetoric and glib determinism, the Nun's Priest offers both an exuberant mock-heroic tone and a far more circumspect approach to some philosophical issues which, as we have seen, were regarded by his contemporaries as highly contentious. Just as his characters refuse to be wholly confined by the hard-line approach to theology, so they cannot easily be accommodated to the wire-drawn distinctions of medieval logic. As he speculates as to whether Chauntecleer's fall was determined by Fortune or not, so the Nun's Priest at once rehearses and satirizes the numbing terms of the professional theologians:

> Witnesse on hym that any parfit clerk is,
> That in scole is greet altercacioun
> In this mateere, and greet disputisoun,
> And hath been of an hundred thousand men.
> But I ne kan nat bulte it to the bren

As kan the hooly doctour Augustyn,
Or Boece, or the Bisshop Bradwardyn,
Wheither that Goddes worthy forwityng
Streyneth me nedely for to doon a thyng, –
'Nedely' clepe I symple necessitee;
Or elles, if free choys be graunted me
To do that same thyng, or do it noght,
Though God forwoot it er that it was wroght;
Or if his wityng streyneth never a deel
But by necessitee condicioneel.
I wol nat han to do of swich mateere;
My tale is of a cok, as ye may heere . . .

parfit: fully trained   *scole:* universities or cathedral schools
bulte it to the bren: sift it all out   *Boece:* Boethius
forwityng: foreknowledge   *streyneth:* constrains   *nedely:* of necessity
symple necessitee: straightforward determinism   *never a deel:* not at all
necessitee condicioneel: moderate determinism

Authorities are cited only to be pushed into the background. Fiction –
sense rather than 'sentence' – seems to take command. The difficulties of
interpretation are emphasized at the expense of easy answers.

A similar scepticism is revealed in the portrayal of both Pertelote and
the widow. While, after Chauntecleer's 'fall', the Nun's Priest can re-
hearse the clichés of that anti-feminism which saw all women as 'types'
of Eve, the Nun's Priest himself refuses to give his consent to these. His
formal indictment of women is required by the rhetoric of the poem but
is offered without the consent of his heart. He prefers to pass over the
matter, referring those interested to various 'auctours' whom he does
not specify. There is here a benevolent scepticism – a refusal to toe the
hard line – but this should not lead us to think that the Nun's Priest is
sentimentally humanistic. The difficulties he has with his image of the
widow illustrate this.

While her initial presentation is indeed dignified and most engaging,
the widow is a somewhat different figure when, roused to the defence of
her property, she and her daughters pursue the thieving fox with a great
outburst of comic noise. This is compared with that made by Jack Straw
and the murdering crowds of the Peasants' Revolt. Chaucer briefly –
and on one of the very few occasions in his poetry – touches the world of
the *Vox Clamantis*. Scepticism forces the Nun's Priest to see the bad as
well as the good, while his relativism in an age of apparently strict
methods of interpretation makes his final and conventional request that
we should separate the 'fruyt' from the 'chaf' of his tale a very complex

matter indeed. Starting out as the most anonymous of the pilgrims, the Nun's Priest blossoms to become one of Chaucer's most subtle presentations.

The literary dexterity shown by the Nun's Priest is again adapted in *The Pardoner's Tale* and its Prologue to issues of the utmost seriousness. The poem is nonetheless one of Chaucer's most exuberant creations. The Pardoner – a character vividly and ironically embodying all seven of the Deadly Sins – mesmerizes his audience with a wilfully inverted sermon delivered by an apparently damned soul. When he afterwards scavenges for their money, he is exposed, criticized and pardoned by their common humanity. Chaucer here allows a familiar and much despised figure to reveal himself through parody, irony and blasphemy. We should also recognize the underlying rhetorical tradition which, following the False-Seeming of the *Roman de la Rose*, allows a character to reveal his inner life in such a comic way.

The Pardoner, it emerges, is a eunuch yet a would-be sensualist. (Both ideas are consonant with the suggestions of homosexuality that cluster about him and suggest his sinful misuse of Nature's gifts.) He also appears as a grotesque parody of the priesthood who claims to offer the forgiveness of sins even while he staggers on the edge of Hell. His whole performance is an exhibition of how the benign ideas that cluster round the Word of God are savaged by the loquacious trickery of man. As such, the work has an important role in Chaucer's experiments with fiction and in the broader interest of *The Canterbury Tales* as a whole in showing the pilgrimage of many souls across the world to divine truth.

We have seen that sermon rhetoric in the Middle Ages had well-established and elaborate rules. The Pardoner exploits many of these; but it is necessary to appreciate that his entire performance is a parody of the familiar notion of the devout, learned cleric, disciplined by religious practice, fulfilling what Aquinas had called the highest of the ecclesiastical functions while being directly inspired by the Holy Ghost. The Pardoner, by contrast, is motivated solely by greed and is inspired by drink. Such worldliness leads to a wealth of paradox. As is proper, the Pardoner takes his text from the Vulgate or Latin Bible: *radix malorum est cupiditas*, which we may translate narrowly as 'the love of money is the root of all evil'. This idea he elaborates with compelling *exempla* and a plenitude of vigorous, dramatic rhetoric while telling us that he performs only for cash. He thus preaches against Avarice – the Deadly Sin he most fully personifies. Nonetheless, by offering a 'moral tale' for the wrong reasons, he sometimes – so he says – enhances the faith of those who listen. Evil can only ever be a negative force in Christian theology and, claiming to offer the remission of sins, the Pardoner in fact threatens to damn himself while opening the paths of grace to his congregation.

The Pardoner's tale – which occupies only a third of his performance – moves from parody to blasphemy. It is a savage, concise *exemplum* which opens in a Breughel-like Land of Cockayne where three tavern-haunting 'riotoures', who personify the gluttony, gambling and time-wasting the drunken Pardoner has so vividly analysed, learn of the death of a friend. Roused by his knell – a prefiguring of their own deaths at each other's hands – they set out to destroy Death himself. We should here recall the fourth or anagogical level of interpretation which we have seen applied to *The Man of Law's Tale*, and so gloss the rioters' aim as a profane parody of Christ's triumph over mortality at the Resurrection. The rioters' pathetic, sin-sodden purposes are deflected, however, when an old man who is forbidden to die (he is Chaucer's compelling image of humanity longing for its natural end) tells them of a crock of gold. They run off after it. 'No lenger thanne after Deeth they soughte,' the Pardoner ironically comments as all three hurl themselves, like grotesque heroes from fabliaux, to their own destruction. When they have found the gold beneath a tree which we may like to compare with that in Eden, the youngest is sent off after bread and wine. These we may interpret as a blasphemous parody of the eucharist which the boy – as evil as the others – laces with rat poison. He is killed on his return, but the others consume his poisoned victuals. *The Pardoner's Tale* thus illustrates its text with chilling logic and shows that the wages of sin are death indeed.

The Parson's Tale – the last of the pilgrims' offerings – presents the remedy for sin and deserves our attention for a number of reasons. First, it is an early example of Middle English devotional prose written by a layman. Secondly, its analysis of true penitence and the Seven Deadly Sins provides an important insight into many of the commonly held religious beliefs of the Middle Ages. But there are two further interesting aspects. First, the Parson – a fictional figure himself – refuses to have anything to do with fiction. In his stern sincerity, founded on Scripture and doctrine, he opts for analytic prose, for 'moralitee and virtuous mateere' rather than fable. In so doing, he brings to a devout conclusion the wide-ranging and often very daring experiments we have seen made in *The Canterbury Tales* between literary invention and divine truth, between man's word and God's. The secular speculations of the opening *Knight's Tale*, for example, are resolved in traditional piety as we move from Athens to Canterbury, from the city of man to the image of the city of God. Secondly, and in a manner wholly appropriate, Chaucer appends to the sermon a sincere, conventional retraction of his 'enditynges of worldly vanitees'. It is a moving moment. The great master of medieval English fiction here, at the close of his most various work, dismisses his early poems, the philosophic enquiries of *Troilus and Criseyde*, his fabliaux, romances and dream works. No longer either an inventive poet or an imagined pilgrim, he presents himself as a mortal and kneels contrite before the ultimate truth of Christian salvation, gratefully offering up only his homilies and his pious translations in the hope that 'I may be oon of hem at the day of doom that shalle be saved'. The greatest voice of Middle English fiction is finally silenced in prayer.

CHAPTER 5

CHAUCER'S FRIENDS AND FOLLOWERS

1

Chaucer's genius is so pre-eminent that a few poems not by him at all were early gathered into his collected works. *The Flower and the Leaf* (*c.* 1400), a refined and anonymous secular vision, is perhaps the prettiest of them. The poet, who was almost certainly a woman, rejoices in the pageantry of courtly life and presents two groups of knights and ladies in a delightful setting: a white company with chaplets of woodbine, laurel and hawthorn, and a green company crowned with flowers. These last are the servants of Flora who lived

> But for to hunt and hauke, and pley in medes,
> And many other such idle dedes.

When these people have beautifully sung the praises of the daisy, they faint in the sun and are drenched by a storm, while the virtuous white company stay protected beneath their laurel tree. The moral purpose is firm and unobtrusive, the observation fresh, and the fantasy delightful.

The poems of the 'Chauceriana' are important not only for their quality – *The Cuckoo and the Nightingale*, possibly written by Sir John Clanvowe (d. 1391), is a most polished example of minor polite verse – but for the insight such works as *The Court of Love* give into the aspirations of a highly civilized society, and the influence exerted by all these pieces because of their misattribution to Chaucer. *La Belle Dame Sans-Merci* (*c.* 1350), for example, is an admirable translation of a French original in which the cruel lady of the title asserts her independence in lines that are more readily acceptable today than at the time of their composition, when they caused an acrimonious literary debate, a whole series of replies, refutations and pleadings of the case:

> Free am I now, and free wil I endure;
> To be ruled by mannes governaunce
> For erthely good, nay! that I you ensure!

The lover's eventual death from unrequited passion becomes, in Keats's poem of the same title, a tragedy shot through with a romantic ardour in which the Middle Ages themselves become not just a period of history but an imagined state of the soul.

2

John Gower's enormous English poem, the *Confessio Amantis* ('The Lover's Confession') has inspired no such revival, but in its pleasant if sometimes pedestrian way it uses many of the ideas we have already discussed, reworking these in a comfortable manner that ensured Gower's popularity down to Elizabethan times. Forty-nine manuscripts of the work survive. The poem was begun in about 1386, apparently at the suggestion of Richard II, and was completed four years later. In 1393 the disgust with which Gower viewed Richard's court became such that he re-dedicated the work to Bolingbroke, later Henry IV.

Since the *Confessio Amantis* is a poem of over 33,000 lines, it may be useful to give some general idea of its construction. The work is a *compilatio* of 133 smooth-flowing, moral and unemphatic stories from familiar sources, skilfully re-told in octosyllabic couplets. They were designed both to offer delight and serve as *exempla* in the wider framework of the text. This takes the form of a penitential manual. The Lover's confession to Genius, the priest of Venus, is almost certainly intended in part as a comment on the fashionable association of aristocratic passion and religious devotion. As with much of the best work of the period, the worth of this alliance is subtly explored. While Genius works his way through the Seven Deadly Sins, dividing each into five parts and relating these to courtship, so he both tells his illustrative tales and analyses the Lover's plight. He does this in such a way that he becomes the voice of conscience, prompter of that calm voice of fine feeling or 'gentilesse' which makes sin appear merely gauche and low-bred. We come to see love as an imperative force, but one that should not make man lose either his dignity or his self-control:

> It sit a man be weie of kinde
> To love, bot it is noght kinde . . .
> A man for love his wit to lese

sit: suits   *be weie of kinde:* naturally   *lese:* lose

Reason and an ideal of marriage that is sometimes heroic in intensity should temper passion and so limit the possibilities of sin. Yet, amid this golden mediocrity, the Lover himself is far from lacking in character. He has his moments of frustrated petulance, while Gower also shows him staring devotedly at his lady's 'fingres longe and smale' as she works her embroidery. Again, the Lover describes his weightless feeling as 'I daunce and skippe' at the occasional ball. Although the lady's absolute disdain rules out the possibility of any emotional development between the two, this impasse helps Gower towards a tender final surprise. As his huge poem comes to its close, so the playful identification of the poet with his Lover assumes a gentle, touching melancholy. We slowly realize his age:

> 'That which was whilom grene gras,
> Is welked hey at time now,
> Forthi mi conseil is that thou
> Remembre wel hou thou art old.'

> *whilom:* once   *welked:* withered   *forthi:* therefore

He is verging on the type of the *senex amans*, the foolish elderly lover of convention.

Gower is not invariably bound by the typical, however, and one of his best verse paragraphs – the medium of his quiet excellence – describes the company of aged lovers:

> Me thoghte I sih upon the field,
> Where Elde cam a softe pas
> Toward Venus, ther as sche was.
> With him gret compaignie he ladde,
> Bot noght so manye as Youthe hadde:
> The moste part were of gret Age,
> And that was sene in the visage,
> And noght forthi, so as thei myhte,
> Thei made hem yongly to the sihte:
> Bot yit herde I no pipe there
> To make noise in mannes Ere,
> Bot the Musette I myhte knowe,
> For olde men which souneth lowe,
> With Harpe and Lute and with Citole.
> The hovedance and the Carole,
> In such a wise as love hath bede,
> A softe pas thei dance and trede;
> And with the wommen otherwhile
> With sobre chier among thei smyle,
> For laghtre was ther non on hyh.
> And natheles full wel I syh
> That thei the more queinte it made
> For love, in whom thei weren glade.

sih: saw   *Elde:* Old Age   *visage:* face   *forthi:* therefore
musette: a musical instrument   *citole:* lute   *hovedance:* dance   *pas:* step
queinte: delightful

There is nothing here of the grinding pessimism of the so-called *ubi
sunt* motif (the list of long-dead lovers recited to remind us of our own
deaths) which a lesser poet might have tried. Nor is there that too-
exclusive emphasis on adolescent ardour which is perhaps the most
baleful legacy of *fine amour*. Finally, it is among this company of the
elderly that Gower is eased of his passion. He has suffered much and
heard many tales – among them the excellent *Rosiphelle, Ceyx and
Alcyone* and *Jason and Medea*. Most of these narratives have been
worked with skilful simplicity. Gower had little of Chaucer's virtuoso
playfulness, but he had a feeling for the complexity and variety of experience and presents his women especially with touching pathos. The
Lover's shrift is certainly helped by this tone, and Cupid finally plucks
his fiery dart from his victim. The Lover goes home, if not with all
passion spent then at least with his mind fixed on more serious matters:
the state of England and the pursuit of charity.

The closing sections of the *Confessio Amantis*, like its Prologue, show
Gower in his familiar role as a satirist. As in the *Vox Clamantis*, the
wretched state of England is exposed. Men no longer care for virtue or
good books. The Church is in the hands of simonists and Lollards, justice is corrupt, the third estate is mutinous, and the world's end is nigh.
We live in the last times and can only look back to a golden age, when

> Justice of lawe tho was holde,
> The privilege of regalie
> Was sauf, and al the baronie
> Worschiped was in his astat;
> The citees knewen no debat,
> The poeple stod in obeissance
> Under the reule of governance,
> And pes, which ryhtwisnesse keste,
> With charite tho stod in reste . . .

tho: then   *regalie:* kingship   *baronie:* peerage   *debat:* contention
ryhtwisnesse: righteousness   *keste:* kissed

And it is this wider concept of love that really binds the vast work
together, not just the cupidinous desire of the Lover tempered as the
purity of his will is refined, but the broader concept of charity.

Such social love is central to the vast seventh book of the *Confessio
Amantis* which is nothing less than an encyclopedia presented in the

conventional form of an educational tract for a prince – Alexander, in this case, who is implicitly compared with Richard II and his running riot, free from a restraining hand. That Gower should have inserted this considerable section into his already vast poem suggests that verse was still seen as the natural medium of exposition, and Book VII of the *Confessio Amantis* is indeed a most useful *summa* of commonplace medieval thought. Following Aristotle, Gower divides knowledge into the theoretical, the rhetorical or poetic, and the practical. In this vast compass, he discusses theology and the natural world, physics, geography, astrology and language. The practical element includes ethics, economics and political policy – the education of a prince's morals in particular. A concern with truth and steadfastness, proper liberality and the royal direction of the laws by a monarch who is himself above the law, lead to a discussion of the fourth part of policy which is pity, and the fifth which is chastity. In this way, and with the widest interpretation of love, Gower presents the personal and the public, the corrupt and the ideal, in a work which fulfils his own requirement of vernacular literature, that his poem should be 'a bok for Engelondes sake'.

3

The reputation of John Lydgate (*c.* 1370–1450) has declined dramatically from the time when contemporaries placed him beside Gower and only a little behind Chaucer. 'A voluminous, prosaick and drivelling monk', the eighteenth-century scholar Joseph Ritson called him. Voluminous Lydgate certainly was. Life in the monastery at Bury St Edmunds allowed him to write the 145,000 or so lines of his collected verse, and it was just this facility his contemporaries admired. Lydgate produced work for them in almost every genre. The future Henry V commissioned his *Troybook* which consists of 30,117 lines of epic translated and amplified from Guido delle Colonne. Not to be outdone, the Duke of Gloucester received the 36,365 lines of *The Fall of Princes*. The Earl of Salisbury asked for a translation of Deguileville, and the resulting *Pilgrimage of Man* runs to 24,832 lines. John Braine once defined the professional writer as a person who counts words. With Lydgate, it is easier to count lines; but it is the professionalism that is important and may account for the 'prosaick'. We have seen that English prose at this period did not have the facility to deal with all subjects. Verse was still a more natural medium for exposition. Gower wrote his versified encyclopedia; Lydgate, following a still hugely popular trend, wrote works on etiquette which contain such lines as 'pike nat they nase', and issued a 'dietary' or guide to good health which was the most widely circulated of all his texts. He also wrote short didactic plays or interludes.

The need for information and the uncertainty of prose account for much of Lydgate's work but they do not wholly explain his style or what to us must appear as his excessive prolixity. The purpose of the latter he described himself:

> Ffor a stori which is nat pleynli told,
> But constreyned vndir wordes fewe,
> Ffor lak off trouth, wher thei be newe or old,
> Men be report kan nat the mater shewe.
> Thes ookes grete be nat downe ihewe
> Ffirst at a strok, but bi longe processe;
> Nor longe stories a woord may nat expresse.

> *ihewe:* hewn

This is the precise opposite of Chaucer's sometimes ironically expressed concern with brevity as the soul of wit, but it is well to remember the words of another eighteenth-century critic at this point – a man who also happened to be a greater poet than Lydgate. 'It is folly to judge of the understanding and of the patience of those times by our own,' wrote Thomas Gray. 'They loved, I will not say tediousness, but length and a chain of circumstances in narration.' Further, while Lydgate's ear was happy with the monotonous and his grammar was far from scrupulous, he had also been brought up on the manuals of rhetoric. So had Chaucer; but poets are born, not made, and even when Lydgate read the works of the man he so touchingly admired and tried to imitate, he ransacked him for elements that we perhaps now least regard: 'the gold dewe-dropis of rethorik so fine'. In reading the early poems of Chaucer especially in his search for 'aureate' or self-consciously literary terms, Lydgate and his contemporaries tried to restrain the greatest of Middle English poets in their own late Gothic fold. Their master's freedom was beyond them. This 'medievalizing' of Chaucer was widespread, and many poets were tempted by 'aureate' terms, sometimes with fine results. With Lydgate, such an interest leads to what is at times an almost abstract poetry (and this may well be the point), a verse so disembodied and generalized as to be about hardly anything except its own effects:

> The nyght ypassed, at spryngyng of the day,
> Whan that the larke with a blissed lay
> Gan to salue the lusty rowes rede
> Of Phebus char, that so freschely sprede
> Upon the bordure of the orient.

> *salue:* greet *char:* chariot

This is a technique perfectly adapted to saying very little over many lines, thereby creating a generalized, unproblematic fuzz of courtly sentiment, political and moral pessimism, anti-feminist satire, or whatever else was required. In such ways 'sentence' becomes cliché, commonplace platitude. Perhaps it is only in his poems to the Virgin that Lydgate's style, acquiring a liturgical, hieratic splendour, achieves an imaginative if rather curious effect.

4

Thomas Hoccleve (*c.* 1368–*c.* 1450) – a less voluminous and more attractive poet than Lydgate – was a scrivener who complained of the tedium of the copyist's craft. Not for him and his colleagues were the chat and whistling of the ordinary workshop:

> We stowpe and stare upon the shepes skyn,
> And keepe muste our song and wordes in.

Hoccleve tried his hand at serious didactic work and dedicated his *Regement of Princes* – a piece of conventional moral instruction – to Henry V. Hoccleve was also a translator, but it is in his works of touching self-portrayal, enlivened as they are by vivid observation, that his best work often lies. He has his moments of humour and can describe his plump mistress's figure as being as comely as a football. *La male Regle de T. Hoccleve* (*c.* 1405–6), while it cannot match Villon, is a pleasant account of harmless youthful follies. The picture of the poet's mental collapse offered in his *Complaint* is as emotive as an honest account of such things should be:

> . . . Men seiden, I loked as a wilde steer,
> And so my looke aboute I gan to throwe.
> Min heed to hie anothir seide I beer:
> 'Ful bukkissh is his brayn, wel may I trowe!'
> And seyde the thridde – and apt is in the rowe
> To site of hem that resounles reed
> Can geve – 'No sadnesse is in his heed.'

bukkissh: frenzied   *trowe:* believe   *thridde:* third person   *rowe:* company
reed: counsel   *sadnesse:* stability

5

Chaucer's achievement was most fruitfully developed half a century after his death and in a country he almost certainly never visited. The best of the so-called 'Scottish Chaucerians' – James I, Dunbar, Henryson and Gavin Douglas, the translator of Virgil – are greater poets than either Lydgate or Hoccleve, but we should measure their achievement not simply in terms of their relationship to England, but in the context of European poetry and their own native traditions and language. They borrowed much, but their genius was their own.

Scotland also had a considerable output of verse chronicle, and in Barbour's *Bruce* (*c*. 1380), an old-fashioned chronicle of nationalism that is not without its moments of vivid description, the native language is used and is rightly called 'Inglis'. The name differentiates the tongue from Gaelic. The political independence of Scotland ensured that 'Inglis' developed separately, however, and by 1450 there was a vigorous body of poetry in what is now termed 'Middle Scots'.

Some of the best poetry in Middle Scots was written by the Scottish Chaucerians but owed little to Chaucer's direct influence. Anthologies assembled in the sixteenth century contain such lively descriptions of peasant humour as *Christis Kirk on the Grene*, attributed to James I (1394–1437), and it is this king, long imprisoned in England, who was almost certainly responsible for the first Scottish work in the courtly tradition: *The Kingis Quair* ('The King's Book'). This is a poem that beautifully describes the progress of a love affair from the moment of the gaoled hero's first glimpse of his beloved as she walks in a nearby garden, through anguish and illumination, to a rapt praise of the power of love. While the work derives much from Chaucer (from *Troilus and Criseyde* and *The Knight's Tale* especially), it is powerfully original and beautifully constructed.

The poem starts with the restless poet's reading of Boethius and, summoned by a matins bell, his subsequent recitation of what befell him. As with Palamon and Arcite, the chance sight of a beautiful girl in a springtime garden near his prison causes a sudden and desperate pang:

> For quhich sodayn abate anon astert
> The blude of all my body to my hert.

abate: faintness

Combining the roles of the two young men in Chaucer's poem, the king is unsure whether his beloved is a goddess or an earthly woman:

> 'A, suete, ar ye a warldly creature,
> Or hevinly thing in liknesse of nature?

> 'Or ar ye god Cupidis owin princesse
> And cummyn ar to louse me out of band?

Or ar ye verray Nature the goddesse
That have depaynted with your hevinly hand
This gardyn full of flouris, as they stand?
Quhat sall I think, allace, quhat reverence
Sall I minister to your excellence?

'Gif ye a goddesse be, and that ye like
To do me payne, I may it noght astert.
Gif ye be warldly wight that dooth me sike
Quhy lest God mak you so, my derrest hert,
To do a sely prisoner thus smert,
That lufis yow all and wote of noght bot wo?
And therfore merci, suete, sen it is so.'

astert: escape   *sike:* sigh

A series of exquisitely refined and tender stages follow in which the poet begs the nightingale to sing in his lady's honour. A dream sequence is then offered. In this, the poet visits first the house of Venus where lovers both secular and 'folk of religioun' present their petitions, and then the temple of Minerva where he learns that love should be virtuous and steadfast. Finally he meets Fortune, who looks on him favourably. A white dove brings the poet a message of comfort from Venus, while, in the excellent and highly ornate conclusion, the poet blesses the fair chain of love that binds all living creatures together. The familiar themes of imprisonment, passion and philosophic enquiry lead to final happiness and a very beautiful celebration of the personal sentiments and broader implications of *fine amour*.

6

The narrative skills of Robert Henryson (*c.* 1424–*c.* 1505) are outstanding. Very little is known about him personally beyond the fact that in a country where three universities had been founded by the fifteenth century, Henryson had a degree and possibly held the then revered post of schoolmaster at Dunfermline, an important cultural centre favoured by the court. And it is with the courtly tradition that Henryson is most at home. He wrote a number of religious and moral pieces as well as a deeply considered version of the Eurydice myth. Something of his delicacy appears in *Robene and Makene*, a poem of pastoral courtship in which a simple shepherd is unaware of the sufferings Makene's love for him is causing her and of his own consequent cruelty. Finally the tables are turned and the poet points the moral:

> 'Robene, thow hes hard soung and say
> In gestis and storeis auld,
> The man that will nocht quhen he may
> Sall haif nocht quhen he wald.'

gestis: narratives

If Henryson was indeed a schoolmaster, then the fables of Aesop would have been particularly familiar to him. There is no trace of staleness in his re-workings, however. They are shrewd, energetic and comic. Henryson's purpose was, he states ironically, 'to make ane maner of translation . . . in hamelie language and in termis rude'. In fact, he was a rhetorician of exceptional competence. He also had a keen knowledge of animal life and of the human foibles his animals represent. Boethius and the Bestiaries had shown how sin corresponds to the animal element in man, and Henryson develops this idea with great humanity. He knows the daily grind of 'the pure [poor] pepill . . . of quhome the lyfe is half ane purgatorie'. He also writes powerfully of the vices of the rich. *The Sheep and the Dog* exposes legal injustices, while *The Wolf and the Wedder* is as vividly anthropomorphic as *The Nun's Priest's Tale* itself. The little foibles of social class are charmingly expressed as the Town Mouse, invited to a rustic feast of nuts and candle-ends, declares:

> 'My fair sister . . . have me excusit.
> This rude dyat and I can not accord;
> To tender meit my stomok is ay usit,
> For quhylis I fair alsweill as ony Lord;
> Thir wydderit peis, and nuttis, or thay be bord,
> Wil I brek my teith, and mak my wame fful sklender,
> Quhilk wes before usit to meitis tender.'

wydderit: withered   *or thay be bord:* before they are chewed   *wame:* stomach

In all, *The Morall Fabillis of Esope the Phrygian* show us a frail and uncertain world, corrupt, cruel, clearly seen and criticized, and yet lightened by delicacy and shrewd understanding.

Henryson's most powerful achievement, however – a poem at once derived from Chaucer and wholly independent – is *The Testament of Cresseid*. This is the story of Chaucer's heroine:

> Quhen Diomeid had all his appetyte,
> And mair, fulfillit of this fair ladie . . .

That 'and mair' is devastating. It points to the fixed and unillusioned stare, the sometimes terse but always compassionate realism of the whole work.

Henryson presents his narrator as an unhappy poet, a would-be *senex amans*, reading Chaucer by his winter fireside with a glass of wine. First he describes Cresseid's return to her father when she has been jilted by Diomeid, Calchas's kindly reception of her, and Cresseid's regrets. The effect is strong, very tender and humane. The fallen woman's shame and the father's simple solicitude suggest dignity even in humiliation. The suffering is reproach enough. But, in her resentment, Cresseid curses the gods, and, in her dream of the great pageant of the deities that follows, we are led to feel the dreadful power and petulance of these astrological forces. Cupid feels that he and his mother have been insulted:

> 'Lo,' quod Cupide, 'quha will blaspheme the name
> Of his awin god, outher in word or deid,
> To all goddis he dois baith lak and schame,
> And suld have bitter panis to his meid.
> I say this by yon wretchit Cresseid,
> The quhilk throw me was sum tyme flour of lufe,
> Me and my mother starklie can reprufe,
>
> 'Saying of hir greit infelicitie
> I was the caus, and my mother Venus,
> Ane blind goddes hir cald that micht not se,
> With sclander and defame injurious.
> Thus hir leving unclene and lecherous
> Scho wald retorte on me and my mother,
> To quhome I schew my grace abone all uther.'

> *meid:* reward *the quhilk:* who

Cresseid is struck with leprosy:

> And quhen scho saw hir face sa deformait,
> Gif scho in hart was wa aneuch, God wait!

> *wa aneuch:* sufficiently pained

A little child comes to tell her that supper is ready, and afterwards, with great simplicity, Henryson describes Cresseid's father taking her to the lepers' hospital. Against this background – plain, tragic, human – her complaint to 'frivoll fortune' becomes very powerful. Indeed, in its combination of the personal and the formal, it is one of the loveliest pieces of rhetoric in medieval verse:

> 'My cleir voice and courtlie carrolling,
> Quhair I was wont with ladyis for to sing,
> Is rawk as ruik full hiddeous, hoir and hace;
> My plesand port, all utheris precelling,
> Of lustines I was hald maist conding –

Now is deformit the figour of my face;
To luik on it na leid now lyking hes.
Sowpit in syte, I say with sair siching,
Ludgeit amang the lipper leid: "Allace!"

rawk as ruik: raucous as a rook *hoir and hace:* grating and hoarse
precelling: preceding *conding:* worthy *leid:* lord
sowpit in syte, etc.: horrible to look at, I say with sore sighing, lodged among the ugly lepers
'alas!'

But this is not all the poem has to offer. Troilus later rides past.
Cresseid, thick-sighted from disease, does not recognize him. He, even
through her disfigurement, is reminded of the woman he once knew:

Than upon him scho kest up baith hir ene –
And with ane blenk it come into his thocht
That he sumtime hir face befoir had sene.
Bot scho was in sic plye he knew hir nocht;
Yit than hir luik into his mynd it brocht
The sweit visage and amorous blenking
Of fair Cresseid, sumtyme his awin darling.

blenk: glance *plye:* plight

Compassionate memory prompts him to offer her money. Told who her
benefactor is, Cresseid dies of remorse. Some say that Troilus himself
raised a tomb to her. The 'golden letteris' carved on the stone are a
perfect expression of an absolute and tragic generosity of spirit:

'Lo, fair ladyis! Cresseid of Troyis toun,
Sumtyme countit the flour of womanheid,
Under this stane, lait lipper, lyis deid.'

lait lipper: late leper

The great lover tries to immortalize his feckless beloved as the victim of
a tragic destiny. He makes no mention of her deceit.

7

The Testament of Cresseid is a sublime and tragic achievement. The
assured range of its language and the combination of skilful narrative,
pathos and unblinking philosophic inquiry make it one of the most
humane works of medieval English poetry. It has a grandeur quite
unmatched by the other Scottish Chaucerians. Yet in the widely ranging work of William Dunbar (*c.* 1456–*c.* 1513) there is to be found
something of that marvellous mix of contraries it is tempting to call

typically Gothic, save that no medieval poet – least of all Chaucer – is quite like Dunbar.

The Chaucerian influence can be traced in some of Dunbar's formal, courtly set-pieces: *The Golden Targe*, for example, and the slightly more subtle *Thrisill and the Rois*. The last is a poem which draws on obvious heraldic symbolism to celebrate the marriage of the Scottish king to an English princess. It is a poem by a professional poet and succeeds in the difficult task of complimenting a courtly occasion without being too fawning. Its 'aureate' terms give the work a certain sonorous beauty, but in the following poem (a more assured technical achievement), such artificial language becomes like spun gold – extraordinarily contrived, yet gold all the same:

> Hale, sterne superne! Hale, in eterne,
> In Godis sicht to schyne!
> Lucerne in derne for to discerne
> Be glory and grace devyne;
> Hodiern, modern, sempitern,
> Angelicall regyne!
> Our tern inferne for to dispern
> Helpe, rialest rosyne.
> *Ave Maria, gracia plena!*
> Haile, fresche floure femynyne!
> Yerne us, guberne, virgin matern,
> Of reuth baith rute and ryne.

sterne superne: high star *lucerne in derne:* light in darkness *hodiern:* of today
sempitern: eternal *regyne:* queen *tern inferne for to dispern:* our infernal woes to relieve
rosyne: rose *yerne:* guide *guberne:* govern *reuth:* pity *ryne:* rind or bark

It may perhaps be a form of sincere devotion to make something so elaborate in honour of the Virgin, but the real sincerity is perhaps in the devotion to an artifice Swinburne might have envied. It is also characteristic of Dunbar that he can turn the language of devotion to secular purposes. In his *Dregy* or 'Dirge', he adapts the Office for the Dead into an expression of pity for those of his provincial colleagues languishing in the purgatory of Stirling rather than taking part in the 'mirrines' of Edinburgh. Again, when Dunbar attempts to describe the standard theme of the Seven Deadly Sins, drawing on dramatic and sermon traditions, he can be ribald and satiric. A satiric tone is found again – alongside a strong sense of personal outrage – in his address *To the Merchantis of Edinburgh* who have let his favourite city become corrupt and dirty, full of beggars and flat-toned minstrels. But it is in *The Tretis of the Tua Mariit Wemen and the Wedo* that Dunbar's satiric bawdy, the influence of the Chaucer of *The Wife of Bath's Tale*, and the French courtly and fabliau traditions are most skilfully combined. The poem also uses the alliterative line with great technical virtuosity. Though independent of the 'alliterative revival' proper, the work is the comic masterpiece of medieval alliterative verse.

The poem begins in the beautiful landscape of convention and offers a view of 'thre gay ladeis'. Two are the wives of lords, while the third is a widow who asks what 'mirth' the others find in their marriages – whether these are a penance or a joy to them. So far, so courtly. Perhaps we are to be treated to a refined discussion of marriage and *fine amour*, perhaps even the praise of holy chastity as a state superior to earthly love. Not a bit of it. Unaware of the male presence of the narrator, the women indulge in the coarsest abuse of their husbands. The first is married to the *vieux jaloux*, or

> . . . ane wallidrag, ane worme, ane auld wobat carle,
> A waistit wolroun, na worth bot wourdis to clatter;
> Ane bumbart, ane dron bee, ane bag full of flewme,
> Ane skabbit skarth, ane scorpioun, ane scutarde behind;
> To see him scart his awin skyn grit scunner I think.

wallidrag: sloven   *wobat carle:* caterpillar man   *bumbart:* drone   *skarth:* cormorant
scutarde: shitter   *scart:* scratch   *scunner:* disgust

The second is shackled with an exhausted lecher. Pleased to have discovered that each is in a similarly dreadful plight, the Widow then offers them advice gained from her own experience of two husbands: an old fool and a vulgar merchant. The most blatant and calculated cynicism is combined with *sententiae* of great formal beauty, and the whole becomes a skilful playing with the conventions of love debate and fabliau. For the Widow, her single state is delightful. Far from recognizing the alleged spiritual superiority of widowhood to the married life, she declares in language that ironically echoes Psalm 30 and the Easter hymns:

> Now done is my dolly nyght, my day is upsprungin,
> Adew dolour, adew! my daynte now begynis:
> Now am I a wedow, I wise and weill am at ese.

dolly: miserable   *daynte:* delight

In *The Tua Mariit Wemen and the Wedo*, Dunbar comes closest to that self-delighting play with convention that is so important to medieval poetry, and if he is coarser-grained than Chaucer he is nonetheless capable of some fine effects.

At the opposite pole stand Dunbar's hymns to the Virgin. In the hands of a great poet, convention can be a form of freedom, an arena for imaginative experiment. It is a measure of Dunbar's diversity that, in addition to the poems already described, he is also capable of a touching personal expression, a moving elegiac tone, and an assured mood of religious triumph.

On an incidental, personal level, Dunbar can write such touching minor verse as *On His Heid-ake*. The *Meditatioun in Wyntir*, however, is a powerful expression of the self-mothering solicitude which comes with

> . . . thir dirk and drublie dayis,
> Quhone sabill all the hevin arrayis
> With mystie vapouris, cluddis, and skyis,
> Nature all curage me denyis
> Off sangis, ballattis, and of playis.

> *sabill:* sable, black   *curage:* heart   *sangis:* songs   *ballattis:* ballads

The pessimism deepens with the winter. Serious allegorical figures lecture the poet on the purposes of life and its end. He has no money, no wife 'nor luiffis blys'. The penitent tone of worldly unhappiness is wholly convincing, but the fresh insight and genius come with the last stanza:

> Yit, quhone the nycht begynnis to schort,
> It dois my spreit sum pairt confort,
> Off thocht oppressit with the schowris.
> Cum, lustie symmer! with thi flowris,
> That I may leif in sum disport.

It is as committed poet and devout Christian that we can leave this energetically various man. While the 'flyting' of Dunbar and Kennedy is a poem of fine and uproarious abuse, the reverse of this mood is found in *The Lament for the Makaris* (or 'Poets'), a haunting poem on the transience of earthly things. The knell-like tolling of its refrain combines a personal fear of death with a vision of worldwide destruction. This leads to a consideration of the most lamentable deaths of all – those of the lords of language:

> He hes done petuously devour,
> The noble Chaucer, of makaris flour,
> The Monk of Bery, and Gower, all thre;
>   *Timor mortis conturbat me.*

> *The Monk of Bery:* Lydgate
> *Timor mortis conturbat me:* The fear of death harries me

Finally, in Dunbar's greatest religious lyric, with drama and an unstated personal sense of relief, the poet presents the triumph of Easter and suggests his grateful place among the congregation of the faithful:

> Done is a battell on the dragon blak,
> Our campioun Chryst confountet hes his force;
> The yettis of hell ar brokin with a crak,
> The signe triumphall rasit is of the croce,
> The divillis trymmillis with hiddous voce,
> The saulis ar borrowit and to the blis can go,
> Chryst with his blud our ransonis dois indoce:
> *Surrexit Dominus de sepulchro.*

> *yettis:* gates   *trymmillis:* trembles   *saulis:* souls   *indoce:* endorse
> *Surrexit Dominus de sepulchro:* God is risen from the grave

CHAPTER 6

ALLITERATIVE POETRY

1

During the period in which Chaucer was writing, poets from the great houses of the North and West Midlands especially – parts of the country that had earlier nurtured Layamon and the 'Katherine Homilist' – were revitalizing alliterative verse. There is much debate as to how far these authors were directly exploiting Old English traditions, but, however obscure its origins, their work encompasses chronicle and romance as well as biblical paraphrase, religious vision and satire, to comprise some of the very finest Middle English poetry. Indeed, the achievements of Langland and the anonymous Gawain-poet stand comparison with Chaucer.

It may be helpful first to describe the Middle English alliterative line. In its basic form, this consists of four stressed syllables (of which the first three usually begin with the same consonant or any vowel) and an undetermined number of unaccented syllables. The alliterating stresses are usually placed in pairs across a caesura and may be increased from four or be as light as two. This is clearly a very flexible and energetic measure – Chaucer's Parson refers to it dismissively as 'rum, ram, ruf by lettre' – but, drawing partly on alliterative vernacular and Latin prose as well as on rhymed French poetry, the Middle English measure is capable of conveying many moods and even an exquisite refinement. The vocabulary employed often has a preponderance of Old English elements and shows a considerable interest in stock phrases, archaisms and a poetic diction rich in necessary synonyms. The following stanza from *Sir Gawain and the Green Knight* (*c.* 1385) suggests many of these qualities:

> þis kyng lay at Camylot vpon Krystmasse
> With mony luflych lorde, ledez of þe best –
> Rekenly of þe Rounde Table alle þo rich breþer –
> With rych reuel oryȝt and rechles merþes.
> þer tournayed tulkes by tymez ful mony,
> Justed ful jolilé þise gentyle kniȝtes,
> Syþen kayred to þe court, caroles to make;
> For þer þe fest watz ilyche ful fiften dayes,

With alle þe mete and þe mirþe þat men couþe avyse:
Such glaum ande gle glorious to here,
Dere dyn vpon day, daunsyng on ny3tes –
Al watz hap vpon he3e in hallez and chambrez
With lordez and ladies, as leuest him þo3t.
With all þe wele of þe worlde þay woned þer samen,
þe most kyd kny3tez vnder Krystes Seluen
And þe louelokkest ladies þat euer lif haden,
And he þe comlokest kyng, þat þe court haldes;
For al watz þis fayre folk in her first age,
    On sille,
   þe hapnest vnder heuen,
   Kyng hy3est mon of wylle –
Hit were now gret nye to neuen
So hardy a here on hille.

(*The king kept his court at Camelot that Christmas with many fine lords and manly liegemen – all rightly reckoned as the Round Table's brotherhood – with sumptuous celebration and carefree mirth. Many a fellow fought in the tournaments, these gentle knights joyfully jousted, then proceeded to the court to sing and dance carols, for it was there that the feast was held for fifteen days, with all the meat and the mirth that men could devise. Such garrulous glee was glorious to hear, a fine din by day and dancing by night – the height of happiness in the halls and the chambers, with lords and ladies as they most liked it. With all the happiness on earth they housed there together, the noblest knights under Christ himself, and the loveliest ladies that ever lived, and the comeliest king who ever held court. All these fair folk were in the first flush of youth in this hall, the happiest under Heaven, and their king of the finest – it would be hard to find today so handsome a host on a hill [i.e. in a castle].*)

There is nothing remotely provincial about this lively, very civilized enjoyment of a courtly and religious festival. While the verse form perhaps owes something to the English alliterative tradition of the *Brut*, the detailed pageantry derives much from the long family line stemming from Wace. Arthur's feasts are one of the conventional subjects of this poetry (there is little here that Chrétien would not have recognized) and the gorgeousness of this one is surpassed only by that in the alliterative *Morte Arthure*. Here are music, love and youthful energy, delights that lie at the very heart of courtly romance. As the 'gentyle kni3tes' beguile their time before the arrival of the necessary Christmas 'wonder' to test their worth, we are encouraged to feel that this is a place where the 'luflych lorde' is a gentleman and his qualities stem from graceful admiration of the flower of chivalry: 'Krystes Seluen'. Secular and sacred are thus in harmony under a mighty king. But, like all such golden ages, this is a paradise lost. The quietly admonishing voice of the poet at the close acknowledges that his art has roots in a more troubled, fallen world.

While alliterative verse makes a direct appeal to the ear and shows many qualities characteristic of an oral culture, the intricate subtlety of much of the finest work suggests that composition in studious and self-conscious solitude which we have seen to be a mark of Chaucer's verse. Again, just as Chaucer's career starts with direct translation, so what may well be one of the earliest alliterative romances is a version of a twelfth-century French original. It is also something of a surprise, for, while *William of Palerne* (before 1361) is imbued with the refined sentiment and concern with true nobility we might expect from its source, the plot is very largely in the hands of a benevolent werewolf who guards the fate of the hero and his beloved Melior until they regain their rightful kingdom. At the close, and in a passage which suggests the fascination with man and the supernatural characteristic of many of these works, the werewolf himself is returned to his true status as Alphouns, son of the King of Spain. Most unusually for an alliterative romance, we know that this very free translation was commissioned by Humphrey de Bohun, sixth Earl of Hereford, a magnate whose family were patrons of a famous group of manuscript illustrators. Such facts point to an easy familiarity with international Gothic culture among the great families of the west.

They also anticipate an interest in one of the most popular 'worthies' of the medieval chivalric imagination: Alexander the Great. Three alliterative versions of his supposed exploits survive (two of them fragmentary), and all are versions of Latin originals. While enjoying the purely fabulous nature of the events described and the possibilities offered for elaborating descriptions of battles and sieges, these poems also reveal a moral concern with establishing their hero as an image of restless worldly achievement, measuring him sometimes critically against the more tranquil ideals of those he conquers. It is as such a tireless but flawed warrior that the defeated Alexander (shown in a conventional image as crushed beneath the wheel of Fortune) greets the hero of one of the most important of all the surviving alliterative poems – King Arthur:

> 'That ever I regnede on þir rog, me rewes it ever!
> Was never roye so riche that regnede in erthe!
> Whene I rode in my rowte, roughte I noghte ells,
> Bot reuaye, and revell, and rawnson the pople.
> And thus I drifte forthe my dayes, whills I dreghe myghte,
> And therefore derflyche I am dampnede for ever.'

(*'I rue forever that I reigned on this wheel! No king so rich ever ruled on earth! When I rode with my retinue I recked little but hawking by rivers and revel and ransom. Thus I drew out my days as long as I could, and for this I am dreadfully damned without end.'*)

2

This dire warning takes us near the heart of the alliterative *Morte Arthure* (*c*. 1360) and its familiar medieval themes of the nature of the good king and the fall of princes, the instability of Fortune and the punishment of worldly pride. It cannot of itself, however, suggest the transforming energy with which these conventions are handled. While Chaucer's Monk collected an anthology of such stories in his rarely visited cell, defining tragedy as the tale of one who stood 'in greet prosperitee' but who fell from so high a state 'into myserie, and endeth wrecchedly', no one was moved by his lugubrious recitations and many indeed were bored. But the alliterative *Morte Arthure* cannot fail to involve us. The unknown poet delights in the full brilliance of heroic glory, revealing how the personal splendour of Arthur, the gleaming eyes, the magnanimity, wrath and heroic valour of this 'the comlyeste of knyghtehode þat undyre Cryste lyffes', merge into cruel, reckless greed and God-forsaking pride as he wages an unjust war. This leads to the final expression of Arthur's anguish over Gawain's corpse and to the end not just of his empire, his dynasty and his marriage, but of his own life also. The starkness of Arthur's death is offset by no mystical promise of return. The wheel of Fortune has simply, crushingly, come full circle.

The unique qualities of the alliterative *Morte Arthure* lie in its tragic force and the way in which the anonymous poet handles the elements on which his work draws. His background is wide-ranging, for it seems sometimes as if the large-boned heroes of Old English epic and French *chanson de geste*, touched by romance, have here acquired a better schooling in theology and manners. They are courteous to women – to the wives, queens and distraught mothers they encounter – but romantic love and the refining intricacies of private passion barely touch them. Their real affection is for their king and their king's for glory. Though Gawain emerges as the sovereign exemplar of chivalry, the poet both criticizes and sees pathos in his being, like a Saxon hero, 'most eager for fame'. The other warriors too, though the poet calls them 'kynde men and courtays, and couthe of courte thewes', describe their fellowship as 'the ryotous men and þe riche of þe rounde table'. If they belong to Camelot, they would not have been wholly out of place in Heorot. Indeed, there is much in the poem that suggests the heroic ethos of *Brut* and even *Beowulf*.

For example, at the start of the work, when the Roman ambassadors come to demand tribute from Arthur, there is a barbaric magnificence about his feast which is reminiscent of the Old English work, as well as a calculated rather than a natural courtesy in Arthur's behaviour. The king vows his revenge on the Romans with a thunderous voice, ignorant of the forthcoming catastrophe. The eager bravery of his men has about it elements at once feudal and reminiscent (to a modern audience at least) of that older, Saxon loyalty of a liegeman to his lord as the giver of gifts. Again, when Arthur has gathered his army together, placed his kingdom and his queen in the treacherous hands of Mordred and entered France, the heroic struggle with the monster of Saint-Michel, while similar to some of the fabulous encounters of romance, has about it a primitivism which can be sensed again in Beowulf's encounter with Grendel. There is also something in the scene of that folk-lore element present in Beowulf's final struggle. The description of Arthur's sword slashing the innards of the ogre 'just to þe genitales, and jaggede þam in sondre' is more basic than much romance would allow. The poem nonetheless shares with that genre an extensive interest in what Milton acidly called the 'tedious havoc' of military prowess.

But if the alliterative *Morte Arthure* looks back to older traditions, it also reflects something of the magnificence of fourteenth-century royal life, the violence and splendour of the court of Edward III, for example, with its lavish display of wealth, prowess and personal and political misfortune. Arthur, dressed in his rose-embroidered doublet and ruby-trimmed gloves, is a mirror of kingship, and the poem itself is addressed to those who love to hear of 'elders of alde tym and of theire awke [strange] dedys'.

It may be helpful briefly to discuss this background. Under Edward III, the English court had become famous throughout Europe. A chronicler described the royal face shining like a god's and added that to see him, or even dream of him, was to conjure up joyous images. All this was conventional, and frequently such images as came to the writer's mind were those of a mythical past – of Arthur and the Round Table, for instance. Hence the place of literature in augmenting ideas of material splendour and moral force – ideas of real significance.

We have seen that in the feudal society of the Middle Ages an elaborate ideal of aristocratic life dominated ethical and political thought. The social order, it was usually believed, had been determined by God, and the supremacy of princes had a divine justification. The highest tasks in the state belonged to such men as of right. In turn, it was their duty to protect the Church, succour the people and combat tyranny and violence. Born to such influence – and regardless of how they exercised it – the nobility then decorated their lives with a vision of their own splendour and imitated an ideal past. The heroes of history and literature inspired them to chivalry, kindled a longing for praise, and awoke the desire for fame. Such dreams even had a part to play in real life. Richard II, together with his uncles, the Dukes of Lancaster, York and Gloucester, challenged the King of France and his uncles to settle their differences by personal combat. Later, Henry V was similarly to challenge the Dauphin before the Battle of Agincourt. To act by such notions as these was to see politics and history as Arthur sees them – as matters of family status and personal pride. And pride, proverbially, must fall. The lives of other medieval princes were a constant reminder of this. For some years the court of Edward III detained King John of France and his peers while they waited for their ransoms to be paid. The history of Burgundy is similarly full of violent reversals in the lives of its rulers. Nearer home, Richard II, the unfortunate grandson of Edward III, was to be not only deposed but secretly murdered. Medieval courtly life was thus often violent, cruel and extreme. Robes and furred gowns offered little protection from political realities; rather, they enhanced the ambitions of those who ruled. 'Princes are men,' wrote the contemporary chronicler Chastellain, 'and as their affairs are high and perilous, their natures are subject to many passions . . . their hearts are veritable dwelling-places for these, because of their pride in reigning'. He could almost have been describing Arthur himself, for the poet of the alliterative *Morte Arthure*, skilfully exploiting the vast literature on the education, nature and responsibilities of kingship, relates his hero's political catastrophe to moral weakness.

In the palmy days of early triumph, Arthur is careful to lay his success on God's Providence. The victories over the monster of Saint-Michel and the Roman Lucius are both signs of the Lord's favour, but later triumphs stem from pride and greed. The dream of world domination, the quest for empire that was also Geoffrey's theme in his *Historia Regnum Britanniae*, is seen once again as an act of mere egoistic assertion. Its success is not part of God's plan. And, just as Arthur's early victories had been prefigured in a dream, so later defeats are prophesied in a second one. The poet has subtly changed the register of his poem from the ebullient confidence of the opening, through greed and calculation to the point where we begin to feel forces other than human prowess – Fortune's punishment of sin, in particular – asserting their power and draining initiative from Arthur's endeavour. When the king has had his dream of the wheel of Fortune and seen the fickleness of that lady herself, he shivers with a wholly uncharacteristic fear of death. The wise men he calls to interpret his vision confirm his worries. It is a fine moment when Arthur turns his back on these men and skulks into the fields accompanied only by his dog. But his fate is closing round him. A repentant British knight appears and tells him of Mordred's treachery, and Arthur's fury and sadness mingle in a tremendous, fatal desire for revenge. It is to this his magnificence has led.

The closing sections of the poem are characterized by a fitful but desperate energy. The shining worth of Gawain's chivalry is revealed in escapades that can only lead to his destruction. Mordred – watching his own evil disintegrate before him – praises Gawain as he dies, while Arthur, supporting Gawain's corpse, realizes what splendour has been destroyed in this wholesale slaughter, the obliteration of his entire world:

> 'Kyng comly with crowne, in care am I leuyed;
> All my lordschipe lawe in lande es layde vndyre!
> That me has gyfen gwerdons, be grace of hym seluen,
> Mayntenyde my manhede be myghte of theire handes,
> Made me manly one molde, and mayster in erthe;
> In a tenefull tym this torfere was rereryde,
> That for a traytoure has tynte all my trewe lordys.
> Here rystys the riche blude of the rownde table,
> Rebukkede with a rebawde, and rewthe es the more!
> I may helples one hethe house be myn one,
> Alls a wafull wedowe at wanttes hir beryn,
> I may werye and wepe, and wrynge myn handys,
> For my wytt and my wyrchipe awaye es for euer.'

(Crowned with kingly glory, I am left with cares. All my lordliness is now laid low in the dust. You who gave me gifts out of your grace, made me master of the world and maintained my manhood by the might of your hand; in a wretched time this woe was wrought that through a traitor my true lords are destroyed. Here rests the noble blood of the Round Table, destroyed by a villain – grief is the greater! I can only live helpless alone on a heath like a woeful widow who lacks her children, waste away weeping and wringing my hands, for my understanding and glory are gone now for ever.)

There remains only Arthur's death and funeral, the last events in the fall of this prince.

3

The chivalrous Gawain of the *Morte Arthure* is the hero of one of the central masterpieces of Middle English literature: *Sir Gawain and the Green Knight* (*c*. 1385). This poem is preserved in the British Library in a unique manuscript which also contains *Pearl*, *Patience* and *Cleanness*. While there is no conclusive evidence to suggest that all are by the same author, similarities of theme and sensibility point to a single hand. Above all, the poems reveal a scrupulous and very beautiful sense of intellectual and moral order. This is often reflected in a mastery of form. Appreciative of the highly coloured appeal of his world, the Gawain-poet's sense of physical beauty merges into a concern with social, moral and religious virtues. These are then analysed through characters at once exemplary but flawed, human yet in contact with the more than man. For all of them, struggle brings a deeper knowledge of penitence and faithful humility.

In *Sir Gawain and the Green Knight*, these serious matters are handled with a lightness that is at one with both the work's courtly tone and its likely festive purpose as a New Year's entertainment. The poem belongs to the romance world of Arthurian legend and is a delicate critique of the chivalric ideal. The plot uses many motifs the French tradition had made familiar, weaving these together with an artistic intelligence that creates a subtle and suspenseful narrative as well as allowing for a quiet awareness of the great themes that underlie this. *Matière* and *sens* are beautifully combined.

The last quality is made clear by the way in which the poet prepares his Arthurian setting. He places his poem against the broadest of historical vistas – the idea of the rise and fall of empire that had been popularized by Geoffrey of Monmouth and which gave England a history focused on the ideal of chivalry. Briefly recapitulating the fall of Troy, the founding of Rome, the landing in England of Felix Brutus and the eventual appearance of Arthur, we are given a broad impression of man in the great cycles of his history. We are also shown the collapse of greatness through human limitation and the failure to uphold the poem's dominant moral value – 'trawþe'. This is that truth which, as we saw in our analysis of Chaucer, develops from a plain statement of the real nature of things, through personal integrity, to a faith in God's truth. This last at once preserves the order of the universe and offers salvation to the individual. Such are the values of Christian and chivalric society.

Against these wide, very serious perspectives, the poet then places his picture of the youthful gaiety of Camelot in its prime, its Christmas celebrations and high civilization of the heart and soul. The best of times becomes more precious for our awareness of mutability and is tempered by our appreciation of moral weakness. As we have seen, the poet gently repeats this idea at the end of his stanza describing the seasonal revelry. He thereby reminds us of the eventual passing of Camelot through moral turpitude and so prepares us for what he will reveal of his hero's slight but signficant moral blemish. The poet's delight in courtly perfection is thus moderated by an awareness of human failing that is at once universal and particular, concerned with all time and this time. In such ways he relates what will be his picture of the most insidious temptations that afflict chivalry to the broadest concerns of human history. If Gawain, the flower of chivalry, stands for all that is best in Camelot, the poet also shows he has received the blemishing touch of moral weakness. This, while forgivable in his exemplary case, will one day lead to the fall of an entire empire.

For the moment, however, everything appears as youthful innocence. The contrast between earnest and game that is so central to the poem is thus established and becomes yet more apparent with the thunderous arrival of the Green Knight himself, a subtly ambivalent figure at once beautiful and horrific, fantastic and sinister. As yet, we know nothing of the demonic circumstances in which he is enmeshed. All we have been told is that Arthur has delayed the feast until he is presented with a marvel. Now, with the coming of the primitive, potent yet threatening figure, he thinks he has what he wants. The Green Knight – his colour perhaps symbolizing the 'trawþe' or integrity he will test – advances on the king, demanding from what he sees as the beardless youngster the right to a Christmas game.

That game will be both a seasonal diversion and a game of life and death, testing the world of Camelot to its core in unexpected ways. It also combines the comic and the macabre, the playful and the deadly serious. What it consists of is the ancient theme of the 'beheading game', familiar from some of the Celtic stories of the hero Cuchulain which inspired Chrétien and French romance. As in the sources, the Green Knight proposes that one of the courtiers cut off his head and then, a year and a day later, appear at the Green Knight's chapel to receive a similar stroke. The challenge is at once absurd and terrifying. For the moment, however, neither the courtiers nor the poet's audience are aware of the true layers of menace that lie behind it.

It is at this dramatic point that we are introduced to the hero. With the convoluted syntax of the secretly proud but apparently courteous, Gawain begs Arthur for the right to take up the challenge, to play the game. He is granted this, and the Green Knight bares his neck. The axe blade falls and the ghastly head rolls to the floor, where the courtiers prod it with their feet. So easy a victory hardly seems a game at all until, staggering forward, the Green Knight snatches up his head, jumps to his horse and, pointing his severed visage to the feast, reminds Gawain of his promise. A central aspect of 'trawþe' is honouring one's word and, with a reminder of this, the Green Knight disappears into the mapless world of faery. Arthur turns to comfort his frightened queen, declaring with more bravado than confidence, perhaps, that 'wel bycommes such craft vpon Cristmasse'. This may be so, but as the first 'fit' or section closes, the poet shows how for Gawain the game is already becoming a matter of the utmost earnest.

As the first fit opened with the great cycles of human history, so the second describes the narrower annual round of the Church and calendar years. It is now 1 November, the feast of All Saints, the day to commemorate the dead and sing the *Dies irae*. As Gawain prepares to ride out on an *aventure* that will test the very core of his being, so the romance themes of quest and trial, the marvellous, the courteous and the devout are placed in the natural sequence of time. We are made aware of the cycle of the seasons and liturgical festivals, the progress of this year into next, what was into what will be. This element in the poem is one of the loveliest and most reassuring aspects of the sacramental and ritualistic culture to which the poet was so deeply responsive. It suggests that while courtly ceremony may give life a certain beauty, only faith can guide and give it purpose.

Gawain's faith, the spiritual aspect of his 'trawþe', is appropriately suggested by heraldic and religious emblems: the pentangle emblazoned on the outside of his shield and the picture of the Virgin limned on its inside. His armour is at once a physical and a metaphysical protection, for a contemporary audience might well have seen it in terms of 'the whole armour of God' described by St Paul in Ephesians – the central text for the image of the *miles Christi*, the knight of Christ:

> Therefore take the whole armour of God, that you may be able to withstand in the evil day, and having done all, to stand. Stand, therefore, having girded your loins with truth, and having put on the breastplate of righteousness, and having shod your feet with the equipment of the gospel of peace; besides all these, taking the shield of faith, with which you can quench all the flaming darts of the evil one.

The image of Mary and the endless interlacing of the golden pentangle suggest the range of values which make up 'trawþe' and 'cheualrye'. Since they are also central to the poem it will be useful to examine them here, bearing in mind that their social, military and Christian origins are given the burnish of courtesy.

In such a moral world as this, sin rather dangerously becomes associated with 'vylany' – the behaviour of the churlish boor. However, if the vocabulary borrows something of the language of hierarchy, the values themselves suggest a profound spiritual idealism. This is supplemented by physical strength – Gawain's 'fyve fyngres' – and natural abilities – his 'fyve wyttez'. These disciplined aspects of his 'sensitive soul' in turn serve a faith in Christ, his five wounds, and the five joys of the Virgin.

Lastly come five more subtle values which are all concerned with a refined and loving relationship to the community. The first of these is 'fraunchyse', the freedom which expresses itself as that confident generosity of spirit, the open-hearted and noble charity which is so central to *The Franklin's Tale*. The second value is again related to charity, for 'felaȝschyp' is that loving kindness which at its broadest ranges from not being stuffy or bitter to a visionary awareness of the love which binds all humankind together. 'Clannes' is another of those values which the medieval mind, with its refusal wholly to divorce the physical from the metaphysical, gave the widest interpretation. It suggests at one and the same time that a gentleman cleans his fingernails and washes behind his ears (contrary to popular ideas of medieval hygiene, Gawain bathes regularly) while also being an aspect of spiritual purity very dear to the poet of *Cleanness*. The idea has now shrunk to proverb lore. Cleanliness, we were told, is next to godliness. That another of Gawain's virtues is 'cortaysye' goes without saying, though it is worth pointing out that it is only one among five and that to stress it at the expense of the others is seriously to misunderstand his integrity. This in turn would be nothing without 'pite', that compassion which is perhaps the most significant legacy of the Christian faith. Armed with these physical, moral and spiritual weapons, the noble Gawain sets off on his search for the Green Knight.

In its combination of fantasy, self-conscious literary humour and devotion, the description of Gawain's quest is one of the great moments of Middle English poetry:

> Mony klyf he ouerclambe in contrayez straunge.
> Fer floten fro his frendez, fremedly he rydez.
> At vche warþe oþer water þer þe wyȝe passed
> He fonde a foo hym byfore, bot ferly hit were,
> And þat so foule and so felle þat feȝt hym byhode.
> So mony meruayl bi mount þer þe mon fyndez

Hit were to tore for to telle of þe tenþe dole.
Sumwhyle wyth wormez he werrez and with wolues als,
Sumwhyle wyth wodwos þat woned in þe knarrez,
Boþe wyth bullez and bercz, and borez oþerquyle,
And etaynez þat hym anelede of þe heȝe felle.
Nade he ben duȝty and dryȝe and Dryȝtyn had serued,
Douteles he hade ben ded and dreped ful ofte.
For werre wrathed hym not so much þat wynter nas wors,
When þe colde cler water fro þe cloudez schadde
And frcs er hit falle myȝt to þe fale erþe.
Ner slayn wyth þe slete he sleped in his yrnes
Mo nyȝtez þen innoghe, in naked rokkez
þeras claterande fro þe crest þe colde borne rennez
And henged heȝe ouer his hede in hard iiseikkles.
þus in peryl and payne and plytes ful harde
Bi contray caryez þis knyȝt tyl Krystmasse Euen,
    Alone.
      þe knyȝt wel þat tyde
      To Mary made his mone
      þat ho hym red to ryde
      And wysse hym to sum wone.

(*He clambered over many a cliff in unknown countries, far from his friends, journeying as a stranger. At each river or water he forded on his way he found a foe before him, unless by a marvel, and that so foul and fierce that he was forced to fight. So many marvels did he meet among the mountains that it would be tedious to tell a tenth part of them. Sometimes with dragons he fought and sometimes with wolves, sometimes with wild men who dwelt in the crags, both with bulls and bears and sometimes with boars and with ogres that challenged him on the high fells. Had he not been doughty, enduring and devout, doubtless he would have been dead and done for many a time. Yet the warring worried him less for the winter was worse when the cold clear water cascaded from the clouds and froze before it could fall to the pale earth. Near slain by the sleet, he slept in his armour, more than enough nights among the naked rocks where the cold streams clattered down from the steep crests and then hung high over his head in hard icicles. Thus in peril and in pain and in dreadful plight this knight covered the country until Christmas Eve, alone. Ardently that evening the knight prayed to Mary and begged her to guide him and show him to some shelter.*)

Compared with the description of Camelot at play, this stanza suggests the range of the poet's achievement and illustrates how earnest the Christmas game has become.

It is on Christmas Eve that Gawain comes suddenly upon a castle, turreted and crenellated with all the fantastication of a building in a manuscript illumination. It seems – and the idea of appearance is fundamental – to be a place enjoying the highest courtly values and *douceur de vivre*, a haven of courtesy where Gawain is appreciated for his breeding by both the courtiers and the vast proprietor of the place. Though experience of romance may have taught us to be wary of giants, it would take an audience blessed with greater perception than Gawain can muster to imagine that the huge figure of Sir Bertilak might be related to the huge figure of the Green Knight. Besides, the elaborate courtesy of the one is a very different matter from the behaviour of the other.

The castle is also a place of keen religious observance. During his stay Gawain attends mass every day (this would have been quite usual) and on the first occasion he encounters a hideous old woman attending his host's beautiful young wife. The combination of serious religious devotion and aristocratic behaviour here is a refined instance of the good manners, piety and flirtation that seem to characterize life in the castle. It is a combination – difficult, perhaps, readily to appreciate – of chastity without priggishness, pleasure without sin. But if it is a game, it is also a precarious balance.

The second fit ends with an impression of the high refinement of life in the castle and the agreement that Gawain will rest there before going on to the Green Chapel and his ominous appointment. Meanwhile, his host is set on hunting, and he and Gawain agree on an 'exchange of winnings'. Sir Bertilak will offer his bag or 'gomen' for whatever Gawain receives during the course of the day in his host's absence. Another promise is exchanged, another game agreed. It all seems like an innocent diversion before the great test. The Green Chapel, we have been told, is not far away.

The third fit narrows the time-scheme more sharply still. It presents Gawain's three-day temptation in the castle. Each morning, while her husband is out hunting, the lady of the place comes to Gawain's bedroom and offers him her body. To appreciate fully the drama of this, we need to remind ourselves that the young knight is under sentence of almost certain death, a fact which inevitably heightens the allure of the proffered temptation. That each time he actually resists the acceptable and even conventional adultery of *fine amour* reveals both the Gawain-poet's sophisticated literary playfulness and, more seriously, the very high value he sets on chastity.

Behind this last lies a complex of ideas wholly opposed to stultifying promiscuity; the biblical notion that sex is a powerful force intimately connected with sin for example, and, in particular, that casual lovemaking, in these circumstances especially, would be an expression of mere cupidinous desire rather than charity. It would be an act wholly opposed to the Christian elements in chivalry. The imminent prospect of death should lead not to a quick seizing of worldly delight but to serious thoughts of salvation. We have seen that on each of the three days Gawain stays in the castle he attends mass. However, to appreciate the subtlety of the temptation it is necessary to expose the suspense element in the plot.

It is only at the end of the poem that Gawain is told the precise nature of the world in which he has been staying. It is a place of enchantment. Sir Bertilak is revealed as none other than the Green Knight, while both he and his wife are under the power of Morgan-le-Fey, the hostess's hideous companion. (She is also Arthur's half-sister and, through the complexities of genealogy, Gawain's aunt.) It is Morgan-le-Fey, with her sheer malevolence towards Camelot, who sent Sir Bertilak to the Christmas feast to test the prowess of the knights, and it is under her supervision that the temptations have taken place. Sir Bertilak is fully aware of what has transpired on each occasion and, when he reveals the origins of his bewitchment to Gawain, he also exposes that combination of the sexual and the diabolic which is at once a motif from romance and an image of spiritual peril. Intercourse with spirits assures certain damnation, and the propinquity of the hostess to the fearful history the Green Knight relates suggests the true danger in which Gawain has been placed.

The particular deftness of the third fit lies in the fact that both Gawain and the audience have been led to believe that the real test will take place at the Green Chapel. The sexual temptation at first appears little more than a moral interlude. This is the world of faery, however. Things are not what they seem. 'Trawþe' is not self-evident. It is the temptations in the bedroom that are the real challenge, and it is precisely Gawain's unpreparedness – the fact that the hostess's blandishments appear a relatively minor matter – that makes them so subtly dangerous. We should see how they work.

On each of three mornings, the hostess slips into the knight's bedroom and with playful words (the combination of game and earnest is again made evident) challenges his chastity. To her personal charms and the youth of Gawain are added the facts that the lady's husband is out hunting and that romance convention permitted such sexual *aventure*. But Gawain, as we have seen, resists. He does so with a courtesy, a social deftness, that at once reveals him as the flower of chivalry while, unknown to him, he also saves his soul:

> þus hym frayned þat fre and fondet hym ofte,
> For to haf wonnen hym to woȝe, whatso scho þoȝt ellez;
> Bot he defended hym so fayr þat no faut semed,

> Ne non euel on nawþer halue, nawþer þay wysten
>   Bot blysse.

(*The fine lady tempted him and tried him with questions to tempt him to woe, whatever else she thought, but he defended himself so fairly that no fault appeared. There was evil on neither side, but only bliss.*)

The chivalrous 'luf-talkyng' of *fine amour* is presented as both a temptation and the means by which temptation may be courteously avoided. It is a game and a powerful risk. The mortal dangers of the situation are further emphasized by the descriptions of Sir Bertilak's hunting a deer, a boar and a fox. These parallel the pursuit of Gawain's destruction.

Gawain plays the elegant but perilous game of courtesy with the lady, receiving from her on the first two days nothing more than a kiss, a delight which he then exchanges after Sir Bertilak's hunt for the day's bag. It is the temptation on the third day that is especially perilous, however. Gawain is trapped between possible discourtesy and possible damnation:

> He cared for his cortaysye, lest craþayn he were,
> And more for his meschef ȝif he schulde make synne
> And be traytor to þat tolke þat þat telde aȝt.

(*He was concerned for his courtesy lest he should be called caitiff, but more for his sake if he should fall into sin and be treacherous to his host.*)

On the third day the familiar kiss is again proffered, but a love token – a green girdle – is also secretly exchanged. The girdle – its colour at once prompting thoughts of the Green Knight and symbolizing the 'trawþe' or integrity that Gawain so values – supposedly has the power to make its wearer immune to the fatal blow. As a result, the knight keeps its possession a secret from his host. It is not sexual desire that places Gawain in the greatest peril, therefore, but the acceptance of this gift and his failure to honour his word and the moral and spiritual values emblazoned on his shield. This failure is his 'vntrawþe'. It symbolizes 'couardise and couetyse', Gawain's love of life before honour and his erroneous belief that salvation is guaranteed by what the audience would have recognized as a conventional love token and not by the workings of God. It is probable that the full significance of his error does not dawn on Gawain for the present. Great artist that the poet is, he reserves this revelation for the final section.

The last fit narrows the passing of time to the change of a night into a day which is also the change of the old year into the new and, with this, the full revelation of the meaning of the Christmas game. Gawain rides out into the bitter cold and to his appointment at the sinister chapel. Unaware

of the nature of the castle and its hosts, he courteously blesses them for
their charity and commends them to God. Then, as he makes his way
across the desolate landscape, he is offered one more temptation. Protected, as he believes, by the girdle, he refuses his guide's offer of silence if he
rides away and baulks the test. Instead, with an affirmation of bravery
and faith which ironically underlines his moral confusion, he declares:

> 'Grant merci,' quoþ Gawayn, and gruchyng he sayde,
> 'Wel worth þe, wyȝe, þat woldez my gode,
> And þat lelly me layne I leue wel þou woldez;
> Bot helde þou hit neuer so holde, and I here passed,
> Founded for ferde for to fle, in fourme þat þou tellez,
> I were a knyȝt kowarde, I myȝt not be excused.
> Bot I wyl to þe chapel, for chaunce þat may falle,
> And talk wyth þat ilk tulk þe tale þat me lyste,
> Worþe hit wele oþer wo, as þe Wyrde lykez
>   Hit hafe.
>   þaȝe he be a sturn knape
>   To stiȝtel, and stad with staue,
>   Ful wel con Dryȝtyn schape
>   His seruauntez for to saue.'

*('Thanks,' said Gawain, somewhat aggrieved, 'well may you thrive, sir, who wish for
my well-being, and I believe that you would keep my secret safe. But however quiet
you kept it, if I quit this place and fled from the fellow in fear as you advise, I would
be a cowardly knight quite beyond excuse, so I'll go to the Green Chapel and take
what fate sends and have what words I choose with the same. Let weal or woe come
as my Fate decides it. Though he be a fearful fellow, wielding his weapon, the Lord
can shape matters to save his servants.')*

Outwardly his faith is in the Lord and, as a Christian knight, in divine
'trawþe' and the 'whole armour of God'. Secretly, there is the girdle
wrapped round his waist. The flower of chivalry has been brought to this
degree of moral confusion.

At the Green Chapel – no Christian place but an ancient tumulus
howling with the thin and savage wind – Gawain feels the presence of
evil and senses that the 'game' has been an attempt to lure him to
destruction. The full significance of the passage from Ephesians begins
to become clear. We see why Gawain should have put his faith in the
physical and metaphysical strength of his armour – in God's 'trawþe'.
He is to fight 'against principalities, against powers, against rulers of
the darkness of this world, against spiritual wickedness in high places'.
He should indeed trust to 'the whole armour of God' rather than the
deceptive green girdle.

Deeply frightened despite his secret counter-charm, Gawain bares his neck to receive the blow. Three times the axe 'glydande adoun on glode [in a flash] hym to schende'. Twice the blade is suspended. On the third occasion it cuts a light nick in Gawain's flesh. What does this mean? On the first two days of his temptation Gawain emerged unscathed. The wound delivered by the third blow is a token of Gawain's 'vntrawþe', his taking the girdle. The Green Knight, speaking now as a gentleman capable of 'fraunchise', 'felaȝschyp', 'cortaysye' and 'pite', absolves what he sees as Gawain's mild error:

> 'þou art confessed so clene, beknowen of þy mysses,
> And hatz þe penaunce apert of þe poynt of myn egge,
> I halde þe polysed of þat plyȝt and pured as clene
> As þou hadez neuer forfeted syþen þou watz fyrst borne.'

(*'You are so cleanly confessed, and all your faults declared, and have clearly suffered your penance by the edge of my axe, I hold you to be shriven as clean as if you had never committed a sin since the day you were born.'*)

On the social level of courtesy this is just and generous, but, in so far as the social virtues of chivalry are inseparable from its religious ones, Gawain cannot accept that *tout comprendre est tout pardonner*. Human forgiveness is not enough. A woman has tempted him to secure his 'salvation' through deceit. The girdle's warrant of safety has delighted his eyes and heart, and led his will to pervert his reason. His 'vileyne' – his social discourtesy – is a sin, and, as with all sin, a recapitulation of the Fall. The flower of chivalry is but a man, weak and acquainted with 'vntrawþe'. In his shame and sorrow, Gawain likens himself to Adam and those other Old Testament 'types' of him: Solomon, Samson and David, all of whom were fondly led into error by female charm. But yet, among such exalted peers, 'Me þink me burde be excused.' After his confession and contrition, he perhaps merits absolution. There is hope to the last. As for the girdle, 'inn syngne of my surfet I scal se hit ofte'.

The chastened Gawain returns to Camelot. Deeply ashamed, he blushingly tells the court of his *aventure*. With the delicate and playful moral seriousness which characterizes the poem, the girdle that for Gawain is a symbol of 'couardise and couetyse' becomes, among the descendants of Brutus, a trophy symbolic of knightly virtue. We must wonder at such a suggestive ambiguity. The poet, however, too refined to point a moral, leaves the matter to us. His Christmas game playfully invites a courteous discussion of some of the great issues of human history, ethics and salvation.

4

The three other works preserved with *Sir Gawain and the Green Knight* are more overtly theological in character and may be approached via a poem that has sometimes been attributed to their author. *St Erkenwald* (*c.* 1386) is an excellent example both of the artistry brought to the saint's life in this period and of the popularization of what to us may seem abstruse theological problems. As with *The Prioress's Tale*, the central miracle in the poem concerns the preservation of a corpse, but where Chaucer's poem deals with the concept of the Holy Innocents, *St Erkenwald* is a pious *exemplum* illustrating another central ecclesiastical issue: the salvation of the righteous pagan.

The theological problem is essentially this. What is the nature of God's justice if men, deprived by accident of birth from a knowledge of Christ, live lives of exemplary virtue but are nonetheless consigned to limbo after death because in life they were unable to partake of the sacraments? Those dying before the Crucifixion were allegedly freed during an event recounted in what is now regarded as the apocryphal Book of Nicodemus. This tells how, during the three days of his entombment, Christ harrowed Hell, winning the souls of righteous pagans from Satan's grasp. It is a scene marvellously portrayed in the Miracle Plays and one essential also to *Piers Ploughman* and Wyclif. But what of those righteous souls who died in ignorance after the Harrowing of Hell? Surely it is wrong that they should suffer?

It was not usually enough for medieval man to believe that such people could be saved by 'oonliche love and leautee [justice]' – in other words, by the direct intervention of God. This would imply that God is prepared to exercise his absolute power and save men simply on account of their good works, thereby ignoring the necessity of faith, the Church and the sacraments. Such a belief came to be considered a heresy. For those wishing to stay within the bosom of the Church, a combination of natural merit, divine grace and sacramental office was required. This is what *St Erkenwald* presents.

During the rebuilding of St Paul's, an uncorrupted body is excavated. Wonder is roused in all levels of society. But mere intellectual effort – the searching of old records – cannot provide even so much as a name for the corpse. Only through the prayerful intercession of the saintly Bishop Erkenwald (a minister under the evangelizing Augustine of Canterbury) does the corpse reveal that he was a just but pagan judge, in other words the embodiment of unenlightened human excellence whose corpse has been preserved as a divine reward for merit. As a devout Christian,

Erkenwald is moved to tears by the tale, while, as a priest, he offers baptism to the man. The saint's tear of compassion – his human pity – is at one with his sacerdotal role. The tear, the holy water and the words of baptism free the judge's soul and, as he enters Heaven, so his body corrupts. Through the sacraments of the Church, human merit has earned remission from limbo, a soul has been saved, human and divine justice reconciled, the power of the Church demonstrated and the faith of the people enhanced by a miracle that reveals God's special care for the virtuous English.

5

Where *St Erkenwald* suggests important theological issues through a pious legend, *Patience* is an exemplary biblical paraphrase couched in the form of a sermon. Through the story of Jonah, it asks us to consider man in terms of the ideals of forbearance and submission expounded in the Beatitudes. It also portrays man's frequent falling into wrath, one of the Seven Deadly Sins. Lastly, the work discusses the terms of man's relation to God.

It may be helpful to deal with this last aspect first. In our discussion of the philosophic basis of Chaucer's concern with free-will, we saw that orthodox fourteenth-century theologians in England, rejecting a purely rationalistic approach to God (an approach which seemed to present him as tied by his own rules of cause and effect), had elaborated a concern with revealed truth and God's freedom to intervene in the steady processes of nature. Building on a distinction already made by St Thomas Aquinas, they showed that while God had entered into a covenant with men which promised salvation to those who fulfilled their side of the contract, God was by no means invariably bound by this – his *potentia ordinata*. To ensure his own freedom, God was said to be able to breach his contract with man and, through his absolute freedom – his *potentia absoluta* – reveal the mysterious workings of his grace. Since this last was a matter of faith and revelation and so was not readily amenable to logical analysis, philosophic interest shifted to the terms of God's contract with man and man's responsibilities under the terms of that agreement. This – the 'new philosophy' or the *via moderna* – emphasized the place of human initiative at the expense of seeing man as a second cause, moved by the Prime Mover. *Patience* in some respects adjusts the balance, for in re-telling the story of Jonah the Gawain-poet found a narrative that was an ideal medium for discussing both the *potentia ordinata* and the *potentia absoluta*. He thereby places his representative human figure on the broadest canvas.

The sermon begins in the approved manner with a citation of a scriptural text (in this case the Beatitudes), discusses this in an abstract way while highlighting the particular importance of patient poverty, and then relates this virtue to the poet himself. He is, so he tells us, a poor man who must be patient if he is to be happy in the service of his demanding master. With gently ironic courtesy, the poet applies his 'sentence' to himself. He stirs his master's compassion, and suggests that their relationship is to be seen in terms of the strictest feudal analogy – as God is to man so is his lord to him. The moral of the story of Jonah the poet is about to tell has thus a personal and social as well as a theological application. Indeed, all three are inseparable.

The first part of the *exemplum* tells how the Lord spoke to Jonah, commanding him to go to Nineveh where he was to upbraid the people for their 'vileyne' and advise them of the imminent destruction of their city. Jonah will do no such thing. The task is far too dangerous. He tries intemperately to flee to Tarshish, and justifies his cowardice with the absurd idea that, since Heaven is so far away, God will not be able to see him.

The journey to Tarshish involves a sea voyage, and the poet provides a lively description of a well-manned vessel setting out. On the literal, descriptive level, the stanzas are excellent. However, recalling that the poem is a sermon, we may like to remember *The Man of Law's Tale* and ask if the boat, the subsequent storm and Jonah's famous swallowing by the whale have deeper significance.

It will be recalled that, on the allegorical level, Constance's journey in a rudderless boat in *The Man of Law's Tale* symbolized the ship of the Church bringing faith to the heathens. Jonah's voyage is a precise antitype to this. He is running away from his religious duties, absurdly confident that God cannot see him. A reference to the Psalms, however, reminds us that:

> 'O folez in folk, felez oþerwhyle
> And vnderstondes vmbestounde, þaȝ ȝe be stapen in folé:
> Hope ȝe þat He heres not þat eres alle made?
> Hit may not be þat He is blynde þat bigged vche yȝe.'

(*'O foolish folk, you must face this fact and understand sooner or later, though you are steeped in your folly: think you He hears not who made all ears? It cannot be that he is blind who made every eye.'*)

While in the early days of the voyage the boat sails calmly, God soon exercises his *potentia absoluta*, interfering in the processes of nature with a violent storm that the poet has great delight in describing. Jonah, smugly confident,

> Slypped vpon a sloumbe-slepe, and sloberande he routes.

(*He fell into a deep slumber and snored as he slept.*)

This is a vivid picture of spiritual forgetfulness and the very image of the wrong way to conduct life amid the storms of Fortune. Thus the 'moral' interpretation of the scene allows us to read it as an antitype of true faith. The watchful pagans, however, acknowledge that they have an enemy of God on board, realize that Jonah is the culprit, and throw their now penitent passenger overboard. In other words, they treat Jonah as he himself had feared the people of Nineveh would. Nonetheless, since grace will not be cheated, the pagans convert to the true God as their ship of faith, rid of its sinner, sails on over a calmer sea.

We saw that, on the anagogical level, the faithful Constance's voyage represented the passing of the soul through nature to the banquet of the blessed in eternity. No such paradise awaits Jonah. Rather, he becomes food for fishes – in particular, the whale. He does not go up to Heaven but, in his faithless state, falls down into an image or 'type' of Hell. The poet's description of the whale's digestive tract sufficiently relates the stench of the one to the sulphurous pits of the other. The rushing of the waters and the three days of dread exactly suggest the force of divine wrath, while Jonah's prayer – the poet's translation of the psalm *De profundis clamavi* – suggests a real and desperate devotion. Such faith in the mercy of God is justified. Without his intervention, Jonah would have died. He is saved, however, by an exercise of the *potentia absoluta*:

> þe hyȝe Heuen-Kyng, þurȝ His honde myȝt,
> Warded þis wrech man in warlowes guttez,
> What lede moȝt leue bi lawe of any kynde,
> þat any lyf myȝt be lent so longe hym withinne?
> Bot he watz sokored by þat Syre þat syttes so hiȝe,
> þaȝ were wanlez of wele in wombe of þat fissche,
> And also dryuen þurȝ þe depe and in derk walterez.

(*The king of high Heaven, through the might of his hand, watched over this wretched man in the guts of the whale, for how could he have been preserved for so long in there by natural law? He was succoured by the Lord that sits on high, though his fortune was forlorn in the fish's belly as it dived in the deep, dark waters.*)

As Christ rose again after three days in the tomb, so Jonah – who was often seen as an Old Testament character prefiguring Christ – emerges from the whale, again on the third day. He goes humbly to Nineveh and upbraids the people, who then confess and are saved.

Jonah is furious. Did he not have an agreement with God? Was he not told that Nineveh would be destroyed? Where are the blood and brimstone of destruction? That his lack of patience makes him angry with the Lord who has saved the truly penitent underlines Jonah's sinful folly. He fails to see that by breaking his agreement – the *potentia ordinata* – God in fact has shown his mercy. Still hoping to chide Him into action, however, Jonah sits sulking ridiculously above Nineveh and awaits its imminent destruction. Instead, God weaves a beautiful arbour for him in which the reluctant prophet takes immoderate delight. Just as he had failed to be patient in adversity, so he now refuses to be what the Church Fathers called *humilis in prosperis* – moderate in prosperity. He rejoices in the gifts of God's bounty – in nature, not the God of nature. That night the arbour is destroyed. Jonah is again furious, but, as God points out,

> 'Is þis ryȝtwys, þou renk, alle þy ronk noyse,
> So wroth for a wodbynde to wax so sone?'

(*'Is it right, O man, to raise all this noise because of a mere woodbine?'*)

The Lord then compares what Jonah sees as the wanton destruction of his arbour with what would have been the far more cruel annihilation of the innocents in Nineveh. Lastly, God points the moral of the whole:

> 'Be noȝt so gryndel, godman, bot go forth þy wayes,
> Be preue and be pacient in payne and in joye;
> For he þat is to rakel to renden his cloþez
> Mot efte sitte with more vnsounde to sewe hem togeder.'

(*'Be less furious, my fine fellow, but go forth on your way and be patient whether things are well or ill; for he who rashly rips up his clothes must later sit with more trouble to sew them together again.'*)

The poet finishes by applying the morality to himself. Humility, penitence and charity are once more emphasized.

6

Where *Patience* tells a single biblical narrative, *Cleanness* consists of three main Old Testament *exempla* and a number of subsidiary episodes. These are supplemented by a fine re-telling of the parable of the wedding feast, and several of the poet's own homiletic passages. This huge and

apparently ungainly structure is given coherence by a theme again drawn
from the Beatitudes: 'Blessed are the pure in heart; for they shall see
God.' The text is illustrated in two ways.

The virtue of purity is first shown negatively through an extended
account of the Flood, when God destroyed the whole world for its
'fylþe', then through the powerful picture of the destruction of Sodom
and Gomorrha, and lastly through a description of Belshazzar's feast
and the collapse of his empire after he had polluted the sacred vessels
stolen by his father from the Temple in Jerusalem. Medieval exegesis
allowed for each of these events to be read as literal narratives, morally
for their description of sin, allegorically for their picture of God's
punishment of sin, and anagogically as prefiguring the wrath of the Last
Judgement. As a result, they can all be applied to every period in the
divine plan for the universe: the past, the present and the prophesied
end.

Against these negative and vividly realized pictures of moral impurity
are then set portraits of the virtuous struggling against sin: Noah,
Abraham, Lot, Daniel, Belshazzar's wife and the repentant Nebuchadnezzar. These characters' Old Testament rectitude is enhanced by an
elegant homiletic passage on Christ as the ideal 'type' of cleanness who
can inspire and save those living under the new law. The idea of salvation
is also memorably expressed in the opening parable of the wedding feast
and its picture of the guests enjoying the banquet of the blessed in
Paradise. In these ways, the poet draws his theme together and balances
his Old Testament picture of a vengeful God lamenting and punishing
the sins of mankind with his New Testament image of Christ promising
salvation. The Lord's vengeance and mercy, man's 'fylþe' and 'clannes',
are thus revealed in a universal perspective. As the poet says at the end,

> I haf yow þro schewed
> þat vnclannes tocleues in corage dere
> Of þat wynnelych Lorde þat wonyes in heuen,
> Entyses Hym to be tene, teldes vp His wrake;
> Ande clannes is His comfort, and coyntyse He louyes,
> And þose þat seme arn and swete schyn se His face.
> þat we gon gay in oure gere þat grace He vus sende,
> þat we may serue in His syȝt, þer solace neuer blynnez.

*(I have shown you that uncleanness cuts in twain the courteous heart of the gracious
Lord that lives in Heaven, rouses his wrath and raises his vengeance. But purity is
his comfort, and wisdom he loves. Those who are seemly and sweetly shine shall see
his face. May we be granted the grace to go in gay garments and to serve in his sight,
where solace never ceases.)*

As we might expect, the poem gives the central concept of 'clannes' the broadest interpretation. Cleanness suggests far more than an absence of dirt and sin. It conveys what is fresh, innocent, morally righteous and natural. It implies integrity, and both physical and spiritual grace. These merge with a view of the proper conduct of earthly life as a devout imitation of the courts of Heaven where 'clannes' is an expression of ceremonious and courteous purity – in other words, of God's law: 'He is so clene in His courte, þe Kyng þat al weldez.' This is a purity that priests should imitate and banqueting guests aspire to. Cleanness thus unites the religious and the secular.

For the moment, concentrating only on the literal level of the text, we should note the imaginative power with which the individual scenes are realized: the drama of the Flood, the cliffs of Sodom fluttering like the leaves of a book as the city is destroyed, the glorious description of the roast meats being carried into Belshazzar's feast to the sound of pipes and kettle-drums. However, it is to the moral level of interpretation we should turn if we want to glimpse something of the poet's deeper purpose, and to do this effectively we need to recognize the theological concept of sin as violence against God and nature. Dante – whom the poet probably read – expressed the matter thus:

> Puossi far forza nella dietade,
> col cuor negando e bestemmiando quella,
> e spregiando natura e sua bontade.

(*One can do violence to the deity with heart negating and blaspheming him, and disdaining nature and its goodness.*)

Negating and violating the deity is the origin of the sin in the poet's first *exemplum*: the fall of Lucifer. The archangel's sinful ambition is seen by the poet as 'fylþe', and this is a matter made more comprehensible when we know that breaking divine law was seen conventionally as a besmirching of the special sanctity of that law. When the poet comes to his description of the Flood, however, we are shown the second term in Dante's equation, for here 'clannes' suggests psychological and emotional purity, chastity rather than promiscuity, the following of natural law:

> þer watz no law to hem layd bot loke to kynde,
> And kepe to hit, and alle hit cors clanly fulfylle.

(*They were enjoined to follow none but natural law and to abide by it and fulfil its requirements.*)

In the giant age before the Flood only Noah ruled himself properly, passing his days in fear of the Lord and in continence. Such a view of chaste sexuality is important and must be recognized as no joyless puritanism. Indeed the poet offers his praise of erotic joy through the words of God himself. He shows how lawful love-making shares in the purity of Paradise:

> 'I compast hem a kynde crafte and kende hit hem derne,
> And armed hit in Myn ordenaunce oddely dere,
> And dyȝt drwry þerinne, doole alþer-swettest,
> And þe play of paramorez I portrayed Myseluen,
> And made þerto a maner myriest of oþer:
> When two true togeder had tyȝed hemseluen,
> Bytwene a male and his make such merþe schulde come,
> Welnyȝe pure paradys moȝt preue no better.'

('*I created a natural way and secretly taught them, holding it specially dear among my laws, making mating a matter of marvellous sweetness. The embrace of lovers was born of my brain and I made it the most delightful deed of all. When two together were truly wedded, there should be such mirth between a man and his mate that the purity of paradise could hardly prove better.*')

It is such natural and sanctified cleanness that Noah's contemporaries and the inhabitants of Sodom and Gomorrha refuse. Since the sins of the cities of the plain are of importance to much medieval literature, a short discussion of them may be useful.

As physical entities, the destroyed cities were a source of awe and travellers' tales, and the Gawain-poet derives much of his knowledge from that great imaginative guidebook of the Middle Ages: Mandeville's *Travels*. As a focus of moral – or immoral – interest, however, the exegetes were less interested in Sodom as a place or with sodomy as an act of lust than with homosexuality as the expression of a more general concern with the perversion of God's law. Homosexual deeds themselves were subsumed by Aquinas under *luxuria*, the seventh Deadly Sin, and are seen partly as such by the Gawain-poet. In so far as homosexuality was thought to be repugnant to human nature and reason, it was believed by St Augustine to pollute our friendship with God. As such, homosexuality is self-evidently sinful and worthy of punishment. Further, when 'unnatural' sex threatened to violate a consecrated person – in this instance the three angelic visitors to Lot, who were seen by many exegetes as a prefiguration of the Trinity – homosexuality was an expression of irreligion and, more especially, of sacrilege. As the standard medieval definition expresses the matter: 'They commit sacrilege who through ignorance confound or through negligence violate or offend the sanctity of a divine law.' As Aquinas and others realized, this concept of sacrilege derived from the original definition of *sacrilegium* as the theft from a temple of those things consecrated to divine service. It is this notion that unites the story of the pollution of the sacred vessels at Belshazzar's feast with the other main *exempla* in the poem. All three stories can then be placed alongside the fall of Lucifer as illustrating sins of violence against God and nature. Hence the particular fury of their punishment.

It is also right to see Belshazzar's orgy as an antitype or grotesque parody of the opening parable of the wedding feast. The orgy has a barbaric splendour which we are asked to see as the triumph of sin over reason, as the drunken king orders the holy vessels to be brought to his feast. The exegetes again may have seen these as images of man as a vessel consecrated to God. The actual vessels themselves, however, are filled with wine and offered to Belshazzar's lolling concubines. They are desecrated. In his fury, God causes the writing on the wall to appear, and Belshazzar's brutal destruction. Violence against God is matched by violence from God. It is the law of the Old Testament.

Only a faith in Christ can bring lasting salvation, and the beautiful homily on cleanness that follows the destruction of Sodom and Gomorrha presents Christ as an exemplary type of purity to be imitated and who offers hope of eternal life:

> ȝis, þat Mayster is mercyable, þaȝ þou be man fenny,
> And al tomarred in myrc whyle þou on molde lyuyes;
> þou may schyne þurȝ schryfte, þaȝ þou haf schome serued,
> And pure þe with penaunce tyl þou a perle worþe.

(*This Master is merciful though a man be defiled, smeared with muck while he lives on the earth. Through shrift you may shine, though you have deserved shame, and be made pure with penance until you are clean as a pearl.*)

To be like the virtuous patriarchs and even more like Christ is the moral message of the poem, telling us *quid agas*, how to act.

When we have read the letter of the poem, seen how to behave and what to believe, the anagogical sense emerges. We are shown the end of the world. The three great scenes of destruction we have witnessed prefigure Doomsday, while the parable of the wedding feast shows how the good and clean – but not the filthy guest who is thrown down to Hell – are invited to the ceremonious banquet of the blessed. Thus at the end of time, through clean living and the saving grace of Christ, the pure in heart are shown to be truly blessed for, at their festival of eternal delight, they see God.

7

The Gawain-poet is sometimes known by the title given to the first piece in his collection: *Pearl*. This work is an elegy for an innocent (a girl of two called either Pearl or, from the Latin, Margaret) and a dream vision in which her distraught father is granted a revelation of his daughter beatified as a courtly young lady. His pearl of great price, lost to the world, has become through her purity and the lapidary symbolism beloved of the Middle Ages a part of the perfection of Heaven. Her father's encounter with her is at once a solace, an enquiry into the nature of grace, and an admonition to the living patiently to accept the ways of God. The poet's assured and intricate artistic intelligence, his courteous theology and delight in material splendour are combined with a moving sense of man in his human limits and promised glory. *Pearl* is beyond question one of the supreme achievements of Middle English poetry.

A stanza from the opening section suggests something of these qualities. The poet and father (later to be revealed as a jeweller) is mourning disconsolately for the loss of his Pearl:.

> To þat spot þat I in speche expoun
> I entred in þat erber grene,
> In Augoste in a hyȝ seysoun,
> Quen corne is coruen wyth crokez kene.
> On huyle þer perle hit trendeled doun
> Schadowed þis wortez ful schyre and schene:
> Gilofre, gyngure, and gromylyoun,
> And pyonys powdered ay bytwene.
> Ȝif hit watz semly on to sene,
> A fayrre flayr ȝet fro hit flot,
> Þer wonys þat worþyly, I wot and wene,
> My precious perle wythouten spot.

(That spot that I have spoken of – the arbour green – I entered in at the height of August when the corn is cut with sharp sickles. The grave where Pearl was lost from view was shaded with beautiful, shining plants: gillyflower, ginger and gromwell, with peonies powdered in between. It was lovely to behold, yet a fairer fragrance from it flowed where lives my loveliest, I know full well, my precious Pearl without a spot.)

A number of points are immediately striking. First of all there is the elegiac loveliness of the seventh and eighth lines and the way in which their appeal to the eye and ear is modulated into an appeal to the most subtle of our senses and the one against whose wordless promptings we have least defence. The fragrance of the spices insists on feelings of the precious, of preservation and even of the divine. Peonies, we should note,

were thought sovereign against melancholy, while 'powdered' is a heraldic term that suggests profusion. Nature – the book of God – speaks to
the poet of divine consolation, but in his grief he is deaf to her significance. He watches the Lammastide harvest, but the gathering of the
wheat prompts no thoughts of the harvest of salvation. The 'crokez
kene' belong, perhaps, to a grimmer reaper. The father can only look
down at the burial-place of his child, forgetting the biblical lesson that a
grain of wheat abides alone unless it falls to the ground and is buried,
when it will bring forth rich fruit. For the present, the father's thoughts
are merely of lying in cold obstruction to rot. Though a jeweller, he
forgets that pearls are incorruptible and what blemishes they receive are
cleaned by a little wine – the chalice of the eucharist. Mourning in the
bright garden of the world, his only refuge is in courtesy, the noble
abundance of the flowers and the graceful language of *fine amour* – the
expression of grief in terms of courtly love:

> I dewyne, fordolked of luf-daungere.

> *(I faint away, grievously smitten by the remoteness of my beloved.)*

'For I am sick for love'; this phrase from the Canticles points back to
St Bernard and his interpretation of the Song of Songs as the soul's
longing for Christ. In his anguish, the grieving poet loses consciousness.
He wakes to a profound revelation. *Ego dormio, et cor meum vigilat,* 'I
sleep and my heart waketh' – a second phrase from the Canticles returns
us to one of the origins of the dream vision in the Scriptures and the idea
that the poet's own dream will be a *visio* – a revelation of divine
truth.

As Pearl's father, now wakened in spirit, stands amid the fabulous
trees and crystal rocks of the Earthly Paradise, he eventually glimpses
his daughter on the distant shore of Heaven. The water that divides
them is the demarcation between what living men may know and what
they can glimpse of an eternity only to be entered after death. The
rapture of seeing the transformed loveliness of his daughter causes the
dreamer physical pain, but at last, unable as yet to value the metaphysical
in her physical beauty, he perceives her in terms of the perfect lady of
romance. The limits of his understanding are thus made clear.

Whether through conscious allusion or the community of ideas, this
passage is irresistibly reminiscent of the closing cantos of the *Purgatorio*
where Dante glimpses Beatrice on the edge of the Earthly Paradise. In the
Divine Comedy, it will be recalled, Dante had scaled Mount Purgatory
and found his will 'free, upright and healthy'. He has attained the heights

that unaided mortal reason can scale. He is almost ready for his revelation of that spiritual truth 'which transcends human reason'. Before his beloved can instruct him, however, Dante has to make his shrift and be immersed in the restoring innocence of Lethe. Only then can he fully participate in the heavenly life. However, where Dante ascends ever closer to the Godhead, the dreaming narrator of *Pearl* is not granted so comprehensive an initiation. He is allowed to glimpse the perfection of Heaven but not to ford the stream. Instead, he has patiently to accept his human limitations. Despite his desperate attempts to enter Paradise, he is returned to this world. He comes back to a place of suffering. With his faith refreshed and with a surer knowledge of the nature of innocence and mercy he can, however, now endure as a patient Christian living in hope.

The fifth section of *Pearl* begins with the incomparable expression of the father's grief at the loss of his daughter. The passage is at once wholly convincing on the human level and foolish – even sinfully despairing – in the eyes of eternity. Once again, we are made aware of how the dreamer's limited understanding is responsible for his immoderate grief. His daughter upbraids him for this: 'Me þynk ȝe put in a mad porpose.'

With this stern admonition to the 'jueler gente' several traditions from the dream vision are subtly fused. First the inability of the dreamer fully to understand his dream is suggested, but suggested in a way that makes his naivety less a matter of gentle comedy than of genuine incomprehension, a picture of a mind numb with pain. The device is at once conventional and moving. Secondly, the monitory figure of Pearl is the typical figure of *auctoritas* from the true *visio*, but she is also the poet's daughter. Her heavenly transformation allows for what would have been unthinkable in terms of earthly manners – the daughter criticizes her father's misplaced despair and points out his errrors:

> 'þou says þou trawez me in þis dene
> Bycawse þou may with yȝen me se;
> Anoþer, þou says in þys countré
> þyself schal won with me ryȝt here;
> þe þrydde, to passe þys water fre:
> þat may no joyfol jueler.'

(*'You say that you believe I am actually in this field because you can see me with your own eyes; you also say that you intend to remain with me here, and thirdly that you intend to cross this freely flowing water – but no joyful jeweller may do that.'*)

The father does not as yet understand that while Pearl has her rightful place in Paradise, his own egoistic desire to ford the stream and remain by her side is an impossibility. His extreme emotion is wholly understandable on a human level, and inevitably arouses our sympathy. He is still in the grip of immoderate grief, however, and the passions of his soul must be calmed by truth as it is revealed to him through his daughter. For the moment, the narrator is still only an earthly jeweller, judging value with his sight rather than his inward eye. He has much to learn in his progress from craftsman to devout Christian, from the valuer of the earthly worth of jewels to an imitator of the merchant in the parable who sold everything to buy that great biblical symbol of grace – the pearl beyond price.

To begin his education, his daughter first urges a complete and humble faith in a benevolent God. Then, after the welcome expression of her father's humility, she explains how, in beatitude, she is the Bride of Christ the Lamb of God, the equal of the Virgin herself. The dreamer is astounded at this, but Pearl continues by saying (in imagery that we have seen to be the special province of the Gawain-poet) that courtesy is the rule of the courts of Heaven. Salvation has been courteously extended to her. To the astonished father it seems merely unjust that a child of two years should share an equality of heavenly bliss with such as he who have suffered on earth a long life of penance. Pearl then uses the parable of the labourers in the vineyard to explain how, just as both the late-comers and the industrious were equally rewarded, so those who die too young even to learn the rudiments of faith can share an equality of grace with the Virgin. Grace is not earned, but is God's gift to reformed sinners and the innocent alike. It is Pearl's purity – the spiritual and richly symbolic qualities inherent in her name – that have ensured her rightful place among the 144,000 virgin brides of Christ the Lamb of God mentioned in Revelation.

Pearl then describes her marriage to the Lamb with a mystical intensity in which the images of human and earthly love are refined into spiritual rapture:

> 'My makelez Lambe þat al may bete,'
> Quoþ scho, 'my dere Destyné,
> Me ches to Hys make, alþaȝ vnmete
> Sumtyme semed þat assemblé.
> When I wente fro yor worlde wete
> He calde me to Hys bonerté:
> "Cum hyder to Me, My lemman swete,
> For mote ne spot is non in þe."
> He gef me myȝt and also bewté;

> In Hys blod He wesch my wede on dese,
> And coronde clene in vergynté,
> And pyȝt me in perlez maskellez.'

(*'My spotless Lamb surpassing all,' she said, 'my dear Destiny, chose me for his bride, though such a union may have seemed inappropriate when I went from your wet world. He called me forth to his grace: "Come hither, my dearly beloved, for there is no spot or flaw in you." He gave me the power and the grace, bathing my clothes in his blood on the dais, crowned me clean in virginity and dressed me in matchless pearls.'*)

She also tells of the Crucifixion and, again from the vision of St John the Divine, of the Lamb's exaltation in Heaven, the antitype of the earthly Jerusalem where he was slain. Pearl now shows her father the celestial city itself, and her description of the adoration of the Lamb especially is a remarkable passage of chaste yet sumptuous beauty, of detail and spellbinding wonder. This very intensity is in itself mystical. A passage from Walter Hilton describes the meaning of the visionary's glimpse of the New Jerusalem:

> Ghostly to our purpose, Jerusalem is as mickle for to say as sight of peace, and betokeneth contemplation in perfect love of God. For contemplation is not else but a sight of Jhesu, which is very peace.

ghostly: spiritual *mickle:* much

For the poet, gazing rapturously:

> The Lombe delyt non lyste to wene;
> þaȝ He were hurt and wounde hade,
> In His sembelaunt watz neuer sene,
> So wern His glentez gloryous glade.
> I loked among His meyny schene
> How þay wyth lyf wern laste and lade;
> þen saȝ I þer my lyttel quene
> þat I wende had standen by me in sclade.
> Lorde, much of mirþe watz þat ho made
> Among her ferez þat watz so quyt!
> þat syȝt me gart to þenk to wade
> For luf-longyng in gret delyt.

(*The delight of the Lamb was plain, though He was wounded. There was no sign of suffering. His look shone so gloriously. I looked at His shining followers and the superabundant life they had. Then I saw there my little queen who I thought had been standing by me in the glade. Lord, what mirth she made, so pure among her peers. The sight moved the wish to wade across the waters because of the great delight of my love-longing.*)

The technical virtuosity and human drama of this stanza are remarkable and closely related. Not only does the light alliterative measure fall with a natural emphasis, but the verse reveals that intricate rhyming pattern which is sustained through all the 101 stanzas. To this should be added what the rhetoricians called *concatenatio*, concatenation or the linking of the groups of five stanzas – six in the case of section fifteen – by a refrain which echoes the first line of the verse in the succeeding group. To complete this circularity, the earthly Pearl, 'plesaunte to prynces paye' at the opening, becomes the pearl beyond price offered to the princely Christ at the close. Through the course of the poem, worldly mourning is transformed by both a mystical glimpse of other-worldly joy and a recognition of the virtue of patient humility. In appreciating the form of the work we also come to appreciate the broad sweep of its theology. We will not do so fully, however, unless we recognize how comprehensively this match of theme and form is developed. We must now turn to sacred mathematics and to God as the great arithmetician.

The Middle Ages inherited from Pythagoras, Plato and the apocryphal books of Solomon the idea that numbers hold a mystical significance. In this poem of 101 twelve-line stanzas, the grand total of 1,212 lines is designed to relate in just such a fashion to the dreamer's mystical view of the New Jerusalem. We have seen that the celestial city itself is described in the terms used by St John the Divine. It is built on twelve tiers of differing precious stones. It is twelve miles across, guarded by twelve gates and peopled by the 144,000 virgins, amongst whom Pearl herself is one. Each stanza and the combination of them all exactly match a mystical harmony. Such silent structures – properly termed 'numerological' – characterize many works from this period down to those of Spenser, Milton and Dryden. In the case of *Pearl* the poem is shaped, in the noble words of Sir Thomas Browne, 'according to the ordainer of order and mystical mathematics of the city of Heaven'. A passage from St Augustine helps us to see yet further into the effect of the whole: 'The soul truly becomes better,' St Augustine wrote, 'when it turns away from the carnal senses and is reformed by the divine numbers of wisdom. For thus it is said in Holy Scripture: "I have made the circuit in order to know and contemplate and seek wisdom and number."' It is so in *Pearl*. As is appropriate for a jeweller and a mystic, the poet has here fashioned an exquisite reliquary in words and number in which to enshrine his vision of beatitude.

8

Romance, theology and mystic vision are not the only subjects of alliterative verse. Poets who employed the form also examined their society in satires which unite a hatred of social and spiritual abuse with a savage condemnation of the age. Much of this work is of more historical interest than literary merit, however. It reflects a period which experienced the bitterest defeats of the Hundred Years War, the rise of the Lollards, the Black Death and the Peasants' Revolt. This was also an age of numerous guides to godly living, and the basis of the greater part of satire and 'complaint' poetry is ultimately religious. Indeed, many of its salient ideas are endlessly repeated in sermons and sermon handbooks.

Many of the satires themselves reveal an earnestly didactic involvement with matters of theological, political and ethical interest. When they attack the abuses of the age such works are properly known as 'complaint'. The grinding expense and cynicism caused by the later stages of the French wars, for example, produced some trenchant satires on the decline of chivalric standards. A poem contemporary with *Sir Gawain and the Green Knight* contrasts a poor but worthy follower of the older ways with a new class of smooth-operating courtiers. A number of more important works in this mode can also be related to the central masterpiece of the genre: Langland's *Piers Ploughman*.

Many of these satires use the dream vision as a means of examining society, and what is probably one of the earliest examples of the 'alliterative revival', a piece written near the home of the Gawain-poet himself, is just such a poem. *Winner and Waster* (*c.* 1350) is an incomplete work which uses dream vision and allegory to discuss contrasting attitudes to national wealth and social responsibility. In a beautiful landscape, a poet troubled by the status of his art sees the armies of Winner and Waster drawn up before the silk tent of Edward III. The poem then examines the economic and social abuses of getting and spending. After an acrimonious 'flyting', the king eventually declares that Winner should side with the Church, Waster with the merchants of Cheapside.

The Parliament of the Three Ages comes from the same period and area – perhaps even from the same pen. In this work Old Age catalogues the vices of Youth and Middle Age not just in economic terms but against a disproportionately long and gloomy expectation of death. This sends the dreamer soberly back to town.

Mention should also be made here of three much longer pieces: the *Simonie* (c. 1360) and *Richard the Redeless*, which is attached to *Mum and the Soothsegger* (*c.* 1400) – a title to be rendered as 'Silence and

Truthteller'. This is an incomplete visionary dream quest which urges the informed and pious gentry to speak out from the heart, advise Richard II, and punish noble wastrels. Many of these poems show how concern over a corrupt Church and state could be expressed through traditional allegories, powerful reportage and the alliterative line. The greatest of such works, however – indeed, the original of many and one of the most important surviving Middle English poems – is the *Piers Ploughman* of William Langland.

9

Over fifty surviving manuscript copies of *Piers Ploughman* witness to the poem's contemporary popularity. Just one of these confirms the poet to have been William Langland. We may deduce that he was born in Shropshire around 1332, the possibly illegitimate son of a landowner who helped fund his basic theological training. Langland remained in minor orders, a member of the Church's literature proletariat, and lived close to the poverty that formed so important a part of his vision. He tells us in his poem that he came to London, resided with his wife on Cornhill for a time, and scraped a living singing masses for the dead:

> Thus ich a-waked, god wot · whanne ich wonede on Cornehulle,
> Kytte and ich in a cote · clothed as a lollere ...
> 'Whanne ich onge was' quath ich · 'meny er hennes,
> My fader and my frendes · founden me to scole,
> Tyl ich wiste wyterliche · what holy wryt menede,
> And what is best for the body · as the bok telleth,
> And sykerest for the soule · by so ich wolle continue.
> And ut fond ich neuere in faith · sytthen my frendes deyden,
> Lyf that me lyked · bote in thes longe clothes.
> Yf ich by laboure schoulde lyue · and lyflode deseruen,
> That labour ich lerned best · ther-with lyue ich sholde;
>   *In eadem uocatione in qua uocati estis, manete*
> And ich lyue in Londone · and on London bothe,
> The lomes that ich laboure with · and lyflode deserue
> Ys *pater-noster* and my prymer · *placebo* and *dirige*,
> And my sauter som tyme · and my seuene psalmes.
> Thus ich singe for hure soules · of suche as me helpen,
> And tho that fynden me my fode · vouchen safe, ich trowe,
> To be welcome whanne ich come · other-while in a monthe,
> Now with hym and now with hure · and thus-gate ich begge
> With-oute bagge other botel - bote my wombe one,
> And al-so me more ouer · me thynketh, syre Reson,

Men sholde constrayne no clerke · to knauene werkes;
For by laws of *Leuitici* · that oure lorde ordeynede,
Clerkes that aren crouned · of kynde vnderstondyng
Sholde nother swynke ne swete · ne swere at enquestes . . .'

(*Thus I awoke, and found myself on Cornhill, where I lived with Kit in a cottage, dressed like a beggar . . . 'Many years ago, when I was a boy,' I answered, 'my father and friends found the means to send me to school, so that I came to understand Holy Scripture, and was taught all that's best for my body and safest for my soul – provided, of course, that I persevere in it. And though the friends who helped me then have since died, I have never found any life that suited me, except in these long, clerical robes. If I'm to earn a living, I must earn it by doing the job that I've learned best, for it is written, "Let every man abide in the same calling wherein he was called."*

'So I live in London and also on London, and the tools that I work with are my Paternoster and Prayer Book, and sometimes my Book of Offices for the Dead, and my Psalter, and Seven Penitential Psalms. And with these I sing for the souls of those who help me; and I expect the folk who provide me with food, to make me welcome when I visit them once or twice a month. So I go on my rounds, now to his house and now to hers, and that is how I do my begging – with neither bag nor bottle, but only my stomach to carry all my supplies! What is more, Sir Reason, I am convinced that you should never force a man in Holy Orders to do manual work. For it says in Leviticus, the Law of God, that men whose natural gifts lead them to take Orders should not toil or sweat, or serve on juries . . .')

This autobiographical passage – a world away from the courtly self-effacement of Chaucer or the Gawain-poet – is a moving picture of dogged if sometimes truculent humility, of an integrity of spirit maintained amid physical difficulty. It also reveals a measure of resentment at the way the poorest clergy were treated, and helps us appreciate Langland's further self-portraits as a restless, even compulsive intellectual. He often shows himself a lanky, critical, bitter outsider, and lastly as a visionary concerned with the purest form of the devout life. His poem – which modern scholarship has shown exists in three versions – was his life's work. The A-text was composed before 1370 but abandoned only to be extensively reworked into the B-text, which was then further emended.

The second or B-text redaction (1377–9) is the most appropriate with which to start. Here, subsumed into the generalized, allegorical figure of Will the narrator of dream visions, Langland presents a man at first alienated from many of the forces of contemporary influence by his insight into corruption, both lay and clerical. Will is also shown as a Christian of strong intellect, a man passionately involved in current theological controversies but increasingly aware of the inadequacies of the life of reason alone. Both as an individual and a personification of the will, the narrator is a figure in many ways representative of his time. We see him longing for spiritual vision and harried by the question Bunyan's hero was later to ask: What must I do to save my soul? As Will progresses through the twenty passus or 'steps' of his poem, so in a demanding series of ten dream visions and dreams within dreams, the allegorized forces of medieval society, its intellectual life and means of salvation, are revealed against the mounting crisis of Will's spiritual growth and his search for the purest form of the Christian life.

The complexity of such a structure is clearly considerable and it must be said that *Piers Ploughman* is a far from easy poem. Its difficulties are increased by the fact that although it is the product of a most powerful verbal and theological imagination, of a writer able vividly to recreate the sights and sounds of his contemporary scene, the deeper purposes of his work – its search for an intuitive understanding of spiritual truth, its fluctuating, many-layered allegory, its diffuse form which owes much to the medieval sermon and mystical prose, and, above all, its intellectual and theological personifications – are the creation of a poet deeply interested in exposition, and whose work relies to a considerable extent on familiarity with what is to us often unfamiliar material. This will be clear even from a bare and necessarily simplistic outline.

We should note first how the poem starts in the secular world, moves inward through intellectual doubt, and then, with an increasing emphasis on the spiritual, allies the dreamer's search for truth to the Passion. This broad development from social criticism through reason to faith is of great importance, and, while it is dramatically involving to the highest degree, it has some of its roots at least in that divide we have seen medieval philosophers open up between the strictly logical analysis of theological concepts and the need for faith and revelation. At the heart of *Piers Ploughman*, Eastertide brings Will a vision of true charity. He recognizes Christ's power to save and man's potential if he responds to grace. He glimpses the truth that can set him free. This passus (number XVIII) contains some of the most dramatic Middle English verse and touches the sublime. However, the corruption on which the poem lavishes so much of its satire threatens these insights at the very moment the Church has been founded. Perfection is not for this world. As the work describes the history of the early Church and the attacks of clerical worldliness or anti-Christ, so the poem ends neither with certainty nor with entry into the celestial city, but rather with a resolve to search once more for a true model of the devout life amid the world's sin.

The last lines of the poem return us to its beginning. As with *Pearl*, such circularity is an important aspect of the work's purposes. We should now examine these in more detail.

Will, the seeker after marvels, first falls asleep on the Malvern Hills. He has a vision of mankind on a plain between the tower of Truth and the dungeons of Hell:

> In a somer seson, whan softe was the sonne,
> I shoop me into shroudes as I a sheep were
> In habite as an heremite unholy of workes,
> Wente wide in this world wondres to here.
> Ac on a May morwenynge on Malverne hilles
> Me bifel a ferly, of Fairye me thoghte.
> I was wery forwandred and wente me to reste
> Under a brood bank by a bourne syde;
> And as I lay and lenede and loked on the watres,
> I slombered into a slepyng, it sweyed so murye.
>   Thanne gan I meten a merveillous swevene –
> That I was in a wildernesse, wiste I nevere where.
> A[c] as I biheeld into the eest an heigh to the sonne,
> I seigh a tour on a toft trieliche ymaked,
> A deep dale bynethe, a dongeon therinne,
> With depe diches and derke and dredfulle of sighte.
> A fair feeld ful of folk fond I ther bitwene –
> Of alle manere of men, the meene and the riche,
> Werchynge and wandrynge as the world asketh.

(*One summer season, when the sun was warm, I rigged myself out in shaggy woollen clothes, as if I were a shepherd; and in the garb of an easy-living hermit I set out to roam far and wide through the world, hoping to hear of marvels. But on a morning in May, among the Malvern Hills, a strange thing happened to me, as though by magic. For I was tired out by my wanderings, and as I lay down to rest under a broad bank by the side of a stream, and leaned over gazing into the water, it sounded so pleasant that I fell asleep.*

And I dreamt a marvellous dream: I was in a wilderness, I could not tell where, and looking eastwards I saw a tower high up against the sun, and splendidly built on top of a hill; and far beneath it was a great gulf, with a dungeon in it, surrounded by deep, dark pits, dreadful to see. But between the tower and the gulf I saw a smooth plain, thronged with all kinds of people, high and low together, moving busily about their worldly affairs.)

This is a particularly vivid reworking of the traditional dream vision formula, but Will's closer inspection – a critical, bustling panorama of medieval society – reveals anti-Christ's widespread corruption and a consequent worldliness in the Church, the law and Parliament. In Passus I, Holy Church informs Will about the proper use of wealth, and, in reply to his anxious question about how he may save his soul, tells him that Truth is man's greatest treasure, is to be identified with the God of the Trinity who is love, and should be sought through the natural knowledge of the heart. In this statement we see brought together many of the poem's central themes. In particular we see the nature of truth which, for medieval thinkers, united man's potential excellence to God's love and salvation and was a matter both of the intellect (or *ratio*) and of intuitive knowledge (*intellectus*). Holy Church states the matter thus:

> 'Whan alle tresors arn tried,' quod she, 'Treuthe is the beste.
> I do it on *Deus caritas* to deme the sothe;
> It is as dereworthe a drury as deere God hymselven.
> Who is trewe of his tonge and telleth noon oother,
> And dooth the werkes therwith and wilneth no man ille,
> He is a god by the Gospel, agrounde and olofte,
> And ylik to Oure Lord, by Seint Lukes wordes.
> The clerkes that knowen this sholde kennen it aboute,
> For Cristen and uncristen cleymeth it echone.'

('When all treasures are tested,' she said, 'Truth is the best. And to prove it and test what is true, I appeal to the text "God is love". For Truth is as precious a jewel as our dear Lord himself. For he who speaks nothing but the truth, and acts by it, wishing no man ill, is like Christ, a God on earth and in Heaven – those are St Luke's words. Men of learning who know this teaching should proclaim it everywhere; for Christians and heathens are alike crying out for it.')

Much of the rest of the poem will be a record of Will's attempts to experience the reality of these seemingly simple statements and his efforts to get beyond forms of words to a vision of salvation founded on that patient, hopeful and loving faith which, as St Paul declared, lightens the eyes of the hearts of believers.

Having identified Truth with the God of Love and shown that Truth itself is written in the heart (all concepts familiar from St Paul), Will is then shown falsehood operating in the secular sphere. He sees the allegorical figure of Mede, or financial reward, whose existence encourages the corruption symbolized by her forced marriage to Fraud. When Mede arrives at court, the king tries to wed her to Conscience who naturally refuses her, and, instead of succumbing to temptation, provides a messianic vision of future purity. After a sharply observed trial which exposes the corruption of the secular sphere, the king vows to follow Reason and Conscience in all things. With this optimistic correction of everyday society, the first vision (Prologue and Passus I–IV) ends.

The second vision (Passus V–VII) shows an already corrupting society turning to inner values. It begins with Reason's sermon on everyday vices, followed by the confession of the Seven Deadly Sins. These grotesques, allegorical figures who live amid the closely detailed, cartoon-like filth of contemporary life, acquire a near heroic beastliness and represent an aspect of Langland's art that is justly popular. In his presentation of Gluttony, for example, we are made to feel the sheer profusion of life among the regulars of a sordid London pub. They are both medieval and timeless, at once a crowd and individuals. Amid them all, the Breughel-like figure of Gluttony swills his beer, vomits and reels his stinking passage home until, racked with a hangover and remorse, he stumbles into self-pity and repentance:

Now bigynneth Gloton for to go to shrifte,
And kaireth hym to kirkewarde his coupe to shewe.
Ac Beton the Brewestere bad hym good morwe
And asked hym with that, whiderward he wolde.
　'To holy chirche,' quod he, 'for to here masse,
And sithen I wole be shryven, and synne no moore.'
'I have good ale, gossib,' quod she, 'Gloton, woltow assaye?'
　'Hastow,' quod he, 'any hote spices?'
　'I have pepir and pione,' quod she, 'and a pound of garleek,
A ferthyngworth of fenel seed for fastynge dayes.'
　Thanne goth Gloton in, and grete othes after.
Cesse the Souteresse sat on the benche,
Watte the Warner and his wif bothe,
Tymme the Tynkere and tweyne of his [knave]es,
Hikke the Hakeneyman and Hugh the Nedlere,
Clarice of Cokkeslane and the Clerk of the chirche,
Sire Piers of Pridie and Pernele of Flaundres,
Dawe the Dykere, and a dozeyne othere –
A Ribibour, a Ratoner, a Rakiere of Chepe,
A Ropere, a Redyngkyng, and Rose the Dysshere,
Godefray of Garlekhithe and Griffyn the Walshe . . .
　There was laughynge and lourynge and 'Lat go the cuppe!'
[Bargaynes and beverages bigonne to arise;]
Til Gloton had yglubbed a galon and a gille.
His guttes bigonne to gothelen as two gredy sowes;
He pissed a potel in a Paternoster-while,
And blew his rounde ruwet at his ruggebones ende,
That alle that herde that horn helde his nose after
And wisshed it hadde ben wexed with a wispe of firses!
　He myghte neither steppe ne stonde er he his staf hadde,
And thanne gan he to go like a glemannes bicche
Som tyme aside and som tyme arere,
As whoso leith lynes for to lacche foweles.

And when he drough to the dore, thanne dymmed hise eighen;
He [thr]umbled on the thresshfold and threw to the erthe.
Clement the Cobelere kaughte hym by the myddel
For to liften hym olofte, and leyde hym on his knowes.
Ac Gloton was a gret cherl and a grym in the liftyng,
And koughed up a cawdel in Clementes lappe.
Is noon so hungry hound in Hertfordshire
Dorste lape of that levynge, so unlovely it smaughte!
 With al the wo of this world, his wif and his wenche
Baren hym to his bed and broughte hym therinne;
And after al this excesse he had an accidie,
That he sleep Saterday and Sonday, till sonne yede to reste.
Thanne waked he of his wynkyng and wiped hise eighen;
The first word that he spak was – 'Where is the bolle?'
His wif [and his wit] edwyte[d] hym tho how wikkedly he lyvede,
And Repentaunce right so rebuked hym that tyme:
'As thow with wordes and werkes hast wroght yvele in thi lyve,
Shryve thee and be shamed therof, and shewe it with thi mouthe.'
 'I, Gloton,' quod the gome, 'gilty me yelde . . .'

(And then Glutton set out to go to Confession. But as he sauntered along to the church, he was hailed by Betty, the ale-wife, who asked him where he was going.

'To Holy Church,' he replied, 'to hear Mass and go to Confession; then I shan't commit any more sins.'

'I've got some good ale here, Glutton,' she said. 'Why don't you come and try it, ducky?'

'Have you got hot spices in your bag?'

'Yes, I've got pepper, and peony-seeds and a pound of garlic – or would you rather have a ha'porth of fennel-seed, as it's a fish-day?'

So Glutton entered the pub and Great Oaths followed him. He found Cissie, the shoe-maker, sitting on the bench, and Wat the gamekeeper with his wife, and Tim the tinker with two of his apprentices, and Hick the hackneyman, and Hugh the haberdasher, and Clarice the whore of Cock Lane, with the parish clerk, and Davy the ditcher, and Father Peter of Prie-Dieu Abbey with Peacock the Flemish wench, and a dozen others, not to mention a fiddler, and a ratcatcher, and a Cheapside scavenger, a rope-maker, and a trooper. Then there was Rose the pewterer, Godfrey of Garlick-Hithe, Griffiths the Welshman . . .

Then there were scowls and roars of laughter and cries of 'Pass round the cup!' and so they sat shouting and singing till time for vespers. By that time, Glutton had put down more than a gallon of ale, and his guts were beginning to rumble like a couple of greedy sows. Then, before you had time to say the Our Father, he had pissed a couple of quarts, and blown such a blast on the round horn of his rump, that all who heard it had to hold their noses, and wish to God he would plug it with a bunch of gorse!

He could neither walk nor stand without his stick. And once he got going, he moved like a blind minstrel's bitch, or like a fowler laying his lines, sometimes sideways, sometimes backwards. And when he drew near to the door, his eyes grew glazed, and he stumbled on the threshold and fell flat on the ground. Then Clement the cobbler seized him round the middle to lift him up, and got him on to his knees. But Glutton was a big fellow, and he took some lifting; and to make matters worse, he was sick in Clement's lap, and his vomit smelt so foul that the hungriest hound in Hertfordshire would never have lapped it up.

At last, with endless trouble, his wife and daughter managed to carry him home and get him into bed. And after all this dissipation, he fell into a stupor, and slept throughout Saturday and Sunday. Then at sunset on Sunday he woke up, and as he wiped his bleary eyes, the first words he uttered were, 'Who's had the tankard?'

Then his wife scolded him for his wicked life, and Repentance joined in, saying, 'You know you have sinned in word and deed, so confess yourself, and show some shame and make an act of contrition.'

'I, Glutton, confess that I am guilty . . .')

This is the very nightmare of indulgence, its sinfulness measured by our own disgust.

But Langland is a far more various poet than this, and at the close of Passus V, when newly repentant mankind has set out on its pilgrimage towards Truth and inevitably got lost, Piers Ploughman makes his first appearance. Few heroes are more elusive or gather to themselves a greater range of allusion. We may like to compare Piers at this point with Chaucer's Ploughman – a figure also familiar from complaint poetry – who represents the Christian values of the secular life, a vision of Truth gained through hard work and faithful charity guided by Conscience and 'Kynde Wit' or that 'Natural Instinct' which some called *intellectus*:

> 'Peter!' quod a Plowman, and putte forth his hed,
> 'I knowe hym as kyndely as clerc doth hise bokes.
> Conscience and Kynde Wit kenned me to his place
> And diden me suren hym si[ththen] to serven hym for evere,
> Bothe to sowe and to sette the while I swynke myghte.
> I have ben his folwere al this fourty wynter –
> Bothe ysowen his seed and suwed hise beestes,
> Withinne and withouten waited his profit,
> Idyke[d] and id[o]lve, ido that he hoteth.
> Som tyme I sowe and som tyme I thresshe,
> In taillours craft and tynkeris craft, what Truthe kan devyse,
> I weve and I wynde and do what Truthe hoteth.
> For though I seye it myself, I serve hym to paye;
> I have myn hire of hym wel and outherwhiles moore.
> He is the presteste paiere that povere men knoweth;
> He with haltnoon hewe his hire that he ne hath it at even.
> He is as lowe as a lomb and lovelich of speche.

And if ye wilneth to wite where that he dwelleth,
I [wol] wisse yow [wel right] to his place.'

(*'By St Peter!' said a ploughman, pushing his way through the crowd, 'I know Him,
as well as a scholar knows his books. Conscience and Natural Instinct showed me
the way to His place, and they made me swear to serve Him for ever, and do His
sowing and planting for as long as I can work. I've been His man for the last forty
years, I've sown His seed and herded His beasts and looked after all His affairs,
indoors and out. I ditch and dig, sow and thresh, and do whatever Truth tells me –
tailoring and tinkering, spinning and weaving – I put my hand to anything He bids me.*

*'And Truth is pleased with my work, though I say it myself. He pays me well, and
sometimes gives me extra; for He's as ready with His wages as any poor man could
wish, and never fails to pay His men each night. Besides, He's as mild as a lamb, and
always speaks to you kindly. – So if you would like to know where He lives, I'll put
you on the track in no time.'*)

This vision of the workaday Piers should always be borne in mind, even
when he is called to far greater allegorical functions. Before considering
a continuation of the pilgrimage, however, Piers sets mankind – English
society after the Black Death – to necessary work. Even the aristocracy
agree to this, but when the labourers begin to shirk, Piers calls up
Hunger to chastise them. A pardon for all the working Christian
community is then received from Truth, but when it is read out it appears
to offer no forgiveness to backsliders but consists merely of phrases from
the Athanasian Creed which state that those who do well will be saved,
while those who sin will be damned. Piers tears the pardon to shreds. He
knows that man cannot rely simply on his own resources to do well:

And Piers for pure tene pulled it atweyne
And seide, *'Si ambulavero in medio umbre mortis
Non timebo mala, quoniam tu mecum es.*
'I shal cessen of my sowyng,' quod Piers, 'and swynke noght so harde,
Ne aboute my bely joye so bisy be na moore;
Of preieres and of penaunce my plough shal ben herafter,
And wepen whan I sholde slepe, though whete breed me faille.'

(*Then Piers, in sheer rage, tore the Pardon in two, and said: '"Yea, though I walk
through the valley of the shadow of death, I will fear no evil: For Thou art with me."*
*'I shall cease sowing,' said Piers, 'and not work so hard, nor be so concerned
about my belly any more. Prayers and penance shall be my plough hereafter, and I
shall weep when I should sleep, though I have no white bread.*)

Prayer, contrition and the absolute faith epitomized by the quotation
from Psalm 23 are essential. They are the only ways of leading life
properly and doing well. As Piers argues with the priest who brought
the pardon, so the need for a more spiritual insight into Dowel – an

allegorical figure representing right conduct and one of the great variously-defined allegories of the poem – is discussed.

The question of doing well – which is unresolved for the moment – we have seen to be one of the central concerns of contemporary theology. Could man, by his natural power to follow the requirements of the covenant between himself and God, merit salvation through his own efforts? Later in the poem we shall see the dreamer's progress develop beyond this basic concern with right behaviour, and on through acts of mercy to those informed with true charity, and the final reception of saving grace. The life of the spirit provides the answers to the life of the mind. For the moment, however, the noise of the disagreement wakes the narrator, and we are shown the puzzled Will back in the everyday world thinking that to do well is indeed better than relying simply on pardons and the sacraments. But what – or who – is Dowel? What is this way of behaving that leads the soul to salvation? Will's search for an answer – which for most editors marks the end of the so-called *visio* or Langland's 'Vision of Piers Ploughman', and the start of the *vita* or 'Life of Dowel, Dobet and Dobest' – takes us to the central sections of the work.

Will at first thinks he can discover Dowel through the intellect. In his third vision, which occupies the sometimes over-long section of Passus VIII–XII, Will encounters the figure of Thought who at once allies Dowel to Dobet (or 'Do Better') and Dobest. Thought provides definitions of these three which will be constantly redefined in this section – never to Will's complete satisfaction – until, after Passus XIII, he begins to abandon his lust for knowledge and surrenders in humility to God's purposes. Before this can happen, however, he has to meet more of the allegorized forces of medieval intellectual life since at this stage of his spiritual enquiry the intellect is still his most active faculty. Thought introduces Will to Wit – or 'Intelligence' – who lectures him on chastity and giving to the needy, while his wife, the strident Lady Study, reproaches her husband for teaching a mere dilettante theologian. Study then directs Will to Clergie ('Learning') and to Scripture. A satire on the spiritual ignorance of the learned leads Will to despise such people and resign his aggrieved trust to the simple, unquestioning forms of faith. Then, in the B-text redaction, Will falls into a deeper sleep and for forty-five years leads a worldly life until he reaches frightened old age and is deserted by the fairweather friars. Scripture now returns to admonish him, while Trajan – a virtuous pagan freed from Hell by God's mercy on his natural goodness and thus a prefiguration of the great act of love in Passus XVIII in which the souls of all the virtuous pagans and Old Testament partriarchs are redeemed – preaches to Will on the superiority of charity over mere learning. A further very lovely vision of God's care for the natural world leads Will to believe that only man is vile. Will's despondency is then assuaged by Ymaginatyf – a figure suggesting the ability to hold ideas in the mind – who wakes him from his inner dream, defines Dobest as charity, and shows him the proper place of the mind, the priesthood, and how the just are saved. Will is now moving away from intellectual pride, and his fourth vision (Passus XIII–XIV) – in some respects the beginning of the life of Dobet – marks a great turning-point in the whole poem.

Will falls to dreaming again and has a vision in which Conscience invites him to dinner with Clergie, Scripture, and a great divine. The last figure is a vivid satire on a boorishly imperious and hypocritical don who despises what he hears of Piers Ploughman's advocacy of divine love. Will, forced to sit at a less important table with Patience, eventually leaves Clergie or Learning behind to set out as a pilgrim with the God-given graces of Conscience and Patience. They then meet with Activa Vita, the man-of-the-world personified in one Hawkyn, a baker who has soiled his allegorical coat of baptism with the Seven Deadly Sins. In some respects the intellect has merely returned Will to the world of the first and second visions. He needs a more spiritual understanding. Patience lectures Hawkyn on poverty and, with his subsequent contrition and the start of the truly devout life instigated this time by Patience rather than Reason, the fourth vision ends. The poem now turns increasingly to spiritual values and to the pursuit of the divine as advocated by the anonymous author of *The Cloud of Unknowing* (c. 1380): 'by love may he be getyn and holdyn'.

The renewed pursuit requires the awakening of charity. Anima, a diffuse figure suggesting aspects of the human soul in whom the spiritual and the intellectual are combined, appears to Will, rebukes his excessive intellectualism and provides not only a long discourse on charity and the responsibilities and failings of the priesthood, but also the suggestion that Piers Ploughman – a figure whose increasing spiritual stature has already been mentioned – can, like Christ and his apostolic successors, detect true charity not in externals but by knowing the heart. This 'kynde knowyng' – the apprehension of the divine through natural spiritual insight and love rather than the intellect – we have seen is central to the poem. So is the gradual identification of Piers with the Redeemer, an identification which emphasizes both the humanity of Christ and the spiritual potential of man. As a preparation for this, Passus XVI contains an inner vision of Piers as the guardian of the Tree of Charity. The elusive symbolism of this section suggests how both human history and the faith of the individual soul are focused on the incarnation of the God of Love in Jesus. When Will wakes from this inner vision, he finds that it is the season of Lent. The subsequent stages of his spiritual growth will now be linked to the Passion, seen both as a literal history told with a full awareness of its allegorical, tropological and mystical significance, and also as the heart of the mass. To prepare for this supreme moment, Abraham instructs Will in faith, Moses in hope, while the story of the Good Samaritan – a figure whose loving-kindness reveals him as a 'type' of Christ and hence of Piers also – shows Will that charity is indeed the greatest virtue.

The Samaritan also provides a discourse on the nature of the Trinity, and it is the second person of the Trinity – God the Son revealed in his humanity as both Jesus and the knightly Piers come to joust with Satan – who is the central figure of the sixth vision (Passus XVIII). In many respects this is the most moving section of the whole poem: a vision of God and man united in pure charity towards which all so far has been moving. Here is Langland's picture of Calvary:

> '*Crucifige!*' quod a cachepol, 'I warante hym a wicche!'
> '*Tolle, tolle!*' quod another, and took of kene thornes,
> And bigan of [gr]ene thorn a garland to make,
> And sette it sore on his heed and seide in envye,
> '*Aye, raby!*' quod that ribaud – and threw reedes at hym,
> Nailed hym with thre nailes naked on the roode,
> And poison on a poole thei putte up to hise lippes,
> And beden hym drynken his deeth-yvel – hise dayes were ydone –
> And [seiden], 'If that thow sotil be, help now thiselve;
> If thow be Crist and kynges sone, com down of the roode;
> Thanne shul we leve that lif thee loveth and wol noght lete thee deye!'
> '*Consummatum est,*' quod Crist, and comsede for to swoune,
> Pitousliche and pale as a prison that deieth;
> The lord of lif and of light tho leide hise eighen togideres.
> The day for drede withdrough and derk bicam the sonne.
> The wal waggede and cleef, and al the world quaved.
> Dede men for that dene come out of depe graves,
> And tolde why that tempeste so longe tyme durede.

('*Crucify Him!*' cried an officer, 'I'll swear He's a sorcerer.'

'*Off with Him! Take Him away!*' yelled another, and seizing some sharp thorns, he made a wreath and rammed it on His head, mocking Him with cries of, 'Hail, Rabbi!' and thrusting reeds at Him.

Then they nailed Him, with three nails, naked, to the Cross, and putting poison to His lips, at the end of a pole, they told Him to drink his death-drink for His days were over. '*But if you're a magician,*' they said, '*come down from the cross; then we'll believe that Life loves you so much, he won't let you die!*'

Christ said, 'It is finished,' and began to grow fearfully pale, like a prisoner on the point of death. And so the Lord of Life and of Light closed His eyes. Then at once the daylight fled in fear and the sun became dark; the wall of the Temple shook and split, and the whole earth quaked.

On hearing this dreadful sound, the dead came forth from their deep graves, and spoke to the living, to tell them why the storm raged for so long.)

The relatively plain alliterative line proves itself swift, flexible and capable of rousing deep feelings. The grotesque activity of the crowd reinforces the passivity of the tortured Saviour suffering to redeem their very brutality. The cruel Latin phrases they shout – and Langland's verse, like much medieval lyric, is often characterized by what is properly called a macaronic combination of Latin and Middle English – contrasts with Christ's last words. The image of God as a pale human prisoner and yet the 'lord of lif' brings poetry and theology together in an exact pathos. The contrast between the closing eyes and the sudden darkness of the world expresses both an individual death and its universal significance. In all, the biblical and sublime are here properly and powerfully at one with the directly observed. Poetry itself becomes a form of 'kynde knowyng'. As we watch – wondering and appalled like Will himself – so the vivid literal impression of the death of Piers–Jesus merges with the conventional layers of medieval textual interpretation to suggest that all life should be such a loving sacrifice, a mystical dying in an ecstasy of communion with God, and the fact – soon to be discussed by the figures of Mercy, Truth, Righteousness and Peace – that the Crucifixion will be followed by a victory over death.

This great theme is attempted not by a description of the Resurrection, but by presenting a scene which was widely used in medieval art – the Harrowing of Hell. This incident was derived from the apocryphal Book of Nicodemus and presented Christ's supposed descent into Hell in order to bind Lucifer and, through a triumph of mercy and justice, to free the souls of righteous pagans and Old Testament patriarchs. In *Piers Ploughman*, this is both a moment of high drama and an allegory of Christ's breaking into the darkness of man's soul to rescue it from the bondage of sin:

> 'And now I se wher a soule cometh [silynge hiderward]
> With glorie and with gret light – God it is, I woot well!
> I rede we fle,' quod he, 'faste alle hennes –
> For us were bettre noght be than biden his sighte.
> For thi lesynges, Lucifer, lost is al oure praye.
> First thorugh the we fellen fro hevene so heighe;
> For we leved thi lesynges, we lopen out alle with thee;

And now for thi laste lesynge, ylorn we have Adam,
And al oure lordshipe, I leve, a londe and a watre:
Nunc princeps huius mundi eicietur foras.'
    Eft the light bad unlouke, and Lucifer answerde,
'Quis est iste?
'What lord artow?' quod Lucifer. The light soone seide,
'Rex glori[a]e,
The lord of myght and of mayn and alle manere vertues –
Dominus virtutum.
Dukes of this dymme place, anoon undo thise yates,
That Crist may come in, the Kynges sone of Hevene!'
    And with that breeth helle brak, with Belialles barres –
For any wye or warde, wide open the yates.
    Patriarkes and prophetes, *populus in tenebris,*
Songen Seint Johanes song, *'Ecce Agnus Dei!'*
Lucifer loke ne myghte, so light hym ablente.
    And tho that Oure Lord lovede, into his light he laughte,
And seide to Sathan, 'Lo! here my soule to amendes
For alle synfulle soules, to save tho that ben worthi.
Myne thei ben and of me – I may the bet hem cleyme.
Although reson recorde, and right of myselve,
That if thei ete the appul, alle sholde deye,
I bihighte hem noght here helle for evere.'

('*And now I can see a soul sailing towards us, blazing with light and glory – I am certain it is God. Quickly, we must escape while we can; it would be more than our lives are worth to let Him find us here. It is you, Lucifer, with your lies, that have lost us all our prey. It was all your fault that we fell from the heights of heaven in the first place; not one of us would have leapt out after you, if we hadn't swallowed your talk. And now, thanks to your latest invention, we have lost Adam, and, more than likely, all our dominion over land and sea – "now shall the prince of this world be cast out".*'

Then again the light bade them unlock the gates, and Lucifer answered saying, 'What Lord art thou?' – '"Who is this king . . . ?"'

'The King of Glory,' answered the Light at once; 'the Lord of power and might, and king of every virtue. Unbar the gates quickly, you lords of this dreary place, so that Christ, the Son of the King of Heaven, may enter.'

With that word, Hell itself, and all the bars of Belial burst asunder, and the gates flew open in the face of the guards, and all the patriarchs and prophets, 'the people that sat in darkness', sang aloud the hymn of St John the Baptist – 'Ecce agnus Dei – Behold the Lamb of God.' But Lucifer could not look to see, for the Light had blinded his eyes. And then our Lord caught up into His Light all those that loved Him; and turning to Satan, He said:

'Behold, here is my soul as a ransom for all these sinful souls, to redeem those that are worthy. They are mine; they come from me, and therefore I have the better claim

on them. I do not deny that, in strict justice, they were condemned to die if they ate the apple. But I did not sentence them to stay in Hell for ever.')

Awakening from this vision of victory, Will is now touchingly enthusiastic in his desire to receive communion:

> I wakede,
> And called Kytte my wif and Calote my doghter:
> 'Ariseth and reverenceth Goddes resurexion,
> And crepeth to the cros on knees, and kisseth it for a juwel!
> For Goddes blissede body it bar for oure boote,
> And it afereth the fend – for swich is the myghte,
> May no grisly goost glide there it shadweth!'

(*I woke, and called out to my wife Kitty and my daughter Kate, 'Get up, and come to honour God's resurrection. Creep to the cross on your knees and kiss it as a priceless jewel! for it bore God's blessed body for our salvation, and such is its power that the devil shrinks from it in terror, and evil spirits dare not glide beneath its shadow.'*)

The penultimate vision (Passus XIX) occurs during the mass and shows the risen Christ appearing to his disciples, identifying Piers himself with St Peter and the Apostles with the life of Dobest. The early history of the Church and the manifold gifts of Grace are then described, but soon after the founding of the Church the spirit of Anti-Christ becomes active. The poem moves quickly from the sublime through the historical to show the weakening of faith. The final vision (Passus XX) returns us to the present day and shows spiritual corruption nearly complete. Despite old age and even a warning plague, the Church – symbolized here by the Castle of Unity – has been all but destroyed by spiritual sloth and greed. These vices are personified in a friar who sells forgiveness for cash and asks for no amendment. We are back in the world of the opening of the poem. Only Conscience is left – the one stout man – to set off once more on the search for Piers Ploughman, the perfect exemplar of the Christian life who knows the Truth of God through love alone.

CHAPTER 7

POPULAR ROMANCE, BALLAD
AND LYRIC

1

The entertainment provided by the Early Middle English romances was continued through a numerous progeny. *King Alisaunder* – following the conventional interpretation of the life of that worthy – is cast in the epic mode and shows both the splendour and futility of earthly achievement as its hero expands his empire through ever more marvellous kingdoms, only to die young and, as was ominously foretold, have his lands broken up on his death. While this poem is a lengthened and modified version of a twelfth-century Anglo-Norman original, *Yvain and Gawain* is a translation of Chrétien de Troyes which, simplifying the intricacy of its original and largely ignoring its analysis of the rival claims of chivalry and romantic passion, has nonetheless some charm and delicacy. *Matière*, however, has gained the upper hand. *Sir Tristrem* and *Sir Perceval de Galles* also deal with Arthurian matters, but in both poems the emphasis is once again on simple effects – sentiment rather than tragedy in the first case, farcical naivety rather than holy innocence in the other. The great qualities of the medieval German versions of these two tales is quite unguessed at. Rather more successful are those adventure stories of lovers happily reunited after suffering and danger, such as *Floris and Blancheflour* from the beginning of the period or *The Squire of Low Degree* from its close. One poem in this manner is, indeed, a small masterpiece.

Sir Orfeo is a minstrel's tale about the power of love and his own art over the mirror-cold spectres of the land of faery. Distantly related to the classical story of Orpheus and owing much to Celtic enchantment, the French *lai* and the common stock of folk-lore motifs, the poem is above all a skilfully achieved work of art. It synthesizes the material on which it draws to create a poem more emotionally sophisticated than its surface might suggest. The plot of *Sir Orfeo* advances from the description of the harpist king's happy marriage to Dame Herodis or Eurydice, through narrative elements that have both a convincing drama and a psychological coherence, to present a final happy ending. The pattern is thus one of union, dislocation and wholeness regained.

The joy of a fully integrated life is suggested at the start by Orfeo's skilful harping, his kingly status and his marriage. This description of serene content – of art, power and love – leads easily to a passage of courtly refinement in which the queen and her ladies go maying. Eventually they sit down to rest and Herodis falls asleep 'under a fair ympetree'. The grafted trunk of the tree is, in folk-lore, a conventional conductor between this and the other world. Herodis eventually wakes in terror:

> Ac as sone as she gan awake,
> She crid and lothly bere gan make;
> She froted hir honden and hir feet
> And crached hir visage – it bled wete.
> Hir riche robe hie all to-rett
> And was reveysed out of hir wit.

lothly bere: horrible outcry   *froted:* rubbed   *crached:* scratched
hie all to-rett: tore to shreds

The violence of seeming lunacy exactly conveys supernatural horror, while the fact that the reason for the queen's outburst is not immediately explained makes it the more awful. Later, Herodis tells the grieving king that she has received an absolute order to leave him. In her dream, her soul has been seized by the king of the underworld. She must return to the tree tomorrow. Not even Orfeo and his 'wele ten hundred knights' can prevent her seizure, which the poet describes with a brevity that makes it particularly sinister.

The inconsolable Orfeo now abdicates and lives 'with wilde bestes in holtes hore'. He has lost his love and left majesty behind. His feral existence powerfully suggests his shattered wholeness:

> Nothing he fint that him is ais,
> Bot ever he liveth in gret malais.
> He that hadde y-werd the fowe and gris
> And on bed the purper bis,
> Now on hard hethe he lith;
> With leves and gresse he him writh.

fint: finds   *malais:* discomfort   *y-werd the fowe and gris:* worn the variegated and grey fur
bis: linen   *writh:* covers

Only art remains. The wild man charms the beasts with his music, and sometimes, in the hot afternoons, glimpses the world of faery, hearing its horns faintly blowing. He notices that the spectral company are dressed for the hunt, but they catch nothing and disappear 'he nist wheder they bicome'. Such events have a sad and sinister purposelessness, the sterile energy of the spiritually inert. Eventually, among these shades, Orfeo glimpses his wife. As she weeps in mute recognition, the others hasten her away. The king, swinging his harp on his back, defiantly follows. He makes his way through the underworld – a landscape the poet describes with a powerful half beguiling, half eerie effect – then, saying he is a minstrel, he knocks boldly at the castle gate. Once inside, he sees the 'folk that were thider y-brought':

> Sum stode withouten hade
> And sum non armes nade,
> And sum thurch the body hadde wounde,
> And sum lay wode, y-bounde,
> And sum armed on hors sete,
> And sum astrangled as they ete,
> And sum were in water adreint,
> And sum with fire all forshreint.
> Wives ther lay on child-bedde,
> Sum ded and sum awedde;
> And wonder fele ther lay bisides,
> Right as they slepe her undertides.
> Eche was thus in this warld y-nome,
> With fairy thider y-come.
> Ther he seighe his owhen wif,
> Dame Herodis, his lef lif . . .

hade: head   *wode:* mad   *adreint:* drowned   *forshreint:* shrivelled   *awedde:* mad
wonder fele: very many   *Eche was thus, etc.:* Each had been seized in this world and had
gone thither through enchantment   *lef:* dear

Orfeo strides on through this dreary and awful place and obliges its ruler to listen to his playing. The lord of the underworld is so ravished by this that he promises Orfeo any reward he cares to name. Orfeo, of course, asks for Herodis. At this point the anonymous author achieves one of his finest effects. The king refuses Orfeo's request. The mortal ruler, however, tells him it is a disgrace to renege on one's word. Herodis is immediately released. Art, love and courtesy have secured human happiness. The couple return to their earthly kingdom and, in a scene of touching pathos, Orfeo regains his realm.

2

Enchantment is also a frequent subject of the ballads, those narrative and originally oral poems which Addison declared to be 'full of that majestic simplicity which we admire in the greatest of the ancient poets'.

Some ballads can be confidently assigned to the Middle Ages, though it should be borne in mind that all these poems stem from a continuous and primarily unwritten tradition broken only in the last century. As a result of their oral nature, variations abound. There are over twenty textual variants of some of the ballads, many of them dating from the seventeenth and eighteenth centuries. Such problems are matters of important scholarly detail, but a passage from Sir Philip Sidney eloquently reminds us both of the original manner of the ballads' performance and the exhilaration they can still arouse:

> I never heard the old song of Percy and Douglas that I found not my heart moved more than with a trumpet; yet it is sung by some blind crowder, with no rougher voice than rude style.

crowder: Welsh fiddler

Sidney's response was the right one, and the ballads have often served to win true poets from too precious a muse. Their themes are timelessly engaging: love, magic, murder, family hatred and revenge. These issues are usually presented in quatrains and with great narrative economy. Sometimes there are dramatic, abrupt transitions, and the ballads are frequently constructed with the help of refrains and traditional formulas.

In the following lines, the Queen of Elfland sweeps a besotted Thomas the Rhymer away with her:

> O they rade on, and farther on,
>   And they waded rivers abune the knee;
> And they saw neither sun nor moon,
>   But they heard the roaring of the sea.
>
> It was mirk, mirk night, there was nae starlight,
>   They waded thro' blude to the knee;
> For a' the blude that's shed on the earth
>   Rins through the springs o' that countrie.

The poet is in thrall, and, as the couple wade through the rivers of blood and ride 'the Road to fair Elfland', so the perils of magic and infatuation mingle in the sinister dark. In what may be a later and literary addition, Thomas himself is shown as having chosen this awe-inspiring route in preference to the better-known paths of pleasure or virtue. He has made the poet's choice of daring emotional experiment. To do so, he has been made to swear a vow of silence. If he breaks it, he will not return to his 'ain countree' for many years. The Queen of Elfland then plucks an apple for him – the symbolism is plain enough – and tells him that 'it will give thee the tongue that can never lee'. The indignant Thomas at once exercises his poet's right to speak and invent. His tongue, he declares, is his own. He is wrong. As Thomas opens his mouth, he is trapped and diminished by the chill world of faery. Imaginative power mingles with a strong and primitive sense that language is deeply involved with magic. The making of poetry is seen as something as dangerous and elemental as the subjects of the ballads themselves.

James Harris – a work sometimes known as *The Demon Lover* – connects the traditional theme of the broken promise with the devil's revenge. The heroine is asked to fulfil a vow to marry made seven years before. Though she has wedded another in the meantime, she eventually leaves both her husband and her children:

> She has taken up her two little babes,
>   Kissed them baith cheek and chin:
> O fair ye weel, my ain two babes,
>   For I'll never see you again.
>
> She set her foot upon the ship,
>   No mariners could she behold;
> But the sails were o the taffetie,
>   And the masts o the beaten gold.
>
> They had not sailed a league, a league,
>   A league but barely three,
> When dismal grew his countenance,
>   And drumlie grew his ee.
>
> They had not sailed a league, a league,
>   A league but barely three,
> Until she espied his cloven foot,
>   And she wept right bitterlie.

drumlie: gloomy

The sharp juxtapositions of pathos, grand passion, the sinister and the outright horrible are remarkable. They lead eventually to the high drama of the devil's destruction of the woman.

The primitive and the sinister are again the subjects of *The Unquiet Grave* and *The Wife of Usher's Well*. In this last poem, a bereaved mother is visited by the ghosts of her three sons. They spend the hours of darkness with her, but:

> The cock doth craw, the day doth daw,
>   The channerin worm doth chide;
> Gin we be mist out o our place,
>   A sair pain we maun bide.

> Fare ye weel, my mother dear!
> Fareweel to barn and byre!
> And fare ye weel, the bonny lass
> That kindles my mother's fire!

channerin: fretting   *sair:* sore

Perhaps the most intense personal drama in the ballads comes in *Edward, Edward*. This poem is a confrontation between a young noble and his mother in which the woman slowly wrings from her son the confession that he has murdered his father. The refrains, the repeated but subtly varied content of the stanzas and the crisp visual images all enliven the horrific dialogue. We listen as lies and deceit give way first to the truth, then to cursing and finally to a vision of unconfined despair.

When the mother asks why Edward's sword is dripping with blood, we immediately imagine him standing in front of her, the signs of his guilt all too evident. At first he lies, claiming that he has killed his hawk. The mother's response is subtle and cruel. She does not say directly that her son is lying but simply declares: 'Your hawk's blude was never sae red.' She clearly enjoys watching the young man's suffering. Again he tries to lie, declaring this time that he has killed his horse, who was 'sae fair and free'. But this excuse is not good enough either. The sadistic mother, relishing the torture she is inflicting, declares that Edward's horse was old and that he has others. The mounting pain now becomes almost unbearable, and Edward at last confesses his crime:

> I hae kill'd my father dear,
> Mither, mither;
> O I hae kill'd my father dear,
> Alas, and wae is me, O!

The mother's cold nature once more asserts its ruthlessness. She says nothing about the deed itself, nothing about her own feelings and nothing at all about the murdered man. She merely increases Edward's anguish by asking him what penance he will do. He tells her that he will sail away. His mother finds in this answer yet a further means of torturing him. What will the young man do with this fine house when he has fled? The suggestion is that he will find life wretched without his wealth and his home. The young man's answer is spat out in defiance. He declares that he will let his house stand where it is until it falls down. Again, the mother is unmoved. Her delight lies, as always, in increasing her son's torment. She has made him confess. She has told him that he will have to undergo penance. She has suggested that if he runs away his life will be wretched without his possessions. Now she asks him how his wife and children will survive. The young man's guilt rises to a hysterical pitch. So intense is his suffering that for the moment he denies all responsibility for his family. With defiant bitterness he hurls his answer at his mother:

> The warld's room: let them beg through life,
>   Mither, mither;
> The warld's room: let them beg through life;
>   For them never mair will I see, O.

The mother has removed all the young man's supports. She has exposed the raw nerve of his guilt and watched him writhe in emotional anguish. Finally she refers to herself. She asks Edward what he will leave to her now that he is going into exile. His answer is of a terrible savagery:

> The curse of hell frae me sall ye bear,
>   Mither, mither;
> The curse of hell frae me sall ye bear:
>   Sic counsels ye gave to me, O!

In a poem whose tension has mounted stanza by stanza, it is only in the last line that the full and dreadful truth is revealed. We shiver in horror as we come to realize the depths of this woman's depravity. She has not only urged her son to murder his father but has enjoyed extracting his terrible confession, syllable by syllable.

In strong contrast, comedy is the subject of many of the ballads concerning Robin Hood, and is a note found again in *Jock o' the Side*, a tale of a Border raid. *Chevy Chase* and *Edom o' Gordon* are also concerned with warfare and the tragedies of Border skirmishes, but it is in what Coleridge called 'the grand old ballad of Sir Patrick Spens' that we perhaps see this poetry at its most effective. The opening image of the king sitting in Dunfermline town 'drinking the blude-red wine' combines power and comfort in a way that contrasts with the forthcoming drama. The great figure of authority asks for a 'skeely skipper' to sail his new ship and is told by an 'eldren lord' that

> 'Sir Patrick Spens is the best sailor
>   That ever sail'd the sea.'

The king issues his orders and, as Sir Patrick receives them, so romantic mission, danger, treachery and death are brought together. The fourth stanza tells us of the purpose of the journey:

> 'To Noroway, to Noroway,
>   To Noroway o'er the faem;

> The king's daughter o' Noroway,
>   'Tis thou must bring her hame.'

But as Sir Patrick reads the king's letter he realizes that he has been trapped in a web of intrigue and certain destruction. A storm breaks almost immediately. The quick succession of sharply observed details suggests the confusion of the tempest, while the hopeless attempt to caulk the ship with 'silken claith' exactly expresses the fatal confrontation of the elements and the luxury of the courtly world. This builds to satire and then to tragedy:

> O laith, laith were our gude Scots lords
>   To wet their cork-heel'd shoon;
> But lang or a' the play was play'd
>   They wat their hats adoon.
>
> And mony was the feather bed
>   That flatter'd on the faem;
> And mony was the gude lord's son
>   That never mair cam hame.
>
> O' lang, lang may the ladies sit,
>   Wi' their fans into their hand,
> Before they see Sir Patrick Spens
>   Come sailing to the strand!
>
> And lang, lang may the maidens sit,
>   Wi' their gowd kames in their hair,
> A-waiting for their ain dear loves!
>   For them they'll see nae mair.

3

The ballads were originally composed for the singing voice. This is also true of a large number of medieval lyrics. Nearly forty short poems written before 1400 survive with their music, and, in the case of one of the most famous of them, with Latin instructions for the manner of its performance as well. The lyric we are to discuss is especially famous for being the first poem printed in the version of *The Oxford Book of English Verse* edited by Sir Arthur Quiller-Couch. Its selection and placing there have led to its acceptance by generations as the first 'real' English poem.

> *Sing, cuccu, nu! Sing, cuccu!*
> *Sing, cuccu! Sing, cuccu, nu!*
>
> Sumer is icumen in –

lhude sing, cuccu!
Groweþ sed and bloweþ med
and sprinþ þe wude nu.
Sing, cuccu!

Awe bleteþ after lomb,
lhouþ after calve cu;
Bulluc sterteþ, bucke verteþ –
murþe sing, cuccu!
Cuccu, cuccu!

Wel þu singest, cuccu;
ne swik þu naver nu.

sed: seed   *med:* mead, field   *lhouþ:* cow   *verteþ:* farts
ne swik þu naver nu: don't ever stop now

The text itself raises a number of problems. As Professor Stevens has written: 'Medieval lyrics do not grow in neatly printed books arranged in lines and stanzas with full-stops, commas and the rest. They have to be edited. And every edition is an interpretation.' To this problem of presenting a modern ordering of the text and its possible meanings is frequently added the further difficulty: the fact that the scribe himself was often far from accurate. We have seen that Chaucer was particularly aware of this, and in his poem to Adam, his own scrivener, complained of errors of transcription which not only involved tedious correction but appeared to the riled author as sheer negligence. The scribe of *Sumer is icumen in* seems to have been fairly careful, though he originally wrote line thirteen in the conventional syntactical form: 'Wel singest þu, cuccu'. Helped partly by alterations to the musical notation made by a later hand which relate the long notes of the music to the stressed syllables of the poem, we can see how in performance his original version leads to a wholly incorrect emphasis being placed on the second syllable of 'singest'. It is more likely that the line should read: 'Wel þu singest, cuccu', and it is in this corrected form that the poem has been reprinted. In such ways textual accuracy advances.

What may appear rather more surprising, however, is the fact that along with the English words (the only vernacular ones in the manuscript) appears a Latin lyric which fits the music but is wholly different in tone:

(*Resurrexit Dominus.*
Dominus Resurrexit.)

Perspice, Christicola –
quae dignacio!
Caelicus agricola,

pro vitis vicio,
filio

non parcens exposuit
mortis exicio;
qui captivos semivivos
a supplicio
vitae donat

et secum coronat
in caeli solio.

([*The Lord has risen.*] *Pay heed, Christian – what an honour! The heavenly hus-*
bandman, because of a blemish in the vine-branch, did not spare his son but exposed
him to the destruction of death; and he [*i.e. the son*] *restores from torment to life the*
half-living captives [*i.e. of Hell*] *and crowns them together with himself on the*
throne of Heaven.)

What are we to make of this? Does the fact that the English words are
written first suggest that the Latin poem is some sort of pious revision?
A *contrafactum*, the writing of new words to old tunes, was after all a well-
recognized medieval practice. This is not necessarily the case, and there is
indeed a severely practical reason for the order adopted, one which is
illustrated by the problems other scribes had with other manuscripts. An
English text quite simply takes up more space than a French or Latin one.
However, if the English version is written first, there will be ample room left
for the others and so problems of aligning the English with the Latin or
French and both with the music will be avoided.

But we must ask if the presence of two poems so very different in tone
suggests the work of two authors. Once again, this is not necessarily the
case. There are good literary arguments, based on genre, which suggest,
since personal expression was not the fundamental issue, that there was
no deep-seated ambivalence in the mind of the author, no last-minute
retraction. Indeed, in view of the essentially learned origins of the music,
it seems quite possible that both lyrics were written by the same man,
that he perhaps composed the Latin version first, and also wrote the
music.

We have mentioned that fairly elaborate instructions were provided
for the performance of this, and from these it emerges that the song was
intended for six singers, two providing the *rondellus* in which the voices
rise and fall through an identical range of pitch and then exchange parts,
the remaining four voices, following their leader with the same tune,
providing the *rota*. In performance, the musical effect is particularly
delightful and elaborate, but, since our concern is principally with the

English version of the words, two further points – both of which suggest a pleasantly wry sense of humour on the part of the author and composer – should be mentioned. First, the five notes on which the composition is based – *fgfga* – are the same as the five notes of *Regina coeli*, an antiphon or response sung by a divided choir in the Easter season and containing suggestions of redemption that reappear in the refrain of the Latin version. There is a light irony, to say the least, when the familiar tune of such mighty words is sung to the cuckoo refrain.

And it is that insistent cuckoo song which, in performance, suggests the final irony. 'Cuccu' is the note of cuckoldry, while the base word 'verteþ' is far less suggestive of pastoral simplicity or the high refinement of a literary spring than of the farmyard helter-skelter of animals in rut. This is the true subject of the English poem – a subject, it should be said, that is not dismissively or joylessly presented, but is offered with a wry wisdom. Through the combination of words and music, some of the great themes of Middle English poetry are presented: redemption, love, adultery and the more elemental instincts that underline *fine amour*.

In its tiny compass, *Sumer is icumen in* is an epitome of a whole range of medieval concerns that are developed in other lyrics. For whom were these poems intended? This question raises the difficult problem of the distinction to be drawn between popular and more obviously courtly traditions, and highlights the fact that much of what may have been truly popular has been lost. However, some excellent popular poems have been preserved by the chance use of the parchment on which they were written as the fly-leaf of a learned manuscript. *Maiden in the moor lay* is one of the most attractive of them.

The carol or dance song is defined by having a self-contained refrain or 'burden' repeated after each verse. Though the courtiers at Camelot beguiled their Christmas season with singing and dancing such carols at the start of *Sir Gawain and the Green Knight*, we should bear in mind first that the carol was not restricted to Christmas and secondly that many medieval poems we now know as 'Christmas carols' – *I sing of a maiden*, for example – are not strictly carols at all since they lack the necessary refrain. Again, while carols were clearly an acceptable court entertainment, they were not an exclusively aristocratic prerogative. Chaucer's Summoner, for instance, sings the 'stif burdoun' to the love song fluted by the Pardoner. Their tune is thus a true carol, but neither of its performers would have gained entry to Camelot.

The lyrics that form a fully courtly tradition are relatively few in number and are often the work of named poets. They are partly to be distinguished by their reliance on French elements in international court culture. As we might expect, it is Chaucer who is a principal exponent of the form. Of the three major types of French courtly lyric – the *rondeau*, *virelai* and *ballade* – Chaucer offers the exquisite *rondeau* from *The Parliament of Fowls* and a number of *ballades* both moral and, in the case of *Merciless Beauty*, concerned ostensibly with *fine amour*. This lyric is a clever parody of the whole ethos.

The dependence of the English courtly lyric on France is well illustrated by the work of a poet from the middle of the fifteenth century. Charles d'Orléans, captured at Agincourt, remained in England until about 1440 and probably wrote what are the first full sequences of love poems in the English language. They are both wide-ranging in subject-matter and varied in quality. The death of his first mistress, for example, gave rise to such fine poems as *In the forest of Noyous Heveynes*, but the easy and cynical wit with which the poet combines the themes of religious devotion and *fine amour* is particularly fresh in *The Lover's Confession*:

> My gostly fadir, y me confesse
> First to God and then to yow
> That at a wyndow, wot ye how,
> I stale a cosse of gret swetnes;
> Which don was out avisynes –
> But hit is doon, not undoon now.
> My gostly fadir y me confesse
> First to God and then to yow.
> But y restore it shall, dowtles,
> Ageyn, if so be that y mow –
> And that, God, y make avow –
> And ellis y axe foryefnes.
> My gostly fadir y me confesse
> First to God and then to yow.

gostly: spiritual   *wot:* know   *stale a cosse:* stole a kiss   *avisynes:* knowingly   *axe:* ask

The *aube*, or poem of lovers parting at dawn, is comparatively rare in English, but is found most perfectly in the third book of *Troilus and Criseyde*. More common is the complaint of the betrayed maiden, a theme also to be found in the ballads. Analogous in manner is the *pastourelle*, in which a knight meets a country girl and makes advances to her. In a poem such as that now called *The Meeting in the Wood* from the Harley Lyrics, the offer is accepted.

We have seen that the majority of the love poems in the Harley Lyrics, though conventional, are fresh and nearly always celebrations of the lady's virtue and beauty. It is a praise of these qualities that lies at their centre rather than a complex concern with the inner workings of the lover's mind. When such a procedure was continued over a long time, the inevitable result was a certain staleness, and by the fifteenth century many love poems – while still serving their social purpose in the intricacies of courtship – have become rather tired. It is to the comic songs (a tradition quite as early as the Harley Lyrics), to works of harmless bawdy such as *I have a gentil cok*, and to nonsense and burlesque pieces like the *Praise of his Lady* attributed to Hoccleve, that we should turn for richer rewards. In addition, there are vivid pictures of city life to be found in *London Lickpenny*, while a famous alliterative lyric exploits the possibilities of onomatopoeia:

> Swarte-smeked smethes, smatered with smoke,
> Drive me to deth with den of here dintes:
> Swich nois on nightes ne herd men never,
> What knavene cry and clatering of knockes!
> The cammede kongons cryen after 'Col! col!'
> And blowen here bellewes that all here brain brestes.

(*Smoke-blackened smiths, begrimed with smoke, drive me to death with the din of their blows: no man ever heard such a noise by night, what crying of workmen and clattering of blows! The snub-nosed changelings cry out for 'Coal! Coal!' and blow their bellows until their brains burst.*)

Bryng us in good ale is a fine drinking song, and nonsense lyrics such as *When netilles in winter bere roses rede* are amusing and imaginative precedents for Donne's *Go and catch a falling star*. Yet further lyrics such as *Jankin at the Agnus* touch on the world of fabliau.

A more serious note is sounded by many short poems. It is heard, for example, in three of Chaucer's minor works: *Lak of Stedfastnesse*, with its reflection of the uncertain England of the 1380s; his moral ballade *Gentilesse* which explores the teaching of Dante that is offered again by the loathly lady in *The Wife of Bath's Tale*; and the excellent *Truth: Ballade de Bon Conseil* which examines some of the Boethian issues glanced at in *The Franklin's Tale*:

> That thee is sent, receyve in buxumnesse;
> The wrastling for this world axeth a fal.
> Her is non hom, her nis but wildernesse:
> Forth, pilgrim, forth! Forth, beste, out of thy stal!
> Know thy contree, look up, thank God of al;
> Hold the heye wey, and lat thy gost thee lede;
> And trouthe thee shal delivere, it is no drede.

> *buxumnesse:* submissiveness   *wrastling:* striving   *gost:* spirit, soul

This stanza, less macabre in its contempt for earthly things than many from the period, shows nonetheless a sure knowledge of the bewildering futility of life in a cruel and insecure world, a world where man – both an animal and a pilgrim – lives as a sojourner amid sin. Only the vast edifice of *Ecclesia*, the international body of the Church with its seemingly endless proliferation of rites, its corruptions and self-divisions, stood between the soul and damnation. It is to the religious lyrics we should now turn.

4

We have seen that the religious saturation of medieval life is an essential element in our understanding of all its works. This is particularly true of the devotional lyrics. The all-pervading presence of religious sentiment suggests a world where truth is not an earthly thing – a matter of experience and patient experiment – but something passionately spiritual and other-worldly, something to be glimpsed through self-abasement, faith and the sacraments. It is to be known finally only in the clean courts of Heaven. As a consequence, the mortal world is one where, in the words of Johan Huizinga, 'there is not an object or an action, however trivial, that is not constantly correlated with Christ or salvation'. Or, we might add, with the painful brevity of life:

> Child, thou ert a pilgrim in wikidnes iborn,
> Thou wandrest in this false world, thou loke the biforn.
> Deth ssal com with a blast ute of a wel dim horn,
> Adamis kin dun to cast, him silf hath ido beforn.
>   Lollai, lollai, litil child, so wo the worp Adam,
>   In the lond of Paradis throgh wikidnes of Satan.
>
> Child, thou nert a pilgrim bot an uncuthe gest,
> Thi dawes beth itold, thi jurneis beth ikest;
> Whoder thou salt wend North other Est,
> Deth the sal betide with bitter bale in brest.
>   Lollai, lollai, litil child, this wo Adam the wroght,
>   Whan he of the appil ete, and Eve hit him betoght.

ute: out   *ido:* done   *so wo the worp Adam:* thus Adam contrived thee woe   *nert:* are not
uncuthe: unknown   *thi dawes:* the number of your days   *ikest:* reckoned
betoght: gave it to him

The child weeps, ignorant but not innocent of original sin. Great spiritual forces will play round it from now until the hour of its death and passage to eternity. Carried uncomprehendingly to its baptism, the infant was stopped at the door of the church while the priest muttered the first words of faith it heard and in a Latin which, though the child might never come fully to understand it, would serve as a second language quite as familiar and perhaps more consoling than its mother tongue. Only when the priest had called on the redeeming power of the Church and expelled the devil could the child be carried to the font and join the confraternity of the Church. If the child was a boy it was a 'type' of Adam, if a girl, she inherited the curse of Eve.

Growing up through the cycle of the Church year with its regular intonation of the Bible, the psalter and the liturgy, with their constant reminders of God's wrath on those who commit the Seven Deadly Sins (a wrath mollified, it was hoped, by the intercession of the saints and the Virgin), the elaborate patterns of ritual which connected man to the divine sank down into the common core of being. No part of life was left untouched, and this accounts for the intimate acquaintance with a wide variety of devotional forms and Latin texts which found their way into the lyrics. These range from translations of passages from St Augustine to this beautiful combination of Middle English prayer and traditional Latin epithet made in honour of the Virgin:

> Of on that is so fayr and bright
> *Velud maris stella,*
> Brighter than the dayis light,
> *Parens et puella,*
> Ic crie to the, thou se to me!
> Levedy, preye thi sone for me,
> *Tam pia,*
> That ic mote come to the,
> *Maria.*

velud maris stella: as the star of the sea   *Parens et puella:* mother and maiden
levedy: lady   *tam pia:* so devoted

This stanza, with its deft combination of divine radiance, human need and a hoped-for intercession whereby the sinning soul may be brought to salvation, reveals something of the religious tenor of the period. It also suggests a number of other factors central to many of the religious lyrics. It will be helpful to deal with the critical matters first. For example, the 'I' of the fifth line cries with such simple intensity that the reader immediately identifies with it and, as he does so, the poem can become a prayer. It is thus a part of daily piety, a highly charged meditation that enhances the faith of those who read it. Something of this relation between poem and audience is again suggested by the words written beside a similar piece: 'a more devout prayere fond I never of the passioun, who so woulde devoutly say hitte,' wrote an anonymous hand. The words imply an audience who saw the affective power of poetry not just as an end in itself but as a means to Heaven. The note also suggests that such works were read not in great numbers at a time but slowly, piously, as is fitting for the prayers and meditations that they are.

Many of the lyrics illustrate the cycle of the Church year. The Annunciation, for example, called forth some of the most beautiful devotional lyrics of the Middle Ages. Poems such as *I syng of a mayden* suggest the purity and wonder of the Immaculate Conception, while the birth of Christ himself is a constant source of grateful wonder and divine paradox:

> Adam lay ibowndyn, bowndyn in a bond,
> Fowre thowsand wynter thowt he not to long.
>
> And al was for an appil, an appil that he tok,
> As clerkes fyndyn wretyn in here book.
>
> Ne hadde the appil take ben, the appil take ben,
> Ne hadde never our Lady a ben hevene qwen.
>
> Blyssid be the tyme that appil take was,
> Therfore we mown syngyn '*Deo gracias!*'

Deo gracias!: The Lord be praised!

This is the *felix culpa*, the 'happy sin' by which man's error led to the glories attendant on his salvation. Yet, while such optimism is an appropriate mood for Christmas, the progress of the Church year towards Easter drew individuals and the community as a whole into the ascetic rituals of Lent. Once again, these rituals indicate the way in which the practice of faith saturated every aspect of medieval life.

Since 1215, all Catholic peoples have been required to make at least an annual acknowledgement of their sins, and the season of Lent especially was designed to rouse feelings of contrition. Beneath the consoling figures of Christ, the Virgin and the saints – now veiled in funeral purple as if hidden from the world and inaccessible to man – preachers turned to their congregations. They urged through high drama and a battery of rhetorical techniques the necessity for remorseless self-examination. Entire medieval communities, peoples easily moved to extremes of emotion, began the dismal probing of their guilt. The most intimate aspects of life were touched upon. Fasting meant that between Ash

Wednesday and Holy Saturday the eating of meat was prohibited, while on the more personal level of abstinence, though the Church no longer forbade intercourse between married couples for the whole season of Lent, there remained a total ban for some days before the Easter communion itself. It was repeatedly urged that the Lenten acknow- ledgement of sin – the contrition, penance and satisfaction required – should be public acts, acts often performed in some visible part of the church. When absolution was finally granted, it was signified by the laying-on of hands. The whole sacrament represented the passage of the baptized but sinning individual into a state of grace, a reconciliation with his God and the Christian community. He was now ready for the Easter communion, that supreme moment of the Church year which Langland so powerfully recreates in *Piers Ploughman*.

Many of the greatest medieval religious lyrics have their origins in this Easter penitential ardour and its promise of joy; many also reveal an especially intense visualization of the Passion itself:

> Of sharp thorne I have worne a crowne on my hed,
> So rubbid, so bobbid, so rufulle, so red,
> Sore payned, sore strayned, and for thi love ded,
> Unfayned, not demed, my blod for the shed,
> My fete and handis sore,
> With sturde naylis bore;
> What myght I suffer more
> Then I have sufferde, man, for the?
> Com when thou wilt, and welcome to me.

bobbid: buffeted   *rufulle:* sorrowful

In the last stanza of this poem – *Wofully araide* – the Lord of Life greets mankind as his 'dere brother'. Redemption is offered through the request for fraternal love.

There is a powerful simplicity in this poem and an inextinguishable charity, but it would be wrong to assume that all the lyrics speak only with an obvious directness. They frequently draw on the widest resources and quietly re-shape these to exquisite effect. Such a process can be traced in one of the great lyric poems of the period, a work most often known by its Latin refrain: *Quia amore langueo*.

5

This is a poem at once courtly and biblical in its references. The intensity of its drama is also inspired by developments in medieval English mysticism in which the 'behaldyng and ȝernyng of þe thynges of heven' was held to lead to a profound, intuitive understanding of salvation. In *Quia amore langueo*, a 'cleer siȝt' of God – what Dame Julian of Norwich called a 'shewing' – offers a mystical understanding of the Incarnation and Passion as the poet beholds his suffering Redeemer and learns of his longing for man's soul.

The Latin refrain of *Quia amore langueo* directs us to the Song of Songs: 'I charge you, O daughters of Jerusalem, if you find my beloved, that ye tell him, that *I am sick of love.*' Such imagery will be sustained throughout the poem and is dependent upon St Bernard's interpretation of the Song of Songs as the expression of Christ's longing for the sinful soul of man. Such a combination of the erotic and the spiritual is complemented here by the courtly imagery used. As in St Bernard and *The Ancrene Riwle*, Christ is the lover-knight who eventually gives his life for his lady – the human soul.

We are shown in the lyric how God searches for man's love, and also how man himself is searching for a 'treulofe'. Their meeting is inevitable. In the opening stanza the narrator presents himself as a questing hero from a *chanson d'aventure* who is searching for a passionate encounter:

> In the vaile of restles mynd
> > I sowght in mownteyn and in mede,
> Trustyng a treulofe for to fynd.
> > Upon an hyll than toke I hede,
> > A voise I herd (and nere I yede)
> In gret dolour complaynyng tho,
> > 'See, dere soule, my sydes blede,
> *Quia amore langueo.*'

yede: went   *Quia amore langueo:* because I languish with love

The pursuit of a 'treulofe' thus at first appears courtly and might even be thought of as purely secular. The landscape is certainly reminiscent of those from romance, but it is a particularly delicate insight in the first line which admits that this landscape is also metaphorical, the 'vaile of restles mynd' where imagined physical events are an expression of an emotional reality. Yet the effect is far from being confined to that of the world of *aventure*. The restless imagined journey can also be compared with the quest of the anguished soul in the Song of Songs: 'By night on my bed I sought him whom my soul loveth: I sought him, but I found him not.' With the help of St Bernard, such an erotic quest becomes a spiritual search. Man's deepest need is for *caritas* rather than *cupiditas* and, in the familiar words of St Augustine, 'our hearts are restless till they rest in

Thee'. In *Quia amore langueo* the questing knight of the *chanson d'aventure* is thus set beside the questing soul of religious tradition.

The lamentation of Christ is also presented at first as the 'complaint' of a chivalric hero. He suffers in longing for the human soul as a lover does for his lady:

> I loved hyr thus;
> Bycause I wold on no wyse dissevere
> I left my kyngdome gloriouse.
> I purveyd hyr a paleis preciouse.
> She flytt, I folowyd; I luffed her soo
> That I suffred thes paynes piteouse,
> *Quia amore langueo.*

dissevere: part

We seem to be in a courtly world like that in which Chaucer encountered his man in black. This man too is 'semely', regal, 'graciose'. (He is, after all, the King of Kings.) As he speaks, so he also becomes the distressed Christ familiar from painting, perhaps as *ecce homo* sitting below his cross, the 'tree'. The narrator then draws close to the suffering Christ and asks the cause of his 'paynyng'. There follows Christ's *complaint d'amor* in which the languages of courtly passion and the Canticles again merge to become an expression of Christ's profound longing for the human soul. This pursuit is attended with difficulties, however, and, in terms of the imagery of *fine amour*, sin or the rejection of Christ is now seen as being 'daungerouse'. This is the language of the *Roman de la Rose*.

Christ's 'complaint' develops subtly from the initial impression of 'she flytt, I folowyd; I luffed her soo' through the wounds and delays of courtship until his ineffable Passion merges with the image of the soul as the *sponsa dei*, the Bride of Christ. As it does so, the clothing of 'grace and hevenly lyght' offered to the soul is contrasted with the surcoat of blood, the bloody gloves and feet of Christ the King made the most degraded of men. Such sharply realized physical detail – so typical of late medieval devotion – again merges with aspects of courtly life and reminiscences of the Song of Songs. This reaches its first climax in the eighth stanza where, with help from St Bernard, the wound in Christ's side becomes 'the clefts of the rock' in the Canticles where the lover longs to hear his 'dove' – for 'sweet is thy voice, and thy countenance is comely'. But, as Christ tells us, the human soul remains unmoved:

> I sitt on an hille for to se farre,
> I loke to the vayle; my spouse I see:

> Now rynne she awayward, now cummyth she narre,
>   Yet fro myn eye-syght she may nat be.

Again, we might like to compare this image of the fleeing soul to the roe-like beloved of the Canticles who 'cometh leaping upon the mountains, skipping upon the hills'. Christ offers her the pleasures of the world in the form of a beautiful garden that we might see as the Earthly Paradise. He also offers her spiritual comfort, the means by which she may be made 'clene'. All this she again refuses. 'I may of unkyndnes the apple [accuse],' Christ eventually declares – the refined courtesy of this is exquisite – but he nonetheless confines himself to waiting on the soul's 'jantilnesse' just as a courtly lover should.

By a paradox familiar to the mystics, it is only when the soul has finally laid aside fleshly things that she is ready for the conjugal bed of her divine lover:

> Wold she lokc onys owt of hyr howse
>   Of flesshely affecciouns and unclennesse!
>   Hyr bed is made, hyr bolstar is in blysse,
> Her chambre is chosen – suche ar no moo!
>   Loke owt at the wyndows of kyndnesse,
> *Quia amore langueo.*

> 'My spouse is in hir chambre, hald yowr pease,
>   Make no noyse, but lat hyr slepe.
> My babe shall sofre noo disease,
>   I may not here my dere childe wepe,
>   For with my pappe I shall hyr kepe.
> No wondyr though I tend hyr to –
>   Thys hoole in my syde had never ben so depe
> But *quia amore langueo.*

> *bolstar:* pillow   *pappe:* breast

When the soul has indeed laid aside her guilty revelling in the things of this world – her 'unclennesse' – and, in the words of the Beatitudes, can 'behold God', she becomes the true Bride of Christ. The imagery of the Song of Songs laps her in an exquisite rest.

It is with such married love that the poem closes. Starting in the courtly world and with the possibilities of *fine amour*, allying these characteristics to the restless heart's pursuit of *caritas* and the vividly realized image of the suffering Christ as the noble lover of the human soul, the poem proceeds through a conventional picture of courtship in which the soul's rebuffs – her 'daungerouse' behaviour – are equated with sin. It ends with the proper image of 'treulofe' – that marriage in which Christ is the soul's compassionate husband:

'Wax not wery, myn owne dere wyfe!
  What mede is aye to lyffe in counfort?
For in tribulacioun I ryn more ryfe
  Ofter tymes than in disport –
  In welth, in woo, ever I support.
Than dere soule, go never me fro! –
  Thy mede is markyd whan thow art mort,
Quia amore langueo.

mede: reward, good   *mort:* dead

Words from the marriage service suggest the vow whereby a mortal is to his wife as Christ is to the immortal soul, its comforter and safeguard. The soul, it is suggested, has been made for God as 'the woman for the man'. For St Paul, this kindly if dependent relationship of wife to husband, soul to God, was an image of the universal peace and perfection when the whole community of Christians is married to its Redeemer: 'Wives, submit yourselves unto your husbands, as unto the Lord ... Therefore the church is subject unto Christ, so let the wives be to their husbands in every thing. Husbands, love your wives, even as Christ also loved the church.' The opening quest is resolved in marriage; the wandering soul has found its home.

6

The drama of Calvary is frequently intensified in the lyrics by the presence of the grieving Mary. This scene, though present in the Bible, owes much to the thirteenth-century sequence of poems on the Virgin's sorrows probably composed by the Franciscan Jacapone da Todi and known from its opening words: *Stabat mater dolorosa.* The radiant Virgin of the Annunciation becomes the anguished mother of the *pietà*:

Sodenly afraide, half wakyng, half slepyng,
And gretly dismayde – a wooman sate weepyng,

With favoure in hir face ferr passyng my reason,
And of hir sore weepyng this was the enchesone:
Hir soon in hir lap lay, she seid, slayne by treason.
Yif wepyng myght ripe bee, it seemyd than in season.
  'Jesu!' so she sobbid –
  So hir soon was bobbid,
  And of his lif robbid –
Saying thies wordes, as I say thee:
'Who cannot wepe, come lerne at me.'

enchesone: cause

The obvious meditative function here is to break into the hardened heart and, by showing the intense grief of a human mother, make the reader aware of the reality of salvation through his awakened feelings. The lyric also makes clear the important place of Marian devotion in the medieval Church, and we should examine its background.

The Virgin, though playing so small a part in the Gospels themselves, is a central figure of Roman Catholic theology. She was capable of inspiring a devotion of the greatest refinement or the utmost simplicity. St Bernard was her troubadour, Henry V her suppliant. The Mystery Plays reveal the intense love – at once domestic and sublime – in which she was held by all peoples in the Middle Ages. In Protestant belief the Virgin's status has been drastically restricted to the number of words written about her in the New Testament, but the Roman Catholic augmentation of her cult is one of our most direct and living links with the Middle Ages.

Four articles of dogma pertain to the Virgin. Her divine motherhood and her virginity – factors both necessary for the incarnation of God in human form but free from original sin – were promulgated by the early Church and are all but universally accepted. Two further articles of faith: the Immaculate Conception whereby Mary herself is declared to be without taint, and the Assumption – her transfer, body and soul, to Heaven, whether after a physical death or not – were also widely accepted in the Middle Ages but only formulated officially in 1854 and 1950 respectively. Around her divine status then gather a host of subsidiary images and devotional specialities. Mary is, for example, the Star of the Sea, the Queen of Heaven and – most memorably expressed in the prayer of St Bernard at the end of the *Paradiso* – the bride of her own son. Numerous appearances and uncounted miracles are attributed to her. The ease with which her comforting presence was experienced by the people of the Middle Ages contained in it the seeds of both an intense vulgarity and a soaring beauty of spirit, while the cult of the *mater dolorosa* stressed the participation of the purest of all women in the common round of human misery. 'Of all mothers,' wrote St Bridget of Sweden (d. 1373), 'Mary was the most afflicted, by reason of her foreknowledge of Christ's bitter passion.' For St Bernard, Mary was martyred on Calvary not in the body but in the spirit, and the pain drew forth unlimited grace for mankind. Standing at the foot of the cross, she received the human race in trust as St John was placed in her keeping and she in his. As *magna mater*, Mary personifies the Church, thus making all believers her children. And it is in her maternal role and

especially in her sorrow that the Virgin is most dramatically presented in
the lyrics:

> Therfor, women, be town and strete
>   Your childur handis when ye beholde,
> Theyr brest, theire body, and theire fete,
>   Then gode hit were on my son thynk ye wolde,
>   How care has made my hert ful colde
> To se my son, with nayle and speyre,
>   With scourge and thornys manyfolde,
> Woundit and ded, my dere son dere.

The intense religious saturation of medieval daily life could hardly be
more clear or poignant.

7

Death, so public and dramatized in the Middle Ages, is the definitive
comment on the futility of a proud and worldly life. The clinking bell
carried before the coffin in *The Pardoner's Tale* sounds through the
whole of medieval culture and it tolled interminably during what was
believed to be the divine punishment of the plague. While neighbours
and relations had their part to play in the complex rites of passage, the
dying themselves were left with their prayers and priests to face the
spiritual ordeals of another world for which the suffering and temptation
of this had been but a preparation:

> O dredeful deth, come, make an ende!
>   Come unto me and do thy cure!
> Thy payne no tunge can comprehende,
>   That I fele, wooful creature.
>   O lorde, how longe shall it endure?
> Whenne shall I goo this worlde fro,
> Out of this bitter payne and woo?

To remind everyone of the inevitable end, a host of paintings, carvings,
sermons, poems and works on the art of dying dwelt on *memento mori*.
Lovers in medieval Paris strolled through the ossuaries and stared at the
upturned skulls. The grave was neither a fine nor a private place, and the
dance of death invited all to join. The requiem mass told of the wrath of
God and the hope of salvation. Finally, the death of each individual
reminds those that survive of their own mortality and the day of
Doom:

... at the laste day thei shullen aryse
And come byfore the juge sovereyne,
To you conjoyned in a wonder wise,
In good accord withouten any peyne
And in this joye eternally remeyne:
What joy is here ye schul assaye and see –
Honoured be the hye mageste!

CHAPTER 8

MEDIEVAL DRAMA

1

While the great wealth of medieval lyric can be drawn on to illustrate moments in the Church year and the existence of the individual within it, Morality Plays such as the incomplete *Pride of Life*, *The Castle of Perseverance* (*c.* 1405–25), *Mankind*, *Wisdom* (both *c.* 1460–70) and *Everyman* (*c.* 1500) present right conduct through dramatized allegory. This takes the form of a *psychomachia* or battle of the vices and virtues, a mode of fundamental importance to the medieval mind.

The manuscript in which *The Castle of Perseverance* is preserved also contains a much-disputed plan of the staging. This suggests the presence of five scaffolds grouped around a large circle. The eastern scaffold is God's and lies in the direction of the holy city of Jerusalem. The western scaffold represents Mundus, or the World. In the north is the home of the Devil, while the south is the location of the Flesh. Finally, in the north-east – and so between the Devil and salvation – stands the scaffold devoted to Avarice. In the centre of the circle made by these five scaffolds stood a single tower or castle. This was open at its base and in it stood a deathbed with a cupboard at its foot. The tower – a conventional image of spiritual security – was also surrounded by a ditch full of water. The audience grouped itself around these fixed points across which the action was then played out.

That action took the form of a journey which symbolized a spiritual sequence of great and long-standing importance. Here we might turn to a sermon attributed to St Bernard in which we are shown the life of man from youth to age. In the weakness of his youth, man wanders from the paradise of Good Conscience into sin. This state he briefly relishes until, guided by Hope and Fear, he journeys to the Castle of Wisdom where he is prepared for his reunion with God. At the end of the sermon, St Bernard summarizes the four stages of this journey:

First man is needy and foolish, then headlong and heedless in prosperity, then anxious and fearful in adversity; lastly he is foreseeing, instructed and made perfect in the kingdom of Charity.

This sequence of innocence, temptation, fall, the life of sin, and then of realization and repentance leading to salvation, is found in many works. For example, it underlies Deguileville's *Le Pèlerinage de la Vie Humaine* (which Lydgate translated in 1426 as *The Pilgrimage of Man*) and it recurs in the construction of the first book of Spenser's *Faerie Queen* (1590). It also lies at the heart of *The Castle of Perseverance*.

At the start of the play proper, the figures of the World, the Flesh and the Devil boast of the powers with which they threaten man. Humanum Genus, Mankind himself, then appears, 'ful feynt and febyl'. His Good and Bad Angels attend him while he makes his journey towards Mundus. This suggests Mankind's spiritual journey towards sin. Backbiter then lures Mankind towards the scaffold of Avarice – a figure of central importance to the play – where he is joined by the remaining Deadly Sins, each of which describes himself with great vigour. Here is part of the speech of Invidia or Envy:

> Whanne Wrath gynnyth walke in ony wyde wonys,
> Envye flet as a fox and folwyth on faste.
> Whanne thou steryst[e] or staryst[e] or stumble up-on stonys,
> I lepe as a lyon; me is loth to be the laste.
> Ya, I breyde byttyr balys in body and in bonys,
> I frete myn herte and in kare I me kast.

wyde wonys: abroad, about   *balys:* torments   *steryst[e] or staryst[e]:* stir or stare about

Since the Seven Deadly Sins play so prominent a role in medieval literature, a brief account of their origins and function may be useful. Such an account will also help to illustrate how *The Castle of Perseverance* stands in the main tradition of the popular Christian doctrine it is concerned to illustrate.

The most widely accepted hierarchy of the Seven Deadly Sins was that suggested by Gregory the Great in the late sixth century, which placed pride at the root of wrath, envy, avarice, sloth, gluttony and luxury. This is the list and – substantially – the order that Chaucer adopted when he included a treatise on the Sins in *The Parson's Tale*. In *The Castle of Perseverance*, we have seen that avarice has taken the initiative from pride. This was a fairly common change in the late Middle Ages, and it may perhaps be connected with the move away from a society described according to the strict hierarchy of feudalism to one where money was attaining an importance verging on that of inherited rank. However that may be, the Seven Deadly Sins continued to provide a most influential way of describing sinful man's behaviour and so urging on him the importance of confession and penance. St Thomas Aquinas, for example, considered the Deadly Sins to be among the final causes which give rise to all mankind's other errors. As the Parson declares: 'been they cleped chieftaines for-as-muche as they been chief, and springers of alle othere sinnes'. They are thus the fundamental errors which, in the familiar pattern, pervert the will away from what the reason knows to be man's proper good and incline it instead to something which only appears to be good – worldly pride or sexual indulgence, for example. Such things are sinful because they place earthly pleasure before obedience to God.

The concept of the Seven Deadly Sins was a popular and effective means of analysing man's conduct, and the Church required that it should be widely disseminated. The result was a profusion of imagined recreations of the Sins and a concern with them that entered deep into the popular imagination – so deep, in fact, as to give the Sins an importance perhaps greater than their position in theology truly warranted. In *The Castle of Perseverance* they hold Mankind in thrall, and we see him getting ever more self-indulgent and aggressive, ever more mean, as he shows himself 'headlong and heedless in prosperity'. Finally, his Good Angel asks for the help of Confession and Penitence. The latter strikes him with a lance and makes him descend from the scaffold of Avarice. 'A seed of sorrow is in me set,' Mankind declares. When he has been shriven he enters the castle itself, and is attended by the Seven Virtues: Humility, Patience, Charity, Abstinence, Chastity, Solicitude and Liberality, each of whom delivers a sermon on the proper way of avoiding the appropriate vice.

Mankind has passed through innocence, temptation, his fall and the life of sin, to realization and repentance. Now when he is apparently ensconced with the Seven Virtues, his castle is attacked by the forces of the World, the Flesh and the Devil. This second section of the play is essentially a spectacle. Flesh, for example, enters on horseback along with the Sins, while Humanum Genus and the Virtues prepare themselves in the castle. The Good and Bad Angels look down on the scene and, as the lively siege takes place with plenty of physical contact and the loud, comic lament of injuries, so there are no less than twenty-two actors on the stage. Mankind is still in his vigorous middle years, however, and he and the Virtues eventually win the day by showering their opposites with rose petals. But Avarice has one last trick.

Humanum Genus has at last grown old, and Avarice plays on what was conventionally seen as the money-loving vices of the aged. True to type, Mankind descends from the castle (despite the protests of the

Virtues) and, when he takes money from Avarice, falls into his power.

The scene now moves to the deathbed at the foot of the castle. Death himself enters and, in a tableau of great power, strikes Mankind to the heart. Man calls on the World to help him, but Mundus only sends his sinister servant Garcio who, with savage glee, deprives Man of his goods. As Humanum Genus dies, his soul is about to be snatched to Hell by his Bad Angel. Damnation as the reward of sin seems assured. But, at the last, Man calls on God for mercy:

> Now my lyfe I have lore.
> Myn hert brekyth, I syhe sore.
> A word may I speke no more.
> I putte me in Goddys mercy.

Such a cry does not go unheard. Pity, Truth, Justice and Peace – the four daughters of God – go to their Father's scaffold and discuss the fate of Man's soul. In other words, they institute a debate on justice and mercy. God finally decides in favour of Man and the four daughters save his soul from the Devil's scaffold and bring it to God's. Salvation – the purpose of life's pilgrimage – has thus been achieved.

The Castle of Perseverance shows the whole life of man against the dramatized forces of sin and redemption. In its far smaller compass, *Everyman* presents a tableau of the preparation for death. Death himself appears to the hero and summons him before God to make a reckoning of his life and account for the use he has made of the goods that have been lent him. Accounting terminology characterizes much of the language of the play and is given emblematic form in the account-book itself which Everyman carries. Like the servants in the parable, Everyman is going to be obliged to render an account of what he has made of his 'talents'. At first, Everyman turns fearfully to the things of this world for support, but, as Felawship, Kynrede, Goddes (i.e. 'Worldly Goods' or 'Possessions'), Beauty, Strength, Discrecyioun and Five Wittes desert him, so we feel his intense isolation and the heavy burden of moral responsibility. His 'pylgrymage' to God becomes an awesome matter indeed and in the end, when he has received instruction and confessed, only his Good Dedes can help him. These are the true fruits of the talents that have been lent him. At the close, Everyman commends his soul to God in perfect faith and in the wish to die. He begs to be saved and is received into Heaven at the last:

> Come excellente electe spouse to Jesu!
> Here above thou shalte go,

Bycause of thy synguler vertue.
  Now the soule is taken the body fro
Thy rekenynge is crystall clere;
Now shalte thou into the hevenly spere,
Unto the whiche all ye shall come
That lyveth well before the daye of dome.

2

The great cycles of Mystery Plays conform explicitly to the Christian
pattern of history from the creation of the world, through Old Testament
events that prefigure those in the New, and on to the Gospels and
Doomsday. In an age when the study of the Bible text was deliberately
restricted, the Mystery Plays were designed to make all sections of the
laity re-experience emotionally what intellectually they already knew of
the Christian story. Just as carvings and windows in cathedrals and
greater churches told sermons in stone and stained glass, so the Mystery
Plays told biblical truths in verse and action. In addition to a number of
fragments, four major English dramatic cycles survive more or less intact:
Chester (*c*. 1375), York (before 1378), the Towneley plays from Wakefield (mss. *c*. 1450), and the so-called 'N-Town' plays (mss. 1468) once
wrongly ascribed to Coventry. Each has its origins in the ecclesiastical
Feast of Corpus Christi which thus provides an essential background.

The Feast of Corpus Christi is of French origin. It was extended to the
whole Church in 1264, but only became fully effective by a decree of
the Council of Vienne in 1311. The Feast was designed to focus special
devotion on the eucharist, on the events that led up to and followed
from its institution, and on the majesty of the risen Christ. The invitatory
for the matins of the Feast has a repeated refrain that brings these ideas
together: 'Let us adore Christ the King, ruler over the nations; he has
given richness of spirit to those who consume him.' In other words, the
risen Christ offers his saving body in the communion and is King over
the universe. For the Old Testament past he provided earthly rulers who
imperfectly prefigured his own embodiment of kingship, shown living
obediently under divine law in the New. For succeeding times – our
times, in fact – his Word is the ultimate law, giving to the one universal
community of mankind its various places in a hierarchy of obedience.
To contravene this is to sin. Sin may be forgiven through Christ's
sacrifice, while the risen Christ as both King and Judge asserts his
authority over the unrepentant at Doomsday.

It is with such a vision that all the cycles close. We see the damnation of the wicked and the salvation of what St Augustine called, in a passage used as one of the Corpus Christi lessons, 'that very society of saints in which there will be peace and full and perfect unity'. While the audience watch this vision, so as individuals they are drawn into the whole progress and final end of history. They are shown their place in the community of mankind, the body of believers. This is literally the Church and typologically the body of Christ. By presenting the universal history of mankind – often with a full awareness of comedy – and by making each spectator feel more fully a part of the Church and Christ, the Mystery cycles augment the Corpus Christi devotion. We watch the creation and fall of man, the corruption of Old Testament society, the life of the Redeemer and the end of all. As we do so, we come to see the overwhelming importance of Christ's sacrifice and the 'precious, awesome and unspeakable mystery' of the communion by which we can share in the benefits derived from that sacrifice. Finally, we tremble at the wrath of God, remember our sins and are grateful for the body of Christ through which these can be absolved. As with the lyrics, the very powerful artistic effects achieved in many of the plays are not ends in themselves but a means of bringing faith alive.

3

While the theological background to the presentation of the Mystery Plays is clear – we will see later how individual works fit into the cycles as a whole – the manner of their staging is less certain. Most were performed by local guilds or associations of craftsmen (a 'mystery' is another term for a skilled trade) which also charged a levy of between a penny and fourpence on their members to cover costs. This was known as the 'pageant silver' and was entrusted to annually elected pageant masters. Sometimes the pageant masters were also required to assess the qualities of aspiring actors. At York, this duty was supervised by the town council.

The action of the plays took place in the open air, on and around raised stages (the *loci*) which were either stationary scaffolds or moveable wagons known as 'pageants'. A description of the pageant used by the Norwich Grocers is particularly useful here: 'a Pageant, yt is to saye, a House of Waynskott paynted and buylded on a Carte with foure whelys ... A square topp to sett over ye sayde House.' When the action did not take place on this – as is implied, for example, by the famous stage direction: 'here Erode ragis in the pagond and in the strete also' – then such an unlocalized area was given the Latin name *platea*.

The greatest problem about the staging of the Mystery Plays – and one that has not been conclusively solved – is whether the pageant carts were rolled past a stationary audience or (and this seems certain in at least some cases) whether they were grouped, most probably in circles, around a central *platea*, the audience moving from one group of *loci* to the next. The latter was evidently the form of staging adopted for *The Conversion of St Paul* since, just before Saul sets out on the road to Damascus, a figure called Poeta announces:

> ffynally of this stacyon thus we mak a conclusyon
> besechyng thys audyens to folow and succede
> with all your delygens this generall processyon.

Riding into the *platea* of the succeeding group of *loci*, Saul is struck blind. His followers then 'lede forth Sale in-to a place' or *locus* where he receives his baptism from Ananias. Since the play is referred to in the text as a 'processyon', it was evidently the audience and the actors who processed rather than the individual pageants.

4

We should now turn to the plays themselves. This passage from the Chester *Abraham and Isaac* is in many ways a useful introduction:

> ISAAK: Father, I am all readye
> To doe your bydding moste mekeleie,
> To beare this woode [full] bowne am I,
> As you comaund me.

> ABRAHAM: O Isaak, Isaak, my derling deare,
> My blessing [now] I geve the here,
> Take up this faggot with good cheare,
> And on thy backe yt bringe,
> And fire with me I will take.
> ISAAK. Your byddinge I will not forsake;
> Father, I will never slake
> To fulfill your byddinge.

> ABRAHAM: Now Isaake, sonne, goe we our waye
> To yonder mowntayne, if that we maye.
> ISAAK: My deere father, I will assaye
> To follow you full fayne.
> ABRAHAM: O! my hart will break in three,

> To heare thy wordes I have pyttie;
> As thou wilt, lord, so must yt be:
> To thee I will be bayne.
>
> Laye downe thy faggot, my owne sonne deere.
> ISAAK: All ready, father, loe yt is here.
> But why make you so heavie cheare?
> Are you any thing adred?
> Father, if it be your will,
> Where is the beast that we shall kill?
> ABRAHAM: Therof, sonne, is none upon this hill,
> That I see here in this steed.
>
> ISAAK: Father, I am full sore afraide
> To see you beare this drawen sworde.
> I hope for all middle-yorde,
> You will not slaye your childe.
> ABRAHAM: Dread not thou, my childe, I red;
> Our lord will send of his godhead
> Some maner beast into this stydd,
> Ether tayme or wylde.

middle-yorde: the world   *stydd:* place

What is immediately striking about this passage is the homely tone of the pathos. This is a quality that also characterizes the lyrics and, since it is of such evident importance to many of the explicitly religious works of the Middle Ages, we should investigate the origins of what we might call this Christian rhetoric. It stems, quite naturally, from the Bible. Christ did not choose to be born in a palace but in a stable. He selected his disciples from among the artisans of Judaea. The greater part of his teaching was delivered to the poor and concerned the virtues of poverty and humility. Christ was executed with common thieves. Further, the record of his works is not a magisterial example of classical prose which carefully avoids the ordinary things of life for calculated literary effects. It is direct and profoundly moving. It also concerns the greatest possible event in history. To many – including St Augustine, who had been a professor of classical rhetoric – it was a considerable problem that Scripture was deeply emotional, overwhelming in its significance, and yet, by classical standards at least, inartistic. Its content might be sublime, but its style was not an example of *sermo sublimis*. As St Augustine wrote:

. . . I made up my mind to examine the holy Scriptures and see what kind of books they were. I discovered something that was at once beyond the understanding of the proud and hidden from the eyes of children. Its gait was humble, but the heights it reached were sublime. It was enfolded in mysteries, and I was not the kind of man to enter into it or bow my head to follow where it led. But these were not the feelings I had when I first read the Scriptures. To me they seemed quite unworthy of comparison with the stately prose of Cicero, because I had too much conceit to accept their simplicity and not enough insight to penetrate their depths . . . Their plain language and simple style make them accessible to everyone, yet it absorbs the attention of the learned. By this means it gathers all men in the wide sweep of its net, and some pass safely through the narrow mesh and come to you. They are not many, but they would be fewer still if it were not that this book stands out alone on so high a peak of authority and yet draws so great a throng in the embrace of its holy humility.

Scripture is thus sufficiently direct for the simple to share its message with a faithful heart. It also contains 'mysteries' that can only be solved by the advanced intellect, by the mind rejoicing not in its own powers but illuminated by faith. Scripture is at once humble and sublime, and in this it exactly corresponds to the incarnation of Christ – the Word of God – himself. As St Bernard expresses the matter: 'that the Word of God, dwelling in the sublime, should descend to us, was first prompted by humility'. Christian rhetoric – revealing the sublime in humble words – is an exact mirror of its content. The simple, affecting language of the Mystery Plays further reflects this tradition. The hearts of the audience are won to faith by the emotional directness of the way in which the events leading to their salvation are described. These events have the same 'surface' as their own existence. Abraham and Isaac are at once Old Testament characters and members of the Chester Guild of Barbers and Wax Chandlers. They are people from everyday life.

But the 'mysteries' St Augustine discovered and elucidated in Scripture also have their important part to play in the drama. Indeed, they are central to the passage quoted from *Abraham and Isaac*.

The particular issue which concerns us here is what has come to be known as the 'figural' interpretation of scriptural history. This is a view of Old Testament events which firmly places God as the supreme author of man's destiny, rather than, for example, chance, fortune, military power or commercial development. It is also a view in which the events of Jewish history in particular are seen as imperfectly foreshadowing the greatest moments of human history in general – the incarnation of Christ as man, his death and Resurrection. An event such as the sacrifice of Isaac can thus be seen as a 'figure' foretelling the Crucifixion. It is both a human drama prophetic of the New Testament and an *exemplum* of proper, devout behaviour at all times. Writing of Abraham's place in this framework, St Augustine declares: 'Abraham our father was a faithful man who lived in those far-off days. He trusted in God and was justified by his faith . . . Whatever Scripture says about Abraham is both literal fact and prophecy.' We should now ask how this division between fact and prophecy relates to the *Abraham and Isaac* plays of the various cycles, and, in particular, to the extract chosen from the Chester version.

The 'literal fact' of the story is the Old Testament narrative itself which all six surviving versions of the play recreate. Each begins with an extensive Prologue. In the Wakefield play, the whole of human history since the Fall is recounted, while the Chester version opens with a note of quiet faith and triumph. With the help of the Lord, Abraham has won a victory over enemy kings who have been attacking the as yet unpolluted Sodom, where Abraham's brother Lot has been living. Abraham has gained a considerable amount of booty with his military success, and, as he gives thanks to God, he promises a tenth of his spoils to Melchisadech 'that here kinge is and God's priest also'. Melchisadech, himself delighted by the victory, now hastens to Abraham in order

> My office to fulfill,
> And present hym with bread and wyne
> For grace of God is him withine;
> Speedes fast for love myne!

Both Abraham and Lot receive this gift of bread and wine – an obvious 'figure' of the eucharist – and offer their tithes. Abraham is then left alone.

He desperately wants a son. Both he and his wife are elderly people, but nonetheless God promises Abraham a line of legitimate descendants who will be more numerous than the stars in the sky, a progeny which will include One that 'all mankind shall forbye [redeem]'. God then requires that Abraham be 'trewe', and commands that all his future sons be circumcised. Abraham gives thanks.

Since the Mystery cycles concern biblical events seen in the light of eternity, there is no need for them to preserve the unities of time and place. Decades can pass between scenes that follow each other in performance almost without a break. This in its turn can considerably heighten the dramatic effect. For example, the incident that succeeds God's promise to Abraham is his command that his loyal servant slay the very son he has so devoutly requested:

> Take, Isaack, thy sonne by name,
> That thou lovest best of all,
> And in sacrafice offer him to me
> Upon that hill, besyde thee.
> Abraham, I will that it be so
> For ought that may befalle.

Abraham immediately agrees. To look for conflict – the essence of most drama – is entirely to miss the point. A modern or medieval audience may well be horrified by God's command, but what is required of them is that they admire a man who gives absolute priority to unquestioning devotion. By being stronger than the normal human reactions we inevitably bring to the scene, Abraham becomes an *exemplum* of faith. Such a mood of obedience also characterizes the scene of the attempted sacrifice from the Chester *Abraham and Isaac*. It in no way diminishes its humanity. Indeed, the emotional recognition of what absolute faith involves is deeply moving.

Abraham and Isaac make their way to the hill where the innocent boy will be sacrificed. The father gives his instructions. The son is loving and dutiful as he carries the faggots on his back. For all that we know the happy outcome – the fact that God will provide a ram for the sacrifice – the sense of doom that hangs over the scene is very powerful and is made all the more so by the presence of the unsuspecting boy and the father's anguished lifting of his hands and subsequent brief soliloquy. This is, in fact, a prayer. Isaac's concern at his father's distress and his questions about the absence of a sacrificial victim are in the best manner sentimental and melodramatic. Abraham's blunt reply meanwhile disguises a world of woe. Then, suddenly, the boy has an intuition of what is to happen. His fear wrings his father's heart. But Abraham's reply once again reinforces the theme of faith. His absolute trust in God seems to amount to a knowledge of what will come to pass. He is sure that another victim will be found. Before this can happen, however, what appears as the unbearable and even gratuitous cruelty of God's command must be followed to the letter. The father has unwavering faith, but for the moment Isaac is just a confused and frightened child. He wishes his mother were there; she would surely save him. However, as the boy learns that his sacrifice is God's wish, so he submits. With heartrending innocence and overflowing charity, he bids his father take comfort in his other sons. The grotesque binding of the victim takes place. The simple, physical terror here is made the more awful for the apparent injustice, yet there rises above it an absolute purity of faith and feeling. Only with the drawing of Abraham's sword do the redeeming angels finally come and point to the sacrificial lamb. God himself then appears to praise Abraham's strength of purpose.

The 'figural' meaning of these events is pointed out during the course of the Chester play by an Expositor. His interpretation accords with that provided by St Augustine, and this was also the way in which the Old Testament narrative was expounded in the service of Quinquagesima – the second Sunday in Lent. Indeed, throughout the period leading up to Easter, the Church lessons provided the congregation with the whole biblical history of man, dividing this into seven ages. These in their turn determine the selection of episodes in the Mystery Plays. These periods are: Adam to Noah, Noah to Abraham, Abraham to Moses, Moses to David, David and on to the return from the Captivity (this period of the prophets is summarized in the 'Balaam play' of the Chester cycle), and so to the life of Christ and the Last Judgement. Each of the Old Testament ages is an ever clearer figure of the coming of Christ. As St Augustine declared of Abraham's time, we find in it 'more evident promises from God which we now see fulfilled in Christ'. For example, God promised Abraham that he would found a great nation and that it would live in Canaan in perpetuity. This nation would be the Jews amongst whom Christ would be born. Again, for St Augustine (as for the Expositor of the Chester Mystery) Abraham's receiving bread and wine from Melchisadech was a clear prefiguration of the eucharist. Most important of all, the Chester Expositor provides the standard interpretation of the sacrifice of Isaac in terms of the life of Christ. He sees Abraham as a 'type' or figure of God who offers his Son as a pledge of salvation. Isaac, obedient to his father, is thus a prefiguration of Jesus:

> This deed you se done here in this place,
> In example of Ihesu done yt was,
> That for to wyn mankinde grace
> Was sacrifised on the [rode].

> By Abraham I may understand
> The Father of heaven that can fand
> With his sonnes blood to breake that band,
> The devil had brought us too.
> By Isaak understand I may
> Ihesu that was obedyent aye,
> His fathers will to worke alway,
> His death for to underfonge.

underfonge: endure

In fact, this correspondence is worked out in rather more detail than the Chester Expositor suggests and derives from the interpretation of the episode provided by St Augustine in the *De Civitate Dei*. St Augustine first expounds the moral meaning of Abraham's test, revealing it as an *exemplum* of faith:

... Abraham was tempted in the matter of the sacrifice of his beloved son Isaac, so that his beautiful obedience might be put to the proof, and he be brought to the knowledge, not of God, but of future ages. It is to be observed that temptation does not always imply anything blameworthy, since the testing that brings approval is a matter for rejoicing. And as a general rule, there is no other way in which the human spirit can acquire self-knowledge except by trying its own strength in answering, not in word but in deed, what may be called the interrogation of temptation. And then, if God acknowledges the task performed, there is an example of a spirit truly devoted to God, with the solidity given by the strength of grace, instead of the inflation of an empty boast.

Abraham, we can be sure, could never have believed that God delights in human victims; and yet the thunder of a divine command must be obeyed without argument.

Having explained the purpose behind God's seemingly unreasonable command, St Augustine then deals with the problem of the promise to Abraham that his race and name would be perpetuated through the very boy he is about to sacrifice. To overcome this difficulty, St Augustine turns to a passage in the Epistle to the Romans and explains that Abraham already knows that God does not mean that it is his actual bodily sons who will carry on his line, but his metaphorical ones – in other words, those people who have been drawn to God:

The Apostle explains the force of 'through Isaac your descendants will carry on your name' in this way: 'It does not mean that the sons of the flesh are the sons of God: it is the sons of the promise who are counted as his descendants.' Consequently, the sons of the promise are called in Isaac to be the descendants of Abraham, that is they are called by grace and gathered together in Christ. The devout father therefore clung to this promise faithfully, and since it had to be fulfilled through the son God ordered to be slain, he did not doubt that a son who could be granted to him when he had ceased to hope could also be restored to him after he had been sacrificed.

The precise details of the scene of sacrifice also have their part to play in this prefigurative pattern. Thus the hill on which the sacrifice takes place is a 'type' of Calvary and the faggots foreshadow the cross. It follows that Abraham and Isaac too must each be a 'type':

A type of whom? It can only be of Him of whom the Apostle says, 'He did not spare his own son, but handed him over for us all.' This is why, as the Lord carried his cross, so Isaac himself carried to the place of sacrifice the wood on which he too was to be placed. Moreover, after the father had been prevented from striking his son, since it was not right that Isaac should be slain, who was the ram whose immolation completed the sacrifice by blood of symbolic significance? Bear in mind that when Abraham saw the ram it was caught by the thorns in a thicket. Who, then, was symbolized by that ram but Jesus, crowned with Jewish thorns before he was offered in sacrifice?

In the Chester version, the ram caught in the thicket has been changed to a lamb – the Lamb of God – who is joyfully slain as a prefiguration of the Passion of Christ. Similarly, in the Quinquagesima service, the story of Abraham and Isaac is followed by Luke's account of how Jesus told his disciples of his forthcoming sacrifice in Jerusalem. We can thus see how the plays unite Scripture, the teaching of the Church and abstruse theology in a manner that brings the essential points home clearly and forcibly to a largely illiterate audience.

5

Christ as the Lamb of God is also the central image of what is perhaps the greatest of the Mystery dramas: *The Second Shepherd's Play* from the Towneley cycle. This is the work of an unnamed reviser from the first half of the fifteenth century who also worked on *Cain and Abel*, *Noah*, *The First Shepherds' Play*, *Herod* and the *Coliphizacio* or 'Scourging of Christ'. His skill with the nine-line alliterative stanza, with characterization, with varied dramatic effects, and – above all, perhaps – his truly inventive use of scriptural exegesis have earned him his name as the 'Wakefield Master'. He is one of the geniuses of English drama.

The subject of *The Second Shepherds' Play* is, of course, the adoration of the baby Jesus by the shepherds. What is particularly remarkable about the piece is the way in which the shrewdly observed realism of the work is related dramatically to the interpretation of the incarnation of Christ as both the Good Shepherd and the Lamb of God. Christ is the Saviour who, typologically, is the fulfilment of the shepherds' own craft. By virtue of this role, the shepherds – as the earliest Christian believers – become his sheep. Christ is also the sacrificial Lamb who offers redemption and so gives purpose to the shepherds' lives. Further, through the excellently constructed, farcical incident of Mak the sheep-thief, these Christian themes are placed in the context of the devil's power to steal and corrupt the goodness of the world. The biblical text which brings this sequence of imagery together comes from the tenth chapter of St John's gospel: 'The thief comes only to steal and kill and destroy; I come that they may have life, and have it abundantly. I am the good shepherd. The good shepherd lays down his life for the sheep.'

Let us see how this works. The play begins in the world of the three human shepherds: Coll, Gyb and Daw. Each has an extended, powerful soliloquy which shows the harshness of the life of the poor in the fallen world:

> Lord, what these weders ar cold! And I am yll happyd.
> I am nere hande dold, so long have I nappyd;
> My legys thay fold, my fyngers ar chappyd.
> It is not as I wold, for I am al lappyd
> In sorow.

Here is an existence apparently without human or divine relief, where 'thys gentley men' oppress the overtaxed agricultural labourers and 'wo is hym that grefe or onys agane says'. This is the substance of contemporary 'complaint' poetry cast in the idiom of the people. The second and third shepherds repeat its tone. The ungratefulness of human life is their subject, too. Gyb then laments the pains of marriage in terms derived from conventional medieval anti-feminism, while Daw sees life and the world passing 'ever in drede and brekyll as glas'. Though formal and conventional in content, the direct and sharp observation of these soliloquies brings them vividly to life – a suffering, hard-done-by, timeless existence. Daw, the youngest of the shepherds, now tells us he is hungry. He protests against the conditions of his employment but gains no sympathy from the others. There is not a trace of sentimentality here. Coll and Gyb are hard but not unkind men in a hard and unkind world. All three have the relief of their music, however – the part-song which they now perform. While music helps structure the play (in this case rounding off the first section), we shall see that it also has a far deeper significance.

Mak the sheep-stealer now enters in disguise, complaining not of his earthly master but about God and the insupportable burden of God's bounty revealed to him in the form of his large family. Though the shepherds immediately see through his disguise, Mak maintains his ridiculous and arrogant pose as the 'yoman' of a great king. By his disdain, he becomes the antitype of the charitable angel of the Nativity sent by the King of Kings. As the wary shepherds compare Mak with the devil, we begin to see something of the range of associations that gather about him. Mak eventually lies down in feigned sleep among the shepherds, then, drawing a circle round them and muttering an incantation, he goes to steal a sheep – a parodic image of the Lamb of God. Beneath the comic action, the diabolic suggestions already touched upon begin to build up as the audience is led to compare Mak's theft to the devil stealing grace from mankind. For the very human and hungry Mak, however, his theft is a form of worldly salvation. He and his large family will be able to eat and sustain their wicked selves through a stolen physical lamb rather than nourish their spiritual selves through the spiritual Lamb of God offered in the eucharist.

On his return home, Mak's quick-witted wife Gyll realizes the danger that the theft has put them in and suggests a stratagem which – like the other Mak episodes – is at once a farce and a parody of Christian imagery. The couple will bind the feet of the sheep, place it in a cradle, and, if the shepherds come searching for it, pretend it is another child newly born to them. By placing the stolen lamb with its bound feet in the cradle, the couple at once suggest the image of the lamb with bound feet that conventionally symbolized the Crucifixion and also the Nativity of Christ in the humble stable at Bethlehem. In each case, their wicked yet farcical actions are a hollow parody of the divine.

As we have seen, it is fundamental to Christian thought that sin can achieve nothing of itself and can only parody the spiritual. It is so here. His loot apparently secure, Mak returns to the shepherds, pretends to be asleep among them and then, when they have woken up, wanders home. His alibi, it seems, is sound. On his return, his wife – once again reinforcing the diabolic imagery – calls him 'Syr Gyle'.

Needless to say, the shepherds discover that one of their sheep is missing and hurry, distraught, to Mak's house. He at once starts singing a grotesque lullaby – it is perhaps meant to remind us of the hymns of the Nativity and is certainly the lowest musical point in the play, the one furthest away from the divine harmony of Heaven. His wife meanwhile feigns the agonies of childbirth. Even this grotesque incident can be made into a parody of the eucharist:

> A, my medyll!
> I pray to God so mylde,
> If ever I you begyld,
> That I ete this chylde
> That lygys in this credyll.

Having failed to find their sheep, the disappointed shepherds eventually leave with their apologies. Then they remember their charity. They have given nothing to the newborn child and so return to Mak's cottage. Through the exercise of charity, they discover the truth – their lamb in

Mak's cradle. The alleged human baby, they find, has a 'long snoute' like a devil's child, but when Mak claims it has been enchanted into the form of a sheep, we are intended to see this as a parody of the spiritual miracle by which Christ became the Lamb of God. The good shepherds then retrieve their lost sheep from the image of the devil's lair and signify their triumph over Mak by tossing him in a blanket.

Having won a victory over this farcical image of the devil, the shepherds sleep once again. The angels now appear to them, singing *Gloria in excelsis* with a music whose complexity – so much greater than the shepherds' own and so wholeheartedly approved of by them – we should understand as the heavenly harmony itself descending to these poor men in the Yorkshire dales. They at once obey the angels' command and hasten to Bethlehem. As they present the true Lamb of God with the most touchingly simple presents, a 'bob of cherys', a bird and a ball – presents symbolic of the incarnation, Resurrection, and Christ as King over the orb of the world – so they are drawn into the true spiritual mystery, and away from the discouraged worldly suffering of their opening soliloquies.

6

The Passion itself – the actual sacrifice of the Lamb of God – is most powerfully realized by a second anonymous master of medieval drama, a writer who has been named the 'York Realist'. Like the author of the Wakefield plays in the Towneley cycle, he was a reviser of previously existing work to which he brought both his learning and his special genius for vivid and often very physical detail. The York Realist is also an expert with convincing dialogue. This in turn deepens his characterization of vain and bestial humanity. Such traits are always contrasted with the still purity of Christ. The York Realist's *Dream of Pilate's Wife*, for example – his dramatization of Christ's trial – exemplifies this particularly well. We hear the proud, gluttonous and lascivious worldly prince, his arrogant wife and her obnoxious son. We also see – for he barely speaks – the silent figure of Christ, dignified in his reticence amid so much squalor. He is the Prince of Heaven who gives his life to save such loathsome humanity.

In the York cycle, the scene of the Crucifixion was played by the guild of 'Pynneres and Paynters'. Since the first were makers of nails, their presence here is horribly apt, and the contrast maintained throughout between the unrelieved brutality of the soldiers competing with each other in the pain they can inflict – their dialogue brief, colloquial, appallingly factual – and the serene, forgiving Christ is outstandingly powerful. Christ is God made man willingly going to his death. He silently places himself on the cross and, as the soldiers gather round him, we see humanity at its most degraded.

After the Crucifixion plays come the death and burial of Christ, the Harrowing of Hell (a scene which probably influenced Langland), the Resurrection and the events leading to Pentecost. The Towneley cycle omits the scenes of the death, assumption and coronation of the Virgin. It has been conjectured that these were removed during the Reformation when opinion turned violently against the cult of Mary. In other cycles, however, the drama of Marian devotion is recreated with an excellent combination of pathos, comedy and triumph.

All the cycles close with Doomsday. This was invariably presented with great elaboration – the York version, for example, has thirty-eight parts – and in it the whole of human history is recapitulated, judged and brought to its conclusion.

The action takes place in Heaven, earth and Hell. At the opening of the York version, God tells of his creation of the world, describes the Fall, his sending his son as a sacrifice and man's continuing ingratitude, his 'folie'. In exasperation, God decides to bring his creation to an end. The good and evil souls rise from their graves, either blessing God or in fear and trembling. Christ then appears as Judge and King. He relates the story of his Passion and takes his 'blissid childre' to his right hand. These are the redeemed who have performed the seven acts of mercy:

> Whenne I was hungery ye me fedde;
> To slake my thirste youre harte was free;
> Whanne I was clothles ye me cledde;
> Ye wolde no sorowe uppon me see.
> In harde presse whan I was stedde,
> Of my paynes ye hadde pitee;
> Full seke whan I was brought in bedde,
> Kyndely ye come to coumforte me.
>
> Whanne I was wikke and werieste
> Ye herbered me full hartefully;
> Full gladde thann were ye of youre geste,
> And pleynd my poverte piteuously.
> Be-lyve ye brought me of the beste,
> And made my bedde full esyly;
> Therfore in hevene schall be youre reste,
> In joie and blisse to be me by.

geste: guest

The blessed have been saved. As they enter the serene company of the saints, the Mystery cycles close on the border of infinity. We have watched the whole progress of the universe; we have seen faith, wickedness, the promise of redemption and the damnation of evil. Physical life is no more, and the final image offered by the plays is of the angels choiring an unearthly music at the end of time.

CHAPTER 9

MIDDLE ENGLISH PROSE

1

Both medieval drama and the sermons of the period have their origins in the clerical duty to instruct the people on the avoidance of sin and on following the paths of righteousness. The sermon, being the older form, also provided much of the material and many of the techniques employed by the Miracle and Mystery Plays. The vivid emotions, realistic detail, comedy, satire and colloquial language of *The Second Shepherds' Play* in the Towneley cycle, for example, owe much to the techniques of the preachers, as does the play's use of analogy, 'figural' interpretation and biblical reference. The vivid realization of a suffering Christ in the following passage further suggests how preachers could inspire such various figures as Langland and the York Realist:

> He was betun and buffetid, scorned and scourgid, that unnethis was ther left ony hoole platte of his skyn, fro the top to the too, that a man my3te have sette in the point of a nedil. But al his bodi rane out as a strem of blood. He was crowned with a crowne of thornes for dispite. And whanne the crowne, as clerkis seien, wolde not stik fast and iust doun on his heed for the longe thornes and stronge, thei toke staves and betun it down, til the thornes thrilliden the brayne panne. He was naylyd hond and foot with scharp nailis and ruggid, for his peyne schulde be the more; and so, at the last, he sufferid moost peynful deeth, hanging ful schamefulli on the cros.

unnethis: scarcely

Drawing large crowds and fixing such scenes deep in the medieval mind, the preachers and their sermons are of the greatest influence. We have already seen how the sermon provides the form for many of the *Canterbury Tales,* much of *Piers Ploughman*, and the homilies of the Gawain-poet, but, as a final and specific example of the relation of the sermon to the drama, it should be noted that the speech of the risen Lazarus in the Towneley cycle is almost identical with a sermon on the fate of the dead delivered by the influential Dominican preacher John Bromyard. The relationship between the two forms could hardly be more pronounced.

Preaching was thus a matter of central importance to the culture of the Middle Ages. St Thomas Aquinas, the man who gave definitive form to the scholastic theology of the Church, called it 'the noblest of all the ecclesiastical functions', and declared that preachers are 'the mouth of Christ'. It is from New Testament practice that medieval traditions of preaching largely stem. This suggests once again the central place of the Bible in medieval literature.

The synoptic gospels lay great emphasis on Christ's ordering his disciples to preach and on portraying Christ himself as a model for this. For example, Christ used both direct instruction and parables. Many medieval sermons in turn deal with matters of theology, sometimes at an advanced level, while a great number of the most attractive offer exemplary stories.

Such an exalted concept of preaching clearly placed huge responsibilities on the preacher. He needed considerable knowledge, skill in communication and the clear personal rectitude that would inspire respect. Ideally these qualities were merged, and it will be useful if we consider them here in relation to a definition of preaching itself.

The twelfth-century writer Alain de Lille (Alanus) regarded preaching as one of the highest activities of the Christian life and that which revealed 'the perfection of the whole man'. Preaching could only be pursued competently by one who was already disciplined by confession, prayer and study. So prepared, he could perform his task, which Alanus defined thus: 'Preaching is an open and public instruction in faith and morals, zealously serving the information of mankind, proceeding by the narrow path of reason and growing from the spring of the sacred text.' Alanus elaborates on this by explaining that preaching must be open and public so that it does not seem to smack of heresy and because it is for the benefit of many people, giving clear information about theological issues and the proper conduct of life. Preaching should be interesting but sober in style, and should draw from the Bible and received teaching.

Since sermons were also regarded as a medicine 'by which the disease of sin is purged' and were intended to rouse the soul from languor and recall it to a life of virtue, it was necessary that the preacher himself should be both a man of moral rectitude and lovable in his own right. It was thus recognized that the personal strengths of the preacher were an important part of his effectiveness. We should bear this in mind when we consider the nature of some of those who deliver sermons in *The Canterbury Tales*. For example, it is obvious that both the Pardoner and the erring and disdainful Monk lack these qualities. By way of contrast, the proper attitude of a preacher, declared one writer, should be 'good will, devout love, and a clear conscience'. A preacher's interior struggles will have taught him 'to act wisely for his own salvation and that of others'. But such personal knowledge is not in itself enough. Deep learning is also essential to effective preaching. 'It is extremely dangerous for a man who has the obligation of preaching ever to stop studying,' declared one writer of a manual on how sermons should be given, but the same authority stated that the intellectual pride that may well go with scholarship should be zealously avoided. He warns the would-be preacher against striving with the more difficult passages of Scripture and enunciating 'grave platitudes in carefully polished phrases, not in order to help his hearers live better, but to feed his own ego by demonstrating that he knows more'. Further, the good and humble preacher should deliver his matter clearly, and above all should avoid tedium and excessive length. St Ambrose declared that a tedious sermon rouses anger, but Chaucer's Monk has clearly forgotten this truth, as the reactions of his bored audience illustrate. The Monk's exhortation to virtue fails because he himself lacks both virtue and technical skill, while the sermon delivered by the Pardoner is successful despite the wickedness and folly of its preacher. It thereby illustrates that evil intentions are a parody of the divine will and of themselves can finally produce nothing but good. Chaucer's poor Parson, on the other hand – a figure who, we have seen, owes much to the image of the priest as an imitation of Christ as the Good Shepherd – is a perfect example of what a preacher should be. We are told that he was 'of holy thoght and werk', that he was a 'lerned' man, devout, loyal to his parishioners, patient of his poverty, while, above all,

> . . . Cristes loore and his apostles twelve
> He taughte, but first he folwed it hymselve.

The concern with homely detail, and a simple and direct ecclesiastical language that as we have seen stems from the Bible and the writings of St Augustine (and, later, those of St Francis of Assisi) help to account for the wealth of exemplary stories many of the sermons contain. Some of these take the form of delightfully observed details of daily life: the mother with her child, the pot boiling by the fire on which the fly never lands, the host welcoming pilgrims into a tavern. All these are then made to yield up their spiritual truths and so suggest once again how deep-seated was the medieval notion of interpreting the things of this world in the light of the next. Allegorical motifs derived from the Scriptures also have a large part to play, as do moralized anecdotes taken from secular and religious history, contemporary life and the imagination.

Many sermons – particularly those preached to university congregations – also had their own rhetoric and involved great elaboration. First of all there was a theme in Latin, usually taken from the Bible. Though this was often no more than a phrase, it was broken down into two or three topics which were then carefully related to one another and supported by citations from a wealth of authorities, both sacred and secular. To provide this information, a number of preacher's handbooks were now being prepared (Bromyard was the compiler of one such) in which topics were listed alphabetically and were followed by a string of associated topics on which the preacher could then find *exempla* which he might put into his sermon. Hence the emphasis is less on personal expression than the able manipulation of the rules. The trained faculties required to appreciate such skills are of the greatest importance not just to the reconstruction of the minds of a medieval congregation listening to a sermon, but also to how such an audience on a secular occasion would have appreciated the oral delivery of a poem. The first listeners to *Troilus and Criseyde* were, after all, used to the intricate artifice of the sermon form.

Some of the liveliest parts of many medieval sermons are satirical. Churchmen, peasants, lawyers, physicians, merchants and bad wives were all the commonplace subjects of satirical diatribes that were often realized with vivid detail. Time and again we can see how deeply influenced poets such as Langland were by these. We might compare his picture of Gluttony, for example, with this passage from a sermon which tells of

glotons sittyng in the taverne, puttynge hire mouthes into the bolle, til thei ben drunke. Thenne thei crien with grete voice, boostynge, swerynge, lyynge and slaunderynge, and al hire evele dedes which thei have doun of many ȝeres afore freschli rehercynge and reioisynge.

This is shrewdly observed and satirizes timeless self-indulgence. Many of the sermons, however, are directed to contemporary abuses, and some of the most powerful prose of the period comes from those sermons which, covering the same ground as much 'complaint' poetry, were written under the influence of Wyclif and the Lollards:

Lordis many tymes don wronges to pore men bi extorcions and unresonable mercymentis and unresonable taxis and taken pore mennus goodis and paien not þerfore but white sticks and dispisen hem and manassen hem and sumtyme beten hem whanne þei axen here peye. And þus lordis devouren pore mennus goodis in glotonye and waste and pride and þei perischen for myschief and hunger and þrist and colde and þere children also. And ȝif here rente be not redily paied here bestis ben stressid and þei pursued wiþouten mercy þouȝ þei be neuere so pore and nedi and overcharged wiþ many children.

mercymentis: payments   *manassen:* menace   *stressid:* arrested

2

The mention of the Lollards raises a number of points that directly affect the literature of the late Middle Ages. The Lollards believed, for example, that it was desirable for the laity to read the Bible both for its teaching on salvation and for the proper ordering of worldly institutions, issues which had previously only been conveyed to the majority through sermons, drama and the visual arts rather than the private study of the text itself. While it is likely that Wyclif's own efforts were intended for the knightly class, it is clear that by the start of the fifteenth century the lesser laity were keenly interested in what became the unified Lollard combination of theological, political and popular radicalism. That this implied some level of literacy is made clear by the order *De Heretico Cumburendo* which authorized the death penalty for the Lollards, and describes how 'they make unlawful conventicles and confederacies, they hold and exercise schools, they make and write books, they do wickedly instruct and inform people'. Coming to prominence in a period of heavy taxation, the exhaustion of the French wars, plague, and what often seemed an alarming degree of social mobility, the literacy that Wyclif and his followers encouraged appeared deeply threatening to both Church and state.

Lollardy raised in particular the question of who should have access to the Bible and how its texts should be interpreted. The danger that the Church perceived in the literate laity having access to vernacular translations of the Bible was that they would read the text without an adequate knowledge of traditional interpretations. Like the Wife of Bath, perhaps, they would be tempted to pit their own experience against authority. We have seen that, in the Wife of Bath's case at least, this danger was rendered nugatory by the fact that her deepest experiences contradicted much of her alleged personal interpretation of Scripture and so illustrated the abiding truth of Holy Writ. However, the right to read the Bible in the vernacular and to criticize society by reference to it – in other words, the right to be literate and articulate – was one for which men and women were now prepared to die. They wished to discuss issues that had previously been reserved for ecclesiastics, to argue about grace, salvation and reward, and to do so from the text itself. It was for such people as these that the Wyclifite translation of the Bible was prepared, and it was these men and women who read the simple, affecting prose of, for example, the tale of the Prodigal Son:

Forsoth his eldere sone was in the feeld, and whanne he cam and neighede to the hous, he herde a symfonye and a croude. And he clepide oon of the seruauntis, and axide what thingis thes weren. And he seide to him, Thi brodir is comen, and thi fadir hath slayn a fat calf, for he resseyued him saf. Forsoth he was wroth, and wolde not entre: therfore his fadir yede out, bigan to preie him. And he answeringe to his fadir seide, Lo, so manye yeeris I serue to thee, and I brak neuere thi commaundement, thou hast neuere yovun a kyde to me, that I schulde ete largely with my frendis. But aftir that this thi sone, which deuouride his substaunce with hooris, cam, thou hast slayn to him a fat calf. And he seide to him, Sone, thou ert euere with me, and alle myne thingis ben thyne. Forsoth it bihofte to ete plenteuously, and for to ioye: for this thi brother was deed, and lyuede ayeyn: he peryschide, and he is founden.

3

Along with the sermons there also survives a body of prose concerned with the religious life of the individual. *The Book of Margery Kempe* (1433) is an account of her spiritual experiences dictated by a woman who could neither read nor write but who nonetheless acquired a wide knowledge of the mystical tradition. This she largely learned from those she persuaded to read to her. However, it is less Margery's scholarship that affects us today – though it does reveal how an extensive acquaintance with continental spirituality could be acquired fairly readily – than her descriptions of her attempts to lead a life of extreme devotion.

Her book opens with an account of the madness that followed the birth of the first of her many children and her subsequent vision of Christ which she did not fully appreciate until worldly problems humbled her. In her newly abject state – a life of constant tears and conspicuous emotionalism – conversations with Christ are reported. Her husband's sexual demands also begin to revolt her, and her life continues as a curious, mawkish combination of hysteria, vision and wide-ranging pilgrimage. Many of her contemporaries found her – understandably enough – a repellent character, and Margery was frequently involved in violent controversies. She was even suspected on occasion of heresy, a charge which she vigorously and successfully rebutted. Her book, the first surviving English autobiography, is a curious document, uneven in quality, and yet one that leaves behind a vivid memory of late medieval religious fervour, with its intimate imaginings of the life of Christ perceived with all the directness of the daily existence with which they so readily merge.

One of the contemporaries from whom Margery Kempe sought advice was a woman whose spiritual life was of an altogether higher order: the anchorite Dame Julian of Norwich. Her book – *Revelations of Divine Love* – exists in two versions. The first is almost certainly an earlier draft of what was later expanded into one of the great works of European mysticism.

Dame Julian's book is her account of a series of 'shewings' or mystical visions that came to her on 13 May 1373. Much of her subsequent life was spent meditating on these. In her book she tells how she had previously begged three graces from God: to remember Christ's Passion, to have bodily sickness, and to receive what she calls three wounds: contrition, compassion and the longing for God. The second of these three graces came suddenly to her on the day of her 'shewings'. These included a vision of the Crucifixion that Dame Julian records with an emphasis on physical realism which we have seen to be typical of the sermons. It is also clear from her book that Julian was an educated woman, well-read in orthodox theology, and that she had the ability to interpret her visions in the fourfold manner of scriptural exegesis. Again – and probably stemming from the tradition of *The Ancrene Riwle* – she places much stress on the courteous nature of Christ. The greatest courtesy that he can extend to his poor servant is to be 'homely' with her, and there is indeed a direct and level-headed quality about Julian, a strength and warm maturity wholly different from Margery Kempe's extremism. Finally, like all the great mystics, Julian realizes the true purpose behind her experiences. In a passage of great formal beauty, patterned with conscious rhetoric, she explains God's intention:

And fro the tyme that it was shewde I desyerde oftyn tymes to wytt in what was oure lord's menyng. And XV yere after and more I was answeryd in gostly understondyng, seyeng thus: 'What, woldest thou witt thy lords menyng in this thyng? Wytt it wele, love was his menyng. Who shewyth it the? Love. Wherefore shewyth he it the? For love. Holde thee therein, thou shalt wytt more in the same. But thou schalt nevyr witt therein other, withoutyn ende. Thus was I lernyd that love is oure lordes menyng.

Dame Julian's description of the Crucifixion is intense yet restrained. That by Richard Rolle (*c.* 1300–1349) in his *Meditation on the Passion* is fervent, effusive and, like so much of the contemplative literature of the period, was written for the inspiration of devout women. Such a style was not approved of by the unknown author of *The Cloud of Unknowing* (*c.* 1380), however. His own approach follows that form of asceticism which, deriving from the pseudo-Dionysius whose work was widely known in the Middle Ages, examines the mysticism of the Negative Way with its insistence that the mind be emptied of all images and should recognize the utter unknowability of God. Thus between the soul and its Creator hangs 'the cloud of unknowing' which gives the work its title. The unnamed author explains his image thus:

. . . wene not, for I clepe it a derknes or a cloude, that it be any cloude congelid of the humours that fleen in the ayre, ne yit any derknes soche as is in thin house on nightes, when thi candel is oute. For soche a derknes & soche a cloude maist thou ymagin with coriousite of witte for to bere before thin iyen in the lightest day of somer; and also ayenswarde in the derkist night of wynter thou mayst ymagin a clere schinyng light. Lat be soche falsheed; I mene not thus. For when I sey derknes I mene a lackyng of knowyng; as alle that thing that thou knowest not, or elles that thou has foryetyn, it is derk to thee, for thou seest it not with thi goostly iye. & for this skile is it not clepid a cloude of the eire, bot a cloude of unknowyng, that is bitwix thee and thi God.

coriousite of witte: inquisitiveness of mind   *skile:* reason

Only loving and mystical prayer can pierce this cloud.

4

The existence of such works as *The Cloud of Unknowing* suggests that, by the close of the fourteenth century, prose rather than verse had become a natural means of recording thoughts and experiences. This is stated explicitly by the translator John of Trevisa, whose patron advised him to write not in verse but 'in prose, for comynlich prose is more clere than ryme, more esy, and more playn to knowe and understonde'. Clarity such as this statement recommends was being achieved partly by vernacular sermons, homilies and works of popular edification, and partly by the need to write such things as wills and practical treatises in ways that were not wholly dependent on manuals of rhetoric. Though such books gave instruction on how to write letters, the great letter-writing families of the period – the Pastons especially – achieved vivid and immediate accounts of troubled everyday life during the Wars of the Roses. Here, for example, is a description from 1478 of a manor court and a disagreement between the Duke of Suffolk and an absent Sir John Paston. The Duke,

beyng ther that daye ther was never no man that playd Herrod in Corpus Crysty play better and more agreable to hys pageaunt than he dud. But ye schall understond that it was after none, and the weder hot, and he so feble for sekenes that hys legges wold not bere hyme, but ther was ij men had gret payn to kepe hym on hys fete; and ther ye were juged. Som sayd, 'Sley'; some sayd, 'Put hym in preson.' And forth com my lord, and he wold met you with a spere, and have none other mendes for the troble at ye have put hym to but your hart blod, and that will be gayt with hys owen handes.

Other needs placed more exacting requirements on prose. For example, the defence offered by Margery Kempe and William Thorpe when accused of Lollardy required the greatest precision if the accused were to save themselves from the stake, while Bishop Pecock – also concerned to refute Lollardy – turned in the manner of the preachers to what he hoped was 'the common pepil's language' in order to expose the fallacies of the heretics. Nonetheless, because the vernacular did not contain many of the concepts Pecock needed, he was forced to invent much of his vocabulary. Few of his coinages have survived, and his neologisms contribute to the opacity of his laboured and pedantic style.

A large quantity of miscellaneous prose survives from the second half of the fifteenth century: treatises on medicines and herbs, on hunting, fishing, games, and so on. There are also a number of accounts of pilgrimages which suggest the extreme difficulties pious men and woman were prepared to face. But the most famous travel book from the period is that by Sir John Mandeville.

Mandeville's *Travels* appears to have originally been written in French and to have been in circulation by the middle of the fourteenth century. Fifty years later it was available in every major European vernacular. Nothing is known of the author beyond what is revealed by the text which relates that Sir John Mandeville was an English knight who, from 1322 to 1356, travelled widely between Egypt and China. There are certainly elements here of the persona – in other words, of the author as a literary device – but the fact that an original from this period was composed in French is no argument against the writer being English. What is really questionable is how far Mandeville travelled at all. Certain arcane details seem to derive from the author's own observations, but many – again in a manner wholly conventional – are taken from a wide range of standard authorities. These are blended with the greatest skill, however, and help to focus attention on the writer's chief themes: the pilgrim voyage to the Holy Land, the corruption of the Church which makes the Christians unworthy of repossessing Palestine, and, most refreshingly, a concern with the innate goodness and piety of many non-Christian peoples – an imaginative sympathy rare indeed at the time. Such a mixture of warmth and curious information must, in part at least, account for the book's wide and long-lasting popularity.

5

The most considerable achievement of late medieval literary prose remains the *Morte Darthur* of Sir Thomas Malory. At the close of his text Malory declares that he finished the work in the ninth year of the reign of Edward IV. This allows us to date its completion between 4 March 1469 and 3 March 1470 and to place it in the context of the exhausted change and confusion of the Wars of the Roses. In his conclusion, Malory also asks his audience to 'pray for me while I am on live [i.e. 'living'] that God send me good deliveraunce'. Elsewhere he describes himself as a 'knyght presonour' and this allows us tentatively to identify him with the Sir Thomas Malory of Newbolt Revel in Warwickshire who, in about 1450, was gaoled for robbery, cattle-raiding, rape and attempted murder. He escaped, was re-imprisoned and then pardoned, and in 1456 he served as Member of Parliament for his shire. After more spells of fighting and imprisonment, Malory died on 14 March 1471. The *Morte Darthur* is the achievement of his last twenty years.

As we might expect of a medieval work, the narrative draws heavily on earlier sources: Geoffrey of Monmouth, Chrétien, and the large cycle of French vernacular romances that followed in Chrétien's wake. Malory also turned frequently to the alliterative *Morte Arthure*, changing the image of Gawain in that work and concentrating on the adultery of Lancelot and Guinevere, thereby introducing a large element of romance into his version. Malory was also influenced by the structure of the English poem, for, just as the alliterative *Morte Arthure* presents an image of kingship set against the revolutions of Fortune's wheel, so Malory's work – using the French romances to elaborate on the splendour and chivalry of Arthur's knights – can be seen as following a threefold movement. First, in Parts I and II, we see the rise of Arthur as we are told the familiar tale of his miraculous birth, his wars of accession, his begetting of Mordred and his marriage to Guinevere. We are then introduced to Lancelot, 'the greatest knight of a sinful man' as Malory calls him, whose life will be so inextricably and tragically involved with that of his king. For the moment, however, the whole company are bound together by the ideals and oath of the Round Table:

Then the king stablished all the knights and gave them that were of lands not rich, he gave them lands, and charged them never to do outrage nother murder, and always to flee treason, also by no mean to be cruel, but to give mercy unto him that asketh mercy, upon pain of forfeiture of their worship and lordship of king Arthur for evermore: and always to do ladies, damsels, and gentlewomen and widows succour; strength them in their rights, and never to enforce them upon pain of death. Also that no man take no battles in a wrongful quarrel for no love ne for no worlds goods. So unto this were all knights sworn of the Table Round, both old and young.

The three succeeding parts tell of the adventures of Lancelot, Gareth and Tristan, and then of Lancelot's being tricked into begetting Galahad. In Part VI, Galahad becomes a knight of the Round Table and members of the company set out in pursuit of the Holy Grail. Galahad succeeds in the quest, but, while the others fail, Lancelot is in part successful. Imperfections among the knights are thus exposed. In the third movement, the wheel of Fortune continues its downward movement. The adultery of Lancelot and Guinevere comes fully into prominence and leads eventually to the downfall of the Round Table. At this point, Lancelot is portrayed as both the greatest of Arthur's knights and a man caught in an irreconcilable paradox: he cannot be both the honourable and loyal follower of his king and the honourable and loyal lover of his master's wife. The object of his passion is at once criminal and destructive, while his love in itself worthy and stable. The following passage beautifully describes this latter ideal:

> For like as winter rasure doth alway erase and deface green summer, so fareth it by unstable love in man and woman. For in many persons there is no stability; for we may see all day, for a little blast of winter's rasure, anon we shall deface and lay apart true love for little or nought, that cost much thing; this is no wisdom nor stability, but it is feebleness of nature and great disworship, whosoever useth this.

Eventually the lovers are obliged to leave Camelot. Arthur's illegitimate son Mordred forces the king to recognize the adultery, and Arthur's honour requires him to pursue Guinevere with the full force of the law. Lancelot's honour, on the other hand, forces him to save the queen and so bring about the destruction of the order of the Round Table. In Arthur's absence, Mordred rebels and is slain in the last battle. The dying king himself is then transported to Avalon. At the close, Lancelot and Guinevere turn to the religious life, so repudiating their previous sinful existence. The paradoxes of merely worldly honour have led to the destruction of a very beautiful ideal of society, but, at the close, the ideas of honour and shame that once provided the lovers' moral universe are finally abandoned for a wholly different set of values. There is true contrition here, while, in the noble words of Sir Ector, there is also a moving lament for what has been lost:

> 'Ah, Lancelot!' he said, 'thou were head of all Christian knights! And now I dare say,' said sir Ector, 'thou sir Lancelot, there thou liest, that thou were never

matched of earthly knight's hand. And thou were the courteoust knight that ever bore shield! And thou were the truest friend to thy lover that ever bestrode horse, and thou were the truest lover of a sinful man that ever loved woman, and thou were the kindest man that ever struck with sword. And thou were the goodliest person that ever came among press of knights, and thou was the meekest man and the gentlest that ever ate in hall among ladies, and thou were the sternest knight to thy mortal foe that ever put spear in the rest.'

Then there was weeping and dolour out of measure.

The *Morte Darthur* was one of the texts later printed by William Caxton (*c.* 1421–91), and it is with the man who introduced printing into England that we may properly end. For much of his life Caxton had been a successful merchant. He learned the art of printing in Cologne (he tells us that he did so at great expense and in order to avoid the tedium of producing copies by hand), and in 1473–4 he issued his first English work: the *Recuyell of the Historyes of Troye*, published in Bruges. In 1476 he moved his press to Westminster, and from there until the time of his death he produced a series of books representative of his and his public's taste for piety and chivalric romance. Much of his work was as a translator – he seems to have worked with extraordinary industry – and the influence of French syntax is very clear in the many prefaces and prologues which he provided for his books. He laboured hard with his style and was clearly responsive to criticisms of his early experiments with an over-ornate vocabulary. It is, however, as a technical innovator that Caxton's real importance lies. While his books themselves were conservative in appearance, Caxton's introduction of the printing press, and with it the possibility of disseminating many identical copies of a single text, signals the close of the manuscript culture of the Middle Ages and heralds the start of the Renaissance.

BIBLIOGRAPHY

This book list does not claim to be comprehensive. It itemizes the more readily available texts and translations as well as those works of criticism the author has found particularly helpful.

EDITIONS AND TRANSLATIONS

i. General Anthologies and Selections

OLD ENGLISH LITERATURE

Sweet's Anglo-Saxon Reader in Prose and Verse, 1876, revised ed. Dorothy Whitelock, Oxford University Press, 1975

Alexander, Michael (trans.), *The Earliest English Poems*, Penguin Books, 1977

Crossley-Holland, Kevin (ed.), *The Anglo-Saxon World: An Anthology*, Oxford University Press, 1984

Swanton, Michael (ed.), *Anglo-Saxon Prose*, Everyman's Library, Dent, 1975

EARLY MIDDLE ENGLISH LITERATURE

Bennett, J. A. W., and G. V. Smithers (eds.), with a glossary by Norman Davis, *Early Middle English Verse and Prose*, Oxford University Press, 1968

MIDDLE ENGLISH LITERATURE

Blake, N. F. (ed.), *Middle English Religious Prose*, Edward Arnold, 1972

Burrow, J. (ed.), *English Verse, 1300–1500*, Longman, 1977

Gray, Douglas (ed.), *The Oxford Book of Late Medieval Verse and Prose*, Oxford University Press, 1985

Sisam, K. (ed.), *Fourteenth-Century Verse and Prose*, Oxford University Press, revised ed. 1955

Sisam, K., and C. Sisam (eds.), *The Oxford Book of Medieval English Verse*, Oxford University Press, 1970

ii. Anthologies of Genres, etc.

DRAMA

P. Happé (ed.), *English Mystery Plays*, Penguin Books, 1975
Four Morality Plays, Penguin Books, 1979

LYRIC

Brown, Carleton (ed.), *English Lyrics of the XIII Century*, Oxford University Press, 1932
   Religious Lyrics of the XIV Century, Oxford University Press, 1924, revised ed. G. V. Smithers, 1952
   Religious Lyrics of the XV Century, Oxford University Press, 1939
Davies, R. T. (ed.), *Medieval English Lyrics: A Critical Anthology*, Faber and Faber, 1963
Gray, Douglas (ed.), *A Selection of Religious Lyrics*, Clarendon Medieval and Tudor Texts, Oxford University Press, 1975
Greene, R. L. (ed.), *A Selection of English Carols*, Clarendon Medieval and Tudor Texts, Oxford University Press, 1977

ROMANCE

Mills, M. (ed.), *Six Middle English Romances*, Dent, 1973
Sands, D. B. (ed.), *Middle English Verse Romances*, Holt, Rinehart & Winston, New York, 1966
Schmidt, A. V. C., and N. Jacobs (eds.), *Medieval English Romances* (2 vols.), Hodder & Stoughton, 1980

iii. Authors and Anonymous Works

AELFRIC. *Aelfric's Colloquies*, ed. G. N. Garmonsway, Methuen's Old English Library, 1947
ALFRED. Useful translations may be found in *Alfred the Great: Asser's 'Life of King Alfred' and Other Contemporary Sources*, trans. Simon Keynes and Michael Lapidge, Penguin Books, 1983
Alliterative Morte Arthure, ed. E. Brock, Early English Text Society, 1871, abridged ed. J. Finlayson, York Medieval Texts, Edward Arnold, 1967
Ancrene Riwle, The, trans. M. B. Salu, Burns & Oates, 1955
Ancrene Wisse, ed. G. Shepherd, Old and Middle English Texts, Manchester University Press, 1960
Anglo-Saxon Chronicle, The, trans. G. N. Garmonsway, Everyman's Library, Dent, 1953
BALLADS. Selection in *The Penguin Book of Ballads*, ed. Geoffrey Grigson, Penguin Books, 1975
Beowulf, trans. Michael Alexander, Penguin Books, 1973
CAEDMON. See *Anglo-Saxon Poetry*, trans. R. K. Gordon, Everyman's Library, Dent, 1954
CAXTON, WILLIAM. *Selections from William Caxton*, ed. N. F. Blake, Oxford University Press, 1973
CHAUCER, GEOFFREY. *The Works of Geoffrey Chaucer*, ed. F. N. Robinson, Oxford University Press, 2nd ed. 1966

The Parlement of Foulys, ed. D. S. Brewer, Old and Middle English Texts, Manchester University Press, 1972

Troilus and Criseyde, ed. Barry Windeatt, Routledge & Kegan Paul, 1985

(There are innumerable secondary editions of individual *Canterbury Tales*.)

Chauceriana, in *The Complete Works of Geoffrey Chaucer*, ed. W. W. Skeat, Oxford University Press, 1897, Vol. VII

Chester Miracle Plays, ed. R. M. Lumiansky and D. Mills, Early English Text Society, 1976

CLANVOWE, SIR JOHN. *The Works of Sir John Clanvowe*, ed. V. J. Scattergood, Cambridge University Press, 1975

The Cloud of Unknowing and The Book of Privy Counselling, ed. P. Hodgson, Early English Text Society, 1944, reprinted 1973

The Cloud of Unknowing and Other Works, trans. Clifton Wolters, Penguin Books, 1978

Cursor Mundi, ed. R. Morris, Early English Text Society, 1874–92

CYNEWULF. See *Anglo-Saxon Poetry*, trans. R. K. Gordon, Everyman's Library, Dent, 1954

DOUGLAS, GAVIN. *Works* (4 vols.), Edinburgh, 1874

Dream of the Rood, The, in *The Earliest English Poems*, trans. Michael Alexander, Penguin Books, 2nd ed. 1977

DUNBAR, WILLIAM. *The Poems of William Dunbar*, ed. W. Mackay Mackenzie, 1932, reprinted Faber and Faber, 1950

Elegies, in *The Earliest English Poems*, trans. Michael Alexander, Penguin Books, 2nd ed. 1977

Everyman, ed. A. C. Cawley, Old and Middle English Texts, Manchester University Press, 1961

GAWAIN-POET. *The Poems of the Pearl Manuscript: Pearl, Cleanness, Patience, Sir Gawain and the Green Knight*, ed. Andrew Malcolm and Ronald Waldron, York Medieval Texts, 2nd series, Edward Arnold, 1978

Cleanness, ed. J. J. Anderson, Old and Middle English Texts, Manchester University Press, 1977

trans. Brian Stone in *The Owl and the Nightingale, Cleanness, St Erkenwald*, Penguin Books, 1971

Sir Gawain and the Green Knight, ed. J. R. R. Tolkien and E. V. Gordon, 2nd ed. revised N. Davis, Oxford University Press, 1967

trans. Brian Stone, *Sir Gawain and the Green Knight*, Penguin Books, 2nd ed. 1974

Patience, ed. J. J. Anderson, Old and Middle English Texts, Manchester University Press, 1969

trans. Brian Stone in *Medieval English Verse*, Penguin Books, revised ed. 1971

Pearl, ed. E. V. Gordon, Oxford University Press, 1955

trans. Brian Stone in *Medieval English Verse*, Penguin Books, revised ed. 1971

GOWER, JOHN. *English Works* (2 vols.), ed. G. C. Macaulay, Early English Text Society, 1900–1901, reprinted 1957

The Major Latin Works, trans. E. W. Stockton, Seattle, 1962

Selections from John Gower, ed. J. A. W. Bennet, Clarendon Medieval and Tudor Texts, Oxford University Press, 1968

Hali Meiðhad, ed. R. M. Wilson, Leeds, 1940

Harley Lyrics, The, ed. G. L. Brook, Old and Middle English English Texts, Manchester University Press, 1956, revised ed. 1978

HENRYSON, ROBERT. *The Poems of Robert Henryson*, ed. D. Fox, Oxford University Press, 1980

HILTON, WALTER. *The Scale of Perfection*, modernized and ed. E. Underhill, London, 1923

HOCCLEVE, THOMAS. *Works*, ed. I. Gollancz, Early English Text Society, 1925, reprinted 1970

JAMES I OF SCOTLAND. *The Kingis Quair*, ed. J. Norton-Smith, Oxford University Press, 1971

JULIAN OF NORWICH. *A Revelation of Divine Love*, ed. M. Glasscoe, Exeter University Press, 1976

trans. Clifton Wolters, *Revelations of Divine Love*, Penguin Books, 1966

KEMPE, MARGERY. *The Book of Margery Kempe*, ed. H. E. Allen and S. B. Meech, Early English Text Society, 1940, reprinted 1961

trans. Barry Windeatt, *The Book of Margery Kempe*, Penguin Books, 1985

LANGLAND, WILLIAM. *The Vision of Piers Ploughman: A Complete Edition of the B-text*, ed. A. V. C. Schmidt, Everyman's Library, Dent, 1978

trans. J. F. Goodridge, *Piers the Ploughman*, Penguin Books, 1959, revised ed. 1966

LAYAMON. *Brut*, ed. G. L. Brook and R. F. Leslie, Early English Text Society, 1963

trans. Eugene Mason, *Wace and Layamon: Arthurian Chronicles*, Everyman's Library, Dent, 1912, reprinted 1962

LYDGATE, JOHN. *Poems* (selections), ed. J. Norton Smith, Clarendon Medieval and Tudor Texts, Oxford University Press, 1966

Macro Plays, ed. M. Eccles, Early English Text Society, 1969

MALORY, SIR THOMAS. *Works* (3 vols.), ed. E. Vinaver, Oxford University Press, 1954, reprinted 1967

The Morte Darthur: Parts Seven and Eight, ed. D. S. Brewer, York Medieval Texts, Edward Arnold, 1968

MANDEVILLE, SIR JOHN. *Travels: The Cotton Text*, ed. M. C. Seymour, Oxford University Press, 1967; *The Egerton Text*, ed. G. F. Warner, Roxburghe Club, 1889

trans. C. W. R. D. Mosley, *The Travels of Sir John Mandeville*, Penguin Books, 1983

Mum and the Soothsegger, ed. M. Day and R. Steele, Early English Text Society, 1936

N-Town Plays, ed. K. S. Block, Early English Text Society, 1922, reprinted 1960

D'ORLEANS, CHARLES. *The English Poems of Charles of Orleans*, Early English Text Society, 1941–6, reprinted 1970

Ormulum, ed. R. M. White and R. Holt, Oxford University Press, 1878

The Owl and the Nightingale, ed. E. G. Stanley, Medieval and Renaissance Library, Nelson, 1960

    trans. Brian Stone in *The Owl and the Nightingale, Cleanness, St Erkenwald*, Penguin Books, 1971

The Parliament of the Three Ages, ed. M. Y. Offord, Early English Text Society, 1959

Paston Letters (6 vols.), ed. J. Gardiner, London, 1904

    The Pastons: A Family in the Wars of the Roses, selection ed. Richard Barber, 1981, reprinted Penguin Books, 1984

RIDDLES. in *The Earliest English Poems*, trans. Michael Alexander, Penguin Books, 1966

Sawles Warde, ed. R. M. Wilson, Leeds University Press, 1938

Sir Orfeo, ed. A. J. Bliss, Oxford University Press, 1954

St Erkenwald, ed. Clifford Peterson, University of Pennsylvania Press, 1977

    trans. Brian Stone in *The Owl and the Nightingale, Cleanness, St Erkenwald*, Penguin Books, 1971

TOWNELEY PLAYS. *The Wakefield Pageants in the Towneley Cycle,* ed. A. C. Cawley. Old and Middle English Texts, Manchester University Press, 1958

Winner and Waster, ed. I. Gollancz, 1920

WYCLIF, JOHN. *English Works*, ed. F. D. Matthew, Early English Text Society, 1880

York Plays, ed. L. Toulmin-Smith, Oxford University Press, 1885

iv. Foreign Language Texts

LATIN

ABELARD. *The Letters of Abelard and Heloise and Historia Calamitatum*, trans. Betty Radice, Penguin Books, 1974

ALANUS DE INSULIS. *The Complaint of Nature*, trans. D. M. Moffat, *Yale Studies*, 36, 1908

ANSELM. *The Prayers and Meditations of St Anselm*, trans. Sister Benedicta Ward, S.L.G., Penguin Books, 1973

AUGUSTINE. *The City of God*, trans. Henry Bettenson, Penguin Books, 1984

    Confessions, trans. R. S. Pine-Coffin, Penguin Books, 1961

BEDE. *A History of the English Church and People*, trans. L. Sherley-Price, Penguin Books, 1955

BOETHIUS. *The Consolation of Philosophy*, trans. E. V. Watts, Penguin Books, 1969

CAPELLANUS, ANDREAS. *The Art of Courtly Love*, trans. J. J. Parry, 1941

CICERO. *Republic*, ed. and trans. C. W. Keyes, Loeb Classical Library, 1928

GEOFFREY OF MONMOUTH. *The History of the Kings of Britain*, trans. Lewis Thorpe, Penguin Books, 1966

MACROBIUS. *Commentary on the Dream of Scipio*, trans. W. H. Stahl, 1952

ROLLE, RICHARD. *The Fire of Love*, trans. Clifton Wolters, Penguin Books, 1972

FRENCH

ARTHUR. *The Death of King Arthur*, trans. James Cable, Penguin Books, 1971
BÉROUL. *The Romance of Tristan and The Tale of Tristan's Madness*, trans. Alan S. Fedrick, Penguin Books, 1970
CHRÉTIEN DE TROYES. *Arthurian Romances*, trans. W. W. Comfort, Everyman's Library, Dent, 1914, reprinted 1975
MARIE DE FRANCE. *Lais of Marie de France*, trans. Glyn S. Burgess and Keith Busby, Penguin Books, 1986
The Quest of the Holy Grail, trans. Pauline Matarasso, Penguin Books, 1969
Roman de la Rose, trans. Charles Dahlberg, University of New England Press, 1983
The Song of Roland, trans. Dorothy Sayers, Penguin Books, 1957
WACE. See Layamon

(There are useful translations of many romances: see Pauline Matarasso, *Aucassin and Nicolette and Other Tales*, Penguin Books, 1971; and E. Mason, *Aucassin and Nicolette and Other Medieval French Romances and Legends*, Everyman's Library, Dent, 1910.)

ITALIAN

BOCCACCIO. *Decameron*, trans. J. M. Rigg, Penguin Books, 1978
   Il Filostrato, trans. R. K. Gordon, in *The Story of Troilus*, University of Toronto Press, 1978
DANTE. *Convivio*, trans. P. H. Wicksteed, Temple Classics, 1903
   Dante's Lyric Poetry, ed. and trans. K. Foster and P. Boyle, Oxford University Press, 1967
   The Divine Comedy (3 vols.), trans. J. Sinclair, Oxford University Press, 1936, 1946, reprinted 1961
   Vita Nuova, trans. Barbara Reynolds, Penguin Books, 1969
PETRARCH. *Petrarch's Lyric Poems*, trans. R. M. Durling, Harvard University Press, Cambridge, Mass., 1976

SECONDARY MATERIAL

Alexander, M., *Old English Literature*, Macmillan, 1983
Atkins, J. W. H., *English Literary Criticism: The Medieval Phase*, Cambridge University Press, 1943
Auerbach, E., *Mimesis*, Princeton University Press, 1953
Axton, R., *European Drama of the Early Middle Ages*, Hutchinson, 1974
Barber, C. L., *The Story of Language*, Pan, 1964
Barlow, F., *The Feudal Kingdom of England 1042–1216*, Longman, 1955, revised ed. 1972
Barney, S. S., *Chaucer's 'Troilus': Essays in Criticism*, Scolar Press, 1980
Baugh, A. C., and T. Cable, *A History of the English Language*, 1951, revised ed. Routledge & Kegan Paul, 1978

Beer, G., *Romance*, Methuen, 1970

Bennett, H. S., *Chaucer and the Fifteenth Century*, Oxford University Press, 1947

Bennett, J. A. W., *The Parlement of Fowles*, Oxford University Press, 1957
  Chaucer's Book of Fame, Oxford University Press, 1968

Blake, N., *The English Language in Medieval Literature*, Methuen, 1977

Bloch, M., *Feudal Society*, trans. L. A. Manyon, Routledge & Kegan Paul, 1961

Bloomfield, M. W., *The Seven Deadly Sins*, Michigan University Press, 1952

Boase, R., *The Origins and Meaning of Courtly Love*, Manchester University Press, 1977

Boitani, P., *English Medieval Narrative in the Thirteenth and Fourteenth Centuries* (trans.), Cambridge University Press, 1982

Boitani, P. (ed.), *Chaucer and the Italian Trecento*, Cambridge University Press, 1983

Bolton, W. F. (ed.), *A History of Literature in the English Language*, Vol. I, *The Middle Ages*, Sphere, 1970

Bossy, J., *Christianity in the West 1400–1700*, Oxford University Press, 1975

Brewer, D. S., *Chaucer*, Longmans, 1953, reprinted 1960
  Gothic Literature, Macmillan, 1983
  (ed.) *Geoffrey Chaucer*, Bell and Sons, 1974
  Chaucer and Chaucerians, Nelson, 1966, reprinted 1970

Brooke, C., *Europe in the Central Middle Ages 962–1154*, Longmans, 1964
  The Twelfth-Century Renaissance, Thames & Hudson, 1969

Burrow, J., *Ricardian Poetry*, Routledge & Kegan Paul, 1971
  Medieval Writers and their Work: Middle English Literature and its Background 1100–1500, Oxford University Press, 1982
  (ed.) *Geoffrey Chaucer: A Critical Anthology*, Penguin Books, 1969

Chadwick, H., *Augustine*, Oxford University Press, 1986

Chambers, E. K., *English Literature at the Close of the Middle Ages*, Oxford University Press, 1945

Chaytor, H. J., *From Script to Print*, Cambridge University Press, 1945, reprinted 1967

Coleman, J., *English Literature in History 1350–1400: Medieval Readers and Writers*, Hutchinson, 1981

Cook, W. R., and R. B. Herzman, *The Medieval World View: An Introduction*, Oxford University Press, 1983

Crossland, J., *Medieval French Literature*, Blackwell, Oxford, 1956

Curry, W. C., *Chaucer and the Medieval Sciences*, 1926, revised ed. George Allen & Unwin, 1960

Curtius, E. R., *European Literature and the Latin Middle Ages*, trans. Willard R. Trask, Routledge & Kegan Paul, 1953

Dronke, P., *The Medieval Lyric*, Hutchinson, 1968

Fisher, J. H., *John Gower, Moral Philosopher and Friend of Chaucer*, New York University Press, 1964

Fleming, J. V., *The 'Roman de la Rose': A Study in Allegory and Iconography*, Princeton University Press, 1969

Gray, D., *Themes and Images in the Medieval English Religious Lyric*, Routledge & Kegan Paul, 1972

Hale, J. R., J. R. L. Highfield and B. Smalley, *Europe in the Late Middle Ages*, Faber and Faber, 1965

Haskins, C. H., *The Renaissance of the Twelfth Century*, 1928, revised ed. Harvard University Press, Cambridge, Mass., 1976

Heer, F., *The Medieval World: Europe 1100–1350*, trans. Janet Sondheimer, New American Library, New York, 1963

Henderson, G., *Gothic*, Penguin Books, 1967

Holmes, G., *Dante*, Oxford University Press, 1980
    The Later Middle Ages 1272–1485, Penguin Books, 1970

Huizinga, J., *The Waning of the Middle Ages*, 1924, reprinted Penguin Books, 1965

Huppé, B. F., and D. W. Robertson, *Fruyt and Chaf: Studies in Chaucer's Allegories*, Princeton University Press, 1963

Kean, P. M., *Chaucer and the Making of English Poetry* (2 vols.), Routledge & Kegan Paul, 1972

Kenny, A., *Wyclif*, Oxford University Press, 1985

Kolve, V. A., *The Play Called Corpus Christi*, Edward Arnold, 1967
    Chaucer and the Imagery of Narrative, Edward Arnold, 1984

Lawlor, J., *Patterns of Love and Courtesy*, Edward Arnold, 1966

Leff, G., *Medieval Thought*, Penguin Books, 1958

Lewis, C., *The Allegory of Love*, Oxford University Press, 1936
    The Discarded Image, Cambridge University Press, 1964

Mâle, E., *The Gothic Image* (trans.), Harper & Row, New York, 1958

Mann, J., *Chaucer and Medieval Estates Satire*, Cambridge University Press, 1973

Mann, N., *Petrarch*, Oxford University Press, 1984

McKisack, M., *The Fourteenth Century 1307–1399*, Oxford University Press, 1959

Murphy, J. J., *Rhetoric in the Middle Ages*, Berkeley, Calif., 1974

Muscatine, C., *Chaucer and the French Tradition*, Berkeley, Calif., 1957, revised ed. 1964

Myers, A. R., *England in the Late Middle Ages*, 1952, revised ed. Penguin Books, 1976

Nimms, M. F., *The 'Poetria Nova' of Geoffrey de Vinsauf*, University of Toronto Press, 1967

Owst, G. R., *Preaching in Medieval England*, Cambridge University Press, 1926
    Literature and Pulpit in Medieval England, Oxford, 1933, reprinted Blackwell, Oxford, 1962

Riehle, D., *The Middle English Mystics*, Routledge & Kegan Paul, 1981

Robertson, D. W., *A Preface to Chaucer*, Princeton University Press, 1962

Robertson, D. W., and B. F. Huppé, *Piers Ploughman and Scriptural Tradition*, Princeton University Press, 1951

Salter, E., *The Knight's Tale and The Clerk's Tale*, Edward Arnold, 1962
    Piers Ploughman: An Introduction, Blackwell, Oxford, 1962

Salu, M. (ed.), *Essays on 'Troilus and Criseyde'*, Brewer, Cambridge, 1979

Spearing, A. C., *Criticism and Medieval Poetry*, Edward Arnold, 1964

Smalley, B., *The Study of the Bible in the Middle Ages*, Oxford University Press, 1952, 3rd revised ed. 1983

Southern, R. W., *The Making of the Middle Ages*, Hutchinson, 1953
  Western Society and the Church in the Middle Ages, Penguin Books, 1970
  The Gawain-poet: A Critical Study, Cambridge University Press, 1970
  Medieval Dream Poetry, Cambridge University Press, 1976

Stevens, J., *Music and Poetry in the Early Tudor Court*, 1961, reprinted Cambridge University Press, 1979
  Medieval Romance: Themes and Approaches, Hutchinson, 1973

Taylor, J., and Alan H. Nelson (eds.), *Medieval English Drama: Essays Critical and Contextual*, Chicago University Press, 1972

Tolkien, J. R. R., *'Beowulf': The Monsters and the Critics*, Proc. British Academy, XII (1936), 3–53

Tuve, R., *Allegorical Imagery*, Princeton University Press, 1966

Tydeman, W., *The Theatre in the Middle Ages*, Cambridge University Press, 1978

Whitelock, D., *The Beginnings of English Society*, 1952, revised ed. Penguin Books, 1974

Wilson, F. P., *The English Drama 1485–1585*, Oxford University Press, 1969

Wilson, R. M., *Early Middle English Literature*, 1939, revised ed. Methuen, 1968

Woolf, R., *The English Mystery Plays*, Routledge & Kegan Paul, 1972
  The English Religious Lyric in the Middle Ages, Oxford University Press, 1968

Wrenn, C. L., *A Study of Old English Literature,* Harrap, 1967

INDEX

FOR THE BEST IN PAPERBACKS, LOOK FOR THE

In every corner of the world, on every subject under the sun, Penguin represents quality and variety – the very best in publishing today.

For complete information about books available from Penguin – including Pelicans, Puffins, Peregrines and Penguin Classics – and how to order them, write to us at the appropriate address below. Please note that for copyright reasons the selection of books varies from country to country.

In the United Kingdom: For a complete list of books available from Penguin in the U.K., please write to *Dept E.P., Penguin Books Ltd, Harmondsworth, Middlesex, UB7 0DA*

In the United States: For a complete list of books available from Penguin in the U.S., please write to *Dept BA, Penguin, 299 Murray Hill Parkway, East Rutherford, New Jersey 07073*

In Canada: For a complete list of books available from Penguin in Canada, please write to *Penguin Books Canada Ltd, 2801 John Street, Markham, Ontario L3R 1B4*

In Australia: For a complete list of books available from Penguin in Australia, please write to the *Marketing Department, Penguin Books Australia Ltd, P.O. Box 257, Ringwood, Victoria 3134*

In New Zealand: For a complete list of books available from Penguin in New Zealand, please write to the *Marketing Department, Penguin Books (NZ) Ltd, Private Bag, Takapuna, Auckland 9*

In India: For a complete list of books available from Penguin, please write to *Penguin Overseas Ltd, 706 Eros Apartments, 56 Nehru Place, New Delhi, 110019*

In Holland: For a complete list of books available from Penguin in Holland, please write to *Penguin Books Nederland B.V., Postbus 195, NL–1380AD Weesp, Netherlands*

In Germany: For a complete list of books available from Penguin, please write to *Penguin Books Ltd, Friedrichstrasse 10 – 12, D–6000 Frankfurt Main 1, Federal Republic of Germany*

In Spain: For a complete list of books available from Penguin in Spain, please write to *Longman Penguin España, Calle San Nicolas 15, E–28013 Madrid, Spain*

FOR THE BEST IN PAPERBACKS, LOOK FOR THE

A CHOICE OF PENGUINS AND PELICANS

Adieux Simone de Beauvoir

This 'farewell to Sartre' by his life-long companion is a 'true labour of love' (the *Listener*) and 'an extraordinary achievement' (*New Statesman*).

British Society 1914–45 John Stevenson

A major contribution to the Pelican Social History of Britain, which 'will undoubtedly be the standard work for students of modern Britain for many years to come' – *The Times Educational Supplement*

The Pelican History of Greek Literature Peter Levi

A remarkable survey covering all the major writers from Homer to Plutarch, with brilliant translations by the author, one of the leading poets of today.

Art and Literature Sigmund Freud

Volume 14 of the Pelican Freud Library contains Freud's major essays on Leonardo, Michelangelo and Dostoevsky, plus shorter pieces on Shakespeare, the nature of creativity and much more.

A History of the Crusades Sir Steven Runciman

This three-volume history of the events which transferred world power to Western Europe – and founded Modern History – has been universally acclaimed as a masterpiece.

A Night to Remember Walter Lord

The classic account of the sinking of the *Titanic*. 'A stunning book, incomparably the best on its subject and one of the most exciting books of this or any year' – *The New York Times*

FOR THE BEST IN PAPERBACKS, LOOK FOR THE

A CHOICE OF PENGUINS AND PELICANS

The Informed Heart   Bruno Bettelheim

Bettelheim draws on his experience in concentration camps to illuminate the dangers inherent in all mass societies in this profound and moving masterpiece.

God and the New Physics   Paul Davies

Can science, now come of age, offer a surer path to God than religion? This 'very interesting' (*New Scientist*) book suggests it can.

Modernism   Malcolm Bradbury and James McFarlane (eds.)

A brilliant collection of essays dealing with all aspects of literature and culture for the period 1890–1930 – from Apollinaire and Brecht to Yeats and Zola.

Rise to Globalism   Stephen E. Ambrose

A clear, up-to-date and well-researched history of American foreign policy since 1938, Volume 8 of the Pelican History of the United States.

The Waning of the Middle Ages   Johan Huizinga

A magnificent study of life, thought and art in 14th and 15th century France and the Netherlands, long established as a classic.

The Penguin Dictionary of Psychology   Arthur S. Reber

Over 17,000 terms from psychology, psychiatry and related fields are given clear, concise and modern definitions.